Before Mestizaje

This book opens new dimensions on the history of race and caste in Latin America through examining the extreme caste groups of Mexico, particularly *lobos, moriscos,* and *coyotes.* In revealing the experiences of members of these and other groups and tracing the implications of their lives in the colonial world, a deeper understanding is rendered of the connection between *mestizaje* (Latin America's modern ideology of racial mixture) and the colonial caste system. Using bigamy records, marriage cases, census documents, and inquisition cases, this book argues that before mestizaje emerged as a primary concept in Latin America, an earlier form of racial mixture, hybridity, and elasticity existed that must be taken seriously as its precursor. *Before Mestizaje* synthesizes the history of race and caste systems, while tracing the evolution and long-term impact of unique caste categories in Mexico.

Ben Vinson III is the Dean of the Columbian College of Arts and Sciences at The George Washington University, Washington, DC. He was formerly the director of the Center of Africana Studies at Johns Hopkins University. Vinson is the author and coauthor of numerous books, including *Bearing Arms for His Majesty: The Free-Colored Militia in Colonial Mexico* (2002) and *African Slavery in Latin America and the Caribbean* (2007). He is the editor in chief of *The Americas: A Quarterly Review of Latin American History.*

Cambridge Latin American Studies

General Editors
KRIS LANE, *Tulane University*
MATTHEW RESTALL, *Pennsylvania State University*

Editor Emeritus
HERBERT S. KLEIN *Gouverneur Morris Emeritus Professor of History, Columbia University and Hoover Research Fellow, Stanford University*

Other Books in the Series

(*continued after the index*)

Before Mestizaje

The Frontiers of Race and Caste in Colonial Mexico

BEN VINSON III

The George Washington University, Washington, DC

CAMBRIDGE
UNIVERSITY PRESS

CAMBRIDGE
UNIVERSITY PRESS

One Liberty Plaza, 20th Floor, New York, NY 10006, USA

Cambridge University Press is part of the University of Cambridge.

It furthers the University's mission by disseminating knowledge in the pursuit of education, learning, and research at the highest international levels of excellence.

www.cambridge.org
Information on this title: www.cambridge.org/9781107670815
DOI: 10.1017/9781139207744

First published 2018

A catalogue record for this publication is available from the British Library.

Library of Congress Cataloging-in-Publication Data
NAMES: Vinson, Ben, III., author.
TITLE: Before mestizaje : the frontiers of race and caste in colonial Mexico / Ben Vinson III (Johns Hopkins University).
DESCRIPTION: New York, NY : Cambridge University Press, 2017. | Series: Cambridge Latin American studies; 105 | Includes bibliographical references and index.
IDENTIFIERS: LCCN 2017009656| ISBN 9781107026438 (hardback) | ISBN 9781107670815 (paperback)
SUBJECTS: LCSH: Mexico – Race relations – History. | Mexico – Social conditions – To 1810. | Mexico – History – Spanish colony, 1540–1810. | Caste – Mexico – History. | Mestizos – Mexico – History. | Racially mixed people – Mexico – History. | Individual differences – Political aspects – Mexico – History. | Group identity – Mexico – History. | Social control – Mexico – History. | BISAC: HISTORY / Latin America / General.
CLASSIFICATION: LCC F1392.A1 V46 2017 | DDC 972/.02–dc23
LC record available at https://lccn.loc.gov/2017009656

ISBN 978-1-107-02643-8 Hardback
ISBN 978-1-107-67081-5 Paperback

To Allyson, Ben, and Brandon

Contents

Figures

Color plates are to be found between pp. 124 and 125

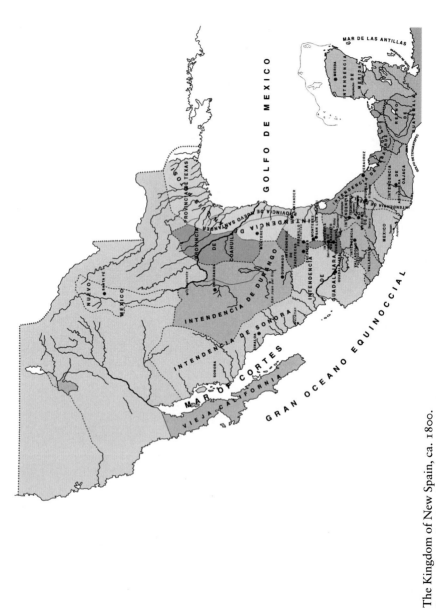

The Kingdom of New Spain, ca. 1800.
Source: Antonio García Cubas, *Reyno de la Nueva España, Atlas pintoresco e histórico de los Estados Unidos Mexicanos*, 1885.
Courtesy of The Newberry Library, Chicago, call no. Ayer 655.59.G2 1885.

Preface

This book began as a simple idea at Harvard more than 15 years ago. Stuart Schwartz, the renowned historian from Yale, was lecturing on campus at Bernard Bailyn's spring workshop on the History of the Atlantic World, which I had the good fortune of attending. The topic was the Latin American caste system, and as is customary for lectures on casta, it was accompanied by a wealth of gripping images, taken from the exquisite series of caste paintings produced in Latin America during colonial times. Many of us in the field routinely use these images in our classes on colonial Latin American history to help students visualize what may seem strange, and to help make intelligible the registers of racial mixture that demarcated difference in the Spanish kingdom. For those of us in the United States, these paintings particularly help us grapple with understanding the differences between a fluid, multilayered conception of race and what have been our own somewhat more stationary views.

There came a point in Stuart Schwartz's lecture where those less familiar with the complexities of Latin American history began to smile. Others looked at some of the images in disbelief. As we moved from mestizos to *moriscos* to *lobos* to *coyotes*, and ultimately, the *salto para atrás*, the audience members could not contain themselves. It seemed obvious: history was crossing a line, becoming visual fiction. Except that was not my reaction. Having recently completed my own book on free-coloreds in the Mexican militias, several of the projected images made me recall what I had seen and read in documents in Mexico's national archives. Lobos, moriscos, coyotes, and chinos, in particular, were familiar indeed, and even plentiful in the colonial record.

In the brief span of the lecture session, I decided that I would write a social history, bringing back to life what seemed to me were largely "forgotten castes." My work on the militias had also led me to believe that rather than being fiction, these groups might have had concrete racial identities. I saw a clear avenue for exploring a hidden history. The project would be quick, so I thought, and the methodology easy: just collect everything that could be had on the forgotten castas from the archives, consider the different domains of existence of these groups, and tell their story. Maybe it would be an article, maybe a book.

What I did not completely understand then, and what I fully comprehend now, is the extent to which their experiences stretched beyond their individual lives. In the way that these categories were utilized in colonial records, there was a greater story – one about caste legacies, footprints, and patterns. The various and often surprising ways in which these fringe casta populations were construed and lived had a dynamic effect on the very system of caste organization under which they were classified, and may have established precedents – faint though they might be – for later, far grander conceptualizations of racial order. These "forgotten castes" – I now term them "extreme castes" – represented the limits of racial mixture and therefore offered clues into what has become known to the world as the ideology of mestizaje. Could it be that in these groups, and their forms of interaction with society, there were lessons for the future, for unlocking hidden registers of mestizaje itself?

As this book slowly began taking shape, it also bespoke trends that have been taking place in the now burgeoning field of Afro-Mexican history. At least in my view, recent scholarship appears to indicate that there was something afoot culturally in Mexico, approximating the genesis of a black cultural sphere, which started thriving as early as the seventeenth century. A black world of intricate ritual practice thrived, fusing elements of African spiritual arts with New World forms. There were sanctioned arenas of so-called black magico-spiritual authority that were well recognized across a wide spectrum of society, bestowing on black populations a discrete status in New Spain. Multiple crown-endorsed institutions such as militias and confraternities were organized for black participation, and these were sometimes veritable incubators of identity, even as they helped blacks assimilate and maneuver within colonial society. Distinct black conceptions of freedom, shaped by absolutism and slavery, were further forged in the conversations that blacks had among their kinship networks. There was an evolving sense of black honor that while mimetically associated with elite culture, remained unique. Colonial black honor was inevitably shaped by the social ceilings, opportunities, and interactions that peoples of African descent had among themselves and with other colonists. Even as blacks occupied interstitial roles in their societies – often brokering between whites and native populations occupationally, socially, and culturally (as in colonial Yucatán) – these midlevel subaltern spaces could nevertheless constitute a rallying source of collectivity that ebbed and flowed as needed. The black cultural sphere that scholars have been uncovering was fragile, pocked with holes, and permeable. Indeed, there were moments when the power of the crown, regional patron-client networks, and even the strength of native communities suffocated the expressions of their cultural world. Nonetheless, scholarship is continuing to reveal an underlying canvass to black life that provided a common texture to the black presence, despite the acknowledgement of real divisions and differences that existed among black populations. The black castas featured in this book, hybridized as they were, meandered in and out of this cultural sphere, revealing its complexity, atomization, and integrity throughout colonial times.

So what began in a dark Harvard classroom as a simple project has now become a tangled exploration into both lives and patterns, into social history and theory, into the social vision of the colonial era, and beyond. The result is for me a curious book. In the pages that follow you will encounter many things: stories of obscure and long-forgotten castas, overlapping and often contradictory notions of social categorizations and social systems, diachronic tales that weave their way from the deep colonial period to the outset of the twentieth century. There is much to learn here about the origins of the caste system, its evolution, and its legacies. I hope that this book will open as many conversations as it tries to reconcile. And I hope it will inspire more thought and research on the links between caste, blackness, and mestizaje. I leave it to you, the reader, to decide these outcomes.

Of course, I owe deep gratitude to many who touched this project along the way. In fact, there are too many people to acknowledge. To Bernard Bailyn, I tender my thanks for accepting me as a full-fledged member of his History of the Atlantic World Seminar in 2002, where the earliest ideas that became this book were aired. I also thank the National Humanities Center in North Carolina for providing me a succession of opportunities to confer with colleagues in a constellation of disciplines and to think, write, and talk about this project with them. I thank Claudia Lomelí Rodríguez and Fabiola Meléndez, my dear friends in Mexico City, who helped me locate and acquire boxes of documents during the periods when I could not be present at the national archives. Tatiana Seijas has been an endless supporter and cheerleader for this project, funneling me references and documents from her forays into various repositories. At various stages of this work, I derived tremendous value from conversations, contact, and friendship with Matthew Restall, Danielle Terrazas Williams, Pablo Sierra, Patrick Carroll, Maria Elisa Velázquez, Juan Manuel de la Serna, Stefan Wheelock, Trey Proctor, Colin Palmer, Jaime Rodríguez, Andrew Fisher, Justin Wolfe, Juliet Hooker, Herman Bennett, Sandy Darity Jr., Zachary R. Morgan, Alejandro de la Fuente, Joan Bristol, Nicole von Germeten, Rachel O'Toole, Kathryn Burns, Leo Garofalo, Gabriel Haslip Viera, and Michele Reid-Vázquez. My graduate students from Johns Hopkins and Penn State – Norah Andrews, Joseph Clark, Katherine Bonil Gómez, and Robert Schwaller – have also been incredibly resonant sounding boards, thought partners, and colleagues. I thank you so much for your generous insights. Barbara Tenenbaum (Tasha) at the Library of Congress has not only been a great friend, but also was incredibly helpful in assisting me in the hunt for rare images and photographs.

Franklin Knight, my treasured colleague at Johns Hopkins, read early drafts of the opening chapters and provided sage guidance and criticism. Sherwin Bryant allowed me to test some of the premises of my argument at Northwestern, and Henry Louis Gates Jr. invited me to present several chapters of this project in the Huggins Lectures at Harvard. I am grateful to them for such memorable opportunities. At George Washington University, where I am now Dean of Arts and Sciences, Patrick Funiciello helped me push this project through to the finish line – I could not have completed it without him. Jill Gisnburg's expert editorial eye also improved the book's flow, and I thank her for her time, dedication, and patience. I also thank Kiara Osiris and Emmanuella, two brilliant high school students in Cambridge who attended the Huggins Lectures and whose questions inspired me to write the Coda of this book.

And, of course, I owe much to my children, Allyson, Ben, and Brandon; my wife, Yolanda; and my mom and dad – you have had to live with this project in more ways than one. Thank you for providing the bedrock upon which I could write this book; it was impossible to do this without you. Finally, much is due to my steadfast mentor Herbert S. Klein. Your inspiration, vitality, prolific energy, and keen interpretive sense have always been my model.

FIGURE I Cuadro de Castas (Caste Chart).
Source: Museo Nacional del Virreinato, Tepotzotlán, Mexcio, 18th Century
(anonymous painter). Castas Painting, Oil on canvas H 148 × W 105 cm,
Courtesy of Art Resource.

FIGURE 2 Mestizo and India Produce Coyote.
Source: Juan Rodríguez Juárez (1675–1728), *De Mestizo, y India Produce Coyote*, ca. 1720, Castas Painting, Oil on canvas H 103.8 × W 146.4 cm, Courtesy of The Hispanic Society of America, New York.

FIGURE 3 Negro and India Produce Lobo.
Source: Juan Rodríguez Juárez (1675–1728), *De Negro, y India Produce Lobo*, ca. 1715; Castas Painting, Oil on canvas, Courtesy of Breamore House, Hampshire, UK/Bridgeman Images.

FIGURE 4 Español and Mulata Produce Morisca.
Source: Juan Rodríguez Juárez (1675–1728), *De Español, y Mulata Produce Morisca*, ca. 1715; Castas Painting, Oil on canvas, Courtesy of Breamore House, Hampshire, UK/Bridgeman Images.

FIGURE 5 Indio y Loba Produce Grifo, Which Is "Tente en el Aire."
Source: Juan Rodríguez Juárez (1675–1728), *De Indio, y Loba Produce Grifo, que es Tente en el Aire*, ca. 1715; Castas Painting, Oil on canvas, Courtesy of Breamore House, Hampshire, UK/Bridgeman Images.

Wayward Mixture: The Problem of Race in the Colonies

From the dawn of Spain's venture into the New World until the end of its colonial regime, Spanish America was gripped by an almost innate need to process, categorize, and label human differences in an effort to manage its vast empire.[1] Whether it was conquistadors seeking to establish grades of difference between themselves and native rulers, or simple artisans striving to distinguish themselves from their peers, people paid careful attention to what others looked like, how they lived, what they wore, and how they behaved. Over time, rules were created to contain transgressions. The wearing of costumes and masks outside of sanctioned events and holidays was soundly discouraged, lest disguises lead

---

[1] Such impulses and desires, particularly acute in the New World, have caused scholars such as Jorge Cañizares-Esguerra to postulate that Spanish America was the first modern society to formulate notions of scientific racism based on biological determinism that assigned essentialist categories to human populations. See "New World, New Stars: Patriotic Astrology and the Invention of Indian and Creole Bodies in Colonial Spanish America, 1600–1650," *American Historical Review* 104, no. 1 (1999): 35. María Elena Martínez observes that the Spanish proclivity to indulge in human categorizations likely had medieval origins, as a means of describing hybrid offspring of the type produced by Christians and Muslims. See Martínez, *Genealogical Fictions: Limpieza de Sangre, Religion, and Gender in Colonial Mexico* (Stanford: Stanford University Press, 2008), 142–143. Additional context can be found in Solange Alberro and Pilar Gonzalbo, *La sociedad novohispana: estereotipos y realidades* (Mexico City: Colegio de México, Centro de Estudios Históricos, 2013). For non-Iberian examples of categorizing populations via biological determinism, particularly during the Enlightenment era, see Thomas Jefferson, *Notes on the State of Virginia* (Raleigh, NC: Alex Catalogue, 1990); and Georges L. Buffon, *Natural History, General and Particular*, trans. William Smellie and William M. Wood (London: T. Cadell and W. Davies, 1812).

to crimes, immorality, and mistaken identities.[2] People who lived as others could be labeled criminals, and those who moved across color boundaries to enjoy privileges not associated with their caste did so at their own peril.[3] When legislation failed to control behavior, social pressure impelled obedience and conformity.

Yet, in spite of the Spanish empire's craving for fixed identities, the truth is that there was great fluidity. It could be seen almost everywhere. In the early days of the conquest, as native regimes collapsed and tumbled, impostors rapidly ascended the ranks of a vanishing native nobility. Along the frontiers and in urban centers, skilled and crafty pretenders found entry into professions for which they were never intended. Mulattoes became priests, blacks became silversmiths, and plebeians of various hues became politicians and landowners of renown. Some petty criminals became native lords. A central catalyst of this social mobility was rampant racial mixture, which represented one of the realities of colonial life most threatening to the construction of an orderly society.

From the perspective of the government and the elite, the proliferation of new racial groups arising from racial mixture presented concrete problems for transferring privileges and defining social station. This was a special concern for the Spaniards since almost immediately after the conquest, what we categorize today as "race" became a means of dividing the spoils. Buttressed by their sense of technological, military, moral, intellectual, and cultural superiority, white Spaniards felt entitled to extract the best that the New World had to offer. To perpetuate this status, they designated themselves *gente de razón*, literally "people of reason," uniquely capable of making rational decisions. Even

---

[2] For an example of legislation prohibiting the use of masks and disguises, see a decree published April 30, 1716, to this effect. Archivo General de la Nación, Mexico (hereafter AGN), General de Parte, vol. 21, exp. 211, fols. 248v–249v. This decree was intended to apply to individuals regardless of caste, gender, or social station. As the Bourbon period progressed, even wearing masks and disguises during sanctioned festivals and other events was curtailed in some locations, among them Mexico City. See Linda A. Curcio-Nagy, *The Great Festivals of Mexico City: Performing Power and Identity* (Albuquerque: University of New Mexico Press, 2004), 117.

[3] One of the most famous cases of transvestitism was that of Catalina de Erauso, who traveled the world and performed incredible deeds as a man. See Erauso, *Lieutenant Nun: Memoir of a Basque Transvestite in the New World*, trans. Michele Stepto and Gabrielle Stepto (Boston: Beacon Press, 1996). Another example of cross-dressing and hermaphroditism can be found in "Sexuality and the Marriage Sacrament," in Richard Kagan and Abigail Dyer, *Inquisitorial Inquiries: Brief Lives of Secret Jews and Other Heretics* (Baltimore: Johns Hopkins Press, 2004), 64–87.

more important, gente de razón were indelibly marked by their Christian faith.[4]

On the other hand, the indigenous population was marked by an inherent inferiority. Considering them heathens or at best novices in the faith, and lacking the trappings of civilization that Europeans most valued (despite their having created dazzling societies), the Spaniards relegated to the *indios* whatever was left. It did not take long for these ideas to translate into a social system: the "dual republic" that divided the people of the New World into a "republic of Spaniards" and a "republic of Indians."[5] Based loosely on the social principles of late medieval Spain where society was organized into an estate system according to hereditary landlord/serf relationships, and borrowing the social stratification underlying the corporate arrangement of Spanish cities, the dual republic was the Spanish attempt to transplant the hierarchies of the Old World onto the racial landscape of the Americas. Indians were to become almost akin to the serfs of Europe, while whiteness stood as a marker of noble status.[6]

The dual republic was not to be realized solely in a juridical sense – it had spatial implications. Early Spanish urban planners developed the concept of the *traza*, in which whites were to be physically separated from the masses of Indians. Mexico City provides an excellent example. Here, shortly after the defeat of the Aztecs, the Spanish population was housed within the confines of thirteen city blocks, located in the center of what had been the capital city of Tenochtitlan. Outside this nucleus, the indigenous population was assigned to live in four barrios, or

---

[4] In 1542, Álvar Núñez Cabeza de Vaca discussed *gente de razón* in his accounts of his early explorations. Enrique Pupo-Walker, *The Narrative of Álvar Núñez Cabeza de Vaca* (Berkeley: University of California Press, 1993), fol. 35r.

[5] An excellent overview of the development of the dual republic system can be found in María Elena Martínez, *Genealogical Fictions*, 61–90. For additional context see Anthony Pagden's discussion about rationality and humanity in *The Fall of Natural Man: The American Indian and the Origins of Comparative Ethnology* (Cambridge: Cambridge University Press, 1982).

[6] One of the great ironies of Iberian white privilege is that in Spain itself, *españoles* could be far from white. For an excellent treatment of the role of Moorish characteristics in early modern Spain, a sense of the complexity of Hispanicity and whiteness, and a study of how others in Europe viewed Spain's racial composition, see Barbara Fuchs, "The Spanish Race," in *Rereading the Black Legend: The Discourses of Religious and Racial Difference in the Renaissance Empires*, ed. Margaret R. Greer, Walter D. Mignolo, and Maureen Quilligan (Chicago: University of Chicago, 2007), 88–98; and Fuchs, *Exotic Nation: Maurophilia and the Construction of Early Modern Spain* (Philadelphia: University of Pennsylvania Press, 2009).

neighborhoods, roughly aligned along the cardinal points of the traza. The traza's architect, Alonso García Bravo, duplicated his plans in Oaxaca.[7] Other trazas came into being shortly thereafter. The patterning of urban space along these lines served not only as an important physical demarcator for the colonial population but also as a vehicle for apportioning privileges. Clustered around the main plaza of each new city were the primary buildings of colonial government and religious authority. The plaza was the hub of urban commerce, itself tied into a web of regional trade networks. Physically locating the white population in close proximity to these structures constituted a strong symbolic statement as to who possessed true economic, political, and moral power in the colonies. However, even within the traza there was gradation. The wealthiest and most important magnates were located nearest to the plaza's key buildings, while lesser Spaniards inhabited the traza's fringes.

With all of its exclusionary tendencies, the dual republic also served as a means of including the indigenous population into the colonial order. Although it relegated Indians to neighborhoods and townships (*pueblos de indios*) outside of the traza, the system still aspired to acculturate them to Spanish governing norms.[8] For instance, each of the four indigenous barrios of Mexico City had its own plaza and elected its own network of governing officials, primarily councilmen (*regidores*) and judges (*alcaldes*). Thus, in theory, the republic system established a separate but integrated social and political order that allowed the indigenous population a certain autonomy under the Spanish regime.[9]

---

[7] Manuel Toussaint, Federico Gómez de Orozco, and Justino Fernández, *Planos de la Ciudad de México, siglos XVI y XVII. Estudio histórico, urbanístico y bibliográfico* (Mexico City: Universidad Nacional Autónoma de México, 1990), 21–22.

[8] One can compare the pueblos de indios with townships inhabited by other types of colonial populations. See Brígida von Mentz, *Pueblos de indios, mulatos y mestizos. Los campesinos y las transformaciones proto-industriales en el Poniente de Morelos* (Mexico City: CIESAS, 1988). The division of the colonial settlements into republics added another dimension to "legal plurality" by opening up legal space for indigenous peoples. See Rachel Sieder and John-Andrew McNeish, *Gender Justice and Legal Pluralities: Latin American and African Perspectives* (Milton Park, Abingdon, Oxon: Routledge, 2013).

[9] The degree of success of the parallel political networks created by the Spaniards in indigenous communities is still a matter of debate. For central Mexico, many of the offices created were reinterpreted by the indigenous population as continuities of preconquest governing structures. See James Lockhart, *The Nahuas after the Conquest: A Social and Cultural History of the Indians of Central Mexico, Sixteenth through Eighteenth Centuries* (Stanford: Stanford University Press, 1992), 30–40.

The dual republic was further conceived as a means of protecting Indians from abuses perpetrated by colonists. A cadre of moral thinkers and colonial bureaucrats feared that extended contact with Spaniards would accentuate the impact of the horrendous demographic decline that had gripped the New World. They believed that local estate owners overworked the indios, thereby diverting them from the tasks they needed for self-sustenance. Perhaps more importantly, such work diverted them from economic activities that would enable them to pay more taxes and tribute to the crown. Prolonged contact with Spaniards also supposedly encouraged looser morals: colonists were deemed quick to seduce or invite Indians to engage in activities that prevented them from achieving their true spiritual potential. Consequently, both bureaucrats and clergymen sought to separate Spaniards and Indians, especially in the sixteenth century.[10] For the clergy, separation facilitated the project of spiritual conversion. For the crown, separation offered the chance to enhance revenue streams that flowed into the royal coffers.

Perhaps the main problem with the republic system was that it was predicated on the persistent and vigilant exercise of maintaining racial purity. But almost from the outset of the colonial period, miscegenation occurred. The lack of Spanish women in the early colonies certainly played a role. Between 1509 and 1539, women represented just 5 to 6 percent of white immigrants to the Spanish Indies. Even as the colonies matured, white female immigration remained low. During the 1560s and 1570s, just under a third of all white immigrants were women.[11] Their dearth placed stress upon the reproductive capability of the "republic of

[10] An excellent examination of these themes can be found in Alonso de Zorita, "Breve y sumaria relación de los señores ... de la Nueva España," in *Nueva colección de documentos para la historia de México*, ed. Joaquín García Icazbalceta (Mexico: Editorial Chávez Hayhoe, 1941).

[11] Spanish women's roles in the New World were different from those in Europe, and important shifts in the status of native women vis-à-vis the efforts of colonization much influenced the status of white women. For a discussion, see Karen Viera-Powers, *Women in the Crucible of the Conquest: The Gendered Genesis of Spanish American Society, 1500–1600* (Albuquerque: University of New Mexico Press, 2005). Of course, the general demands of the New World environment and colonization efforts tended to affect and shape gender dynamics in unexpected ways. While far from constituting gender parity, the depth and multiplicity of roles that women took on in Spanish America has been an important area of scholarship. For an example, see Kimberly Gauderman, *Women's Lives in Colonial Quito: Gender, Law, and Economy in Spanish America* (Austin: University of Texas Press, 2003); Magnus Mörner, *Race Mixture in the History of Latin America* (Boston: Little, Brown and Company, 1967); and Sarah E. Owens and Jane E. Mangan, *Women of the Iberian Atlantic* (Baton Rouge: Louisiana State University Press, 2012).

Spaniards" – it could not completely replicate itself without cross-racial contact. A number of colonists took Indians as brides; three out of every four men did so in the Mexican city of Puebla by 1600.[12] Others, flushed with the sense of entitlement that followed the conquest, chose to sexually exploit native women. By both means, racial mixture quickly became a social reality.

These points say nothing of Africans who entered the colonial landscape. Blacks were part of the earliest expeditions of conquest, serving as soldiers, auxiliaries, cooks, and servants, among other capacities.[13] As early as the 1510s, African slaves were brought to work in the Caribbean, albeit in small numbers. However, it was later, between 1521 and 1639, with the conquests of Mexico and Peru, that Africans began pouring into the New World. As the indigenous population declined because of the effects of disease, blacks came to work on estates along the coasts of both regions. Sugar and viticulture were two particular areas of black labor concentration. Additionally, blacks were instrumental as miners in the early heydays of the silver boom. In urban areas, blacks became indispensable as artisans and domestic laborers.[14] While the exact number of Africans who entered the Spanish colonies is still a matter of debate, the general parameters of the slave trade suggest that well over 200,000 entered the realm during this time; of those, roughly half went to New Spain (Mexico). Nearly 50,000 people of African descent were recorded as working in Mexico by 1650.[15] These figures represent

[12] For an excellent synthetic treatment of the transformation of women's roles during the colonial period, see Susan M. Socolow, *The Women of Colonial Latin America* (New York and Cambridge: Cambridge University Press, 2015): "Nearly one-fourth of first-generation Spanish settlers in sixteenth-century Puebla de los Ángeles married Indian brides" (39).

[13] Matthew Restall, *Seven Myths of the Conquest* (New York: Oxford University Press, 2003); Restall, "Black Conquistadors: Armed Africans in Early Spanish America," *The Americas* 57, no. 2 (2000): 171–205.

[14] Some discussion of the patterns of the early Latin American slave trade can be found in Herbert S. Klein and Ben Vinson III, *African Slavery in Latin America and the Caribbean* (New York and Oxford: Oxford University Press, 2007), especially chapter 2.

[15] See Colin Palmer, *Slaves of the White God: Blacks in Mexico 1570–1650* (Cambridge: Harvard University Press, 1976). In fact, the number of slave imports to Mexico may have been higher. The ports of Campeche and Pánuco were important sites of illegal trade for which we have few statistics. Some insights can be found in María Luisa Herrera Cassasús, *Presencia y esclavitud del negro en la Huasteca* (Mexico: University Autónoma de Tamaulipas/Porrúa, 1988). It is plausible that up to 150,000 slaves had entered Mexico by 1640, which would rank the region second in New World slave imports, behind Brazil. See Frank Proctor III, *"Damned Notions of Liberty": Slavery, Culture, and Power in Colonial Mexico, 1640–1769* (Albuquerque: University of New

tremendous numbers, given the relative size of the white population at the time.[16] The slave gender imbalance, combined with the relative inaccessibility of white women for blacks during this period meant that much of the early miscegenation took place between free Indian women and black males, or between *mestizas* and blacks.[17] The few African women who were brought to the Spanish kingdom often engaged in miscegenation with their masters, frequently by force.

Atop black forced migration came sprinkles of immigrants from Asia. Acapulco, which was a main point of trade for the Manila galleons carrying merchandise from the Orient, brought streams of immigrants, especially from the Philippines and India. While some came voluntarily, others arrived as slaves, supplementing the West African workforce. The Asian slave trade was largely illegal, undergirded with complicated legislative twists. Until definitive actions were taken to abolish Asian slavery at the end of the seventeenth century (especially in 1672), traders managed to import between 60 and 300 individuals per year. Asians, known collectively as *chinos*, were typically sold at great profit but more cheaply than Africans, making them particularly welcome in the Americas.

A vibrant and intense period of trade transpired between 1580 and 1640. In all, tens of thousands of free and enslaved chinos (estimates run from 40,000 to 60,000) entered New Spain during the colonial era alone. Many became peddlers in small goods, barbers, fishermen, construction workers, militiamen, and agricultural workers. Given that barbers also used their skills as surgeons in colonial times, there were a number of Asian physicians.[18] What may be most striking for our purposes is that

Mexico Press, 2010), 15. Note also that Joseph M. Clark's reassessment of the slave trade in Veracruz may substantially revise the total number of slaves that we currently estimate entered New Spain. See "Veracruz and the Caribbean in the Seventeenth Century," (PhD diss.: Johns Hopkins University, 2016). He believes that 155,000 slaves entered New Spain during the height of the slave trade, with 60% coming from West Central Africa.

[16] The white population in Mexico was about 125,000 in 1646. For an elegant synthesis of the number of African slaves brought into the New World, see David Eltis, *The Rise of African Slavery in the Americas* (Cambridge: Cambridge University Press, 2000), 9.

[17] *Mestizo* was the caste label for the offspring of a white and an Indian. *Mestiza* refers to a female mestizo.

[18] The information on Asian populations in New Spain is drawn from magnificent studies by Tatiana Seijas, "Transpacific Servitude: The Asian Slaves of Mexico, 1580–1700," (PhD diss.: Yale University, 2008); and Seijas, *Asian Slaves in Colonial Mexico: From Chinos to Indians* (New York: Cambridge University Press, 2014), especially chapters 1 through 3, which include her estimates of the slave trade (60–61). However, see also Jonathan I. Israel, *Race, Class, and Politics in Colonial Mexico, 1610–1670* (Oxford:

some Asians, specifically Filipinos, were eligible to become members of Indian pueblos and barrios. Hence, upon arrival in the New World they were retrofitted into the dual republic system as indigenous peoples of the Spanish empire.[19] In cities like Acapulco, Puebla, and Mexico City, it was not uncommon to find Asian immigrants recorded as "indios manilos" (Manila Indians), "indios de Filipinas" (Philippine Indians), or "indios chinos" (Indians from the Far East).[20]

Africans, Asians, Native Americans, and Europeans comprised the foundation upon which New World racial mixture would occur. These groups were themselves deeply complex, given that they possessed a seemingly endless variety of national, cultural, and ethnic substrands. Obviously, although the predominant European population in the Spanish empire originated from the Iberian Peninsula, there were also immigrant streams from places like France, England, Italy, the Netherlands, and Germany.[21] Similarly, *indios*, a term invented in part for administrative convenience, functioned to fuse various indigenous New World populations into a manageable category for recordkeeping. In everyday practice, not all Spaniards adopted the term, because they understood its limitations and imprecision as a descriptor. In certain frontier settings, *indio* was used by Spaniards to refer broadly to Hispanicized native populations. More specific (but still not necessarily precise) nomenclature was used to identify subgroups, such as the Pima, Otomí, Mapuche, or Apache.[22]

Oxford University Press, 1975); and Edward R. Slack, "Sinifying New Spain: Cathay's Influence on Colonial Mexico via the *Nao de China*," *Journal of Chinese Overseas* 5, no. 1 (2009): 5–27. Note that I have used Slack's estimates for the arrival of Asians to New Spain on the whole, based on his survey of the literature. See Slack, "The Chinos in New Spain: A Corrective Lens for a Distorted Image," in *Journal of World History* 20, no. 1 (2009): 37.

[19] See Seijas, *Asian Slaves in Colonial Mexico*, 143–173. She observes that after 1672 in particular, when slavery was largely eliminated for chinos, the path was paved even more smoothly for chinos who desired to become members of New Spain's native communities to do so. Their actions in this regard built on the heritage and activities of those freedmen of Asian descent (especially Filipinos) who had successfully transitioned into New Spain's *indio* communities in the sixteenth and early seventeenth centuries.

[20] Some examples include AGN, Padrones, vol. 16, fols. 226 and 245; AGN, Indios, vol. 11, exp. 166, fols. 136v–137v; and AGN, Inquisición, vol. 312, exp. 45, fol. 228.

[21] For the role of other Europeans in Spain's empire, see Henry Kamen, *Empire: How Spain Became a World Power, 1492–1763* (New York: Harper Collins, 2003).

[22] The category "indio" was a Spanish fabrication, and at least in the Americas, it resulted from fusing together several New World ethnic groups into a single, more manageable social category that could facilitate political, economic, cultural, and social dominance. See Robert Jackson, *Race, Caste and Status: Indians in Colonial Spanish America* (Albuquerque: University of New Mexico Press, 1999), 28–29.

Africans, meanwhile, through the jumbling of identities that occurred during the Middle Passage, also came to the New World in variegated fashion. Despite the many ships that brought groups of individuals from regions that had deep historic familiarity with each other (creating a form of ethnic clustering that enabled cross-communication and the preservation of certain African traditions), the broader reality was that the New World produced amalgamations of African populations that had never been seen before.[23] Groups leaving the ports of Africa often traveled under common ethnic identifiers (Bran, Biafara, Fon, Mandinga, for example). However, they might have actually defined the meaning of these ethnicities in transit as they interacted with other Africans. Also likely is that the real meaning of these ethnic group names was realized mainly through the interpersonal interactions of Africans at their destinations, whether across the Atlantic, in Europe, or elsewhere.[24] Similar phenomena could be observed among chinos crossing the Pacific, who not only represented an amalgam of East Asian and Southeast Asian populations but also conjoined small numbers of East Africans who had migrated to the Philippines and India before entering the New World.[25] By the 1700s, in parts of New Spain it had also become vogue to use *chino* to categorize individuals of mixed Native American and African ancestry. Hence, over

[23] Linda M. Heywood and John K. Thornton, *Central Africans, Atlantic Creoles, and the Foundation of the Americas, 1585–1660* (New York: Cambridge University Press, 2007), and Gwendolyn Midlo Hall, *Slavery and African Ethnicities in the Americas: Restoring the Links* (Chapel Hill: University of North Carolina Press, 2005), offer statements on clustering.

[24] Russell Lohse, *Africans into Creoles: Slavery, Ethnicity, and Identity in Colonial Costa Rica* (Albuquerque: University of New Mexico Press, 2014); Herman L. Bennett, *Colonial Blackness: A History of Afro-Mexico* (Bloomington: Indiana University Press, 2009); Michael Angelo Gómez, *Exchanging Our Country Marks: The Transformation of African Identities in the Colonial and Antebellum South* (Chapel Hill: University of North Carolina Press, 1998); John K. Thornton, *A Cultural History of the Atlantic World, 1250–1820* (New York: Cambridge University Press, 2012).

[25] Pascale Girard, "Les Africains aux Philippines aux XVIe et XVIIe siècles," in *Negros, mulatos, zambaigos. Derroteros africanos en los mundos ibéricos*, ed. Berta Ares Queija and Alessandro Stella (Seville: Escuela de Estudios Hispano-Americanos, Consejo Superior de Investigaciones Científicas, 2000), 67–74. Girard notes that by 1636 Manila's population of 1,500 colonists contained between 400 and 500 blacks, causing preoccupation among government officials. Note that these themes touch on the concept and processes of ethnogenesis. For literature on this subject, see Jonathan D. Hill, *History, Power, and Identity: Ethnogenesis in the Americas, 1492–1992* (Iowa City: University of Iowa Press, 1996); Antonio Olliz-Boyd, *The Latin American Identity and the African Diaspora: Ethnogenesis in Context* (Amherst, NY: Cambria Press, 2010); and S. J. K. Wilkerson, "Ethnogenesis of the Huastecs and Totonacs: Early Cultures of North-Central Veracruz at Santa Luisa, Mexico" (PhD diss.: Tulane, 1972).

time, *chino* had come to mean several different things: a person from the Far East, a person who looked like someone from the Far East, someone brown, or someone who possessed a mixture of black and native ancestry.[26]

Skin color, lineage, ethnicity, culture, place of residence, place of birth, geographic mobility – these elements and more compounded the already bewildering task facing Spanish imperial administrators as they attempted to create an "orderly" society.[27] Major metropolitan centers and ports became natural sites for racial and ethnic fusion. It was clear that the dual republic system could not withstand the rapid changes occurring in the colonial population. At stake was the structure of white privilege. Indeed,

---

[26] At least this was the case for Mexico. According to the strict formulas of the caste system, a chino was the offspring of a lobo (already the mixture of an indio with a negra) and a negra. See "Lista de Castas," in *Artes de México* 8 (1990): 79. For more on the shift in the meaning of "chino" in New Spain, see Edward Slack's discussion based on the writings of don Joaquín Antonio de Basarás, who wrote extensively on chinos in Asia and New Spain, and who exemplified this contradiction in a two-volume work titled *Origen, costumbres y estado presente de mexicanos y philipinos. Descripción acompañada de 106 estampas en colores* (Mexico City: Landucci, 2006). See also Slack, "The Chinos in New Spain," 57–61.

[27] It is important to underscore that ethnic differences rapidly expanded the human variety that was endemic in the New World and intensified the work of administrators who were trying to generate common ties and affinities to unite the disparate peoples of the empire. Although the administrators' endgame was not true homogenization in the Americas, they did seek to create cultural bridges that were solid enough to foster fluid imperial operations, financial linkages, and a baseline level of harmony that would minimize violent outbreaks of rebellion and resistance. The hurdles of culture and ethnicity, along with racial complexity, posed a difficult barrier. Ironically, miscegenation offered a tool to overcome these challenges. The physical acts of miscegenation comprised the archetype of cross-cultural contact. In theory, miscegenation could unite individuals who were distant across the racial, cultural, and ethnic continuum. It could also bring into being new people (and hybrid cultures) forged from the shared experiences of their parentage in a specific environment. Yet at the same time mixture presented its own score of issues and tensions, since many factors could shape the cultural and social outcomes of miscegenation. As the progeny of interracial and interethnic unions emerged in the Americas, unequal access to power and privilege, regional demographic imbalances, and variances in how certain groups adapted to their environments led some people and their cultural forms to dominate others. Ultimately, the general tilt of the Spanish Empire was for miscegenation to spawn *criollo* (creole) culture, a distinctly New World product largely anchored in Iberian lifeways but richly informed by other cultural inputs. Much has been written about this. For some examples, see Nestor García Canclini, *Hybrid Cultures: Strategies for Entering and Leaving Modernity*, trans. Christopher L. Chiappari and Silvia L. López (Minneapolis, London: University of Minnesota Press, 1995); Joshua Lund, *The Impure Imagination: Toward a Critical Hybridity in Latin American Writing* (Minneapolis: University of Minnesota Press, 2006); and Ángel Rama and David L. Frye, *Writing across Cultures: Narrative Transculturation in Latin America* (Durham: Duke University Press, 2012).

what did white privilege mean when the legitimate son or daughter of a colonial magnate was racially mixed? How was white privilege to be transferred, or should it be, in the case of such a child? Did the introduction of white admixture elevate the pedigree of the offspring, allowing them to transcend the baser traits associated with nonwhites? Could legitimacy serve to override negative racial characteristics? Were the mixed children of legitimate unions the social equals of those who were not? What about the social station of parentage? Was a child born to an Indian governor's daughter and a white noble significantly superior to another born to a white artisan and a slave? If so, why? And how was the difference to be communicated socially and legislatively?

In the first decades of the sixteenth century, rather than deal directly with the full implications of race mixture, colonial bureaucrats and residents routinely chose to ignore many of the thorniest issues involved. When a Spaniard fathered (or, much less likely, mothered) a child with an Indian, a decision was made as to whether or not to recognize the child as legitimate. Children who were not recognized would be raised in indigenous communities. There they would adopt indigenous customs, worldviews, and language. In effect, these mixed children would become Indians. Children who were recognized as legitimate would be socialized as white, and the fact of racial mixture would be overlooked. The son of Juan Cano and Isabel Moctezuma, the daughter of the last ruling Aztec king, was one such child. Embraced as legitimate, he grew up to become one of the most influential members of the white creole nobility in the 1500s.[28] Initially, colonial authorities did not have any problem with these practices. In fact, they encouraged them; the mixed progeny of white aristocrats would fortify the ruling classes by increasing their constituency. During the early days, the number of whites, actual or honorary, was deemed a valuable resource in the project of implementing Spanish governance.

However, a series of mid-sixteenth-century conspiracies and rebellions, launched by creole and mestizo elites, helped change that perspective. A new attitude toward racial mixture began to emerge gradually between the 1540s and 1570s. It was at this time that the term *mestizo* began appearing with more frequency, becoming virtually synonymous with illegitimacy. The changes in both attitude and racial nomenclature coincided with other changes taking place in colonial society. In the specific

---

[28] *Creole* in the Latin American context comes from the Spanish word *criollo* and simply refers to whites who were born in the Indies.

context of New Spain, the year 1563 marked a coup attempt. Disgruntled estate owners who had participated in the conquest had become disaffected over time, as the colonial government steadily reduced their privileges and opportunities for wealth. Using Martín Cortés, the son of Hernán Cortés, as a figurehead, they plotted to assassinate members of the high bureaucracy and take control for themselves. The coup attempt's significance for understanding how it eroded prevailing racial attitudes rests in the extent of its socio-racial reach. Martín himself was a creole, and others involved included prominent individuals of mixed race. Centered as it was in Mexico City, the plot resonated with key members of government in ways that conspiracies launched elsewhere might not have. Those who were already suspicious about the loyalties of mestizos and creoles now became doubly so. Many of the conspirators were decapitated and had their heads placed on pikes for all to see. Cortés himself was spared.[29]

Another, and perhaps pivotal, colonial force behind the change in racial attitudes was the effect of the growing population of African slaves. It may not be coincidental that the rise of the mestizo category (despite *mestizo* being a term with an Old World history) came as the influx of Africans to the Spanish territories markedly increased.[30] In New Spain, for instance, blacks and whites were virtually at parity in terms of their demographic presence in the middle of the sixteenth century.[31] Nervous

[29] Ramón Osorio y Carbajal, *La conjura de Martín Cortés y otros sucesos de la época colonial* (Mexico City: Departamento del Distrito Federal, Secretaría de Obras y Servicios, 1973). As mestizo agitation was happening in places like Mexico City, there were parallel rebellions taking place in Spain itself during the middle of the seventeenth century, particularly among the moriscos in the Alpujarras region. The crown clearly conceived of these separate struggles as linked. Arguably, one by-product of these closely aligned episodes of resistance is that associations between moors and mestizos became more frequent, leaving a lasting imprint on mestizo identity. Some argue that the birth of the mestizo, in a legislative sense – replete with efforts to control and suppress this population – owes credit to the cauldron of resistance on both sides of the Atlantic. See Kathryn Burns, "Unfixing Race," in *Rereading the Black Legend: The Discourses of Religious and Racial Difference in the Renaissance Empires*, ed. Margaret R. Greer, Walter D. Mignolo, and Maureen Quilligan (Chicago: University of Chicago, 2007), 197–200.

[30] Ruth Hill has shown that in certain regions of southern Spain, *mestizo* was used to label people who were "Christian in name and Muslim in heart." See Hill, "Casta as Culture and the Sociedad de Castas as Literature," in *Interpreting Colonialism*, ed. Byron Wells and Philip Stewart (Oxford: Voltaire Foundation, 2004), 236–237.

[31] There were 20,000 blacks in Mexico in 1550, and there were 20,211 whites in 1560. See Palmer, *Slaves of the White God*, and Patricia Seed, *Amar, honrar y obedecer en el México colonial: conflictos en torno a la elección matrimonial, 1574–1821* (Mexico City: Conaculta; Alianza Editorial, 1991).

bureaucrats worried that if other colored groups joined with the mestizo population, they could easily overwhelm the colony's whites.[32] The government had reason to fear. The colony's black population had proved restless. A number of runaway slaves had been joining rebellious indigenous communities from as early as 1523. In New Galicia, from 1549 through the 1570s, free mulattos, vagabonds, and mestizos joined forces with runaway slaves and Chichimec Indians to launch a series of menacing highway raids. The same transpired in Guanajuato, Penjamo, and San Miguel during the 1560s. Throughout the sixteenth century, numerous runaway slave communities, or *palenques*, were established in Mexico, among them Cañada de los Negros (1576) near León and others outside of Antequera, Huatulco, Veracruz, and Orizaba. The most famous was the community of Yanga, which operated in the vicinity of Veracruz from the 1570s until 1609.

Among the most alarming events of the sixteenth century was a furtive attempt by blacks to overthrow the viceregal government, staged to launch at midnight on September 24, 1537. Blacks in Mexico City, both slave and free, had become aware of Spain's deep commitment to its wars in Europe and believed that if they precipitated a widespread revolt, the crown would be able to send only limited military resources and personnel to counter the uprising. As would become standard in several future revolt attempts, the conspirators elected a black king (probably a confraternity officer), an individual who may well have had royal lineage in Africa. Unfortunately for the rebels, the viceroy had planted among the slave population a number of spies who eventually infiltrated the plot. Hours before the rebellion was to take place, key arrests were made. Bounty hunters tracked and killed other suspects. The authorities of neighboring towns and cities were quickly notified of possible insurrectionary activities within their jurisdictions. In the aftermath of the thwarted uprising, such panic prevailed that a decision was made to build walls around Mexico City to handle potential future insurgencies. Additionally, the city's residents began practicing siege drills to deal with such emergencies. The year 1537 also marked the beginning of a stream of legislation that was directed at monitoring and controlling blacks – with such measures as preventing them from congregating in groups and carrying arms.[33]

---

[32] Israel, *Race, Class, and Politics*, 67–68.

[33] A careful and concise survey of some episodes of African resistance in Mexico is Frank Proctor III, "Slave Rebellion and Liberty in Colonial Mexico," in *Black Mexico: Race and Society from Colonial to Modern Times*, ed. Ben Vinson III and Matthew Restall

These were just the experiences of New Spain. Similar stories could be recounted from throughout the empire. As belligerent black runaway slave activity increased, and as more *palenques* were founded, scholars such as Jane Landers believe that the colonial government considered and partly enacted the creation of a "third republic." Its primary purpose was to augment the old dual republic system to provide a space for blacks.[34] New free-colored townships, built in the aftermath of maroon activity or other forms of resistance, became emblematic features of the republic.[35]

(Albuquerque: University of New Mexico Press: 2009), 21–50. For a general treatment of slave resistance throughout the colony, see Palmer, *Slaves of the White God*, 119–144. For the communities of Yanga and Veracruz, see Octaviano Corro Ramos, *Los cimarrones en Veracruz y la fundación de Amapa* (Veracruz: Comercial, 1951); Juan Laurencio, *Campaña contra Yanga en 1608* (Mexico City: Editorial Citlaltepetl, 1974); Gonzalo Aguirre Beltrán, *El negro esclavo en Nueva España* (Mexico City: Fondo de Cultura Económica, 1994), 179–186; and Antonio Carrión, *Historia de la Ciudad de Puebla de los Angeles*, Vol. 2, 2nd ed. (Puebla: Editorial Jose M. Cajica Jr, SA, 1970), 20–24. For material on less overt forms of slave resistance in Mexico, including marriage strategies, magic, and blasphemy, see Herman L. Bennett, *Africans in Colonial Mexico, Absolutism, Christianity and Afro-Creole Consciousness, 1570–1640* (Bloomington and Indianapolis: Indiana University Press, 2003); Joan C. Bristol, *Christians, Blasphemers, and Witches: Afro-Mexican Ritual Practice in the Seventeenth Century* (Albuquerque: University of New Mexico Press, 2007); Proctor, *Damned Notions of Liberty*, especially chapters 3–6; Javier Villa-Flores, "To Lose One's Soul: Blasphemy and Slavery in New Spain, 1596–1669," *Hispanic American Historical Review* 82, no. 3, (2002): 435–468; and Bennett, *Colonial Blackness*, especially chapter 6 and his discussion on freedom.

[34] Jane G. Landers, "Cimarrón and Citizen: African Ethnicity, Corporate Identity, and the Evolution of Free Black Towns in the Spanish Circum-Caribbean," in *Slaves, Subjects, and Subversives: Blacks in Colonial Latin America*, ed. Jane G. Landers and Barry M. Robinson (Albuquerque: University of New Mexico Press, 2006), 112, 130–132. Note that Landers's evidence comes heavily from late seventeenth-century New Spain. In one telling example, the black governors and officials in the black township of San Miguel Soyaltepeque, in the midst of disputes with local officials, referred to their community as a "república de negros." It seems that the government consciously administered them, and other similar townships, as a separate república.

[35] Although not explicitly referenced by Landers, one can perhaps identify townships like San Diego de Gomera (Guatemala), Vicente de Austria (El Salvador), the Puebla de Pardos (Costa Rica), Esmeraldas (Ecuador), and even El Cobre (Cuba), among others, as constituent parts of a so-called third republic, based on the rights and privileges that blacks enjoyed in these communities and the ways in which their livelihoods were connected through external representations of vassalage, not unlike the pueblos de indios. See Rina Cáceres, *Negros, mulatos, esclavos y libertos en la Costa Rica del siglo XVII* (Mexico: Instituto Panamericano de Geografía e Historia, 2000), 87–97; María Elena Díaz, *The Virgin, the King, and the Royal Slaves of El Cobre: Negotiating Freedom in Colonial Cuba, 1670–1780* (Stanford: Stanford University Press, 2000); Paul Lokken, "Marriage as Slave Emancipation in Seventeenth-Century Rural Guatemala," *The Americas* 58, no. 2 (2001): 186–188; and Charles Beatty Medina, "Caught between Rivals: The Spanish-African Maroon Competition for Captive Indian

While the existence of a *república de negros* proved short-lived at best, what did seem to endure was a deeper evaluation of the meaning of colonial racial mixture. As blacks began fortifying their presence with growth in the mulatto and free-black populations, concerns over social hierarchy intensified. Mestizos and blacks came to be seen as somewhat coterminous categories: both groups were threatening and had to be controlled. All of this took place within a context of growing preoccupation over racial purity and escalating rates of miscegenation.

This book is essentially about the processes and consequences of racial mixture. Much has been written on this topic over the past several decades, but what distinguishes this study is its quest to examine a story less well told. It is nearly common knowledge that Latin American racial complexity ran deep, and that hybridity constitutes a hallmark feature of the region's demography to the point of compelling national ideologies to address notions of racial inclusion (mestizaje). Despite these well-known characteristics, however, we know less about the profundity of racial mixture in colonial times and what the extremities of mixture entailed for society. Such is the focal point of this book.

Racial mixture: its beginnings in the New World spawned a crisis of order; its growth thrust to the fore existential questions on the essence of being. Racial mixture's everyday manifestations introduced a proliferation of new visual codes demarcating human difference, moving scientists, intellectuals, and moralists alike to contemplate the deeper meaning of biological markers. Racial mixture helped toss societies out of balance during the 1500s, a century of rapid and furious change, one of the greatest eras of population contact in human history. Spanish bureaucrats, legal minds, governors, businessmen, and plutocrats responded to what was happening around them, utilizing the primary lexicon and instruments that they had available. They put pen to page. They reasoned that racial mixture needed containment and order. However, much like sand slipping through one's hands while building sandcastles on a beach, as the racial scheme the Spaniards were creating came crumbling around them, the colonial regime rapidly tried rationalizing and rebooting racial mixture through reams of legislation known to the world as the colonial Spanish American caste system. What they didn't know was that this order was fleeting almost in the instant it was being launched, and that its very foundations were far from stable.

Labor in the Region of Esmeraldas during the Late Sixteenth and Early Seventeenth Centuries," *The Americas* 63, no. 1 (2006): 113–136.

As the efforts to build caste unfolded over the course of the colonial era, Spanish socio-racial terminologies grew dramatically. The sheer number of categories and the frameworks developed to explain phenotypic differences exceeded what could be found in the British and Dutch colonies, and quite possibly rivaled all other New World colonial experiences.[36] Using the case of New Spain, the task here is to study groups that represented the outliers of racial mixture – those that have long been considered marginal. Specifically, the book will look most closely at *lobos* (wolves), *moriscos* (Christians of Moorish origin), and *coyotes*; these castes and a number of others are referred to as "extreme castes" to indicate both the profundity of their mixture and their rarity in colonial society. Appendix A identifies nearly 700 essential documents housed in Mexico's Archivo General de la Nación (AGN) that have been used for this study. Although some historians consider these fringe caste groups to be spurious or even fictional, their appearance in the colonial record provokes us to reconsider this view. Is there something we can learn from them about the functioning, goals, and the long-term impact of social categorization systems? Do these caste groups teach us things we might have missed by focusing so much of our scholarly attention on populations that were more abundant in the Spanish colonies? Can we improve our understanding of the Spanish colonial regime by studying caste's boundaries? This book does not pretend that the groups forming its subject matter were universal in Latin America. Lobos, moriscos, and coyotes were not found everywhere. They were not even regularly encountered in New Spain. Rather, each region in the New World has its own extremes, its own frontiers of race and caste. In some places, it was *cuarterones* and *quinterones*; in others it was *zambos* and *zambaigos* (children of a black and an Indian).[37] Regardless of what constituted a colony's caste boundaries, the type of analysis

---

[36] For information on racial classification in the British and Dutch colonial world, see Daniel Livesay, "Children of Uncertain Fortune: Mixed-Race Migration from the West Indies to Britain, 1750–1820" (PhD diss.: University of Michigan, 2010); Willem Klooster, "Subordinate but Proud: Curaçao's Free Blacks and Mulattoes in the Eighteenth Century," *New West Indian Guide* 68, no. 3–4 (1994): 283–300; and James C. Armstrong and Nigel A. Worden, "The Slaves, 1652–1834," in *The Shaping of South African Society, 1652–1840*, ed. Richard Elphick and Hermann Giliomee (Middletown, CT: Maskew Miller Longman, 1989). In general, for the Dutch colonies the most common distinctions were made between blacks and mulattoes. A third category appeared in Curaçao by 1769: the *mustiesen*, that is the offspring of whites and mulattos. But by 1789, these groups were absorbed into the category of mulattos, a process that can be tracked through their militia participation.

[37] These terms can be found in various parts of Central and South America, such as Panama and Peru. For examples, see Queija and Stella, *Negros, mulatos, zambaigos*; and

conducted here for Mexico might well be applied elsewhere, leading to similar conclusions or altogether different answers.

This book, while focusing intently on the colonial period, is also intended to open greater dialogue with more modern eras. It invites us to consider deep historical antecedents that may have set the scene for the emergence of mestizaje, arguably one of the most powerful socio-racial ideologies to emerge in world history during the nineteenth and twentieth centuries. Quite possibly, the way that many caste groups were managed in the colonial period, their impact, and the frameworks in which racial and ethnic difference were articulated, especially at the extremes, may help provide a deeper contextual frame of reference for the ideas upon which mestizaje was based. Note that while *mestizaje* in itself means "racial mixture," I intentionally focus here on mestizaje's influence as an ideology, one that was the product of debates and historical processes emergent in the nineteenth and twentieth centuries. I do not want to suggest that there was always a direct linear connection between certain processes in the colonial period and mestizaje in its modern ideological form. Rather, the configurations may have been more isometric, sometimes leading to connections and sometimes not. The end product is hopefully a project that reveals a great deal about colonial times, while also presaging and laying hitherto unseen foundations for what was to come.

Given these goals, while it may otherwise seem odd to open a book that is largely about colonial Latin American history with a brief foray into more contemporary periods, I believe such a journey will offer valuable material to framing the discussion of the colonial era. It will help us see what is distinctive and useful in constructing a broader socio-racial history. With this in mind, I invite you now to fast-forward into the formal era of modern mestizaje – the aftermath of the colonial period's flourishing racial mixture and fluidity.

Ann Twinam, *Purchasing Whiteness: Pardos, Mulatos, and the Quest for Social Mobility in the Spanish Indies* (Stanford: Stanford University Press, 2015).

2

Mestizaje 1.0: The Moment Mixture Had Modern Meaning

At the outset of the twentieth century, Latin America stood at a critical, transitional moment. Nearly a hundred years of war had ravaged the region, destroying economies and precipitating deep social and political rifts. Yet by 1900, there was much to be optimistic about. Substantial foreign investment, marked by careful attention to the development of infrastructure, complemented an increasingly stable political system that was becoming more inclusive and participatory despite the lingering legacy of authoritarian regimes. The region was on the move, enjoying increased modernization, urbanization, and living standards greater than those of emerging economies in Africa and Asia.

Culturally too, Latin America was coming into its own, showcasing artistic styles that had come into being by melding class and ethnic boundaries, and that in turn molded the national ideologies of the times.[1] However, while Latin America had largely uplifted itself from

---

[1] For the development of Latin America during this period, see John Charles Chasteen, *Born in Blood and Fire: A Concise History of Latin America* (New York: Norton, 2001); David Bushnell and Neill Macaulay, *The Emergence of Latin America in the Nineteenth Century* (New York: Oxford University Press, 1988); Thomas E. Skidmore and Peter H. Smith, *Modern Latin America* (New York: Oxford University Press, 1984); Lawrence A. Clayton and Michael L. Conniff, *History of Modern Latin America* (Fort Worth, TX: Harcourt Brace College Humanities, 1999); Robin D. Moore, *Nationalizing Blackness: Afrocubanismo and Artistic Revolution in Havana, 1920–1940* (Pittsburgh: University of Pittsburgh Press, 1997); and John Charles Chasteen, *National Rhythms, African Roots: The Deep History of Latin American Popular Dance* (Albuquerque: University of New Mexico Press, 2004).

FIGURE 6 "The Cares of a Growing Family."
Source: "The cares of a growing family seen through the Bee's prophescopic scoopograph," New York Public Library, General Research Division, Digital Collections, http://digitalcollections.nypl.org/items/9400421e-c06c-4fc1-e040-e0 0a18065ca1, accessed May 5, 2016. The *Bee* was published in Earlington, Kentucky.

colonial and imperial embraces, it could not escape the phantom of its colonial history (see Figure 6). For close to a century, the region had been working to overcome the stigmas that haunted it, while at the same time trying to absorb positive qualities from the past in its strides towards modernity. Its complex racial composition had posed serious challenges to effective management for the Spanish bureaucracy during colonial times, and from the perspective of most European nations and Latin America's increasingly powerful northern neighbors, race remained a problematic issue (see Figure 7).

Throughout the nineteenth century, conservative and liberal political parties hotly debated and fought wars over the terms of regional progress, pitting colonial-era traditions and institutional privilege (the conservative standpoint) against greater secularization, democratization, equality, and economic freedom (the liberal perspective). For both

FIGURE 7 "Next!" Venezuela Comes In for a Haircut.
Source: *Next!* January 31, 1905, Berryman Political Cartoon Collection,
1896–1949, U.S. National Archives, Record Group 46: Records of the US Senate,
1789–2015.

sides, race stood uncomfortably as a barrier.[2] In an age in which positivist philosophy reigned supreme, social theorists postulated that race

---

[2] In actuality, the liberal and conservative conflicts were considerably more complex,
being often bound in very local and regional subfeuds that did not always neatly
align with the agendas outlined here. See Peter Guardino, *The Time of Liberty: Popular
Political Culture in Oaxaca, 1750–1850* (Durham: Duke University Press, 2005); Charles
A. Hale, *Transmission of Liberalism in Late Nineteenth-Century Mexico* (Princeton:
Princeton University Press, 1989); and Marixa Lasso, *Myths of Harmony: Race and
Republicanism during the Age of Revolution, Colombia, 1795–1821* (Pittsburgh:
University of Pittsburgh Press, 2007). For a hyperlocal example of liberal-conservative
tensions that boiled over into violence between the cities of León and Granada in
Nicaragua, see E. Bradford Burns, *Patriarch and Folk: The Emergence of Nicaragua,
1798–1858* (Cambridge: Harvard University Press, 1991), 5–50.

was both a barometer of the health of nations and a prognosticator of potential future advancement. Simply put, in the eyes of some politicians, intellectuals, and scientists who were deeply influenced by prevailing world opinion, Latin America's large black and native heritage, even if mixed into a hybrid mestizo and mulatto mainstream, threatened to corrode the character of the workforce, the moral capacity of the citizenry, and the region's collective mental acuity.

Social theorists in the nineteenth century strongly reinforced the notion that there were some basic, fundamental variations in humans, plainly visible in the form of race. Such thinking manifested itself in Western intellectual circles as a polygenistic view of human evolution, one that espoused the idea that humans were derived from different lineages, or stock, and thus possessed varying degrees of abilities that were transmissible to their progeny.[3] Using these ideas about human difference, many intellectuals reasoned that races had to be periodically overhauled for the benefit of sustaining orderly societies. For the record, polygenism was not the only major socio-scientific theory of the era. Polygenists routinely faced off against monogenists, who believed that all of humanity shared a common ancestry, on the basis of Judeo-Christian teachings about Adam and Eve.

Defenders of these two viewpoints had collided violently between the sixteenth and nineteenth centuries. Early polygenists such as Isaac de la Peyrère, Giordano Bruno, and François Bernier postulated in the seventeenth century that there had been separate acts of creation accounting for different human types, such as Gentiles, Jews, and Africans. Their opponents, meanwhile, sought increasingly more-scientific explanations of monogenism. The renowned philosopher Pierre-Louis Moreau de Maupertuis, along with his French fellow naturalist, the Comte de Buffon, lodged an important eighteenth-century critique based on the existence of albino populations. The spontaneous appearance of white offspring among dark-skinned peoples (and the absence of the reverse) offered seemingly incontrovertible proof that original man was white. All albinos, whether born in Africa or among native populations in Latin America, were simply reversions, going back to the original human type. Essentially, people could descend from the same family tree but become different over time. Scores of monogenists came to reason that human variance might best be explained by external circumstances such as climate, environment, food, and even engagement in sin.

[3] Peter Wade, *Race and Ethnicity in Latin America* (Chicago: Pluto Press, 1997), 6–12; Michael Banton, *Racial Theories* (Cambridge: Cambridge University Press, 1998).

From at least the fifteenth century, many Christians believed that Africans were black because of a biblical curse against Ham.[4]

As debates raged into the nineteenth century, and as various camps of intellectuals gathered greater mounds of ethnographic and scientific proof to sustain their respective positions about the fundamental origins of human difference, questions began to mount concerning the consequences of prolonged contact between different populations. For both monogenists and polygenists, the fear that humans could be tainted through their interactions (especially sexual ones) continually arrested the conversation. In the eighteenth century, Buffon, as well as the influential Scottish surgeon John Hunter, advanced the idea that human racial mixture could eventually produce infertile offspring, despite ample evidence from the New World to the contrary. These ideas continued to hold influence early into the 1800s.

By the mid-nineteenth century, it had become common for scientists in the West to assert that intermixture's effects varied according to how distant one human group was from another. In other words, the mixture between the Irish and French bore less degenerative consequences than, say, between Africans and Europeans. Scholars such as Edward East further warned that crossbreeding very distant genetic stock increased the danger that any positive traits carried by the dominant

---

[4] Many believed that Ham's descendants were doomed to blackness because Ham saw his drunken father, Noah, naked, with his genitals exposed. The reputed curse of Noah against Cain was believed to have been issued because Cain had killed his brother. The story is a corruption of biblical texts, since it was Adam's son Cain (not Noah's son) who killed his brother, Abel. The misrepresentations and commingling of the stories of Ham and Cain ultimately gave rise to the modern myth of the racial curse of Ham. Even authors who accurately knew both biblical stories proceeded to signify perpetual blackness as the curse bestowed on Ham. Rebecca Earle has discussed convincingly how Gomes Eanes de Zurara, the fifteenth-century Portuguese chronicler and traveler to West Africa, may have been responsible for this error and for widely disseminating it. See Earle, *The Body of the Conquistador: Food, Race, and the Colonial Experience in Spanish America, 1492–1700* (Cambridge: Cambridge University Press, 2012), 191–196. For an excellent treatment of the evolution of polygenist and monogenist thought, as well as albinism's role, see Andrew Curran, "Rethinking Race History: The Role of the Albino in the French Enlightenment Life Sciences," *History and Theory* 48, no. 3 (2009): 151–179, and *The Anatomy of Blackness: Science & Slavery in an Age of Enlightenment* (Baltimore: Johns Hopkins University Press, 2011), 20, 87–113. For an excellent recent treatment of albinism in the colonial period, see Ilona Katzew, "White or Black? Albinism and Spotted Blacks in the Eighteenth-Century Atlantic World," in *Envisioning Others: Race, Color and the Visual in Iberia and Latin America*, ed. Pamela A. Patton (Leiden and Boston: Brill Press, 2016), 142–186. Finally, for more on Ham, see Robin Blackburn, *The Making of New World Slavery: From the Baroque to the Modern, 1492–1800* (London: Verso, 1997), 66–76.

race would become susceptible to permanent rupture and loss, not just deterioration, over a single generation.[5] To guard against these unwanted outcomes, thinkers including Francis Galton liberally juxtaposed and borrowed ideas from the latest scientific findings in search of solutions.

In 1869, Galton published *Hereditary Genius*, which misused Charles Darwin's theory of evolution to argue that careful human breeding could help produce desirable populations. Galton was very optimistic, suggesting that through social instruments and state policies humans could successfully engineer ideal population types, accomplishing results much faster than nature could on its own.[6] His ideas formed the core principles of the eugenics movement, which was further interwoven with the positivist theories of Herbert Spencer and Auguste Comte, to whom the "survival of the fittest" maxim can be credited.[7] Spencerian thought, widely prevalent in the second half of the nineteenth century and very influential in Latin America, used biological metaphors and biological science to explain social phenomena, creating an elaborate classification system of races that ranged from superior (civilized) races, to the semicivilized and barbarous savages.[8] By the end of the nineteenth century, as science strove to understand, classify, and harness nature – and by association the nature of states – it seemed that the human biological composition of Latin America was ultimately signaling that its progress was almost irreparably corrupted and doomed from within. Unless major change happened quickly, Latin

---

[5] Paul Lawrence Farber, *Mixing Races: From Scientific Racism to Modern Evolutionary Ideas* (Baltimore: Johns Hopkins University Press, 2011), 33; Edward East and Donald Jones, *Inbreeding and Outbreeding: Their Genetic and Sociological Significance* (Philadelphia: Lippincott, 1919), 253.

[6] For more on this notion, see Nancy L. Stepan, *The Hour of Eugenics: Race, Gender, and Nation in Latin America* (Ithaca, NY: Cornell University Press, 1991), 22–24; and Francis Galton, *Hereditary Genius* (Bristol, UK: Thoemmes Press, 1998).

[7] Auguste Comte and Gertrud Lenzer, *Auguste Comte and Positivism: The Essential Writings* (New York: Harper & Row, 1975).

[8] Lee Baker, *From Savage to Negro: Anthropology and the Construction of Race, 1896–1954* (Berkeley: University of California Press, 2007), 29–31; Herbert Spencer, *Classification of the Sciences: To Which Are Added Reasons for Dissenting from the Philosophy of M. Comte* (New York: Don Appleton and Company, 1864). Note that Leopoldo Zea has argued that Comtean positivism was influential in Brazil, whereas Spencerian positivism was more influential in the Spanish-speaking world. With its emphasis on the "survival of the fittest," the latter could accommodate more-revolutionary ideologies, such as support for Cuba's break from Spain. See Leopoldo Zea, *The Latin-American Mind* (Norman: University of Oklahoma Press, 1963), 29–30.

America, despite its greatest strides, would never fully join the top tier of nations.[9]

In the early twentieth century, a new series of responses emerged to contest these views. The message of positivism had certainly been persuasive to scores of Latin American statesmen, intellectuals, and social engineers, including individuals of no less repute than Domingo Faustino Sarmiento (president of Argentina), Alcides Arguedas (Bolivian intellectual), Justo Sierra (Mexican politician), Gabindo Barreda (Mexican educator and intellectual), Raimundo Nina Rodrigues (Brazilian physician and intellectual), Alejandro O. Deustua (Peruvian philosopher), and Euclides da Cunha (Brazilian sociologist). But even some of the principal adherents of positivism realized that it could not simply be adopted wholesale. It would have to be massaged and adjusted to Latin American realities and conditions. Of course, being a collage of theories with complex substrands, positivism exhibited the malleability to accommodate some of the alternative viewpoints held by Latin American intellectuals. However, in the latter part of the nineteenth century, and even more so in the early twentieth century, as Latin America increasingly experimented with its own forms of self-categorization in its social and national development, some individuals did not wholly embrace (and often vigorously eschewed) the positivist frameworks emanating from Europe.[10]

It was in this context that thinkers such as Venezuela's Gil Fortul, an avowed positivist, adopted notions like "social race," expressing the belief that while mestizos were unquestionably the population best adapted to living and working in the tropics, Latin America could still benefit from infusions of white immigrants who could enhance the cultural capacity of society at large.[11] Probably without even realizing their source, many

[9] Tremendous expectations had been built up in Latin America by travelers such as Alexander von Humboldt, who noted that Latin America's resources would position her for greatness. The drawbacks and limitations of progress were felt and viewed as doubly problematic, given the rosy forecasts of foreign visitors to Latin America in previous eras. See Von Humboldt, *The Travels and Researches of Alexander von Humboldt: Being a Condensed Narrative of His Journeys in the Equinoctial Regions of America, and in Asiatic Russia: Together with an Analysis of His More Important Investigations* (New York: J. & J. Harper, 1833).

[10] This can be detected in the case of Mexico with the establishment of the Ateneo de la Juventud, the writings of Antonio Saco, and the work of Felix F. Palavicini, *México: historia de su evolución constructiva* (Mexico City: Libro, 1945); see also Antonio Caso, *Discursos a la nación mexicana* (Mexico City: Porrúa, 1922).

[11] Winthrop R. Wright, *Café con Leche: Race, Class, and National Image in Venezuela* (Ann Arbor, MI: UMI Books on Demand, 2003), 54–59. Social race was also important

oppositional ideas arising in this period sprang from a long tradition of Latin American and Iberian resistance to the primary intellectual positions that had governed science and social thinking from at least the seventeenth century. In particular, as European philosophers and naturalists argued about the extent to which the New World was inferior to the Old World, and how its environment, diet, and climate negatively affected its inhabitants, the creole elite – who took these as deeply personal attacks – developed an encompassing epistemological defense of their lifeways. This creole patriotic epistemology, as some have called it, extended into the realms of medicine, astrology, botany, and climatology, among others.[12] Because these defenses were intimately associated with the old colonial order and its hierarchy, they quickly fell from favor in the post-independence period.[13] Yet they were not without influence and were partly resurrected as Latin America designed its late nineteenth-century responses to critiques about its racial heritage, especially surrounding questions of race mixture.

What was palpably new at the turn of the twentieth century was a near-contemporaneous, region-wide crystallization of ideas and opinions regarding racial mixture that had long been in the making. Roughly speaking, in the period stretching from 1893 when the Cuban intellectual José Martí wrote *My Race* – an engaged, passionate, and insightful plea for Cuban unity predicated upon racial harmony – through 1933 when Gilberto Freyre formulated his classic arguments about the evolution of the so-called Brazilian race in the tropics in *Casa grande e senzala*, there was a movement afoot in Latin America that challenged the precepts of pseudoscience. It gave rise to a bold new acceptance in the region of its own racial distinctiveness. The spirit of the era proffered visions of racial mixture that differed in tenor from those found in the earlier nineteenth-century

to thinkers like Freyre who picked up on the term and its usefulness in allowing biological race to be disassociated from cultural and social factors. In this way, one could conveniently extol mixed-race origins while also advocating for new infusions of whites, who would add a smattering of other nonbiological benefits to a populace. On social race, see Charles Wagley, *Race and Class in Rural Brazil* (Paris: UNESCO, 1952).

[12] Jorge Cañizares-Esguerra, *How to Write a History of the New World: Histories, Epistemologies, and Identities in the Eighteenth-Century Atlantic World* (Stanford: Stanford University Press, 2001); Cañizares-Esguerra, "New World, New Stars"; and Carlos López Beltrán, "Hippocratic Bodies: Temperament and Castas in Spanish America (1570–1820)," *Journal of Spanish Cultural Studies* 8, no. 2 (2007): 253–289. These provide excellent material for understanding what Cañizares-Esguerra calls a "creole patriotic epistemology."

[13] David A. Brading, *The Origins of Mexican Nationalism* (Cambridge: Cambridge University Press, 1985); Cañizares-Esguerra, *How to Write a History*, 204–206.

writings of individuals like José Antonio Saco, the noted Cuban nationalist and abolitionist, who argued that racial mixture was necessary for Cuba to avoid the fate of Haiti, a society he believed was hopelessly overrun with blacks.[14] For Saco and thinkers like him, mixture offered an antidote to degeneracy. Measured and controlled breeding, emphasizing the union between white men and black women (as opposed to black men and white women), meant that the progeny of racial mixture could be better managed, since the new mulatto offspring would fall fully under the purview their white fathers.[15]

In essence, Saco, like many of his counterparts, articulated a vision known as "whitening" (*blanqueamiento*), which advocated for mixture without glorifying the cultural roots of the nonwhites essential to the mix. It was even common to openly spurn nonwhite culture.[16] On the other hand, the new and emergent twentieth-century vision of mixture was arguably more idealistic, more celebratory of Latin America's cultural past, and more insistent on articulating the soul of a continent. These works were not without their flaws. José Martí's writings at times indicted Afro-Cubans for their lack of European culture.[17] Freyre's own *Casa grande* centralized the plantation experience, elevating it almost romantically in Brazilian history, while endorsing many of the master-slave relations that later generations of scholars and laypersons would find abominable.[18] In this sense, both Freyre's and Martí's writings and several other works from the period essentially manifested themselves to be

[14] It is important to note the irony of Saco being both an antislavery sympathizer and notably unsympathetic to elevating the position and rights of blacks and the status of blacks more generally in Cuban society. See Manuel Moreno Fraginals and Cedric Belfrage, *The Sugar Mill: The Socioeconomic Complex of Sugar in Cuba, 1760–1860* (New York: Monthly Review Press, 2008).

[15] Lourdes Martínez-Echazabal, "'Mestizaje' and the Discourse of National/Cultural Identity in Latin America, 1845–1959," *Latin American Perspectives: A Journal of Capitalism and Socialism* 25, no. 3 (May 1998): 21–42.

[16] This was a common occurrence. For an example from Colombia, see José Eusebio Caro, Esther Vargas Arbeláez, and Germán Vargas Guillén, *Mecánica social, o, teoría del movimiento humano, considerado en su naturaleza, en sus efectos y en sus causas* (Bogotá: Instituto Caro y Cuervo, 2002).

[17] For full treatment of the multiple cults of personality surrounding Jose Martí, see Lillian Guerra, *The Myth of José Martí: Conflicting Nationalisms in Early Twentieth-Century Cuba* (Chapel Hill: University of North Carolina Press, 2005).

[18] A still useful and perceptive article on Freyre's work and times is Jeffrey D. Needell, "Identity, Race, Gender, and Modernity in the Origins of Gilberto Freyre's Oeuvre," *American Historical Review* 100, no. 1 (February 1995): 51–77. See also David Cleary, "Race, Nationalism, and Social Theory in Brazil: Rethinking Gilberto Freyre," Working Paper TC-99-09, David Rockefeller Center for Latin American Studies, Harvard

paternalistic, focused on indicating how the creole elite would guide disparate populations back to lost grandeur. Distinct racial or ethnic groups could not achieve such a glorious state on their own. Rather (and this is where the power of nationalism came into play), each nation needed to harness all of its constituent groups through a process of recombinant fusion, yielding an outcome wherein the sum of the whole was greater than its parts.[19]

Improved technologies of communication, international travel, and greater access to documents, manifestos, and ideas – alongside a shared awareness of the joint challenges confronting Latin America in the face of global attitudes toward race – facilitated the rapid and concurrent development of these messages in the early twentieth century. Likewise, Latin America's political and economic rise promoted a new and ever more apparent self-confidence, fostering the development of stronger nationalist perspectives, policies, and rhetoric vis-à-vis the greater world. As was splendidly captured in the essay *Ariel*, published in 1900 by the Uruguayan writer José Enrique Rodó, Latin America viewed its exceptionalism as valuable, to be counterpoised against the decadent forms of materialism that were inherent to the supposedly great capitalist societies.[20] Soon afterward, during World War I, the stature of European power cascaded in complete free fall. Not only was European racial supremacy thrown into question by the actions of war, but even the economic grip that countries like Great Britain had over Latin America was evaporating. Conversely, the United States was gaining a stronger foothold south of its borders, punctuated by aggressions in Mexico (1846–48) and Cuba (1898), sparking a number of Latin Americans to fear the imminent installation of a US-style racial system that would actively work to exclude them from participating in the civic and cultural

University, 2005. www.transcomm.ox.ac.uk/working%20papers/cleary.pdf, accessed May 27, 2016.

[19] Valuable discussion on this theme can be found in Peter Wade, *Blackness and Race Mixture: The Dynamics of Racial Identity in Colombia* (Baltimore: Johns Hopkins University Press, 1993), 3–12; and Richard Graham, Thomas E. Skidmore, Aline Helg, and Alan Knight, *The Idea of Race in Latin America, 1870–1940* (Austin: University of Texas Press, 1990). Note that one can compare trends occurring in Latin America with the rise and outcome of ameliorationist discourses that took place in the Anglophone world some time earlier. The extent to which these processes were interrelated and connected to one another is seemingly worth further research. See George Boulukos, *The Grateful Slave: The Emergence of Race in Eighteenth-Century British and American Culture* (Cambridge: Cambridge University Press, 2008).

[20] José Enrique Rodó, *Ariel* (Austin: University of Texas Press, 1988).

lives of their own countries.[21] Undergirding these fears was a burgeoning new reality. Over the course of the nineteenth century, Latin America's civil society had been growing by leaps and bounds, with people of mixed race rising both to important middling positions and posts of deep influence and power. Justifiably, some asked where their place would be in a future clouded by the prevailing racial theories of the day. And what would happen if these views were not opposed?

An emerging crisis within pseudoscience helped offer a language of opposition, as well as the intellectual scaffolding needed to construct the ideas that conveyed Latin America's racial situation as favorable for regional development. Columbia University professor Franz Boas, long heralded as the founder of modern cultural anthropology, was among the global leaders in the charge against pseudoscientific thought. In *The Mind of Primitive Man*, he launched a scathing critique of the myth of European racial purity, revealing that in actuality racial mixture had been transpiring within Europe for centuries.[22] Part of Boas's legacy also involved bringing new light to the role of the environment and culture in shaping human behavioral outcomes, severely delimiting any biologically deterministic assumptions about the correlation between genetics and behavior. Indeed, Boas was a champion of the view that humans of different races fundamentally differed little.

The assault led by Boas brought together a vanguard of scholars and scientists, several of whom were his own students. Into the twentieth century, Melville Herskovits, Margaret Mead, Ruth Benedict, and Ashley Montagu spearheaded discussions and research that would continue to weaken not only eighteenth-century definitions of race, but also flawed nineteenth-century research connecting science, race, and social policies.[23] Notably, Boas visited Mexico City, where he delivered lectures at the National Autonomous University in 1910 and 1911. He trained Manuel Gamio, who proceeded to become one of the prime architects of Mexico's twentieth-century national narrative on racial mixture.[24] Boas's work also helped Latin American thinkers reject arguments surrounding the genetic inferiority of native populations, thereby permitting the incubation of *indigenismo* – an ideology

---

[21] Latin Americans had much to fear as well from US anti-Catholic leanings. See Janice L. Hayes, *The Illusion of Ignorance: Constructing the American Encounter with Mexico, 1877–1920* (Lanham, MD: University Press of America, 2011), 70.

[22] Franz Boas, *The Mind of Primitive Man* (Lexington, Kentucky: Forgotten Books, 2011).

[23] A good and readable survey of racial practices is Farber, *Mixing Races*.

[24] Manuel Gamio, *Forjando Patria* (Mexico City: Porrúa, 1960).

championed in Peru and Mexico that valorized native contributions to the nation-state.[25]

Slowly, the countries of Latin America came forward to test the new social ideas. In the 1920s, Mexico, having endured one of the hemisphere's greatest social revolutions, served as a primary breeding ground for crafting and implementing the new rhetoric. José Vasconcelos (Figure 8), Mexico's first secretary for education in the postrevolutionary period, wrote a seminal work titled *La raza cósmica*, through which he emerged as the principal voice of *mestizaje*. Like many influential concepts, the term was not new when Vasconcelos coined it. By 1831, if not earlier, mestizaje had been used to describe mixture, albeit in the realm of animal breeding.[26] By the late nineteenth century, *mestizaje* was being used in Mexico alongside terms such as *cruzamiento* and *mestización* to describe processes of hybridity in both the human and natural worlds.[27] In the 1870s and 1880s, Mexican intellectuals were also discussing mestizaje in light of a theory of *métissage*, emanating from France, which combined findings from Charles Darwin's *Origins of Species* with thoughts about mixture and heredity in human populations.[28] In 1879,

---

[25] Although Boas's work did help move *indigenismo* forward, Latin American thinkers also borrowed notions embedded in his writings that suggest that while native populations may not have been genetically inferior, they were possibly culturally primitive. See "Mi Andina y Dulce Rita: Women, Indigenism, and the Avant-Garde in César Vallejo," in *Primitivism and Identity in Latin America: Essays on Art, Literature, and Culture*, eds. Erik Camayd-Freixas and José Eduardo González (Tucson: University of Arizona Press, 2000), 241–266.

[26] Marqués de la Vega Armijo, *Observaciones del Excmo. Marqués de la Vega Armijo sobre la mejora de las castas de caballo en España* (Madrid: Don Eusebio Aguado, 1831), 20, 23–24.

[27] *Boletín de Agricultura Minera e Industrias*, October 1, 1891, Mexico City, 56–58; *Semana Mercantíl*, Mexico City, December 13, 1886, 579.

[28] The publication of Darwin's *On the Origins of Species*, particularly the French translations of it by the noted scholar Clémence Royer, drew attention from Mexican intellectuals and influenced the development of the concept of mestizaje. Royer took the liberty of adding a long introduction to Darwin's work wherein she expounded upon his ideas by discussing *métissage*, her own theory of hybridism's impact on humans. Royer would articulate métissage again in other contexts, provoking more debate on what Mexicans discussed as mestizaje. See Clémence Royer, "La question du métissage," *Actes de la Société d'Ethnographie* 10 (Paris, 1886): 49–57. The Mexican thinker R. de Zayas Enríquez critiqued Royer's idea that racial mixture (*métissage*) was responsible for criminality in certain people. See Zayas, "Fisiología del crimen," *El Siglo XIX*, Mexico City, October 30, 1891. R. de Zayas felt that a deep understanding of social causes (as opposed to psychological reasons) was necessary for explaining criminal behavior. For more on Mexican trends in the study of crime, see Pablo Piccato, *City of Suspects: Crime in Mexico City, 1900–1931* (Durham: Duke University Press, 2001). He addresses Zayas on p. 65.

FIGURE 8 *José Vasconcelos and Diego Rivera during an Outdoor Event at Chapultepec Park, Mexico City, 1921.* Black-and-white photograph taken in 1921 by Tina Modotti (1896–1942). José Vasconcelos appears on the left and Diego Rivera to his right.
Source: Reproduced courtesy Galerie Bilderwelt/Bridgeman Images.

the Mexico City newspaper *La Libertad* carried an interesting article that seemed to anticipate Vasconcelos's formulation of mestizaje by several decades. In one of the paper's regular columns titled "Cosas del día" (Items of the Day), a writer reflected on the "true problem facing Mexico." According to the author, the preeminent challenges were economic in nature, and for those concerned that the nation's large native population constituted an additional burden on workforce capacity, there was little to fear:

The Mexican indigenous race has demonstrated in another age the singular aptitude for creating material civilization. It has cultivated noble arts whose vestiges are still latent in their spirit ... [T]he degeneration produced by the conquest is no longer in effect. The principles of natural selection that govern the universe and morals do not work against the native population in Mexico ... [D]ue to *mestizaje* [my emphasis], greater numbers infiltrate the general population daily, such that in time a new natural group of people will emerge that one might genuinely call "*mexicano.*"[29]

Mestizaje here clearly referred to racial mixture in a progressive sense, and as such it promised two goals. First, it offered hope that a new and better day for Mexico was on the horizon through racial mixture, and second, it signaled that the qualities of scorned populations were not only salvageable but potentially positive contributors to nationhood.

In the 1920s, Vasconcelos's *La raza cósmica* consolidated these various lines of thinking, linking them to a dynamic constellation of other ideas. The author's final manuscript was a relatively short treatise – compelling, poetic, and coherent – that was as much a statement of philosophy as a template for action. The work demonstrated broad formative intellectual influences ranging from classical works of antiquity, the Alexandrian School, and Theosophy to more-modern European thinkers (including Herbert Spencer) and philosophers from India. Vasconcelos expressed the conviction that the world was entering a new stage of development and that mankind was transitioning out of an existence in which reason predominated. There existed a higher-level knowledge than science, and in the new "aesthetic age," principles such as joy and love would steer future relationships, decisions, and practices. Unfettered by the constraints of scientific thinking, racial mixture would markedly accelerate.

From this mixture, a new race of people would emerge as dominant – a "cosmic race" fashioned through a Darwinist selection process and shepherded by love. Vasconcelos knew that his new race would be better than anything that had come beforehand, primarily because the best qualities of each group would manifest themselves through mixture. With a visionary stroke, Vasconcelos wrote that Latin America had taken the early lead in this process, bearing one of the world's most

[29] *La Libertad*, "Cosas del día," Mexico City, November 12, 1879.

progressive and racially mixed peoples. The future needed even more intense hybridity and cultural fusion to complete the cycle. But to be fully successful, Vasconcelos cautioned, Latin America would have to remain vigilant against the seductions of the intellect and remain steadfast on the path of love.[30] While Vasconcelos himself would later express ambivalence concerning the power of hybridity to accomplish such lofty goals – as well as skepticism about whether Mexico was indeed emblematic of his "cosmic race" – nevertheless, once his vision was outlined, it rapidly assumed a life of its own.[31]

Outside of Mexico the symbolism of mestizaje would not be lost upon nations seeking similar national metaphors and symbols. Postindependence Cuba, needing to reconcile differences and racial divides within its population, along with Venezuela, Peru, and Brazil (among others), with their substantial mixed-race intelligentsia, eventually developed complementary ideologies.[32] Mestizaje, Brazilian *mestiçagem*, and *mulataje* (stressing the value inherent in the mixture of black and white populations), followed by indigenismo, quickly became iconic markers of regional identity and nationalist sentiment. In truth, as has already been noted, several of the core principles underlying these concepts were far from new and could be identified as far back as colonial times. However, they gained new dimension and force under a confluence of unique historical factors that ignited their power throughout the region. Apart from a few exceptions such as Argentina, the image of the hybridized mestizo personage (*lo mestizo*) evolved between 1930 and 1940 into the prototypical, ideal Latin American somatic type. Mestizaje had become mainstream ideology. Soon thereafter many Latin American countries declared themselves racial democracies, wherein racial discrimination was considered absent and where everyone purportedly possessed equal opportunities to succeed.

[30] José Vasconcelos and Didier T. Jaén, *The Cosmic Race: A Bilingual Edition* (Baltimore: Johns Hopkins University Press, 1997), ix–xxx.

[31] Vasconcelos displayed his reserve in his 1938 book, *El desastre, tercera parte de Ulises criollo, continuación de la tormenta* (Mexico City: Ediciones Botas, 1938). Vasconcelos's split with Plutarco Elías Calles and his loss in the 1932 presidential election also weighed in on his take on the loftier notions of mestizaje. As a Oaxacan, he was never fully a member of the Sonora dynasty. I would like to thank Franklin Knight for this insight.

[32] Aline Helg, *Our Rightful Share: The Afro-Cuban Struggle for Equality, 1886–1912* (Chapel Hill: University of North Carolina Press, 1995); Ada Ferrer, *Insurgent Cuba: Race, Nation, and Revolution, 1868–1898* (Chapel Hill: University of North Carolina Press, 1999); Lillian Guerra, *The Myth of Jose Martí*. See also the perceptive arguments of key texts in the formation of mestizaje in Juan E. de Castro, *Mestizo Nations: Culture, Race, and Conformity in Latin American Literature* (Tucson: University of Arizona Press, 2002).

If anything restrained an individual's advancement, it was their class background that should be faulted, not their race.[33]

Pulling back from this early twentieth-century transitional period to more broadly examine mestizaje and its evolutionary course, we can see additional processes at work. As much as mestizaje was about melding and realigning Latin America's racial heritage with nations' aspirations for the future, and as much as it was about building nationalism, bestowing racial redemption, and forming interregional identity, it also marked a key historical endpoint. Well before mestizaje and mulataje were readily recognizable concepts, other vocabularies had circulated to describe the racial formation processes that Latin America had experienced. Chief among these during late colonial times was the notion of caste (*casta*).

The complicated caste taxonomy (some have called it a system) that was instituted in the 1500s – captured in paintings, wax figurines, and even a genre of poetry – reveals the extent to which colonial-era ideas of difference came from melding both what was transposed onto colonists by Europeans and what grew organically out of the interactions and experiences of the colonists themselves.[34] Although it appears in retrospect to

---

[33] Despite the proclamations of Latin American societies, racism and discrimination persisted within racial democracy. The literature on the subject is vast, but see especially Pierre-Michel Fontaine, *Race, Class, and Power in Brazil* (Los Angeles: University of California, Center for Afro-American Studies, 1985); Melissa Nobles, *Shades of Citizenship: Race and the Census in Modern Politics* (Stanford: Stanford University Press, 2000); Wade, *Blackness and Racial Mixture*; Winthrop Wright, *Café con Leche*; Arlene Dávila, *Latino Spin: Public Image and the Whitewashing of Race* (New York: New York University Press, 2008); and Michael G. Hanchard, *Orpheus and Power: The Movimento Negro of Rio de Janeiro and São Paulo, Brazil, 1945–1988* (Princeton: Princeton University Press, 1998). Arguably, what emerged from mestizaje was the deployment of new intraregional tools for forging cohesion. Latin American identity began to coalesce in new ways, and nations, despite their individual competitions, found themselves sharing more than they had realized. Of course, mestizaje acquired certain national particularities as each nation wrestled with its manifold aspects. Thus there was a common intellectual agenda as the region struggled with key issues, but there was regional specificity that could be built into national dialogues.

[34] Two important contributions to casta painting literature in English are Ilona Katzew, *Casta Painting: Images of Race in Eighteenth-Century Mexico* (New Haven and London: Yale University Press, 2004); and Magali M. Carrera, *Imagining Identity in New Spain: Race, Lineage and the Colonial Body in Portraiture and Casta Paintings* (Austin: University of Texas Press, 2003). See also the work of Melina Pappademos, *Black Political Activism and the Cuban Republic* (Chapel Hill: University of North Carolina Press, 2011); Ruth Hill (who has taken on the topic of casta poetry in some of her work), "Towards an Eighteenth-Century Transatlantic Critical Race Theory," *Literature Compass* 3 (2006): 53–64; and the great nineteenth-century Mexican thinker Lucas

have been a carefully designed set of categories, casta at best offered a rough-hewn architecture for describing the effects of miscegenation. By most accounts, the practice of assigning casta labels to marshal behavior and grant privileges was a difficult, frustrating, and imprecise task. There are numerous explanations for this, many of which will be addressed throughout this book. Suffice it to say here that early twentieth-century mestizaje brought a measure of conclusion and logic to the racial mixture that began in the colonial period through casta relationships and that had effectively ruptured the earlier dual republic system described in Chapter 1. Mestizaje rationalized what had been largely an ad hoc process, providing substantive meaning and direction. Early twentieth-century mestizaje was certainly a product of its time, but it was also a bridge to the past, linking the colonial and modern worlds in ways that made two grand eras of mixture meaningful and intelligible to each other. Ultimately too, mestizaje, perhaps more than anything else, may have finally introduced to Latin America the somatic order that colonial officials had sought so diligently. Of course, it did so at a cost, and in ways that, interestingly, may have been enabled by certain features of the caste regime.

Alamán, who discussed the existence of wax casta figurines in his *Historia de México desde los primeros movimientos que prepararon su independencia en el año de 1808, hasta la época presente* (Mexico City: Instituto Cultural Helénico, 2000).

3

"Castagenesis" and the Moment of Castizaje

One of the fundamental differences between Latin America's colonial and modern periods was the move away from a rather pluralized understanding of socio-racial complexity, one that showcased multiple racial categories, to more singular and harmonized views of race that acknowledged differences but actively sought to bridge them. Although the roots of this divergence extend to colonial times, mestizaje represents its capstone, because it signified both a process that encouraged the ultimate fusion of races and the propagation of a dominant idea to explain and support the phenomenon. Of course, mestizaje did not magically meld individual racial and ethnic groups into their nations or completely erase their identities. In fact, in the early years, as the ideology insinuated itself into the lives of citizens and states, it precipitated contentious struggles among groups who sought to refine the meaning of mestizaje, and who also competed with each other over which identities were to be prioritized within it.[1]

Even as Latin American states began adopting mestizaje as a tool for nation-building, they sometimes still found it useful to allocate discursive space for blackness, indigeneity, and whiteness. Frequently, this came in

---

[1] Peter Wade, "Rethinking 'Mestizaje': Ideology and Lived Experience," *Journal of Latin American Studies* 37, no. 2 (May 2005): 255; Edmund T. Gordon, *Disparate Diasporas: Identity and Politics in an African Nicaraguan Community* (Austin: University of Texas Press, Institute of Latin American Studies, 1998); Wade, *Blackness and Race Mixture*; Kim D. Butler, *Freedoms Given, Freedoms Won: Afro-Brazilians in Post-Abolition São Paulo and Salvador* (New Brunswick, NJ: Rutgers University Press, 1998); Hanchard, *Orpheus and Power*. Note as well that whereas identities were in competition with each other, mestizaje seemed to place a premium on whiteness.

arenas that were not completely within state control, such as culture and religion. Although the examples are legion, the Venezuelan cult of María Lionza nicely displays how representations of blacks, natives, and whites all helped integrate these groups into the larger social body, while also providing special outlets for each of them. The devotions to the Virgin of Guadalupe in Mexico and the Virgen de la Caridad in Cuba offer two more excellent examples, with deep and traceable historical roots that show how each religious form provided an important venue for native and black voices, respectively.[2]

For Latin America's nation-states, keeping all three racial identities functional also allowed mixed-race populations to toggle between them periodically to renew distinctive elements of their heritage. In the context of religious celebrations or cultural events such as the Afro-Venezuelan festival for St. John the Baptist, or in musical and dance spectacles featuring black musical forms like Mexico's African-derived *jarocho* sound and Cuba's *son*, citizens of the nation of any race could participate, celebrate, and exalt these expressions as part of both their own identity and the national patrimony.[3] States too could manipulate individual ethnic and

---

[2] For some basic reference works on these devotions, see Angelina Pollak-Eltz, *María Lionza, mito y culto venezolano, ayer y hoy: 40 años del trabajo en el campo* (Caracas: Universidad Católica Andrés Bello, 2004); David Brading, *Mexican Phoenix, Our Lady of Guadalupe: Image and Tradition across Five Centuries* (Cambridge: Cambridge University Press, 2001); and María Elena Díaz, *The Virgin, the King, and the Royal Slaves of El Cobre: Negotiating Freedom in Colonial Cuba, 1670–1780* (Stanford: Stanford University Press, 2000).

[3] Anita González, *Jarocho's Soul: Cultural Identity and Afro-Mexican Dance* (Lanham, MD: University Press of America, 2004); Robin D. Moore, *Nationalizing Blackness: Afrocubanismo and the Artistic Revolution in Havana, 1920–1940* (Pittsburgh: University of Pittsburgh Press, 1997); David M. Guss, "The Selling of San Juan: The Performance of History in an Afro-Venezuelan Community," *American Ethnologist* 20, no. 3 (1993): 451–473. Note that Guss's article places a special emphasis on how the festival of San Juan has been an important catalyst for community development and renewal amid major challenges facing the Afro-Venezuelan population. He points out too that the festival has offered an important forum for talking about race. By the same token, a casual perusal of literature promoting the festival demonstrates the pride of representing Afro-Venezuelan culture and its dances as a part of national identity. As visitors stream to the festival annually from places like Caracas, there is a sense of renewal and communion with the African heritage, even if it is an imagined one, as individuals participate in the revelry. Further-ranging but more intricate arguments along these lines can be found in Guss, *The Festive State: Race, Ethnicity and Nationalism as Cultural Performance* (Berkeley and Los Angeles: University of California Press, 2000). See also Jesús García, *Caribeñidad: afroespiritualidad y afroepistemología* (Caracas: Ministerio de Cultura, Fundación Editorial el Perro y la Rana, 2006); García, *Afrovenezolanidad: esclavitud, cimarronaje y lucha contemporánea* (Caracas: Ministerio de Educación, Cultura y Deportes: CONAC, 2001); and García,

racial identities strategically to maneuver around and co-opt their citizens. Finally, retaining small enclaves of these populations as living relics, especially blacks and Native Americans, conveniently served the state's purpose of validating the merits of mixture. Especially as long as these groups remained in poverty, the state could use them to juxtapose what were supposedly prototypical black and native lifestyles against those of the racially mixed mainstream. Correspondingly, the benefits of mestizaje could be championed and the thesis could be sustained that blacks and natives were largely marginalized because of factors like educational and class disparities.

In practice, therefore, Latin America's mestizaje may have been more mosaic than not. And, intentionally or not, it may have opportunistically preserved and recreated both blackness and indigeneity. The legacy of these practices has given rise today to a multicultural movement within mestizaje, bringing forth an altogether new-age version (what I call mestizaje 2.0).[4] Groups such as Afro-Latin Americans and Native Americans are seeking to reconcile mestizaje on their own terms through strong social and cultural movements. Nevertheless, due to mestizaje's overwhelming power to coax entire societies into believing its creed, while at the same time masking practices that preserve racial and ethnic distinctions, early twentieth-century mestizaje undoubtedly represented one of the strongest moves toward imagining racial conformity and consensus that Latin America had ever seen, especially as compared to colonial times. Clearly, as the twentieth century progressed, a powerful, unitary racial view of Latin American society had evolved.

Flash back now to the colonial period. There was no such sweeping ideology at play. Casta existed as a comparable ordering framework for notions of race, but it was a splintered concept, with multiple meanings. The so-called caste system also had mysterious origins that clouded its purpose and long-term goals, while interfering with the way it operated on a day-to-day basis. Additionally, not only did casta groups come to

---

Mokongo ma chévere: danzar la historia . . . danzar la memoria. Introducción a las danzas de autodefensa de origen africano (Caracas: Dirección de la Danza, CONAC, Fundación Afroamérica, 2004).

[4] Juliet Hooker discusses the phenomenon of "mestizo multiculturalism," wherein groups such as Afro-Latin Americans are seeking to reconcile mestizaje and multiculturalism on their own terms. See Hooker, *Race and the Politics of Solidarity* (New York: Oxford University Press, 2009), 142. Some vivid examples of the challenge to traditional *mestizaje* can be found in Jean Muteba Rahier, *Black Social Movements in Latin America: From Monocultural Mestizaje to Multiculturalism* (New York: Palgrave-MacMillan Press, 2012).

proliferate during colonial times, but numerous other ways of expressing socio-racial condition also flowered. Beginning with the earliest moments of conquest and extending well into the eighteenth century, an array of ethnoreligious classifications (*morisco, judío, cristiano, converso*), socio-economic designations (*labrador, hidalgo, pechero* [commoner], *caballero*), and geographic descriptors (*vecino, natural, criollo*) that had been circulating in Spain for ages were renewed and reinterpreted in colonial landscapes.[5] Collectively, these descriptions for categorizing human difference came to be known and expressed by sixteenth-century Spanish bureaucrats and laypersons as "géneros de gente" (types of people). This term preceded the spread of concepts such as casta and was widely used in the colonies during the sixteenth century to describe individuals who would later be designated as castas – among them mestizos, mulatos, negros, and others.[6]

When the term *casta* did enter the lexicon of colonial Spanish American society at the beginning of the colonial period, its meaning was rather different from what it would become over time. In its purest sense, the idea of casta, as expressed in Spanish sixteenth- and seventeenth-century writings (especially on the Iberian Peninsula), referred to breeding and lineage, emphasizing taintless purity.[7] Applied first to the world of animal husbandry, the term was later used to describe human behavior, emphasizing practices of "good breeding" that favored legitimate birth and noble status. When transplanted to the Americas, the term's meaning shifted somewhat, referring to the offspring of individuals who were produced by miscegenation. All racially mixed individuals, regardless of hue, were collectively known as castas.[8] Although the concept of casta continued

---

[5] Excellent work examining the early origins of classification schemes in the colonies can be found in Robert C. Schwaller, "Defining Difference in Early Colonial New Spain" (PhD diss.: Penn State University, 2009).

[6] Robert C. Schwaller, *Géneros de Gente in Early Colonial Mexico: Defining Racial Difference* (Norman: University of Oklahoma Press, 2016). See also the discussion on *géneros de gente* in Schwaller, "'For Honor and Defence': Race and the Right to Bear Arms in Early Colonial Mexico," *Colonial Latin American Review* 21, no. 2 (August 2012): 239–266. Another term prefiguring casta in the 1500s was *calidad*, which tended to capture one's overall social status but was also used to describe newly emerging categories of racially mixed individuals. See Joanne Rappaport, *The Disappearing Mestizo: Configuring Difference in the Colonial Kingdom of New Granada* (Durham: Duke University Press, 2014), 60–61.

[7] Real Academia Española, *Diccionario de autoridades*, tomo I (Madrid: Editorial Gredos, SA, 1990 [facsimile edition]), 219–220.

[8] María Elena Martínez, "The Language, Genealogy, and Classification of 'Race' in Colonial Mexico," in *Race and Classification: The Case of Mexican Americans*, ed. Ilona Katzew and

to emphasize breeding and lineage in the New World, the original positive connotations that were associated with it in sixteenth-century Spain gradually faded as colonial elites began viewing segments of the mixed-race population with disdain, and as they consequently began assigning inferiority to certain phenotypes.

Some have suggested that casta started gaining traction as a socioracial term in the 1620s, but records have not emerged to demonstrate such a clear point of genesis for the normalization of its usage in the empire. We also cannot identify any official document or set of documents for decreeing a formal system into existence.[9] There is even debate regarding the degree to which the complex formulas and nomenclature that have become known as the *sistema de castas* were actually ever discussed in that way during the colonial era, and whether the disparate corpus of legislation and social norms that composed what some now describe as a system could truly be consolidated into something recognizable as such. In well-known compilations of colonial laws, legislation governing racially mixed individuals tended to be scattered throughout a vast body of legal opinion and decrees that addressed specific issues confronting the colonies, such as arms use, taxes, public office holding, marital law, and other aspects of public life.[10] While there were certainly laws governing mestizos, indios, negros, and mulatos, one seldom encountered targeted legislation carved out for the rarer castes. That is to say that when it came to groups like moriscos, castizos, coyotes, and lobos, colonial legal guidelines were murkier. Sometimes these groups were singled out by law; at other times their regulation fell under more general rubrics. Put another way, legal differentiation and striation *among* the full range of castes was a rarity. Consequently, extreme castas in particular comprised a bit of a blind spot in colonial legal eyes.

Susan Deans-Smith (Stanford: Stanford University Press, 2009), 29–30. This article offers a superb and concise discussion of the caste system. Ruth Hill has argued that the term *casta* was not synonymous with mixed populations, but the archival evidence I have seen suggests otherwise, at least for Mexico. See Hill, *Hierarchy, Commerce, and Fraud in Bourbon Spanish America: A Postal Inspector's Exposé* (Nashville: Vanderbilt University Press, 2005), 204–205. Hill has indicted Julian Pitt-Rivers for having "reinscribed casta within a modern and postmodern semantics, tearing asunder local roots." Pitt-Rivers, *Race in Latin America: The Concept of "Raza"* (Paris: Plon, 1973).

[9] Robert Schwaller has made the observation that the usage of *casta* became more prominent around the 1620s.

[10] For instance, see the organization of the *Recopilación de leyes de los reynos de las Indias*, 4 vols. (Madrid: Julián de Paredes, 1681).

Early on, the regulation of caste evolved as a distinctly absolutist Hapsburg institution, adopting the practices and governing philosophies of the Hapsburg monarchs and their bureaucracy. There was even a baroque quality to caste, wherein its ornate complexity mirrored the types of governance systems embraced by the Spanish regime.[11] Some might go so far as to proffer that caste regulation was an instantiation of the Hapsburg state. John Lynch's remarks about the nature of absolutism in the sixteenth- and seventeenth-century Spanish context are particularly apropos: "Absolutism was qualified by conditions, and its power was less imposing in practice than it was in theory. It was restricted in the first place by inefficiency... [I]t was also restricted by the existence of local forces."[12] So while modern observers (and even some contemporaries) might be tempted to construe colonial Spanish caste regulation as comprehensive and imposing, there was in truth room for variance between regions and colonies, and the enactment of caste policy was distinctively textured throughout the realm.

Indeed, the influence of local forces on imperial policy may well have determined the true impact of caste regulation. It is not too wild a stretch to claim that the earliest impetus for the design of casta-related laws probably came first from the colonies, with New World officials likely being the primary architects of caste policy. It was fairly common for Spain in this period to react to events in the Indies, resolving issues and matters as they happened. Equally customary was for the crown to sometimes allow local viceregal governments to respond rather definitively to circumstances occurring in their domains. When matters were resolved through local channels, the decisions and decrees issued in one province or colony might very well serve as precedent for handling similar incidents elsewhere in the Indies. In fact, as regional governors and administrators dealt independently with racially mixed groups in their settings, their rulings slowly agglomerated into a body of legal precedent that guided how racially mixed groups were to be handled throughout the Americas. This was likely the birth of the reputed caste system. Some laws complemented one another; others were directly contradictory. Sometimes there was legal redundancy. Sometimes laws were obeyed and enforced; at other

---

[11] José A. Maravall, *Culture of the Baroque: Analysis of a Historical Structure* (Minneapolis: University of Minnesota Press, 1986). I would like to thank Patrick Funiciello for this insight.

[12] John Lynch, *Spain under the Habsburgs* (New York: Oxford University Press, 1964), 289. There is considerable debate as to the periodization of the Hapsburg era and its essential features.

times there was widespread misinterpretation of the law, abuse, or neglect. The jumbled nature of caste regulation made it feel incoherent, but it is likely that coherence was never conceived as its endgame. Lumbering along bit by bit, a patchwork of habits and practices developed alongside caste legislation, serving more like a compass than a direct instrument of control for colonial life. To the best of our knowledge, what resembled a system probably did not begin to coalesce across the empire until around the middle of the seventeenth century. It is important to remember that caste systematization, to the extent that it could be achieved, was impelled by everyday needs in the New World, as well as the efforts of those managing the Spanish realm. Yet even the stance of the kingdom's bureaucrats often proved mutable.[13]

CASTAGENESIS AND THE NATURAL WORLD

In the haze surrounding the origins of caste policy, what does stand clear is that what later became known as the *sociedad de castas*, or *sistema de castas*, concretely reflected an intricate system of beliefs about the natural order of the world and how racial mixture both complicated and affirmed those notions. That is to say that understandings of caste were rooted in basic beliefs about religion, society, and science. The fact that these ideas were constantly evolving, particularly in the realm of science, produced an added fluidity in the concept of casta that would manifest itself over the span of nearly three centuries of colonial rule.

The sixteenth century may have been one of the most elastic moments for caste's conceptualization, since many of the castas appearing in this period were new, frameworks for assigning legal statuses to them were in their infancy, and ideas about how firmly biological properties could impact human bodies were not as strongly planted in the colonial mindset as they would be in later eras.[14] Underwriting some of this elasticity was the power of scientific and medical theories, especially the influence of

---

[13] For some of the points raised in this paragraph, I am in agreement with Robert Schwaller, "Defining Difference," 84–90.

[14] López Beltrán, "Hippocratic Bodies," 272–273. María Elena Martínez has argued that the sixteenth century was likely when lineage, social rank, acculturation, and parental recognition all played a factor in determining caste. By the end of the sixteenth century, lineage had become a far more dominant factor; according to her argument, the concept of caste had more weight in the earlier colonial period than in later times. This line of thought may have also added to the impression that the sociedad de castas was more elastic than later forms. See Martínez, *Genealogical Fictions*, 146.

medieval and early modern interpretations of scientific claims made by two of antiquity's greatest medical thinkers, Galen and Hippocrates. Thanks to their pioneering work, people living in the Hispanic world at this time largely believed that human physiology, temperament, and character were malleable, being subject to a variety of external and internal influences. To maintain good health and a robust constitution, one had to achieve an overall balance of humors appropriate to one's body type. Humors were the four bodily fluids (black bile, yellow bile, phlegm, and blood) that were believed to govern the body by expressing heat, wetness, cold, and dryness. Africans, Indians, and Europeans were thought to have different baseline humoral balances that, in part, accounted for their varied complexions and behavioral attributes. Significantly, humoral balance could be affected by a series of "nonnatural" forces, such as food, climate, air, exercise, sleep, evacuation (for example, bloodletting or menstruation), and emotions. Early science and medicine placed great emphasis on managing these variables in regulating overall health. This "humoral thinking" was prominent in the early colonial period, and when construed alongside the early evolution of casta, it underwrote notions that the new populations appearing in the New World were inherently changeable rather than deterministically fixed.[15]

Ideas of science could not be divorced from religious beliefs, and during this period, the supremacy of Christian thought in Europe deeply affected views of the body, caste, and general differences in physiology. In particular, monogenism, the notion that all humanity had Adam and Eve as its common ancestors, made it heretical to conceive that different branches of human populations could pass their own supposedly innate characteristics to their progeny over time. The belief in monogenism shaped conversations about human difference in ways that encouraged thinkers to affirm core elements of human commonality.[16] When seemingly permanent

[15] Ideas about humoral thinking and the flexibility of the body are extracted from arguments forwarded by Rebecca Earle, *The Body of the Conquistador: Food, Race, and the Colonial Experience in Spanish America* (New York and Cambridge: Cambridge University Press, 2012).

[16] For instance, Amerindians, the Western world's most recognizable "strangers" of the sixteenth century, were frequently written about by monogenists as fundamentally human, and therefore not subject to disassociation from the rest of the world's populations. Their essential humanity meant that Indians had souls and could be subjected to the vast spiritual conversion project that occupied the clergy during the early colonial period. Good summary discussions of various debates and arguments about the origins of Amerindians can be found in Ilona Katzew, "'That This Should Be Published Again in

human differences were encountered in certain populations (and considered transmissible through racial mixture), monogenism placed a heavy burden of proof on the Bible for explaining them. African skin color, for instance, was thought to be the physical marker of a Biblical curse; this helped explain why black skin did not revert back to whiteness (man's presumed "natural" color) when exposed to colder climates. With biblical undergirding, other features were codified as supposedly innate in blacks. Partly contradicting popular Hippocratic-Galenic theories, black bodies were considered less impressionable by nonnatural forces and the effects of humoral imbalances. The personalities of black people were considered more set, their bodies less pliant, and their constitution less changeable than those of Spaniards. These ideas found a home in the early mindset of caste in Spanish America, shaping opinions about mulattos and other blacks of mixed racial heritage who were considered to carry the traits of their African ancestors. Yet on the other hand, Africans arriving in the New World, as well as their offspring, were largely considered Old Christians.[17] As such, they were incorporated as gente de razón, thereby enjoying a different status and legal position from that of the native population in the early colonial world.[18]

Another force influencing the articulation of casta in the early colonial period was the Iberian concern over maintaining blood purity (*limpieza de sangre*). Spaniards had developed this preoccupation during their centuries of close contact with Muslims and alongside their efforts to contain the spread of Judaism. In the fifteenth and early sixteenth centuries, moves to eradicate the Moors from the Iberian Peninsula provided a framework for thinking about hybridity that would ultimately take hold in the colonies. In Spain, as the sixteenth century gradually unfolded, the practice of accepting Jews and Moors into genealogical bloodlines increasingly came to be seen as bearing negative consequences, since the supposed impurities of these faiths were considered

---

the Age of the Enlightenment?' Eighteenth-Century Debates about the Indian Body in Colonial Mexico," in *Race and Classification: The Case of Mexican America*, ed. Ilona Katzew and Susan Deans-Smith (Stanford: Stanford University Press, 2009), especially 75–76.

[17] Africans were members of the *extra ecclesiam*, a Church term used to refer to all individuals who did not profess Christianity. Under Church law, these individuals did enjoy basic rights until the moment they were exposed to Christianity and accepted it, when a new set of rights was granted.

[18] It is debatable just what the advantage of being connected with the gente de razón actually bought blacks, especially the enslaved.

transmissible from parent to child. This held true even if one could prove that a Jew or Moor in the family's lineage had converted to Catholicism. As limpieza de sangre evolved, it affirmed more and more that clean Christian blood had to be guarded vigilantly and that previously relaxed practices of allowing converts to experience full redemption had to be revisited.

Rising to the challenge, the Spanish Inquisition and other Iberian institutions intensified their gatekeeping in the second half of the sixteenth century to better monitor and control heterodoxy. One result in Spain was the adoption of more-calculated and genealogically rooted practices to measure the precise degree to which converts were Old or New Christians. The Inquisition began tabulating individuals as half Christian, one-quarter Christian, one-eighth Christian, one-sixteenth Christian, and so on. The more distant one's Jewish or Moorish ancestry, the more acceptable he or she was deemed to be.[19]

Turning back now to the New World, the Iberian grade of inquest used to discern Christian background would not be replicated in Spanish America, since Jews and Moors were forbidden from traveling to Spain's colonies (though small numbers trickled through).[20] Nevertheless, the ideas and principles that underwrote limpieza de sangre successfully made the journey across the Atlantic. The practice of categorizing individuals by fractions gradually embedded itself in articulations of caste.

When colonists and bureaucrats wrestled with what it meant to be racially mixed, they conjured a legal and social framework that took into consideration what it meant to be one-quarter Spanish, half African, or one-third Indian, and the like. These fractional categories quickly acquired names, and new hybrid populations started blossoming in the New World. Despite the literally infinite possibilities within the racial stock of the Spanish colonies, three main bloodlines formed the core: *españoles* (whites), *indios* (Indians), and *negros/morenos* (blacks).[21]

---

[19] One of the best books to capture the mania that surrounded lineage is Ruth Pike's *Linajudos and Conversos in Seville: Greed and Prejudice in Sixteenth- and Seventeenth-Century Spain* (New York: Peter Lang, 2000). In it, she addresses how a whole group of genealogists arose to serve as expert witnesses to determine one's blood purity.

[20] Portuguese residents were assumed to be New Christians, and thus of questionable blood purity. See Irene Silverblatt, *Modern Inquisitions: Peru and the Colonial Origins of the Civilized World* (Durham: Duke University Press, 2004), 32–34.

[21] For Laura A. Lewis, these core bloodlines correspondingly formed "sanctioned" and "unsanctioned" domains of power and authority in the colonial world. See Lewis, *Hall of Mirrors: Power, Witchcraft, and Caste in Colonial Mexico* (Durham: Duke University Press, 2003).

These groupings, in turn, gave rise to a selection of frequently cited mixtures: mestizos (mixture of white and Indian), mulatos (mixture of white and black), and *pardos* or *zambos* (mixture of black and Indian).[22] Over time, *pardo* became virtually synonymous with *mulato*, thereby losing much of its indigenous referencing (see Chapter 4).[23] A final category found with frequency, at least in colonial Mexico, was that of the *castizo* (mixture of white and mestizo).[24]

In addition to these core classifications, there was a plethora of other possible caste combinations (see Table 3.1). In general, each casta designation was governed by a logic that emphasized genealogical lineage: from knowing one's ancestors, one could supposedly calculate casta. An indio and an español produced a mestizo, a mestizo and an español produced a castizo, and so forth.

The rise of casta nomenclature took an interesting twist as it connected back to sixteenth- and early seventeenth-century scientific thought. Alongside the Hippocratic-Galenic framework, which encouraged people to think about the inherent pliability of human bodies, the prominent stature of astrology as a key science during the first century after the conquest caused many to consider that some of the forces responsible for generating variances among humankind were astral in nature. Of course, astral forces did not spawn the various casta groups – only sexual contact could produce that. But certainly the alignment of the stars induced a supportive climate for human variation, striation, and change.

Here again, construing the New World as different from the Old World mattered. The latitudinal position of the Americas presented a new

---

[22] Of the terms described, *zambo* was the least often encountered in New Spain's colonial records. *Pardo* was more commonly found as a signifier of black and Indian admixture but was a less precise term.

[23] Note that the use of *pardo* to denote indigenous ancestry may have been more common in seventeenth-century Mexico than elsewhere. Even in nearby Guatemala, there was considerable blurring of the terms *mulato* and *pardo* from early moments in the colonial period. See the work of Christopher H. Lutz, *Santiago de Guatemala, 1541–1773: City, Caste, and the Colonial Experience* (Norman: University of Oklahoma Press, 1994); Robinson Herrera, *Natives, Europeans, and Africans in Sixteenth-Century Santiago de Guatemala* (Austin: University of Texas Press, 2003); and María Luisa Herrera Cassasús, *Presencia y esclavitud del negro en la Huasteca* (Mexico: Universidad Autónoma de Tamaulipas/Porrúa, 1988). Conversely, in places like Peru, the term *zambo* to denote black/Indian mixture may have circulated longer than in Mexico. See Berta Ares Queija and Alessandro Stella (eds.), *Negros, mulatos, zambaigos: derroteros africanos en los mundos ibéricos* (Seville: Escuela de Estudios Hispano-Americanos, 2000).

[24] The term was used in colonial Guatemala as well and can be found in parish marriage records from at least the 1720s. See Lutz, *Santiago de Guatemala*.

TABLE 3.1 *Partial List of Caste Combinations in the*
Sistema de Castas

Caste	Racial Mixture
'Ahí te estás'	'No te entiendo' with india
Albarazado	'Tente en el aire' with mulata
Albino	Español with morisca
Barzino	Albarazado with india
Cambujo	Chino with india
Calpamulato	Barzino with India
Mestizo	Mestizo with blanca
Coyote	Indio with mestiza
Coyote mestizo	Chamizo with mestiza
Cuarterón	Blanco with tercerona
Chamizo	Coyota with indio
Chino	Lobo with negra
Cholo	Mestizo with india
Español	Castiza with blanco
Genízaro	Barzino with zambaiga
Galfarro	Negro with mulata
Gíbaro	Lobo with china
Harnizo	Blanco with coyote
Jarocho	Negro with india
Lobo	Indio with negra
Mestindio	Indio with mestiza
Mestizo	Blanco with india
Morisco	Blanco with mulata
'No te entiendo'	'Tente en el aire' with mulata
Saltatrás	Blanco with albino
'Tente en el aire'	Negro with cuarterona
Tresalvo	Indio with mestiza
Zambaigo	Cambujo with india
Zambo	Indio with negra
Zambo prieto	Negro with zamba

Source: "Lista de Castas," *Artes de México*, vol. 8 (1990): 79.

astrological landscape, both unfamiliar and potentially problematic from a European perspective. Its unique stars and alignments were believed to hinder the body and even corrupt the mind. Combined with the New World's humidity, temperature, and food sources, the verdict could not be good for long-term settlers in the Americas and their children. As Old World philosophers, scientists, and naturalists pondered the colonists' fate, arriving at dismal conclusions, the New World's creole elite retaliated. In the early 1600s, through treatises, debates, and other forms of responses, some argued that latent within the European body type were certain "natural" defenses against forces described as debilitative. Consequently, Spanish colonists and their white offspring (*españoles*) could supposedly endure the New World's negative influences, while other populations such as natives were potentially gripped and damaged by them.[25]

Generally speaking, the epistemological defenses raised by the creole elite also hardened the meaning of color in colonial society, because they made it tougher to overcome the characteristics associated with phenotype. Not all phenotypes were viewed with the same level of rigidity. Whites, blacks, and natives were the most often characterized as bearing definitive and distinguishing features, but there was tremendous ambiguity in the spaces between. Necessarily, questions emerged. With whiteness in their bloodstreams, to what extent were populations like mestizos and mulatos immune to the supposedly detrimental environment of the Americas? Just how much whiteness was needed to improve a bloodline? How was indigeneity to be scripted when factored into racial mixture – was it always detrimental, or could it engineer positive outcomes? How about the additive effects of blackness? Did they blend better with whiteness or with native bloodlines? And how was the mixture among hybrid groups to be conceived and reasoned? Such questions resembled and complemented those being asked as miscegenation functionally ruptured the dual republic (see Chapter 1).

Limpieza de sangre provided a useful, albeit incomplete, guide for answering these questions by offering a basic set of religious principles to help think through the implications of racial mixture. In affirming the supremacy of Old Christian roots, limpieza de sangre supported the notion of the overriding superiority of the español category. Hence, most mixture was seen in relation to an español ideal, which represented the embodiment of a pure Christian, optimal human type. By the early seventeenth century, some countervailing theories held that native populations and bloodlines were equally "pure." This was based on the fact that indios, who had arrived in the Indies well before Jesus's

---

[25] Today, some modern scholars believe that these defenses presaged future racial thinking. Because their use of physical and phenotypal criteria was distinct from systems built on biblical justification, these early assertions by Spanish colonists resembled the type of biological arguments that would become the calling card of racial ideologies formulated in the eighteenth century. See Cañizares-Esguerra, "New World, New Stars."

crucifixion, did not have the opportunity to accept Christ into their lives prior to the coming of the Spaniards and could not therefore be indicted for rejecting Christianity in the same way as could Jews and Moors.

While some thinkers nonetheless proceeded to characterize natives as crypto-Jews and idol worshippers, conversations around the purity of their blood helped underwrite the idea that native progeny could be more easily absorbed into whiteness if they repeatedly and exclusively bred with "pure" españoles. Continuous infusions of whiteness could fully "cleanse" indios into whites in as little as three generations. Blacks and blackness, on the other hand, presented problems. Despite being construed as gente de razón, only a thin degree of distance was seen to separate blacks from Jews and Muslims. Already considered incapable of being pure in the religious sense, the idea that blacks were religiously cursed damned them even more. If mixed with native bloodlines, blackness was considered extremely deleterious, especially given the prevailing fears that any union of blacks and natives posed serious threats to the crown's power.[26] Fully framed against the backdrop of ideas about human malleability, the ways in which limpieza de sangre began to characterize the outcome of black, white, and native intermixture helped showcase a vital feature of the caste system: miscegenation could produce both positive and negative outcomes, enabling people to move either up or down the somatic scale, expressing different characteristics and qualities as they traveled along the continuum.

THE BROKEN COLOR OF CASTE

Another central idea that came to inform understandings of casta, especially the effects of miscegenation, was that racial mixture introduced something fundamentally unsettling into an ideal way of being. Mixed-race people were often described as being of "color quebrado" (broken color), particularly when discussed as groups rather than as individuals. This terminology not only helped strengthen the role of color in distinguishing between populations, but it also exposed a host of biases that had long percolated in colonial life. People of color quebrado were routinely and pejoratively referred to as having bad habits (*malas costumbres*). They were considered innately superstitious, which was partly

---

[26] For deeper discussion of these points, see Martínez, *Genealogical Fictions*, 142–170.

attributable to poor upbringing.[27] They were depicted as shiftless and suspicious, prone to lying under oath, inherently untrustworthy, and roundly unreliable from an elite standpoint. Being "quebrado" was equated with having been born with an inescapable defect, as opposed to being born español, which was described as being "of good birth." Even just a dash of racial mixture excluded some people from being considered members of society's upper strata, regardless of their professional pedigrees and accomplishments.[28]

As the colonial period matured, a primary impact of the quebrado label was its destabilizing effect on the mestizo category, which was among those most closely aligned to the revered Hispanic ideal. Mestizos sometimes considered themselves above the rest of the non-españoles (*de calidad privilegiada*) and lobbied for special privileges, immunities, and exemptions. However, circumstances could trigger varied reactions to their racially mixed status and precipitate rapid dips in their rank. There were places, such as the frontier zone of Molango in Mextitlan de la Sierra, where mestizos paid tribute (a tax elsewhere demanded exclusively of indios, mulattos, and blacks), and had done so for centuries.[29] As late as the mid-seventeenth century, the right of mestizos to bear arms was also closely governed, as witnessed in the royal decrees of 1654, 1661, and 1668.[30]

Unsurprisingly, quebrado status was often assigned early in life. In eighteenth-century Mexico City, right from birth, scores of residents were separated into baptismal registries slated for gente de color quebrado, españoles, and indios.[31] Not even castizos, the nearest category to whiteness, could evade the quebrado label.[32] Classifying the population in this way pitted the tradition of identifying castas by familial lineage against caste-labeling practices that were driven by observing phenotype. The tension became unavoidable and escalated monumentally when it

---

[27] See for instance Fr. Francisco Larrea's description of Joseph de Rojas, a mulato or lobo sorcerer who stopped storms with "superstitious signs" and strange utterings. AGN, Inquisición, vol. 1176, exp. 4, fol. 71v.

[28] See arguments raised in the case of Gerónimo Marani, who protested his son's unequal marriage to the mulata (or loba) Bárbara Álvarez. AGN, Inquisición, vol. 1378, exp. 2, fol. 11.

[29] AGN, General de Parte, vol. 73, exp. 216, fols. 235–237v.

[30] For mestizos' petitions for use of arms, see R. C. Schwaller, "For Honor and Defence," especially 247–252.

[31] It was not uncommon for indios to be folded into quebrado registers.

[32] There were parishes in the kingdom, and even in Mexico City, where indios were placed in baptismal registers that included all other non-Spaniards.

was difficult or impossible to gather reliable information on lineage. In a small selection of cases from the 1730s to the 1780s, one can find siblings (by the same parents) of different hues who were routinely placed in different registers, as well as children without parents who were classified as quebrados by default.[33] The Church had clearly intended for the quebrado designation to be determined by lineage, but sometimes lack of access to data inhibited this practice. It is equally evident that some clergy spurned lineage-based assessments, especially when they visually inspected babies and their families as they approached the baptismal font. In 1789, don Joseph Ángel de Gómez y Jaime, a member of the "literary profession," protested his baptismal characterization of 1763. As his case unfolded, he claimed that the officiating priest at his baptism had written an insulting marginal note on his register, asserting that his parents seemed to be mulattoes. As a result, he was placed into the books of the quebrados. Instead, Gómez y Jaime argued that he should have been recorded in the baptismal register of españoles, an oversight that had caused him considerable personal and professional grief.[34]

Not every complication with quebrado status was the clergy's fault. In 1754, Francisca Medina, the wife of a muleteer, was unfortunately compelled to deliver her baby while her husband was away on business. Unable to take the child to be baptized herself, Francisca turned to the baby's godmother to perform the task. When the clergyman asked for the baby's casta, the godmother had a momentary lapse of memory before finally replying that he was a morisco. Furious, Francisca's husband immediately appealed when he returned to Mexico City, claiming that his family had long been known as españoles – the baby therefore could not possibly be a morisco.[35]

In his appeal and others like it, a script appeared to be followed. By and large, litigants who protested the quebrado label asserted that their lineage was "pure" (español), thereby suggesting that any other phenotypical assessment was flawed. To add credence to their cases, members of the community were called to testify. Casta verification always seemed to be a community act, largely because as a social designation casta acquired its greatest meaning in the context of interpersonal and institutional

---

[33] AGN, Indiferente Virreinal, caja 6295, exp. 15, fols. 1–8; AGN, Indiferente Virreinal, caja 4077, exp. 9, fols. 1–6; AGN, Bienes Nacionales, leg. 88, exp. 13, fols. 1–6; AGN, Matrimonios, vol. 87, exp. 4 bis., fols. 14–26.

[34] AGN, Matrimonios, vol. 87, exp. 4 bis, fols. 15–16.

[35] AGN, Clero Regular y Secular, vol. 48, exp. 4, fols. 96–101.

relationships. Witnesses, invariably españoles, were summoned to verify one's parents, and in some cases grandparents. In situations where clergymen had recorded a baby's parents as unknown, clear evidence of ancestry was usually presented. It seemed equally important to stress that the alleged quebrados not only knew their genealogy, but had also been born within wedlock. Affirming legitimacy immediately boosted any case. Children born within wedlock presumably had better access to more accurate genealogical knowledge, and their parents were thought to be more concerned about managing the social boundaries of color. When amassed successfully, these arguments, grounded primarily in lineage-based proofs, routinely trumped evidence of phenotype and frequently moved someone from being quebrado to español. Of course, there were those who vehemently challenged successful appeals. They argued that changes made to original documents as a result of such litigation represented gross falsifications that corroded society by promoting the ambitions of its most undeserving sectors.[36]

Nonetheless, the legal conflicts over quebrado status show how many colonists struggled over prioritizing lineage or phenotype in identity assessments. Another development to surface as the concept of color quebrado expanded in the colonies was the conflation of genealogical assessments with phenotypic ones. As the colonial period progressed, it was also not unusual to find individuals who were not racially mixed being categorized as quebrados, sometimes due to characteristics they supposedly had in common. In eighteenth-century baptismal registers, indios and negros were sometimes included in the books of quebrados in places like Mexico City, most likely on account of their presumed low social station. In Salvatierra during the 1790s, indios, quebrados, and the larger plebeian class were construed as a single interconnected group, a belief stemming largely from the vice of drunkenness that they all purportedly possessed. This trait ostensibly caused problems in the greater jurisdiction.[37] Associations like these could have grave consequences, especially when borne in the minds of senior colonial officials. Despite frequently being separated in legal codes, the pairing of indios with quebrados may have helped account for the strikingly similar punishments they received for certain infractions as well as

---

[36] AGN, Inquisición, vol. 1378, exp. 2, fols. 5–17v.

[37] I draw my example from AGN, Indiferente Virreinal, caja 2486, exp. 18, fols. 1–16. One might also interpret this case as concerning two discrete groups, in this case indios and those designated "de color quebrado."

lower-than-normal tolerance thresholds for legal transgressions by indios.[38]

The same considerations and defects that caused some elites to associate quebrados with other nonwhites also helped puncture long-standing assumptions about who society's gente de razón were. As has been noted, blacks, españoles, and all mixed-race groups were included in this special social category.[39] However, the stigma associated with being color quebrado was marked enough to justify distancing racially mixed castas from whites, thereby reconjuring the meaning of "gente de razón." In some circles, gente de razón became a synonym for whiteness.[40] In others, gente de razón were clearly stratified into an upper tier (whites) and a variety of lower tiers (racially mixed groups and blacks).

Parsing the gente de razón could produce conundrums. On the eve of Easter in 1729, two Jesuit clergymen in the town of Querétaro, Antonio Cortés and Juan de Dios Pruneda, were indicted for spreading false teachings about who was supposed to fast during Lent. At the root of the problem was the challenge that quebrados posed to enacting the rules of the faith and the lack of direction that the Church sometimes provided in guiding them. According to Cortés and Pruneda, only Spaniards whose lineage could be proven on "all four sides" (meaning through both maternal and paternal grandparents) were supposed to fast throughout the entire season. All other gente de razón, namely quebrados, need fast only on Fridays and again on Easter Saturday. The men based their teachings on certain exemptions that Indians enjoyed from fasting, which they then proceeded to decipher, extrapolate, reinterpret, and apply to individuals of mixed blood. While the clergymen's sermons

---

[38] The document referred to here is a published infraction for individuals of color quebrado and indios who had opened a mercury or quicksilver mine. AGN, General de Parte, vol. 41, exp. 329, fols. 253v–254.

[39] Especially in frontier settings where whites were few, native populations might enjoy the distinction of being gente de razón, though that was never the original intent of the designation. Indios who were embraced as gente de razón typically shared the following characteristics: they had accepted Christianity, moved to Spanish settlements, and adopted basic European lifeways. See Gloria E. Miranda, "Racial and Cultural Dimensions of Gente de Razón Status in Spanish and Mexican California," *Southern California Quarterly* 70, no. 3 (1988): 265–278; and Miranda, "Gente de Razón Marriage Patterns in Spanish and Mexican California: A Case Study of Santa Barbara and Los Angeles," *Southern California Quarterly* 63, no. 1 (1981): 1–21. See also AGN, Provincias Internas, vol. 240, exp. 11, exps. 156–166v; and AGN, General de Parte, vol. 38, exp. 10, fols. 19–19v.

[40] AGN, Bienes Nacionales, vol. 113, exp. 10, fols. 39–43; AGN, Provincias Internas, vol. 240, exp. 11, fols. 156–166v.

probably reflected the social beliefs of many in their flock, especially the elite, their teachings were disturbing and potentially heretical from the Church's point of view. Cortés and Pruneda effectively lumped all non-Spaniards into a separate moral class aligned with indios and made españoles the main observers of the details of the Christian faith. Such a moral divide transcended the intentions behind the creation of the social divisions. The Mexican Inquisition perceived Cortés's and Pruneda's teachings to be extremely dangerous, and both were summarily admonished. Church officials underscored that the gente de color quebrado constituted important members of the broader Christian community who needed proper Catholic instruction; they could not be released from basic Christian obligations.[41]

CASTA'S COGNATES

Such were many of the fundamental concepts, ideological frameworks, and principles that undergirded what has become known as the Spanish colonial caste system. By way of recap, certain influences of astrology and early modern science served both to highlight the malleable aspects of caste and to sustain the ingrained mythos of white supremacy. Anchored in considerations of religious purity, limpieza de sangre also affirmed the reigning value of whiteness but added a lineage-based taxonomy to trace genealogical change over time. The notion of color quebrado helped solidify the influence of phenotype in considering how racial mixture was both perceived and explained, while concepts such as gente de razón straddled an uncertain boundary, demonstrating how racially mixed castas were connected with whites (primarily through the link of Christianity and Christian observance), and how they were not.

---

[41] AGN, Inquisición, vol. 826, exp. 42, fols. 413–431v. The following is found in fols. 428v–429: "Digo por ultimo de este mandamiento que todos aquellos y aquellas que no son españoles, o españolas de todos cuatro costados no tienen obligacion de ayunar en todo el año, sino solamente los viernes de Quaresma, y las dos vigilias de Navidad, y el Sabado Santo. Assi parece que se colige de la constitucion del Sumario Pontifice Paulo III, que cita el Concilio Mexicana en el Libro 3, en el Titulo 21, observancimtieuniorum. Y aunque es verdad que el Sumario Pontificie habla de los Indios, y de las Indias, asi Orientales como Occidentales, por ser neófitos, que quiere decir, recién convertidos, es parecer de algunos Theologos dictos, que este privilegio se extienda a todos aquellos y aquellas que no son de todos cuatro costados, puros y netos españoles. De suerte que un solo cuarterón, que tengan de Indios u de negros u de chinos, como son castizos o castizas, moriscos o moriscas, mulatos o mulatas, negros o negras, indios o Indias, todos estos y todas estas no tienen obligación de ayunar en todo el año, sino como dije, solo los viernes de quaresma y solas las dos vigilias de las pascuas de Navidad y Resurrección."

Clearly, as all of these concepts evolved, they began influencing each other. Take the concept of limpieza de sangre, which initially helped steer colonial society's viewpoint on the outcomes of miscegenation but later sometimes found its own definition hijacked by emerging understandings of racial mixture and the taint of quebrado status. In 1792, for instance, when don Gerónimo Marani, the Italian-born director of the court's *coliseo* dance company, protested his son's marriage to Bárbara Álvarez, a reputed mulata or loba, he argued that she did not have limpieza de sangre. By this, it was clear that he was not arguing that she lacked full Christian status. Rather, the case hinged on determining whether the baptismal register that described her as an española was accurate. As the investigation ensued, Mariani's attorney encapsulated the core concern when he wrote, "In this kingdom, *limpieza de sangre* means to not have any mixture of *castas*."[42]

In this situation and others, new renderings of a terminology's meaning did not necessarily displace old ones. Hence, as concepts influenced each other and new interpretations were reached, old and new definitions could coexist, creating additional complications. It should be no surprise, then, that the great cycle of ideas that undergirded casta was subject to strong pendulum shifts, some due to the very evolution of the notion of casta itself. As the colonial period matured, casta increasingly manifested itself to be an unstable idea. The more it was used, the more its explanatory power seemed to slip. Part of the problem had to do with its cognates. Already by the seventeenth century, a person could simultaneously be referred to in a single document by their *nación* (nation), *calidad* (quality), *clase* (class), *condición* (condition), and casta.[43]

When juxtaposed against one another, it grew hard to differentiate between these various categories, since they could be used synonymously. In 1631, for example, don Domingo Carvallo, a resident of Manila (part of the Spanish

---

[42] AGN, Inquisición, vol. 1378, exp. 2, fols 5–17v. On *limpieza de sangre*, see fol. 8: "limpieza de sangre, pues consistiendo en este reyno en no tener mezcla de castas ..."

[43] Between 1774 and 1790, Matías Torres, a slave and resident of Veracruz, was one such individual referred to in this manner. Languishing in jail on various charges ranging from homicide to blasphemy, he was described as a *natural* of Guinea (Africa) whose *calidad* was negro and whose *casta* was Anchino (a specific African ethnic group). His *condición* was described as *esclavo* (slave), while his *oficio* (occupation) was that of *panadero* (bread maker). Throughout the document, his calidad as negro and his casta as Anchino were faithfully recorded. That is, there was some consistency in how Matías was described, but for others the circumstances could be less clear. See AGN, Inquisición, vol. 1274, exp. 7, fols. 427–436.

Empire) was involved in litigation against his slaves. Although they believed their bondage to be temporary, Carvallo maintained that they were indebted to him for life. As a matter of procedure, each slave's *casta* was carefully recorded within the pages of the document; however, don Domingo, the notaries, and apparently everyone else involved in the case, implicitly understood that the way the term *casta* was being utilized was identical to the concept of *nación*. Etymologically derived from the word *nacer* (to be born), the word *nación* frequently marked ethnolinguistic groups who shared a common birthplace and culture.[44] This was precisely the meaning invoked in the Domingo Carvallo affair. Casta had almost nothing to do with describing phenotype and lineage; instead, it virtually mimicked modern understandings of the concept of ethnicity.[45]

Outside of the Philippines, and especially during the seventeenth century, such conceptualizations of casta also applied to scores of African-born slaves who were routinely described with the phrase "de casta y nación" Angola, Anchino, Loanda, Mozambique, Congo, etc.[46] However, many

[44] A good discussion of *nación* can be found in Martínez, *Genealogical Fictions*, 153–154. Claudio Lomnitz-Adler, in *Exits from the Labyrinth: Culture and Ideology in the Mexican National Space* (Berkeley: University of California Press, 1992), has observed that the word *nación* might be best employed as referring to "communities of blood," which makes a great deal of sense in the colonial context. Note that on occasion, the word *nacional* could be used to refer to someone's birthplace, as was the case of Joseph Lázaro, who in 1710 was accused of idolatry. In the documentation he was described as being a vecino of Atocpan, but a "*nacional* de Totlapa." See AGN, Inquisición, vol. 715, exp. 18, fol. 489v. Additionally, the archival record shows that the term *de tierra* could be substituted for *nación*, especially in describing slave populations. For some examples, see AGN, Matrimonios, vol. 170, exp. 1, fols 1–4; vol. 113, exp. 62, fols.162–163v; and vol. 88, exp. 3, fols. 5–6v. A good source on national citizenship is Tamar Herzog, *Defining Nations: Immigrants and Citizens in Early Modern Spain and Spanish America* (New Haven: Yale University Press, 2003).

[45] AGN, Indiferente Virreinal, caja 1355, exp. 34, fols. 1–4v. This document identifies clearly the caste of individuals: Maria Peti (*casta* Vadagachi), Florencia (*casta* Parachiladina), Maria Mansal (*casta* Vadagachi), Manuel Tandaba (*casta* Vaga), Maria Vengui (*casta* Vela), Manuel Vala (*casta* Reti), Manuel Mamudu (*casta* Tolucan), Ignacia (*casta* Plachima), and Mielpecha (*casta* Velala).

[46] There are countless examples in the archival record. See AGN, Indiferente Virreinal, vol. 726, exp. 26, fols. 1–3v (*casta* Loando case); and AGN, Inquisición, vol. 1495, exp. 3, fols. 9–21 (*casta* Mozambique case). Keep in mind that African "ethnicities" were in part fabrications based on categories used by European slave traders in Africa. Gwendolyn Midlo Hall has recently done some good work on African ethnic designations in the New World context. See Midlo Hall, *Slavery and African Ethnicities in the Americas: Restoring the Links* (Chapel Hill: University of North Carolina Press, 2005). Finally, the archival documentation demonstrates that utilizing the term *casta* to refer to nationality/ethnicity might also be applied to people from Japan. Miguel Jerónimo, *de casta Japón*, was sold (probably in the seventeenth century) in the Philippines as an indentured

European-born and criollo slaves – not to mention cohorts of free-coloreds born in the New World – were frequently assigned a nación label that only minimally referenced an ethnicity. In 1661, the Spanish-born slave Pedro España (from Cádiz) was listed as "de nación mulato."[47] Similarly, free-coloreds such as Francisca Ángela from Puebla (1604) and Juan Joseph from San Agustín de las Cuevas (1727) could be found listed as "de nación morisca" and "de nación lobo," respectively.[48] By 1642, senior bureaucrats in New Spain were clearly exhibiting alternative understandings of nación that considered phenotypic characteristics and genealogy to a much greater degree than ethnolinguistic heritages. That year, the viceroy Juan de Palafox y Mendoza wrote an ordinance that applied to all of Mexico's residents, underscoring that none of the colony's "*españoles, mulatos,* and other people of mixed *nación*" should be elected to political office in native villages (*pueblos de indios*).[49] Obviously, the memorandum displayed the extent to which the concept of nación had been influenced by the ideological effects of a century of racial mixture in Mexico.

Hence, to summarize some of the foregoing discussion, for Domingo Carvallo's slaves in the Philippines and for countless African-born bondsmen throughout the Spanish realm, notions of nación greatly affected how casta was to be conceived. But for New Spain's creoles (both enslaved and free), as well as other individuals of mixed race who were born in Europe or the Americas, the precepts of casta began to guide and inform notions of nación. Seemingly, therefore, as Spanish colonialism evolved, it slowly deemphasized ethnic differences among people who were creoles, replacing ethnic differentiation with variables that highlighted color and lineage.[50]

---

servant to Luis Pérez, a Portuguese man, for 40 *reales*. The sale was conducted by Francisco Martínez, who was living in Japan at the time. The bill of sale reveals that Miguel was to serve Luis for a period of five years. After three years, Luis died in Acapulco and all of his goods were embargoed in the port. Miguel was then placed under the stewardship of Martín de Biruiesca a Roo, an official of the Inquisition. He worked for an additional four years before finally notifying the authorities that he had fully satisfied his obligations and desired to be released from bondage. See AGN, Indiferente Virreinal, vol. 6596, exp. 138, fol. 1.

[47] AGN, Inquisición, vol. 705, exp.7, fol. 52.

[48] AGN, Inquisición, vol. 362, second series, exp. 133, fols. 510–511v; AGN, Inquisición, vol. 817, exp. 18, fol. 409.

[49] AGN, Indios, vol. 25, exp. 499, fols. 346v–347v.

[50] The same phenomenon has been observed for Honduras by Melida Velásquez, "El comercio de esclavos en la alcaldía mayor de Tegucigalpa," *Mesoamerica* 22, no. 42 (2001): 218. Since creoles were born within the empire, one could argue that their shared language (Spanish) and knowledge of Hispanic culture muted ethnic differentiation, thereby making color a more meaningful signifier of difference, especially for individuals

As readily as the concepts of *nación* and *casta* were used interchangeably, so too were the designations of *calidad, clase, raza, condición*, and *casta*. Typically, calidad made reference to an individual's honor, socioeconomic standing, community status, and reputation.[51] Although it can be traced to sixteenth-century documents, the melding of calidad and casta is often cited as an eighteenth-century phenomenon.[52] During the 1700s as well, terms such as *clase* and *condición* gained influence in identity classification schemas. When used as correlates for casta, both bore resemblance to the meaning of calidad, but with slightly different emphases. Thanks to the Enlightenment and expanding mercantile capitalism, *clase* probably placed a greater significance on an individual's socioeconomic standing.[53] *Condición*, in contrast, probably tended to accentuate phenotype and lineage.[54]

of mixed race. Of course, groups and individuals who were affiliated with specific indigenous communities and who retained many aspects of their native culture offer a powerful counterexample.

[51] Note that status differences also grew in importance. Robert McCaa, "Calidad, Clase, and Marriage in Colonial Mexico: The Case of Parral, 1788–1790," *Hispanic American Historical Review* 64, no. 3 (1984): 477–501; R. C. Schwaller, "Defining Difference," chap. 2; Richard Boyer, *Cast* [sic] *and Identity in Colonial Mexico: A Proposal and an Example* (Storrs, CT, Providence, RI, and Amherst, MA: Latin American Consortium of New England, 1997).

[52] Rappaport, *Disappearing Mestizo*, 60–61.

[53] Martínez, *Genealogical Fictions*, 247.

[54] Considerable debate can emerge as to whether any of these categories supplanted casta or should be prioritized over casta. The truth is that each took primacy in specific situations. *Calidad*, for instance, was a major term employed in the rhetoric of tribute policy and collection; *condición* entered into the tribute vocabulary as well. *Calidad* also became a featured terminology in some census registers, and there is traceable evidence of other pinpointed usages of this and the other terms in the archives. Regardless, it is clear that casta served as a governing concept by the eighteenth century, if not well before. Casta did not necessarily stand above the other notions, but rather the ways in which those others operated in conjunction with casta, and were tethered to it, meant that they stretched the notion of caste but were never fully severed from it. Thus, the information these concepts conveyed gradually informed casta and became part of its core.

Norah Andrews's dissertation, "Taxing Blackness: Tribute and Free-Colored Community in Colonial Mexico" (PhD diss.: Johns Hopkins University, 2014), is one of the strongest recent arguments conveying the importance of *calidad* as a key colonial terminology, particularly as reflected in tribute policy and collection practices. See also her article "Calidad, Genealogy, and Disputed Free-Colored Tributary Status in New Spain," *The Americas* 73, no. 2 (2016): 139–170. For a specific example of how *casta* and *condición* could be applied in the context of tribute collection, see AGN, Indiferente Virreinal, 1781, caja 599, exp. 16, fols. 1–7v. This document records attempts to determine whether the militiamen listed by Col. Manuel Vaamonte were exempt from paying tribute "por su casta o condición." In the same document, we see the term *calidad* used in ways that bear strong analogy to *casta* and *condición*.

The lines that were blurred between the early concepts of *raza* (race) and *casta* may be some of the most beguiling of all, and among the most troubling from the point of view of modern scholars. There has been grave concern among academics that without carefully understanding each term's separate history, we run the risk of unjustifiably imposing modern ideas about race onto the colonial world.[55] Notwithstanding, there is general consensus that there was great definitional overlap between raza and casta from the fifteenth century through the early moments of the colonial period, since both terms had emerged from ruminations over lineage, nature, and breeding, with a particular emphasis on purity. Overlap continued for much of the sixteenth and early seventeenth centuries, until a major disjuncture occurred when raza and casta started being applied to humans instead of animals. According to some, casta made the transfer more readily, showing an aptitude for changeability. *Raza* lingered as a term that applied more consistently to animals. When it finally made the transition to describing humans, it connoted shame and marked infamy.[56] Especially in Spain, raza grew increasingly associated with descriptions of religious lineage, specifically the heterodoxies implicit in Judaism and Islam. Jews or Moors were seen as having "mala raza" (bad race), in contrast to people who were described as being noble and of "clean casta."[57]

As *raza* continued evolving along this track, *casta* took a different turn, becoming ever less laden with ethnoreligious overtones. Some have argued

---

[55] Américo Castro, *The Spaniards: An Introduction to Their History* (Berkeley: University of California Press, 1971), preface. In this book and others, Castro suggests that we should abandon the term *race* in favor of *caste*. David Nirenberg criticizes this approach as hollow, noting that swapping the two terms without substantially changing their meaning preserves their essentializing qualities and at the same time affords no new utility to either. For another critique of the use of *race*, see the important work of Ruth Hill, "Casta as Culture and the Sociedad de Castas as Literature," in *Interpreting Colonialism*, ed. Byron Wells and Philip Stewart (Oxford: Voltaire Foundation, 2004), 236–237; and Hill, *Hierarchy, Commerce, and Fraud*.

[56] Hill, *Hierarchy, Commerce, and Fraud*, 211–212.

[57] Castro, *The Spaniards*, 51. See his discussion on "good caste," 51–52. Much of the preceding discussion on the religious implications of raza is expertly treated in Martínez's *Genealogical Fictions*. David Nirenberg also captures the essence of the discussion when he writes, "Vocabulary of race grounded in theories of animal husbandry that posited the biological reproduction of somatic and behavioral traits ... underwrote a set of strategies that explained and legitimated the creation and perpetuation of certain hierarchies and discriminations through the language of reproduction." See Nirenberg, "Race and the Middle Ages," in *Rereading the Black Legend: The Discourses of Religious and Racial Difference in Renaissance Empires*, ed. Margaret Greer, Walter Mignolo, and Maureen Quilligan (Chicago: University of Chicago Press, 2008), 77–78, 83.

nonetheless that New World expressions of casta owed much to the foundations laid by these new manifestations of raza. What happened next is an issue of great scholarly contention. It is possible that the distinctions put in place by raza, demarcating Moors and Jews from Christians and setting up discriminatory practices around them, were crucial steps toward framing modern notions of race and racism.[58] Others argue strongly against this view.[59] However one chooses to decipher the ways in which *casta* and *raza* were utilized and overlapped during this period, a clear chronology can be crafted. Starting from being almost indistinct terminologies during the fifteenth and early sixteenth centuries, there was a steady divergence in their meaning as *raza* became more associated with religious lineage and as *casta* arrived in the New World and adapted to local conditions and demographies. While never absolute, some degree of conceptual distance between the terms lasted for about a century. But by the 1700s they began melding again. The reduced zeal in trying to excise Jewish and Islamic heresies, combined with the circulation of new racial ideas from other parts of Europe and the New World, had an impact. In 1726, the dictionary of the Real Academia Española defined *raza* as "the caste or quality of one's lineage."[60] The larger point to bear in mind, however, is that since *raza, nación, calidad, clase, condición*, and related terms were all aligned with *casta* at various points in time, and could even serve as surrogates for it, the very concept of *casta* was subject to substantial variation. Its meaning varied in particular situations and

---

[58] James H. Sweet, "The Iberian Roots of American Racist Thought," *William and Mary Quarterly* 54, no. 1 (January 1997): 143–166.

[59] Based on the dependence in modern concepts of race on locating steadfast, biological codes that supposedly defined a person's essence and being, the terms *raza* and *casta* fell short, at least in their usages prior to the eighteenth century. On the other hand, some believe that the definitions by which we have understood raza and casta are simply too inflexible for the way people lived and thought in the colonial period. The characteristics associated with modern racial thinking – skin color, behavior, physical traits, aptitudes, and other elements – were never seen as constants in the perspective of sixteenth- and seventeenth-century residents of Spain and the Iberian colonies. The principles of human physiology and behavior, then heavily based on Galenic theories of humors and humoral balances, meant that one's diet, environment, and interpersonal relationships could substantially change biological outcomes, rendering notions of biological fixity and certainty difficult. Bearing this in mind, both raza and casta could represent early forms of racial thinking (as we currently construe race), primarily because the contemporary nature of race itself was more relaxed and accommodating. For more, see Hill, *Hierarchy, Commerce, and Fraud*, 200; López Beltrán, "Hippocratic Bodies," 284–285; Earle, *Body of the Conquistador*, 26–30, 187–214; and Burns, "Unfixing Race," in *Rereading the Black Legend*, 188–203, especially 188–190.

[60] Burns, "Unfixing Race," in *Rereading the Black Legend*, 188.

circumstances, being liable to substantial change as different ideologies came into vogue or lost favor over time. The lack of hard rules to anchor the idea of casta, or to regulate its practice, is one reason why some scholars believe that an explicitly defined and regulated caste system never truly materialized.

PROTOMESTIZAJE: THE MOMENT OF CASTIZAJE

The amorphousness of casta is also partly why scholars have hotly debated whether either class or casta influences were more important in determining the general shape of social relations in the colonies. A vast literature exists on describing how people moved in and out of casta categories, mainly by applying the instruments of class and status (*calidad*) to provide access up and down the social scale.[61] An equally intriguing literature explores how casta status became inscribed into law, enabling hops across the social hierarchy.[62] Interestingly, however, as an inherently organic category, subject to great fluidity, the concept of *casta* could live, contract, stretch, and grow. This point, which has often been identified as a weakness of casta, may have actually been its strength.[63] Its elasticity enabled it to survive as an idea and eventually blend with the

[61] An overview can be found in Robert H. Jackson, *Race, Caste, and Status: Indians in Colonial Spanish America* (Albuquerque: University of New Mexico Press, 1999), 3–22. Another interesting summation, targeted at examining questions around "gracias al sacar" documents can be found in Twinam, *Purchasing Whiteness*, 58–66. Recently, important work has provided new ways of envisioning the debate. See Leo Garofalo and Rachel O'Toole, eds., "Constructing Difference in Colonial Latin America," *Journal of Colonialism and Colonial History* 7, no. 1 (Spring 2006); Andrew B. Fisher and Matthew D. O'Hara, *Imperial Subjects: Race and Identity in Colonial Latin America* (Durham and London: Duke University Press, 2009); and Aaron P. Althouse, "Contested Mestizos, Alleged Mulattos: Racial Identity and Caste Hierarchy in Eighteenth-Century Pátzcuaro, Mexico," *The Americas* 62, no. 2 (October 2005): 151–175. My own concern is that given the ad hoc nature in which government and society often functioned in colonial Latin America, especially prior to the eighteenth century and even more so in remote areas, are scholars perhaps asking too much of caste? Why should we expect a caste system to look more coherent than many of the other institutions, social policies, and systems that existed alongside it?

[62] Yanna Yannakakis interestingly discusses how *indio* was considered a legal category when racial notions were not yet fully formed, and Gabriela Ramos brilliantly addresses the legal dimensions of race and how these affect the performance of racial identities before a variety of audiences – among them the state, the public, and the family. See Ramos and Yannakakis, *Indigenous Intellectuals: Knowledge, Power, and Colonial Culture in Mexico and the Andes* (Durham: Duke University Press, 2014).

[63] An excellent critique of the notion of a caste system can be found in Rappaport, *The Disappearing Mestizo*, 225–260.

modern concept of race as it took root in the Hispanic world of the eighteenth and early nineteenth centuries. In the process, casta may have served as a conduit through which older notions of social differentiation were incubated, refined, recoded, and transmitted, finding expression in contemporary manifestations of race in Latin America.[64] As the concept of casta evolved between the sixteenth and early nineteenth centuries, it also emerged as a prime candidate and channel for transmitting the colonial era's multidescriptional socio-racial systems into a more singular one framed within the ideology of mestizaje.[65]

Casta, though, performed different ideological work than *mestizaje*. Both took racial mixture as a basic reality of life and a fundamental starting point for the construction of society. At heart, however, casta attempted to demarcate and accentuate differences between people, in the hope of bringing a stronger social order. Mestizaje placed greater emphasis on commonality and hybridity to engineer order and unity. Casta was also fundamentally an imperial project, rooted in conversations about the functioning of empire.[66] It follows, then, that Spain, Spanishness, and to some extent early concepts of whiteness were unabashedly extolled, despite all three notions being incompletely formulated and understood (even in Europe) for significant portions of the colonial era.[67] Mestizaje, on the other hand, operated within the context of the nation-state and

[64] María Elena Martínez illuminates the way here with her wonderful work demonstrating fundamental transformations in the concept of limpieza de sangre. One possible limitation of her work may be that a greater phenomenon was occurring simultaneously. While limpieza de sangre was a bridge from pre-sixteenth-century conceptions of ethnoreligious difference to those of later periods, its relationship to caste seems to have been reciprocal: caste seems to have both altered perceptions of limpieza de sangre and been much affected by it. Indeed, caste may have been the epiphenomenon in the relationship, meaning that it stood to have a wider consequence on society.

[65] As I have argued previously, it would be wrong to categorize mestizaje as a racially narrow, one-dimensional view. One of the beauties of mestizaje was its capaciousness. Even as it compressed races into its framework, it strived to do so inclusively and is replete with attempts to harmonize them.

[66] Eric Wolf, *Sons of the Shaking Earth* (Chicago: University of Chicago Press, 1959); John Elliott, *Empires of the Atlantic World: Britain and Spain in America, 1492–1830* (New Haven: Yale University Press, 2006), especially chap. 3.

[67] On the formulation of whiteness in relation to the slave trade, see David Eltis, *The Rise of African Slavery in the Americas* (Cambridge: Cambridge University Press, 2000). Tzvetan Todorov is also important in resurrecting the idea of "the other," which is key in the formulation of Spanishness. For an examination of alternative means of constructing Spanish national identity, see Todorov, *The Conquest of America: The Question of the Other* (New York: Harper & Row, 1984). Also see Erin Rowe, *Saint and Nation: Santiago, Teresa of Ávila, and Plural Identities in Early Modern Spain* (University Park: Penn State University Press, 2011). As I observed earlier, I believe that in its aim of

sought to derive meaning from Latin America's own internal experiences rather than the dictates or necessities of the empire. Mestizaje, aimed at fulfilling its nationalistic mission, ultimately embraced racial mixture, centering it epistemologically in ways that would reveal miscegenation's own inherent value.[68]

Mestizaje and *casta* were not necessarily immutable. In the 1990s, historian Joseph Sánchez introduced a term that raised little scholarly attention but seems appropriate for establishing conceptual connections between mestizaje and casta. He suggested that we label the tremendous mobility and fluidity that took place among casta groups as *castizaje*, a word that literally fuses casta and mestizaje together.[69] However, Sánchez then contrasted both notions, contending that while mestizaje served as the platform for generating social mobility in Latin America, castizaje was a concept that helped colonials move beyond the framework of race.[70] Others have since used the term *castizaje* to provide a more nuanced alternative descriptor of racial mixture. For them, *mestizaje* represents a blunter descriptive instrument that overemphasizes white-native miscegenation. Castizaje, on the other hand, can be used to more aptly capture the subtler realities of the black-white-native hybridization of Latin America. Perhaps one of the most reflective recent treatments of castizaje has been written by Joel Morales Cruz. In his view, mestizaje charts a linear, Hegelian-like synthesis of racial mixture into an inevitable, singular outcome: the mestizo. Castizaje, meanwhile, shows more alternative possibilities, since constant and fluid caste interactions could lead to multiple, even ambiguous, outcomes: mestizos, castizos, zambos, etc. In short, for Morales Cruz, castizaje underscores how racial mixture produced plural identities,

---

fulfilling the imperial mission, casta ultimately existed to orient colonial racial mixture toward whiteness.

[68] As I have noted earlier in this chapter, mestizaje did not completely eradicate whitening projects, and for many adherents of mestizaje, whiteness was cherished. The conversations toward achieving it, though, were different than in colonial times.

[69] Joseph P. Sánchez, "Between Mestizaje and Castizaje: An Imperial View of the Spanish Vision of Race and Ethnicity in Colonial New Spain," paper presented at "Mestizaje: A Forum," the National Hispanic Cultural Center, Albuquerque, New Mexico, September 26, 2006.

[70] I have never seen evidence of the term *castizaje* in colonial records for Mexico, and from my viewpoint it is doubtful that the term was ever used in the colonial era. It seems best to conceive of it as a modern construct used to categorize and explain historical events. Regardless, it is described as "one of the dynamics of social control in the colonial period." See Review of Robert H. Jackson, *Race, Caste, and Status: Indians in Colonial Spanish America*, in *Colonial Latin American Historical Review* 8, no. 3 (Summer 1999): 393–394.

whereas mestizaje generated more-homogenous ones.[71] Although not in direct conversation with one another, Sánchez (and those informed by his ideas) would likely agree.

All of these analyses might be missing an important step. The fluidity that undergirded castizaje needs more interrogation, based on greater historical evidence. It is here that understanding the lives, fates, and impact of the extreme castes may be helpful. Colonial racial mobility likely extended deeper and proved more socially profound than we might have initially imagined. And while the multiple permutations of caste that occurred during colonial times may have led to plural identities, the form these took might not be exactly what Sánchez or Morales Cruz had in mind. Before getting to this, if we first simply pause for a moment and envision castizaje as a framework that could encompass *all* forms of casta mobility (not just some of them), then I would argue that this can help us conceive of castizaje as a stage along the route to mestizaje. Hence, castizaje was effectively protomestizaje – that is to say, mestizaje in the making. The grades of casta mobility inherent in castizaje worked to anticipate and shape mestizaje's future by producing core conditions that would help generate its birth. By "casta mobility" I am referring to how miscegenation inadvertently facilitated intergenerational mobility along the casta continuum, such that the children of some caste groups enjoyed a very different identity status than their parents did. I also mean the various legal, social, and cultural methods by which different casta groups altered themselves, including the mechanisms by which mestizos and mulattos became whiter, or how indios became mestizos, and so on. Many of these forms of mobility have been categorized as "passing."[72]

Castizaje certainly encompassed passing, but also much more. It even incorporated a phenomenon that might be best described as caste

---

[71] Joel Morales Cruz, *The Mexican Reformation: Catholic Pluralism, Enlightenment Religion, and the Iglesia de Jesús in Benito Juárez's Mexico (1859–72)* (Eugene, OR: Pickwick, 2011).

[72] An individual who was mulato, pardo, or mestizo but looked white, might "pass" for white. Implied here was that individuals eagerly sought whiteness and developed strategies to attain it, including class ascension tactics; some of this indeed transpired. But as has been pointed out, the effort involved in constructing new family and social networks, and the often meager benefit to be obtained, might have dissuaded some from doing so. To add to the difficulty, the psychological strain of leaping from one major caste or racial grouping to the next must have been immense. The literature on passing is vast; an excellent and more recent treatment is Twinam, *Purchasing Whiteness*. Interesting insights can also be found in Dennis Nodín Valdés, "The Decline of the Sociedad de Castas in Mexico City" (PhD diss.: University of Michigan, 1978).

pluralism. Here I will begin to depart from the insights posited by Sánchez and Morales Cruz. Whereas their version of pluralism emphasizes that a multiplicity of caste categories existed that could be treated distinctly, I would also like to stress that colonists could actually live through several of these statuses in their lifetimes (almost constituting a form of intersectionality). Indeed, the archival record is rich in showing how scores of people lived multiple-casta lives.[73] Passing, of course, captures some of this type of fluidity. But whereas passing engineered changes in caste that were largely intentional – and could involve a great deal of psychological stress, masquerade, and identity theater – the caste pluralism I invoke represented a more natural state of affairs. Its form of caste shifting was not so overtly conscious and was less demanding than trying to pass into another caste.

Caste pluralism was often achieved through passive interpretations of an individual's physical characteristics, and through new renderings of a person's caste that came about as social contexts changed. As people moved from one neighborhood to another, as they traveled throughout the regions of their colonies, and as they moved through the various phases of their lives, many of their casta classifications were altered – by the government, the Church, or their neighbors, friends, and colleagues. As racial mixture intensified and new, more-extreme labels were created, the mobility between proximate caste statuses became easier to achieve as the distances demarcating one classification from another shrank. Consequently, pluralism grew exponentially as caste categories multiplied. Finally, it should be noted that caste pluralism captured another reality: multiple-casta existences could be lived serially, simultaneously, or both. And whitening was not always the goal.

Several cases presented in subsequent chapters of this book will illuminate caste pluralism more fully. However, documenting a few cases here will set the stage for what is to come. Pascuala de Morga, who in 1720 was denounced for bigamy in Mexico City, was in many ways a prime example of the caste-shifting phenomenon. By many she was known as a "china,"

---

[73] A few examples from caste-related documents I have identified will demonstrate the point: AGN, Inquisición, vol. 775, exp. 45, fols. 553–556, refers to a *negro zambo*; Inquisición, vol. 829, exp. 9, fols. 589–611 (*mulata loba*); Inquisición, vol. 875, exp. 5, fols. 101–149v (*mestiza, coyote*, or *morisca*); Inquisición, vol. 890, fols. 52–66v (*coyote* or *mestizo*); Inquisición, vol. 980, exp. 12, n.p. (*mulato morisco*); Inquisición, vol. 1176, exp. 4, fols. 69–79 (*lobo* or *mulato*); Inquisición, vol. 1287, exp. 1, fols. 1–16 (*lobo* or *indio*); Matrimonios, vol. 550, exp. 1, fol. 457 (*loba blanca*); and Bienes Nacionales, vol. 293, exp. 299, n/p (*india loba*).

but she was also described and publicly known to be a parda who "looked like" a loba.[74] Since by this time the term *chino* had acquired overtones of blackness, her ability to be expressed simultaneously as a chino-lobo-pardo represented very plausible movement across the caste continuum. And that she could be expressed as all of these at once was not necessarily unusual.

Bernardo Carrillo was a man who lived as a lobo and an indio. Thrown in jail for bigamy in 1746, he was labeled on his first marriage certificate as a lobo. Whether he had declared lobo as his casta, or whether the priest who performed the nuptials assigned the label to him, is unknown. Whatever the proximate cause may have been, he described himself at the time of his incarceration as an indio, a description seconded by his first wife. She even attested to the fact that shortly prior to contracting the marriage, Bernardo was known as an "indio ladino" working as a servant in Temastián, Jalisco. The inquisitors found themselves in a quandary. If Bernardo was a lobo, his case fell squarely within their purview, and they were wholly liable for sentencing him, keeping him jail, or doing whatever else they reasoned was proper justice. But if Bernardo was an indio, his case belonged under a different jurisdiction, that of the *juez eclesiástico ordinario*. It is unclear whether Bernardo or his wives were aware of the legal implications associated with his indio caste status in this circumstance. After a detailed investigation, including an examination of Bernardo's baptismal records and conversations with residents from his hometown, he was determined to be an indio and subsequently set free. However, even this definitive ruling did not exclude the possibility that he would be identified as a lobo in other social contexts.[75]

In the town of Actopan, Phelipe de Callejas Moreno was born to a mother who was classified variously as a morisca, a morisca blanca, or a mulata blanca. His father was white. Like his mother, Phelipe comfortably straddled several somatic worlds during his lifetime. He married a castiza and even presented himself as a castizo at times. As with many

[74] AGN, Inquisición, vol. 781, exp. 44, fols. 517–523. I thank Tatiana Seijas for calling my attention to this case.

[75] AGN, Inquisición, vol. 921, exp. 15, fols. 221–236. The legal and historical literature on "forum shopping" might be useful for framing some of the legal maneuvering that members of the castas consciously deployed, or passively endured, during the colonial period, particularly as it pertained to their oscillations in caste status. For the historical literature, see Karen Barkey, "Aspects of Legal Pluralism in the Ottoman Empire," in *Legal Pluralism and Empires, 1500–1850*, ed. Lauren A. Benton and Richard J. Ross (New York: New York University Press, 2013), 83–108, especially 95. Again, I thank Patrick Funiciello for pointing out this critical link.

whose caste ambiguity enabled them to move in and out of a state of near-whiteness, problems came when the authorities sought a firmer definition of his casta in order to comply with specific regulations. When census takers visited Actopan (in present-day Hidalgo) in 1726 to compile the tribute roster, Phelipe's black ancestry made him a target for payment. However, his father quickly intervened. He reminded the authorities that in a decree issued sometime prior to the 1726 levy, all mestizos, castizos, and coyotes had been asked to present documentation to prove their casta status (these groups were exempted from paying tribute). Phelipe's father made the case for his son, implying that he was a coyote. His arguments and subsequent witness testimonies proved persuasive. Ultimately, Phelipe was not found to be of an exempt caste, but he was recognized to be a morisco, which was good enough to exempt him from tribute.[76]

Phelipe's struggle and his life of caste pluralism revealed at least two things. First, when the need arose, people could sometimes pass as something different.[77] Second, the exigencies of the Church or state in demanding greater clarification of caste categories sometimes had a reverse effect, inadvertently precipitating both caste pluralism and passing. As people responded to the competing and sometimes conflicting caste queries and pressures of the authorities, they might give very different responses in regard to casta. To some extent this variability destabilized the fixity of caste and its designations. At the same time, relaxations of caste policy and the liberties taken as a result created even more seams in which people could live multiple-caste existences.

Nearly a century after Phelipe's case, Actopan again served as a site of interest in regard to these trends. In 1804, several *vecinos* (leading citizens) lodged a formal complaint with the authorities in Mexico City. A number of men who identified themselves as well-known españoles, and who had in 1802 submitted evidence to verify their casta, complained vociferously when they discovered that the regional subdelegate (*subdelegado*) for tributary assessments had failed to remove them from the town's tribute registers. As their case unfolded, their attorney, José Mariano Covarrubias, eloquently conveyed their position. The most insidious effect of appearing on the roster was the tarnish to their reputations, "which [they consider] far more valuable than their material interests." But Covarrubias also demonstrated how

---

[76] AGN, Ramo Civil, vol. 1106, exp. 6 and 11.

[77] Of course, it is interesting to note that Phelipe's father was the prime catalyst of his attempts to pass so as to avoid tribute payment.

the crown's own goals and image as a supreme and benevolent patriarch were jeopardized by the actions of its legates. Beholden now to paying tribute, Covarruvias's clients suddenly felt "equal to Indians." Hitting home one of his major points, Covarrubias observed that the overly zealous actions of the royal treasury were inspiring the king's agents to "take the men to be amphibians, being *indios* for the purposes of tribute, and *españoles* to contribute in all other matters." Through his insightful and electric metaphor, Covarruvias aptly captured a subtle feature of caste pluralism: racial mixture made it possible to double-count certain individuals. Bureaucrats could plug people into an assortment of categories for the Church and state as needs and opportunities arose. Just as the average colonist could use passing and caste pluralism to tactical advantage, so could Spain's colonial institutions use these instruments to forward the interests of the ruling elite.[78]

***

It is possible that by rewriting the historian's script to prioritize castizaje and its various forms of motion (caste pluralism and passing) we can move beyond spending inordinate time and effort discussing the reputed crisis and limitations of casta that have long been front and center in the caste vs. class debate. Undoubtedly, the weaknesses of the sistema de castas, not to mention its well-documented insufficiency at managing itself, produced shocks and commotion in the general colonial order. But ironically, the greatest impact of these deficiencies was probably not on the caste system per se. Consider instead the possibility that it was castizaje that was most affected, and that the shocks it endured were primarily generative, rather than degenerative, in nature. Recall that casta as a concept was fluid, malleable, even shock-absorbent. It could accommodate adjustments, even to a fault. Almost as soon as casta categories were employed in the colonies, they both caused and compounded confusion. Colonial administrators bemoaned the proliferation of castas, and some openly admitted that they did not know which standards they should use to classify people. Newly arrived administrators in remote posts were especially affected, as they struggled with basic categorizations and pondered the extent to which they needed to impose casta standards or adhere to local labeling customs.

---

[78] AGN, General de Parte, vol. 79, exps. 275–277; fols. 239v–241v. For the "amphibians" metaphor, see fol. 241: "Quieren tenerlos por unos hombre anfibios, que sean indios para tributar y españoles para contribuir lo demás."

This environment likely encouraged the convolution of terminologies and the conflation of *casta* with *calidad, nación, clase,* and other partial cognates described earlier. Further, the confusion and convolution had an increasingly cumulative effect. Let me posit that these tensions in the supposed "system" never broke down something that never completely existed in the first place. Casta was an idea that never stood on solid ground, and few contemporaries would have dared to describe casta networks as a functioning system. Therefore, what likely happened as the various collisions and aftershocks worked themselves through the hierarchy of the imperial government, the Church, and local societies is that they further atomized the notion of casta, to a point where it became virtually indistinct from racial mixture itself. Seen another way, castizaje – that process by which casta groups shifted, transformed, moved, and intermingled with each other – helped push the idea of casta beyond being a segmenting force and into something that captured the spirit of colonial plurality and hybridity in its fullest sense. It was not uncommon to find census documents, government memos, tribute and parish records, traveler's accounts, treatises, and other forms of memoranda in which hybrid peoples were referred to as a group – that is, as "castas." As printing technologies advanced steadily during the eighteenth century, imperial presses generated templates for formulaic official documents that included a pretyped category of casta stenciled in ink. Officials attempting to complete these documents would correspondingly have to compress the multiplicity of groups they encountered into this singular category.[79]

Casta, in demonstrating an ability to personify all of colonial racial mixture, prefigured the essence of what *lo mestizo* would become generations later, under the rubric of mestizaje. One cannot underestimate the long-term value of this conceptual leap. However, even as the term *casta* settled into this new, more encompassing meaning during the colonial period, it never fully lost its other functions and meanings. It could still be called upon to carve any colonial population into minced groups – almost infinitely so. The finest mincing typically took place at the regional and local levels, where knowledge about neighbors and family was more available and where officials were closer to events on the ground. At the viceregal and imperial levels, however, bureaucrats did not penetrate too

---

[79] With these factors at play, it is no surprise that even into the nineteenth century, agglomerations of people of mixed race continued to be known as castas in certain settings. See Marisela Jiménez Ramos, "Black Mexico: Nineteenth Century Discourses of Race and Nation" (PhD diss.: Brown University, 2009).

deeply. By the end of the colonial period, and in fact well before, casta had revealed itself to be a Janus-faced creature. Casta was simultaneously able to look broad and wide at the socio-racial condition of society on the one side, while looking microscopically at levels of detail and difference on the other. These abilities augured well for casta to be able to function operably in colonial settings, while equally proving able to synthesize the multiple strands of socio-racial classification throughout the empire for later use by Latin America's nations. Before mestizaje existed casta, morphing through a conduit of change called castizaje.

4

The Jungle of Casta Extremes

As casta unfolded in everyday situations, it was constantly being recoded, recalibrated, and reinvented. These adaptations were both the process and the result of how colonial subjects saw themselves and the world around them. The recoding had subtle and seemingly infinite variations. There were mulattos, for instance, who were not the progeny of blacks and whites, but of negros and chinos. Such was the case with the children of Andrea and Sebastián, slaves in Mexico City during the 1640s.[1] There were also scores of mulatos who were the descendants of negros and indios.[2] Additionally, the assumption that lobos had clear native bloodlines was not always true. In 1674, when Nicolasa, a loba slave from Mexico City was sold, her deed revealed her parental lineage to be negro and mulatto.[3] There were also cases in which coyotes (technically, the mixture of mestizos and indios) were considered equivalent to mestizos, as well as other situations in which coyotes were analogous to castizos (white and mestizo). As with lobos, regional differences determined just how much native ancestry qualified a person to be a coyote.[4]

Then there was the matter of perspective that generated different opinions on caste even within regions and townships. In 1793, a scuffle

[1] Archivo Histórico de Notarias de la Ciudad de México [hereafter ANM], Martín Sariñana, 4362, fol. 196.
[2] R. C. Schwaller, "'Mulata, Hija de Negro y India': Afro-Indigenous Mulattos in Early Colonial Mexico," *Journal of Social History* 44, no. 3 (Spring 2011): 889–914.
[3] ANM, C. Muñoz, 2525, fol. 1v.
[4] A wonderful example comes from the San Antonio de Xacala hacienda (1749). Here, coyotes were largely the offspring of mestizos and españoles. See AGN, Bienes Nacionales, vol. 113, exp. 10, fols. 39–43v (for Xacala).

broke out between Juan Bautista, an Indian tributary from the small, rural town of San Lucas (in Tenango del Valle), and two white militiamen, Máximo Subersa and Felipe Subersa. During the incident, the integrity of the militiamen's casta was called into question.[5] Juan and Máximo had been packing mules with loads of wheat alongside other indios from the community. When Máximo stopped for a break, Juan urged him to continue working. Insulted by the affront, the request sparked Máximo to fight. Felipe overheard the commotion and ran from his field to help his brother. Together, the militiamen carted Juan off to jail, badly injured with head and foot wounds. As the case unfolded, it became clear that the Subersa brothers had been quite prone to aggressive and abusive behavior in the past. The authorities ultimately did not support their actions and instead released Juan from jail, ensuring that his lost wage earnings were recovered. While the brothers initially had the upper hand in this case due to their local connections and caste status, their actions were eventually overturned.

The case provides a window for us on matters of caste, since as it progressed, it became clear that the militiamen's claims to whiteness were based largely on subjective grounds. Thanks to their prominent roles and alliances in the community, the men conducted themselves as españoles. But from Juan's perspective, and that of other natives living in the district, both men were little more than coyotes, a status that carried a pejorative weight in San Lucas. Certainly doubts over the true caste of the brothers lingered in the minds of the authorities outside San Lucas who deliberated the final resolution of the case.

In short, there were scores of regional, local, and sublocal variances that could make casta status operate differently from place to place. These dissonances could be resolved without great difficulty in many cases, and generally did not threaten the stability of the overall social order. Sometimes the number of variances was simply not large enough to make a substantive dent in the grander scheme. Obviously, the multiple ways in which lobos and mulatos were defined throughout the colony did not rupture the broader meaning of these categories. At other times, there was enough latitude in the construction of casta that regional and local differences could be resolved effectively when dissonances occurred, albeit not to everyone's satisfaction. We can surmise that when the central government opted to favor the local native population's viewpoint of the Subersa brothers' caste status in San Lucas, there were some who

---

[5] AGN, Criminal, vol. 206, fols. 364bis–374.

were displeased. Regardless, by whatever means consensus on casta statuses was achieved (or not), caste dissonances were habitual in the colonial period. Thus, in the typical flow of colonial affairs, reconciling conflicting interpretations over casta did not present itself as a major event. In their frequency, these practices of reconciling casta were rather ordinary – part of the natural order of things.

Casta categories, especially extreme ones, could also be deployed strategically in the colonial period – at times being used almost metaphorically. In these cases the primary intent was not to describe and capture the product of racial mixture, but rather to use some of the extreme registers of casta as a guide for demonstrating how particular situations should be interpreted. Those who utilized caste labels in this way often did so to explain and justify certain behaviors and circumstances to specific constituencies. One provocation that could elicit the use of extreme caste descriptions was deviancy. In the town of Coatepec in 1770, María Dolores Colesiala, labeled a loba, was denounced to the Inquisition for bewitching María López, an española. She had apparently sealed María López's mouth shut by applying a concoction including hair, a pig's tail, and a snake. As the case proceeded, it exposed an intricate feud and smear campaign between the women. María Dolores's reputation was thoroughly derided; she was described as a thief who stole money and petty goods from locals and as an expert in making dolls used for bewitchment. She was also accused of killing several townsmen with her magic. Disturbingly, some locals attested to having seen a witch leaving María Dolores's room at night and reported that these visits were followed by flurries of mischief. The details of the case are captivating, but what is important for our purposes is that María Dolores's casta status shifted, albeit slightly, over the course of the testimony. Some said she was a mestiza; others claimed she was a loba. Whatever the truth, the inquisitors clung to the loba label. Arguably, its association with blackness (Afro-Mexicans were among those most accused of heterodoxy in Mexico) added to the case a dimension of culpability and ire on which the plaintiff capitalized, and which was probably endorsed just as soundly by the Inquisition.[6]

---

[6] AGN, Inquisición, vol. 1097, exp. 8, fols. 218v–233. For more on Afro-Mexicans appearing before the Inquisition, see Frank T. Proctor, *Damned Notions of Liberty: Slavery, Culture, and Power in Colonial Mexico, 1640–1769* (Albuquerque: University of New Mexico Press, 2010); Joan C. Bristol, *Christians, Blasphemers, and Witches*; Laura A. Lewis, *Hall of Mirrors*; and Gonzalo Aguirre Beltrán's classic work on black magic, *Medicina y magia: el proceso de aculturación en la estructura colonial* (Mexico: Instituto Nacional Indigenista, 1963).

In the city of Querétaro in the early 1750s, Mónica Guadalupe Mundurriaga (a mulata) appeared before the Inquisition to denounce Joachin Lozano, a morisco *curandero* (healer) and cigar maker. She confessed that about seven years earlier, Lozano (then a sexton at the church of Santo Domingo) had forced her to have sex with him on three separate occasions. At least once, they fornicated directly on the church altar, where she'd also seen him drink from the holy chalice. Lozano had invited her to do the same. As their relationship grew more intense, Lozano reportedly buried a small statue of a saint in her room, stating that through this act he would be assured that she would never betray him. He then asked her to sign her name in blood on a small piece of paper. Once this act was completed, she would join him in becoming enslaved to the devil. She complied, but instead of using her blood, she substituted red ink. As the ritual act unfolded, she chanted, "I submit to you; I am to be the slave of the devil." Mónica never saw Lozano again until he suddenly appeared during her confession and asked her to renounce her declaration of sin.[7]

Although this fantastical story was packed with inconsistencies, the inquisitors still investigated it. Was Lozano real? Was he the devil? Or was he something else from the supernatural realm? In being described as a morisco, Lozano perhaps credibly appeared to the Inquisition as a trickster figure not unlike the devil or another demon.[8] Other descriptions drawn from Mexico's Inquisition files frequently described the devil as a dark man. Very few described him outright as a morisco, but this portrayal definitely fell within the realm of possibility. Moreover, because Mónica was a mulata, the Inquisition might have therefore been lured into believing that her relationship with the morisco was somehow more plausible, despite the colony-wide ubiquity of sexual relations across Mexico's color divide. At a minimum, by using the term *morisco* in her testimony, Mónica inserted a tangible identifier to her story that could facilitate the Inquisition's ability to locate Lozano, if indeed he was real. Finally, as a morisco, Lozano enjoyed a proximity to whiteness that Mónica might have consciously used to introduce irony to her tale.

---

[7] AGN, Inquisición, vol. 941, exp. 3, fols. 10–30.

[8] For general literature on this topic, see Natalie Zemon Davis, *Trickster Travels: A Sixteenth-Century Muslim between Worlds* (New York: Hill and Wang, 2006); David Coleman, *In the Light of Medieval Spain: Islam, the West, and the Relevance of the Past* (New York: Palgrave Macmillan, 2008), 177; and Brian A. Catlos, *Muslims of Medieval Latin Christendom, c. 1050–1614* (Cambridge and New York: Cambridge University Press, 2014), 280.

In sum, whether she was delusional or not, Monica deployed the morisco typology to useful ends in ways that prompted the authorities to at least partially investigate her claims.

A third and final case to illustrate some of the points raised earlier comes from the jurisdiction of Guadalupe in the late eighteenth century. In January of 1770, Joseph de Rojas, a farmworker described by some as a mulato and by others as a lobo, was denounced by his estate's administrator for "depraved intentions." After two days of hard rain on the hacienda of Santa Ana, Rojas was seen leaving the estate for the countryside, uttering incomprehensible phrases while gesticulating with various signs and figurines. According to firsthand accounts from some of the region's indios, Rojas's actions brought a swift end to the torrential storms that had threatened their crops. Word spread quickly through the local communities, circling back to the hacienda and causing commotion among the natives there. Yet not everyone deemed Rojas a hero. Fears brewed that his wizardry posed a threat to both the spiritual order and the crops themselves. In thwarting the ruinous rains he might have inadvertently precipitated drought conditions that could prove equally damaging to crops. He had to be stopped; the Inquisition was called to investigate.

For our purposes, it is important to know that there was uncertainty surrounding Rojas's casta. He was a mulato in some circles and a lobo in others. In truth, there was probably a great degree of synonymy between the categories in this part of New Spain. But at the same time, the choice of when to use the term *lobo* instead of *mulato* could have also been strategic. One might ask to what extent his characterization as a lobo was meant to connect him to native communities or to raise fears about his influence as a black interloper among local indios. On the other hand, was his occasional characterization as a mulato an effort designed to distance him from being connected to natives and emphasize his links with other members of the region's population? It is revealing that the estate administrator opted to highlight Rojas's status as a lobo. In denouncing Rojas, the administrator may have fully understood the implications for his audience of invoking the term. For some inquisitors, the lobo label would link Rojas to the native world in ways that might influence their overall opinion and even tip the scales in favor of punishment, depending on their outlook on the fraternization of Africans and natives.[9]

Some of my discussion in this case, as in the previous ones, is speculative, based on an informed reading of the archival files. Admittedly, there are

[9] AGN, Inquisición, vol. 1176, exp. 4, fols. 68–79v.

multiple ways to interpret the details of these cases and scores of others like them in the colonial archives. But I believe that my fundamental point remains sound. What some scholars have considered slippages, mistakes, or even an unconscious commingling of casta categories in the colonial record might not have always been so accidental. We should not read lightly over what might seem to be small discrepancies in casta descriptions in the archives, produced by what we might deem to be relaxed approaches to assigning caste labels; nor should we readily seek to smooth them over. In fact, these discrepancies can occasionally offer new angles on the documentation. When colonials blended extreme casta categories with others to describe individuals, I argue, it was sometimes done intentionally to convey information in a different light. The purpose was to subtly alter viewpoints in daily life, to influence the outcomes of disputes, or to otherwise massage narratives conveyed to others for specific ends.[10]

Undeniably, the meaning of casta was stretched continually as it was applied in common encounters. Whether it was through the transformation of casta labels as they acquired different meanings in space and time or through the ways in which casta labels were used as metaphors, a veritable thicket of caste combinations and outcomes came into being. Meanwhile, the steady growth of completely new categories kept apace. There were probably far more caste-based terms in actual use by colonists than even the most ambitious rendering of the caste system has conveyed to date. Some classifications enjoyed only a brief existence, being either too cumbersome to survive in everyday situations or used too rarely in remote parts of the colonies to find their way into the mainstream. Although the archives do not capture all of the more esoteric categories, we can occasionally glimpse them. In Durango during the middle of the eighteenth century, the term *bermejo* (usually used to describe a reddish-brown color) could sometimes appear as an expression of casta or calidad.[11] In 1605, in the obscure town of Cacapo in Michoacán, the term *tresalvo* appears to have been used not only as a surname but also as a caste category for describing hybridized mestizos who were most likely the offspring of mestiza mothers and indio fathers.[12] Úrsula de Povares

[10] Again, casta identities might have been strategically deployed in "legal forum shopping," a means of probing to determine which identity offered the best chances for favorable outcomes in court. See Benton and Ross, *Legal Pluralism and Empires*.

[11] AGN, Inquisición, vol. 1133, exp. 5, fol. 47. Mestizos, certain mulatos, and lobos might at times be described as *bermejo* in color.

[12] AGN, Inquisición, vol. 281, exp. 10, fols. 532–537, 717–719. For a definition of a *tresalvo*, see "Lista de castas," in *Artes de México*, vol. 8 (1990): 79.

was one of these tresalvos. Married to don Gil de Mesa (rumored to be an español), she enjoyed the dual reputation of being mestiza and tresalva. It is unclear the degree to which she and her neighbors actually used the term *tresalvo*, or if it was principally a creation of local government and religious officials.

Among the more unique terminologies used to refer to people of African descent was the caste designation "rayado" (striped). There were very few rayados recorded in colonial Mexico, and of that small number, the best evidence comes from Veracruz and Mexico City during the late seventeenth and early eighteenth centuries. The origin and meaning of *rayado* are unclear. We know that the term commonly referred to specific groups of Indians who inhabited frontier regions and either wore tattoos or were renowned for painting their faces with stripes. In this sense, the term served as a physical descriptor that also recognized aspects of native ethnicity. As waves of Spanish settlers moved into northern Mexico – including Texas, New Mexico, and Kansas – they identified people such as the Wichita, Jumano, and Apache as "indios rayados."[13]

The use of the rayado classification to describe people of African descent was more mysterious. Many Afro-rayados were natives of Africa, and nearly all were described as negro or moreno – emphasizing that they were not racially mixed with other groups.[14] Judging from the physical descriptions found in the archival record of individuals like Blas Prudencia – who was denounced before the Inquisition in Veracruz for bigamy in 1724 – these Afro-rayados did not have any apparent physical markers such as tattoos and facial scarification, and nor did they wear special paints like the indios rayados.[15] The rayado designation may have served principally as an ethnic marker, referring to individuals from the

---

[13] Stan Hoig, *Tribal Wars of the Southern Plains* (Norman: University of Oklahoma Press, 1993), 48–52; Nancy P. Hickerson, "The Linguistic Position of Jumano," *Journal of Anthropological Research* 44, no. 3 (Autumn 1988): 322; Jack D. Forbes, "Unknown Athapaskans: The Identification of the Jano, Jocome, Jumano, Manso, Suma, and Other Indian Tribes of the Southwest," *Ethnohistory* 6, no. 2 (Spring 1959): 137. Note that use of the term *rayados* appeared as early as 1601 in Kansas. Here, the chronicles of Governor General Juan de Oñate recount how he and his 70 men were able to differentiate among Indians because some were rayados (painted or tattooed people, with a stripe from one ear to the other). An earlier use of *rayado* may have appeared in the sixteenth century to commemorate the Christianization of the Apaches in Guanajuato in 1531. A dance was created for this purpose, called "los Apaches," or "los Rayados." See Gertrude Prokosch Kurath, "Mexican Moriscas: A Problem in Dance Acculturation," *Journal of American Folklore* 62, no. 244 (April–June 1949): 90.

[14] *Negro* and *moreno* were two terms that connoted "pure blackness."

[15] AGN, Inquisición, vol. 808, exp. 11 y 12, fol. 478.

"raya de Guinea."[16] Unfortunately, there are few indicators demonstrating exactly where this region was or which people it encompassed. In broad terms, the rayados may have constituted populations from just north and south of the Senegal and Niger Rivers, including the kingdoms of Gago, Foules, Meczara, Genoah, Zanfara, and Cano.[17] There is a slimmer chance that the rayados were from East Africa. The Oromo nation of Ethiopia and Kenya (better known as the Galla) are known to be partly comprised of the Raya people, who live along the eastern borders of the Tigra and Lasta provinces in northeastern Ethiopia.[18]

It is possible that some rayados may have developed their sense of ethnicity while living in the Americas.[19] Blas Prudencia, mentioned earlier, was curiously not described as a rayado until he was an adult and had moved about in the New World, finally arriving in Mexico. In his previous

[16] AGN, Bienes Nacionales, leg. 1229, exp. 4, fols. 13–15.

[17] Information regarding rayados was obtained by examining the following maps: *Afrique: selon les relations les plus nouvelles: dressée sur les mémoires du Sr. de Tillemont: divisée en tousses royaumes et grands états avec un discours sur la nouvelle découverte de la situation des sources du Nil* (Paris: Chez I. B. Nolin, sur le Quay de l'Horloge du Palais vers le Pont Neuf, a l'Enseigne de la Place des Victoires, avec privilège du roy, 1704); *Carte de la Barbarie, de la Nigritie et de la Guinée par Guillaume de l'Isle de l'Académie Royale des Sciences: C. Inselin sculpsit* (Paris: Chez l'Auteur sur le Quai de l'Horloge a l'Aigle d'Or, avec privilège, August 1707); and C. de Berey, *Carte de la partie occidentale de l'Afrique: comprise entre Arguin & Serrelionne où l'on a représenté avec plus de circonstances & d'exactitude que dans aucune carte précédente, non seulement le détail de la côte & les entrées des rivières, mais encore un assez grand détail de l'intérieur des terres, jusqu'à une très grande distance de la mer: ensorte qu'on y indique les divers royaumes & les nations des nègres, le cours des grandes rivières, notamment de Sénéga & Gambie, et les établissements que les nations européennes, François, Portugais, & Anglais, ont sur la côte & dans le pays / dressée sur plusieurs cartes & divers mémoires, par le Sr. d'Anville, géographe ordinaire du roi* (Paris: Chez l'Auteur, Rue St. Honoré vis à vis la Rue de l'Arbre Sec, à la Coupe d'Or, January 1727). See also Robert Norris, *Memoirs of the Reign of Bossa Ahádee, King of Dahomy, an Inland Country of Guiney. To which are added, the author's journey to Abomey, the capital, and a short account of the African slave trade* (London, W. Lowndes, 1789).

[18] Mario I. Aguilar, "Local and Global, Political and Scholarly Knowledge: Diversifying Oromo Studies," *African Affairs* 96, no. 383 (April 1997): 277–280; James McCann, "The Political Economy of Rural Rebellion in Ethiopia: Northern Resistance to Imperial Expansion, 1928–1935," *International Journal of African Historical Studies* 18, no. 4 (1985): 601; I. M. Lewis and P. A. Jewell, "The Peoples and Cultures of Ethiopia," *Proceedings of the Royal Society of London, Series B, Biological Sciences* 194, no. 1114 (August 27, 1976): 11. Note that in the 1880s, the Raya lived west of Zebul and could be considered a South Ethiopian branch. See A. H. Keane, "Ethnology of Egyptian Sudan," *Journal of the Anthropological Institute of Great Britain and Ireland* 14 (1885): 91.

[19] This pattern of identity acquisition outside of Africa has sometimes been described as the creation of an African diasporic identity.

unsettled and unruly life as a slave in Cuba, he was widely known to be a negro criollo (creole black), which was a clear indicator that he had been born somewhere in the Spanish colonies. When he was sold into slavery in Veracruz, he seems to have developed close friendships with rayados like Phelis Rodríguez, which may have had an impact on his identity. His second marriage, to María Margarita (described as being of Congo caste and also a slave of Blas's master) placed him in closer proximity to other Africans, with whom he developed ties. This is not to say that he did not have similar ties to Africans in Cuba; however, there may have been something about his relationships in Mexico that triggered him, and those around him, to identify themselves as being of casta rayado. When Blas acquired his freedom sometime after 1719, he apparently continued to be identified as a rayado. Unfortunately, his premature death at the hands of a presidio soldier outside the walls of Veracruz in 1725 prevents us from hearing his full testimony and charting his genealogy, which might have given us more important clues about the origins of his puzzling identity.[20]

Certainly, one of the more influential black rayados in New Spain was Juan Domingo Rayado of Mexico City. Until the time of his death in 1716, he was a respected member of the black community, a smelter for the royal treasury, and the owner of several properties throughout the city. He also owned a ranch and a small charcoal-making enterprise in an adjacent rural jurisdiction. Domingo Rayado first arrived in Mexico as a slave, having been sold in Africa at a young age. Before he was transplanted across the Atlantic, he also spent time in Spain working for a Captain Francisco de la Campa. It was don Francisco who ended up issuing Domingo Rayado his freedom, paving the way for what would become a remarkable life story. At some point during his time in Mexico City, Domingo Rayado married a fellow rayado, Ana María Cayeteana, also from the "raya de Guinea" – that indiscriminate part of Africa. Through hard work the couple survived difficult times, and she eventually acquired her freedom. They had no natural children, but they did take in a number of orphans, including María Efigenia Esmerejilla, who was described as a "negra amulatada" (a mulattoized black). The child had been left on Domingo Rayado's doorstep at the age of seven. Domingo Rayado became a devout Catholic and a prominent member of the black confraternity of Our Lady of the Immaculate Conception, located in the Hospital of Jesús Nazareno. Perhaps as a symbol of his faith and loyalty to

[20] AGN, Inquisición, vol. 808, exp. 11–12, fols. 458–491v.

the confraternity, he named both his ranch and the charcoal estate after Our Lady of the Immaculate Conception.[21] These businesses were quite successful: on his cattle ranch, he also raised donkeys, horses, and mules, and produced potatoes, barley, and straw. With the proceeds of his enterprises, Domingo Rayado was able to purchase three homes in Mexico City.

What makes Domingo Rayado's case important is the ways in which he interacted with fellow members of the nascent black community in Mexico City. The late seventeenth and early eighteenth centuries were critical times in the development of a black community in the viceregal capital. There were considerable tensions between people who identified themselves as blacks or morenos, and the mixed-race pardos and mulatos. The antagonism could be traced through the principal institutions that convened and organized free-colored life, such as militias and confraternities.[22] It is clear that many of those who considered themselves pure blacks greatly disliked the racially mixed mulattos and pardos, feeling that they did not share their social goals and political interests. There were efforts by both parties to keep the groups separate and in competition with one another for privileges, status, and resources. Over his lifetime, Juan Domingo Rayado became a champion of the pure-black and moreno cause, although one of his own adopted daughters was probably a parda (she in turn married a pardo man).[23]

Through a series of fictive kin relationships and friendship networks, Domingo Rayado became the patron of many morenos in the city. He also appears to have rented out some of his property to new freedmen, in addition to providing them with jobs on his ranch. In this sense, he played a role in facilitating the transition of many blacks from slavery into freedom. Ironically, Domingo Rayado, a former slave, became a slave owner, but he was also a well-known patron of slaves, providing cash loans to help them secure their liberty as well as jobs on his estates to furnish them with income. In his legacy, will, and estate, Domingo Rayado continued to express his affiliation with Mexico City's black-moreno community, ceding some of his property to the black confraternity of Our Lady of the Immaculate Conception. One clause in his testament was designed to

---

[21] The discussion on Domingo Rayado is drawn from AGN, Bienes Nacionales, vol. 787, exp. 1.

[22] For a discussion of the feuds in the context of the militia, see Vinson, *Bearing Arms for His Majesty*, 202–207.

[23] One of Domingo Rayado's nephews, Carlos Domingo Pardo, was probably also a pardo.

ensure that his ranch's operations would exclusively and in perpetuity benefit the special segment of Mexico City's negro and moreno population that had originally been born in Africa. Apart from providing them with a reliable source of employment, he stipulated that some vacant rooms of his properties were to be left open to these men and women as a place of refuge and solace during hard times.

Unfortunately, three decades of legal wrangling between various groups of his inheritors inhibited the full realization of Domingo Rayado's dreams, and this despite his care in selecting executors for his estate who were themselves morenos and negros. Interestingly, many of these individuals were of such low social station that it became difficult for them to persuade the authorities that they possessed sufficient competence to uphold the terms of the will. Some were even slaves, close friends with whom Domingo Rayado had worked in the royal treasury.[24] The authorities raised questions again and again: How could slaves, being property themselves, be allowed to manage the property of others? And, certainly, this was no typical estate. Worth 8,000 pesos in 1718, its value was considerable for the times. Moreover, his executors were responsible not only for initiating contracts for repairs and rents and conducting daily business transactions, but also for providing a proper education for Domingo's children. Such a portfolio of affairs required stature and community respect, qualities generally found lacking in the slaves Rayado had selected to manage his affairs.

Fortunately, among the executors was Captain Pedro de San Joseph, Domingo Rayado's close friend and confidant, who was recognized as one of the most successful and respected morenos in Mexico City during the early eighteenth century. A shrewd merchant and influential militiaman who owned a shop in Mexico City's main plaza, Pedro de San Joseph was also one of the prime protagonists in the power struggle between pardos and morenos over control of the free-colored militias between 1710 and 1724. It was a struggle in which he personally emerged victorious, with an

---

[24] Francisco Javier's master was the *coronel* Juan del Castillo, who held the primary office in the treasury. The extent to which slaves working for the treasury were categorized as royal slaves, as opposed to personal slaves, is unclear. Francisco Javier may have been more of a personal slave than was Domingo Martín, although he did serve the head treasurer directly. Nevertheless, as a royal slave, he may have been at greater liberty to execute contracts. For interesting work on royal slaves and their liberties, including their service on cabildos and their authority to negotiate a variety of contracts, see María Elena Díaz, *The Virgin, the King, and the Royal Slaves of El Cobre* (Stanford: Stanford University Press, 2002).

appointment as commanding captain of all the city's pardo and moreno forces. He applied the same personal drive, zeal, and ambition that made him successful in other circles to managing Domingo Rayado's estate, much to the chagrin of several beneficiaries in the will, who quickly became alienated by Pedro de San Joseph's decisive actions.[25]

Domingo Rayado's decisions regarding his estate reveal much about how his personal connections and ties transcended the typical boundaries of social status that governed colonial society.[26] But more particularly, it shows clearly how a specific caste classification bearing ethnic overtones could gradually transform into something greater. Through personal connections, friendships, business transactions, ties made through slavery, confraternity associations, and workplace affinities, Domingo Rayado's status as a rayado morphed into a broader sense of fellowship with others who were in situations like his own. Over his lifetime, his ethnic and caste designation and self-identification never left him; nor did his status as a moreno. What transpired was that these descriptors converged to generate an attachment to other ethnic Africans who were also morenos.

It is likely that almost nothing about this process was conscious, but rather the result of a series of life choices that Domingo Rayado made tactically, in the heat of the moment, as opposed to strategically. Quite frankly, life's fortunes enabled him to overcome many barriers that impeded the progress of many others like him. His striving to supersede these obstacles – along with the tacit recognition that collective action and common cause could help him improve his situation and the lives of others – may have helped him make some deeper meaning out of the casta and color labels that society had assigned to him. Because of the silences of the archives, and the shortcomings of colonial documents, we

---

[25] Note that despite the status differences among his executors (*albaceas*), Domingo Rayado stated explicitly that all were to have equal say in making decisions regarding the estate. It is worth noting that Domingo Martín may have been closest to Domingo Rayado and was actually assigned the title of *tenedor*. There were special provisions in the will to help care for Domingo Martín's legitimate children, who were Domingo Rayado's fictive kin. Eventually, Domingo Martín acquired his freedom but died shortly thereafter. Following his death, Pedro de San Joseph emerged in 1719 as the lone albacea, since Francisco Javier's master had revoked his obligations to the Rayado estate. For more detail, consult AGN, Bienes Nacionales, vol. 787, exp. 1.

[26] It may have been a common practice among slaves with property (at least those working at the royal treasury) to appoint other slaves as albaceas. Domingo Martín himself had the slave Agustín Manuel serve as his albacea, along with the free-colored militiaman Pedro de San Joseph.

will never fully know his thoughts, but his life and legacy provide valuable clues to the motives behind his behavior.

In lieu of using exceedingly rare terms such as *rayado* and *tresalvo*, colonists often resorted to creating "compound" or "composite" castas that conjoined two or more casta categories. Equally evident was the tendency to supplement casta categories with physical or even geographic descriptors. The ensuing composite then came to serve as a person's formal casta designation. It is in this way that terms such as *mulato achinado* (Chinese-looking mulatto), *chino blanco* (white Chinese), or *mulato morisco* emerged.[27] Some compound casta configurations were remarkably complex. Luis de León, a 14-year-old slave who was liberated by doña Tomasina de la Barreza in Mexico City in August of 1657, was described as a "mulatillo castizo de color chino mestizo" (young mulatto castizo of Chinese-mestizo color).[28] Compound casta descriptions tended to come not from self-description but from people who were in a position to evaluate someone else's casta. These included witnesses in legal cases and matrimonial events, government and ecclesiastical functionaries who made assessments for official accounting purposes, and neighbors and friends who described their acquaintances in social settings and other forums.

In a sample taken from 168 notary records from seventeenth-century Mexico City, we can appreciate the range of recombinant variety by studying casta labels in slave sales (Table 4.1).[29] The table does not capture every case; instead, it spotlights the earliest mention of a specific terminology as it appeared in the notarial sample. Most of the slaves were born in Mexico, but 16-year-old Lorenzo, the "mulato blanco" recorded in 1623, hailed from Seville. Others came from Cádíz, Jamaica, Santo Domingo, Angola, and elsewhere.

From the seventeenth to mid-eighteenth centuries in New Spain, terms like *mulato cocho* ("cooked" black) were used well beyond Mexico City. Mulatos cochos, both slave and free, could be found in Tecamachalco, Apam, Real Minas de Chiguagua (Durango), and Antequera – that is, in the northern, central, western, and eastern reaches of the colony.[30] *Cocho*, like other terms such as *membrillo* (a person with a yellowish complexion

---

[27] ANM, Nicolás Bernal, 461, fol. 12 (example of a *mulato achinado*); ANM, Fernando Veedor, 4618, fol. 32v (example of a *chino blanco*).

[28] ANM, Fernando Veedor, 4601, fol. 212v.

[29] My thanks to Tatiana Seijas for sharing this rich slave database.

[30] AGN, Indiferente Virreinal, caja 5868, exp. 4, fols. 1–2v; caja 5257, exp. 36, fols. 1–3v; caja 4045, exp. 26, fols. 1–2v; vol. 3431, exp. 40, fols. 1–1v.

TABLE 4.1 *Extreme Casta Labels in Slave Sales*

Year	Extreme Casta Labels
1623	Mulato blanco
1626	Mulato prieto
1638	Mulata prieta
1649	Mulata blanca
1650	Mulato, color membrillo
1659	Mulata, color prieta membrillo
1660	Mulato, color membrillo
1662	Mulato albino
1662	Nación berberisca
1662	Negro amulatado
1666	Mulata, color prieto
1666	Mulatilla blanca
1667	Mulato blanco
1670	Mulato, "más blanco que prieto"
1671	Negro cafre de pasa
1672	Mulato morisco blanco
1673	Mulato moreno
1673	Negro, color loro
1677	Negro bicho
1678	Mulato membrillo cocho
1680	Mulata amestizada
1682	Mulatilla prieta
1685	Muleque
1686	Mulata, color cocho
1687	Mulato, color cocho

Source: Derived from Appendix C.

akin to the quince fruit), added great specificity to the descriptive power of casta, providing useful identifiers when core terminologies proved too limited to capture an individual's complete phenotype. Cocho and membrillo seldom appeared as discrete caste categories of their own.[31] And it was no

---

[31] The term *cocho* appears in eighteenth-century witness testimonies from the Inquisition. In the bigamy trial of Juan Joseph Balderas (1783), the witness Miguel Francisco Quijada from Sta. María del Río Verde, described Juan as a "mulato de color cocho, mediana estatura, doblado de pelo." See AGN, Inquisición, vol. 1237, exp. 5, fol. 214. In Mexico City during 1750, the cleric Thomas Kempis testified in the bigamy trial of Miguel Chávez, whom he described as a "mulato prieto" or a "mulato cocho." See AGN, Inquisición, vol. 952, exp. 34, fol. 375. Finally, in New Mexico during 1721, the witness Rafael Telles Xiópn testified in the bigamy trial of Marcos Castañeda, whom he described as "a lo que le parece, lobo, medio indio, de estatura perfecta, como de dos baros, algo

accident that both came in vogue after 1650. The designation mulato cocho increased in use during the early to middle 1700s. Essentially, these were years when the slave trade to Mexico had diminished, with fewer fresh African arrivals entering areas outside of centers like Veracruz and selected ports of the southern coasts, such as Campeche, Mérida, and Bacalar.[32] Indeed, the great bulk of the slave trade to Mexico had largely ended by 1640, after shipments aboard Portuguese vessels had virtually ceased with the dissolution of the union (1580–1640) of the Portuguese and Spanish crowns.

By necessity, the slave population became more racially exogamous, hybridized, and diverse in color after the mid-seventeenth century. The free population of African descent also became increasingly more miscegenated.[33] To capture some of the nuances of these vast phenotypic changes, some found it convenient to combine the lineage-based designations of caste nomenclature with more-explicit phenotypic references and emendations rather than invent additional caste categories or expand the use of terms that already existed but were infrequently applied (such as *cuarterón de mulata* or *calpamulato*). These practices commenced fairly early in the seventeenth century, if not before, but the process intensified, with dips and peaks, as the colonial period wore on. While we can detect these trends in Table 4.1, the shifts and volume surges among extreme casta slaves emerge with greater clarity in Table 4.2.[34]

Terminologies such as *mulato cocho, negro cocho, negro prieto* (dark black), and *mulato amestizado* (mulato with a dash of mestizo

---

cargo de espaldo, de color cocho, de ojos en proporcion, que no se acuerda de color, ... los dientes de arriba los delantados apartados." See AGN, Inquisición, vol. 781, exp. 5, fol. 388v.

[32] Matthew Restall, *The Black Middle: Africans, Mayas, and Spaniards in Colonial Yucatan* (Stanford: Stanford University Press, 2009), 13–26; Proctor, *Damned Notions of Liberty*, 13–36; Patrick J. Carroll, *Blacks in Colonial Veracruz: Race, Ethnicity, and Regional Development* (Austin: University of Texas Press, 2001), 30–34; Dennis N. Valdés, "The Decline of Slavery in Mexico," *The Americas* 44, no. 2 (1987): 167–194; Adriana Naveda Chávez-Hita, *Esclavos negros en las haciendas azucareras de Córdoba, Veracruz, 1690–1830* (Xalapa: Universidad Veracruzana, Centro de Investigaciones Históricas, 1987).

[33] Although it is anchored in the work of scholars like Gonzalo Aguirre Beltrán and Colin Palmer, Herman L. Bennett adopts the useful phrase "mulatto ascendancy" to describe some situations at the end of the seventeenth century. See Bennett, "Lovers, Family, and Friends: The Formation of Afro-Mexico, 1580–1810" (PhD diss.: Duke University, 1993).

[34] Our sample ends in 1696, precluding a complete look at the situation at the turn of the century. Still, the number of extreme castes recorded in notarial receipts between 1690 and 1696 exceeded the entire 27-year period between 1623 and 1650.

TABLE 4.2 *Number of Extreme Casta Slaves in Mexico City, Seventeenth Century*

Years	Extreme Castas
1623–1650	8
1650–1660	19
1660–1670	38
1670–1680	54
1680–1690	39
1690–1696	10

Source: Derived from Appendix C.

features) essentially showcased phenotypes within the caste hierarchical order.[35] As compound and composite castas appeared, however, they directly exposed a tautology embedded in the concept of casta itself. As discussed in Chapter 3, caste classifications were imagined as a means of connecting and tracing lineage and phenotype. Lineage was supposed to be an indicator of phenotype, and phenotype was supposed to illuminate the realities of a person's lineage. In practice, though, phenotype and lineage were inconsistent and unreliable guides to one another, particularly in a social system where there were few de facto controls over miscegenation, and where genealogical knowledge among the masses was often rather limited.[36] Consequently, as miscegenation intensified during colonial times and as once-deep genealogical knowledge of one's ancestors slipped away, a greater need arose to be more precise about understanding phenotype in order to properly understand one's place in the social order. Caste nomenclature evolved accordingly. Some categories – like *mulato cocho*, *mulato prieto*, *mulato membrillo*, and *mulato blanco* – functioned in this vein, helping capture what lineage no longer could. These same qualifiers, however, could have a dual impact. Depending upon who utilized the language, they could help police the boundaries of certain casta classifications, but they could

[35] The term *negro cocho* seems to have been used much more rarely than *mulato cocho* in colonial New Spain. For an example from Mexico City (1752), see AGN, Matrimonios, vol. 109, exp. 94, fols. 397–400. The earliest use of *mulato prieto* I have located is from 1621 in Mexico City. AGN, Matrimonios, vol. 85, exp. 18, fol. 34. A "mulata muy prieta" can be found in AGN, Inquisición, vol. 781, exp. 26, fols. 267–270.

[36] R. Douglas Cope discusses this phenomenon for the urban environment in Mexico City in *The Limits of Racial Domination: Plebian Society in Colonial Mexico City, 1660–1720* (Madison: University of Wisconsin Press, 1994).

also provide social advancement opportunities for the individuals they described.

The mulato experience is revealing in this regard. In the seventeenth century, some slave masters used the term *mulato blanco* (white mulatto) to describe their creole slaves, a number of whom were able to use their light skin color to present themselves as free-coloreds when they ran away from their owners.[37] Hair mattered too; a mulato blanco might be categorized as such because he possessed reddish, sandy, or straight hair. In short, the mulato blanco label helped slave owners maintain their regime and better identify chattel property. However, free-colored men like Lorenzo de Zúñiga in Mexico City began manipulating caste nomenclature for their own purposes. Although it seems that Lorenzo was technically a pardo (brown), he petitioned the court in 1636 and 1637 to permit him the privileges of using a dagger, cape, and sword by asserting that he was a mulato blanco. Of course, he sought to enhance his racial credentials through other measures as well, but his conscious use of the mulato blanco label to describe himself appears to have been a calculated move to make him seem more like an español and thus less of a social threat to the elite.[38] Lorenzo's example was followed by others. Free-coloreds throughout the colony who were mulatos blancos sometimes emphasized their white parentage, noting that this made them superior to ordinary mulatos and negros. Especially when their fathers were white, mulatos blancos could enjoy added privileges in their communities or lobby for unique exemptions typically unavailable to the broader class of mulatos.[39]

The modifications to the term *mulato* that appeared in the seventeenth and eighteenth centuries further imply that during an era of intensifying racial mixture in Mexico, the mulato category proved especially susceptible to destabilization, given its inherently hybrid quality. Preserving the integrity of the mulato group and the functionality of mulato as a meaningful caste designation appeared to be of concern to members of the elite, since mulatos represented an important boundary between blackness and whiteness in ways that other classifications did not.

[37] AGN, Indiferente Virreinal, caja 1975, exp. 1.

[38] R. C. Schwaller, "For Honor and Defence," 258–260, provides excellent contextual material for situating Zúñiga's request. Many mulattos pointed to the nature of their profession, their services to the crown, and their good temperament as credentials for qualifying themselves as worthy subjects who should have access to arms.

[39] AGN, Californias, vol. 58, fols. 82–117v; Armona to Mayorga, September 9, 1781, San Andrés Tuxtla, AGN, Indiferentes de Guerra, vol. 53-A.

Mestizos, for instance, definitely forged a similar divide between whiteness and nativeness. But mestizos were deemed less socially threatening, especially after the end of the sixteenth century.[40] When mestizos engaged in miscegenation with whites, the resulting mixture was construed more positively, as evidenced by their progeny being classified as castizo, which stood near the pinnacle of the caste hierarchy. By contrast, the offspring of mulatos and whites were typically called "moriscos" (or Moorish persons), a term loaded with negative connotations.

Another way to look at the same evidence is to say that creating multiple stripes of mulatos possibly prevented moriscos from providing a viable alternative to the mulatto category. It is likely that this was neither intentional nor strategic. Rather, some simply found it easier, or perhaps more meaningful, to label someone a mulato or a mulato blanco rather than a morisco. Certainly, some efforts may have been more deliberate. But whatever the case, at least until the middle of the 1700s, Mexican society used a complex and mushrooming matrix of terminologies to keep the mulato category from sliding into total disrepair.[41]

Despite society's best interventions, there came a point where a degree of indiscriminate blending and jumbling of multiple caste categories proved inevitable. As explained earlier in this chapter, some of the commingling of caste categories may have been by design, and we must exercise care as scholars in trying to recognize these instances. But just as easily as one might find individuals using descriptions like morisco and mulato with careful discretion, one could point out situations in which the classifications of morisco, mulato, and mulato blanco were substituted indiscriminately for one another. Perhaps even more powerfully, the term *pardo* rapidly evolved into virtually synonymity with *mulato* – most notably in the eighteenth century.[42]

---

[40] R. C. Schwaller, "For Honor and Defence," 251.

[41] This effort involved members of the plebeian sector as much as it did institutional authorities and the elite. Poor neighbors, as much as anyone else, routinely used terms like *mulato blanco* and *mulato prieto* to refer to themselves and each other.

[42] Difficult though it is to state with certainty, I believe that in New Spain the category of *mulato* and its multiple representations may have served as a parameter for the use and definition of the term *pardo*. There were probably many more variations to the term *mulato* than are recounted in this chapter. For instance, the terms *indio mulato* and *india amulatada* are found in the sixteenth and early seventeenth centuries. See AGN, Indiferente Virreinal, caja 6512, exp. 50; AGN, Indios, vol. 6, exp. 989; and AGN, Indiferente Virreinal, caja 5679, exp. 18. For some recent scholarly studies of mulatos who were indios (and vice versa), see R. C. Schwaller, "Mulata, Hijo de Negra y India"; and Patrick J. Carroll, "Black Aliens and Black Natives in New

At least in Mexico, *pardo* was arguably a less closely governed term than *mulato*. The various permutations of mulato were designed to capture specific phenotypic characteristics and variances, but pardo was not frequently used in this way. Occasionally, though, one did encounter terms like *pardo mulato*, which conflated the two categories, or *indio pardo*, which was intended more as a comment on African strains found in native bloodlines than a modifier of "pardoness."[43] Of course, as with other casta groups, pardos could be party to altogether new mixtures: in Texcoco in 1792, children born to pardos and indios were sometimes called "chamizos."[44] While the pardo designation probably first surfaced in Mexico to describe the offspring of blacks and mulattos with native Americans, the term quickly came to signify a blanket category for miscegenated blackness, designating all types of mixture but usually without measuring any degree of hybridization.[45] Also, many pardos in Mexican colonial society were free, giving rise to the commonplace term *pardo libre* ("free pardo").[46] Many mulatos, moriscos, morenos, negros, and even lobos in colonial Mexico carried the same "libre" epithet, but applied to pardos it seemed to flow more naturally. *Pardo* may have even been a preferred euphemism in the eighteenth century for blackness. This was partly because of its relative

---

Spain's Indigenous Communities," in *Black Mexico: Race and Society from Colonial to Modern Times*, ed. Ben Vinson III and Matthew Restall (Albuquerque: University of New Mexico Press, 2009), 72–95. Throughout the Spanish Empire, in the litigation known as the "gracias al sacar" cases, the terms *pardo* and *mulato* were used interchangeably, notwithstanding examples from Cuba and Venezuela where distinctions between the categories were more finely articulated. In Cuba, pardos who were whiter than mulatos could be found; in Venezuela, the opposite was true. See Twinam, *Purchasing Whiteness*, 62–63.

[43] For instance, see the 1733 case of Miguel, a *pardo mulato* from Tala in Jalisco. AGN, Inquisición, vol. 1169, exp. 7, fols. 94–97. For an example of the use of the term *indio pardo*, see the 1785 idolatry case of Pascual de los Santos Casanova from Mérida in Yucatán. AGN, Inquisición, vol. 1256, exp. 1, fols. 1–91.

[44] AGN, Padrones, vol. 43, fols. 242–243v.

[45] I don't want to overstate this argument. *Mulato* could also be used as a general reference for hybridized blackness, as evidenced by censuses from various provinces in the Revillagigedo census (1791–93). Also, depending upon the region, *pardo* could still be used to refer specifically to the mixtures between negros and mulatos, and between negros and indios.

[46] There were pardos who were slaves (mainly in the eighteenth century), but the archival record seems to record more mulatos in slavery. For mentions of pardo slaves, see AGN, Matrimonios, vol. 159, exp. 52, fol. 7v; vol. 32, exp. 77, fols. 405–408; vol. 203, exp. 12, fol. 4; and vol. 224, exp. 2, fols. 5–11.

disassociation from slavery and the softer expression of blackness it connoted (in contrast to more edgy words like *mulato, morisco,* and *lobo*), as well as the social privileges that pardos had begun to accrue. It is clear that pardo militiamen could secure special exemptions during the seventeenth and eighteenth centuries, and that elsewhere in the Spanish realm pardos were able to lobby for privileges that began, to a degree, to approximate those of whiteness.[47]

***

In this chapter, we have looked more closely at the operational use of casta in local society, to gain an understanding of what I suggest was a constant recoding of caste as it was applied in a plethora of colonial circumstances. These recodings ultimately produced a rich density of extreme casta terminologies. As casta unfolded in everyday situations, it yielded both compound castas and exceedingly rare casta labels, some of which served to support community identities. In addition to producing subtle recalibrations of seemingly stable casta groups, it also exposed how elites and plebeians utilized extreme casta labeling for different ends and how casta classifications were used as metaphors to enlighten audiences on specific aspects of societal concern. Casta varied richly across regional landscapes, causing terminological dissonances; this variability and the processes by which it was resolved were not extraordinary in the broad colonial order. Finally, we have appreciated how caste labels (especially at the extremes) ebbed and flowed in popularity over time as demographic realities, social and economic conditions, and even political orders shifted during the course of the colonial period.

We return now to a concept introduced in the Chapter 3 that informs much of what we have explored here: castizaje. I suggest that castizaje was the primary vehicle of casta change during colonial times. I have already argued that casta itself underwent important transformations in the colonial period, largely linked to grand ideological shifts in arenas like science and religion, but also due to transformations associated with the evolution of Spanish colonialism. This chapter has looked at other forms of casta change – those produced typically by micropressures and local concerns rather than imperial

---

[47] Ann Twinam, in *Purchasing Whiteness*, discusses eloquently how pardo status came to be seen as a label of privilege.

dictates. In the aggregate, these casta recodings and their attendant recalibrations created circumstances that facilitated yet more forms of casta mobility, interchange, and fluidity. And these recodings probably helped form the platform that allowed individuals to live (or be construed as living) plural casta lives.

5

Extreme Mixture in a Theater of Numbers

By the late eighteenth century, after nearly three centuries of racial mixture, the colonies of the New World had become a remarkably complex somatic landscape.[1] No single Spanish territory possessed so large a population as Mexico, which also boasted the greatest concentration of individuals of mixed race. The naturalist and traveler Alexander von Humboldt calculated that there were as many as 1,231,000 people of mixed race living in Mexico by the end of the eighteenth century, representing roughly a quarter of the total population.[2] His observations were consistent with other late-colonial enumeration efforts. New Spain's 1777 ecclesiastical census, whose surviving documentation captures a rare snapshot of the archbishopric of Mexico, demonstrates that some of Mexico's key rural and urban centers collectively had a mixed-race population of nearly 213,000 individuals, or just under a fifth of the total population.[3] The diversity captured in the 1777 ecclesiastical count was among the more extensive

---

[1] There were places like Costa Rica and Colombia where the population of blacks and racially mixed groups comprised well over half the population by 1800. In other areas, like Peru, the same groups represented smaller percentages, but their raw numbers soared into the hundreds of thousands. See George R. Andrews, *Afro-Latin America, 1800–2000* (Oxford: Oxford University Press, 2004), 41.

[2] Jacques Lafaye, "La sociedad de castas en la Nueva España," *Artes de México*, no. 8 (Summer 1990): 24–35.

[3] Ernest Sánchez Santiró, *Padrón del Arzobispado de México, 1777* (Mexico City: AGN and Secretaría de Gobernacion, 2003).

to be found in colonial censuses.[4] Twelve different casta groups were
tallied, including certain extreme categories like castizos, moriscos,
lobos, albinos, coyotes, mestindios, and chinos.[5] The dioceses in the
1777 census that were home to the extreme castes are shown on the map
in Figure 9.

In this chapter we look more closely at the demography of the extreme
castas, with an eye toward discovering the story behind the numbers:
What can we learn about their lives, and can we perceive patterns in the
application of caste terminologies? The late eighteenth century, with its
rich vein of census data and its signal importance in the history of colonial
racial mixture, will be the focus here. It was during these twilight years of
the colony that colonial racial mixture was most mature, offering us
a great opportunity to identify and examine the wide range of groups as
they operated in society.

Table 5.1 provides a numerical view of the regional distribution of
extreme castas in the archbishopric of Mexico. Excluding castizos, who
were found in most jurisdictions, the census data reveals that there were
concentrations of other extreme castas in only a handful of curacies in
New Spain's central zones. Lobos had the widest distribution, even
though they were quite sparse in some areas, numbering in the dozens or
less. Chinos, mestindios, and albinos represented the other extreme, being
seldom encountered. Chinos, in fact, were virtually absent beyond the
broader region of Acapulco, while mestindios and albinos were almost
exclusive to Mexico City. Rarely did any single concentration of extreme
castas exceed a hundred persons. Given this situation, it may be best to
conceive of these populations as "adjunct" castas to the general population, rather than as core populations themselves.

It would be a misconception to state that the relatively sparse presence
of these groups, particularly in rural jurisdictions, equated to obscurity
and anonymity. Quite to the contrary, these individuals were likely
known. Most parishes and curacies in the archbishopric were subdivided

---

[4] Sergio Paolo Solano D., "Usos y abusos del censo de 1777–1780. Sociedad, 'razas'
y representaciones sociales en el Nuevo Reino de Granada en el siglo XVIII" (PhD diss.:
Universidad de Cartagena, 2013). Note that the 1777–80 census of New Granada had up
to 13 categories, and the 1790 Peruvian census a total of 9 (82, 95).

[5] Similar trends could be found in New Granada, where the use of terms like *cuarterón* and
quinterón were encountered in the 1777–80 census, albeit in small numbers. In fact,
Solano traces an overall decline in the use of some terminologies in the second half of
the eighteenth century, with fewer appearances of categories like *tercerón, tente en el aíre*,
and *salta para atrás*. See Solano, "Usos y abusos," 152.

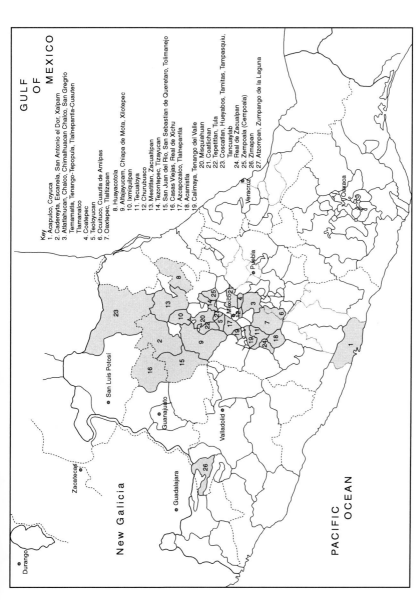

FIGURE 9 Map, Dioceses of the Archbishopric of Mexico that Housed Extreme Castas, Ecclesiastical Census, 1777.
Source: Adapted by the author from Peter Gerhard, *Geografía histórica de la Nueva España, 1519–1821* (Mexico: Universidad Autónoma de México, 1986), 16, and from Ernesto Sánchez Santiró, *Padrón del Arzobispado de México, 1777* (Mexico: Archivo General de la Nación and Secretaría de Gobernación, 2003).

93

TABLE 5.1 *Casta Population, Archbishopric of Mexico, 1777*

Curacy	Albinos	Chinos	Coyotes	Lobos	Mestindios	Moriscos	Total
Acamistla				17			17
Acapulco		121		331			452
Alfajayucam				353		102	455
Atlatlahucan			30	12			42
Atzompan			11				11
Ayotzingo				68			68
Azcapozalco				50			50
Cadereyta			411				411
Calimaya				4			4
Casas Viejas			161	1,228			1,389
Chalco				24			24
Chiapa de Mota						7	7
Chimalhuacan Chalco				56			56
Churubusco				15			15
Ciudad de México (Mexico City)	53		13	266	384	710	1,426
Coatepec				21			21
Coatlichan					61		61
Coscatlan				17			17
Coyuca		388		71			459
Cuautla de Amilpas				90		129	219
Escanela			19				19
Guisquiluca						35	35
Huayacocotla					16		16

(continued)

94

Hueyabos (mission)		25			25
Huichiapan	531	70			601
Ixmiquilpan		7			7
Jiutepec		136			136
Jonacatepec		118		30	148
Mestitlan		13			13
Misquiahuan		106			106
Oaxtepec	34	55		25	114
Ocuituco	4	8		7	19
Real de Xichú		286			286
Real de Zacualpan	40	63		208	311
San Antonio el Dor		11			11
San Gregorio		6			6
San Juan del Río	132	129			261
San Miguel de las Palmas (mission)		46			46
San Sebastián de Querétaro	38	159	38	30	265
Tamazunchale		3			3
Tamitas (mission)		44			44
Tampasquiu (mission)		14			14
Tancuaylab (mission)		204			204
Tecualoya	50	127			177
Temamatla		42			42
Tenango-Tepopula		8			8
Tenango del Valle		22		35	57
Teoloyucan			49		49

(continued)

95

TABLE 5.1 *(continued)*

Curacy	Albinos	Chinos	Coyotes	Lobos	Mestindios	Moriscos	Total
Tepetitlan				17			17
Tezontepec			159				159
Tizayucan				5			5
Tlalnepantla				6			6
Tlalnepantla-Cuautenca			28				28
Tlaltizapan				21		80	101
Tlamanalco				68			68
Tolimanejo						111	111
Tula			20	69			89
Villa de Peña de Francia				42			42
Xalpam				71			71
Xilotepec			22	13			35
Zacualtipan				16			16
Zempoala				6			6
Zimapan			66	32			98
Zumpango de la Laguna				10			10
Total	53	509	1,769	4,701	548	1,509	9,089

Source: Ernest Sánchez Santiró, *Padrón del Arzobispado de México, 1777* (Mexico: Archivo General de la Nación and Secretaría de Gobernación, 2003).

96

into smaller blocs: estates, farms, towns, agricultural properties, hamlets – even single city blocks. Many curacies held between 500 to 1,500 families.[6] Since these families inhabited small nuclei of villages, ranches, and haciendas within the broad territory of their districts, intimate social worlds were constituted within what might seem much vaster spaces. The extreme castas forged ties, friendships, and reputations within these microhabitats. So while the small extreme casta population appeared to be engulfed numerically by the much larger total populations of their regions, the tendency toward segmentation meant that these groups operated within smaller and more concentrated orbits. It is in this milieu that their lives had consequence and meaning.

Lobos and coyotes, at least in the central parts of New Spain, lived rural lives. Even in larger centers such as San Juan del Río (near Querétaro), Tezontepec (near Pachuca), Huichiapan (in Xilotepec), and Cardereyta, their lifestyle was likely to be more rural than urban, since they tended to work on agricultural and ranching properties. Moriscos, meanwhile, were largely though not exclusively city dwellers. Although the extreme castas, like other colonists, were deeply and intricately enmeshed in their local environments, they were not chained to them. Within rural landscapes, as well as towns, there were factors that generated motion. Specific professions, like that of muleteer, were predicated on regional mobility. Day laborers and field hands were known to move from place to place to escape debts and seek better wages. Agricultural crises, droughts, and famines prodded individuals to find sustenance and security in new locales. Mexico City and other larger urban centers of the colony became locus points for travelers.

A survey of approximately 400 extreme casta marriage records from Mexico City for the years 1605 to 1783 provides a telling measure of casta migration. Approximately one-third of the lobos, moriscos, and coyotes who contracted nuptials were not originally from the capital but came from places as disparate as Spain, Cuba, Tarasquillo, Querétaro, and Tolcayucan, as shown in Appendix B. In many instances, the distances traveled were not great, but in others they were considerable. From the records we can capture only part of the range of their travels, because many relocated repeatedly over the course of their lives. Manuel Estrada, a lobo (also described as mulato) who lived and worked in Mexico City at the end of the eighteenth century, offers a good example. A tailor by trade who worked in the shop of Francisco Cova, Estrada

---

[6] This typically corresponded to a population size of between 2,000 and 5,000 individuals.

claimed to have lived in Spain, residing for a period in the port of Cádiz. While in Europe, he reportedly visited France. During his sojourns he had also spent time in Havana and traveled to Veracruz and Puebla. While his colleagues fancied him a liar, the authorities found aspects of the story credible, especially since he may have served in the Spanish navy during a time of deployment and war.[7]

The 1777 census further reveals that certain regions in the colony normalized specific extreme-casta nomenclatures for their locales.[8] In the zone stretching from Huichiapan to Cardereyta (northwest of Mexico City), the term *coyote* was widely used. The reasons for this are almost impossible to determine from the record. What we can say is that at least in Huichiapan itself, coyotes had been strongly represented for almost a century. In fact, in 1718 coyotes constituted Huichiapan's most visible group of nonnative and nonwhite people, having an unusually notable demographic impact as orphans.[9] Nearly one-fifth of the 117 households in the zone's *cabecera* (head town) possessed at least one coyote orphan; several had three or more. Orphans were welcomed in the town, helping provide supplemental labor, support, and sustenance.[10] Whether this trend persisted into the late eighteenth century is hard to ascertain, but assuredly the population of coyotes remained relatively robust throughout the territory.

In Xichú and Casas Viejas, in the jurisdiction of San Luis de la Paz, the emergence of lobos as a normative category seems tied to local demographic and economic conditions. Situated to the north of Querétaro at the juncture of the Bajío (one of Mexico's most fertile plains) and the

---

[7] AGN, Inquisición, vol. 1224, exp. 10, fols. 208–229.

[8] The tendency for some regions to normalize extreme nomenclatures was likely replicated in various corners of the Spanish kingdom. For an example for Bolivia, see Lolita G. Brockington, *Blacks, Indians, and Spaniards in the Eastern Andes: Reclaiming the Forgotten in Colonial Mizque, 1550–1782* (Lincoln: University of Nebraska Press, 2006).

[9] AGN, Bienes Nacionales, vol. 800, legajo 808, exp. 3, fols. 1–37.

[10] Ondina E. González and Bianca Premo, *Raising an Empire: Children in Early Modern Iberia and Colonial Latin America* (Albuquerque: University of New Mexico Press, 2007). In Huichiapan in 1718, eight households headed by single women, widows, or widowers received coyote orphans. Anna de Alexandre, a coyote herself, had seven orphaned children, most of them well into their teens and all appearing to be siblings. Living with her too was a relative, perhaps her sister, who was raising another four orphans of her own, one of them being Juan Maldonado. Already 20 years old, he was capable of handling many of the male roles in the household. Overall, over half the families taking in coyote orphans were married couples, some of whom had their own children. While most members of these couples were also coyotes, several coyote orphans were reared in the households of españoles.

Sierra Gorda mountains, the population here lived on the fringe of a vibrant commercial area in contested frontier territory. Amidst a large indigenous majority, streams of mulattos and blacks found occupations and niche livelihoods. Inevitably, they fraternized with the local native population, bringing forth a mixed-race native/black population.[11] The conditions were ripe for the emergence of lobos, who began to flourish.

Completely different from the other centers in the colony, and grander in scale than any other urban setting in the Spanish kingdom, Mexico City represented a unique environment in the colonial world. With a population ranging between 100,000 and 200,000 in the 1790s, Mexico City was certainly the largest capital under Iberian control and easily one of the great world metropolises.[12] Boasting a workforce of roughly 38,000 individuals and featuring a steady stream of immigrants, the capital was a vibrant and dynamic center whose adult labor pool alone surpassed the size of many urban areas. While the 1777 census allows us to appreciate some of the variety of extreme castas that dwelled there, it is the 1811 municipal census organized by the *juzgado de la policía* (police administration) that affords a closer look at some of these population groups. The census captured information on housing, household structure, casta status, occupation, age, marital status, place of origin, and place of birth.[13] By 1811, Mexico City was subdivided into 32 districts

---

[11] For some information on Xichú and San Luis de la Paz, see John Tutino, *Making a New World: Founding Capitalism in the Bajío and Spanish North America* (Durham and London: Duke University Press, 2011), 411–413.

[12] Population figures for Mexico City in the 1790s are a matter of debate. Viceroy Revillagigedo's census stated that the population stood at 112,000, but contemporaries cited larger numbers. Research has shown that there were possibly as many as 300,000 residents. See Manuel Miño Grijalva, "La población de la Ciudad de México en 1790. Variables económicas y demográficas de una controversia," in *La población de la Ciudad de México en 1790: estructura social, alimentación y vivienda*, ed. Manuel Miño Grijalva and Sonia Pérez Toledo (Mexico: Universidad Autónoma Metropolitana, Unidad Iztapalapa, División de Ciencias Sociales y Humanidades, 2004), 21–74. Sonia Pérez Toledo and Herbert S. Klein have calculated the number to be closer to 117,000. See Pérez Toledo and Klein, *Población y estructura social de la Ciudad de México, 1790–1842* (Mexico City: Universidad Autónoma Metropolitana, Unidad Iztapalapa, División de Ciencias Sociales y Humanidades, Departamento de Filosofía, 2004), 64. Keith Davies's pioneering study calculates the population at 130,000. See Davies, "Tendencias demográficas urbanas durante el siglo XIX en México," *Historia Mexicana* 21, no. 3 (1972): 481–482. Whatever the actual number, the city was extremely large by contemporary standards in the Western world.

[13] An excellent study of the 1811 census is Pérez Toledo and Klein, *Población y estructura social*, especially 91–124.

FIGURE 10 Map of Mexico City, Divided Into 32 Cuarteles, 1782.
Source: John Carter Brown Library, Brown University, Providence, RI.

(*cuarteles menores*), for which census information has survived on only 20
(see Figure 10).

For our purposes, we have looked at 12 cuarteles, with complete family,
occupational, and residential information taken on all of the moriscos,
lobos, coyotes, chinos, and moros. As was seen in the 1777 data, and as
will be seen in the context of marriage documents to be presented later,
moriscos composed the most prevalent of these casta groups in the capital.
From an occupational standpoint, the castes were largely employed in the
artisan and service trades (see Table 5.2).[14] In this sense, they represented
the larger city, for which both of these sectors dominated the employment
arena.[15] The artisanal professions that the extreme castes most commonly

---

[14] Roughly 46 percent of the adult population reported an occupation.
[15] For more on the artisan sector, see Sonia Pérez Toledo, *Los hijos del trabajo: los artesanos
de la Ciudad de México, 1780–1853* (Mexico City: Colegio de México and Universidad
Autónoma Metropolitana Iztapalapa, 1996).

TABLE 5.2 *Occupations of Lobos, Coyotes, Moriscos, Moros, and Chinos in Mexico City, 1811*

	Occupation	Frequency
Aguador	Water carrier	1
Atolera	Atole vendor	1
Carrocero	Coach maker	1
Casera	Apartment manager	1
Cerero	Wax maker	1
Cigarrera	Cigar maker (f.)	6
Cigarrero	Cigar maker (m.)	8
Cochero	Driver	4
Confitero	Confectioner	1
Cocinera	Cook	4
Costurera	Seamstress	1
Criada	Nursemaid	3
Hilandera	Spinner	2
Lavandera	Washerwoman	2
Lutera	[?]	1
Mandadera	Messenger	1
Panadero	Baker	1
Pintor	Painter	1
Portero	Doorman	1
Recamarera	Chambermaid	1
Sangrador	Bloodletter	2
Sastre	Tailor	2
Sirvienta	Servant (f.)	2
Sirviente	Servant (m.)	10
Taburetero	Saddle maker	1
Tejedor	Weaver	1
Viandante	Petty vendor	1
Zapatero	Shoemaker	7
Total, all occupations		68

Source: AGN, Padrones, vols. 53, 54, 55, 56, 57, 58, 60, 62, 62, 63, 64, 65, 66, 67, 68, 69, 70, 71, 72, 73, 78.

entered were those of cigar workers and shoemakers. Again, in this respect they resembled their urban peers. Mexico City's cigar factory employed a tremendous number of workers from the lower classes, especially women. Meanwhile, the profession of shoemaking, along with hat making, offered special opportunities to free people of color.[16] In the service industry, the

[16] Vinson, *Bearing Arms for His Majesty*, chap. 3.

main arena was domestic labor and included servants, coachmen, washer-women, and cooks. There were practitioners of a few skilled and semi-skilled trades in the sample, such as seamstresses and a painter. There was even a moro student. But by and large, the 1811 census shows that the extreme castes represented the very core of the plebeian working class.

The average extreme casta household size was more than six but fewer than seven persons. Thirteen households boasted ten or more members. Collectively, these 13 households represented just a little over one-tenth of the total households but accounted for nearly one-third of the household population found in our sample.[17] In Mexico City during this period, the largest households (those with 15 or more individuals) tended to belong to the elite. Indeed, nearly all of the sample's 13 largest households qualified as elite or upper middle class. Poorer families resided in smaller household arrangements.

The census shows that while some extreme castas lived with Mexico City's upper tier, most lobos, moriscos, coyotes, moros, and chinos were not in families of elite rank, nor were they frequently found as retainers in the largest urban households. Instead, they tended to live in households that were distinctly separated from the upper class. Another important trend is that the majority of lobos, moriscos, coyotes, moros, and chinos were not the heads of the households they lived in. Extreme castes headed just one-third of the families in the sample. Quite simply, most lobos, moriscos, coyotes, moros, and chinos were the spouses, children, kin, friends, coworkers, and boarders of members of the urban poor.[18]

Lobos and coyotes demonstrated the highest probability of being attached as dependents to the urban underclass. Unsurprisingly, their homes, as well as those of most extreme castas, were humble dwellings. Over two-thirds resided in large apartment-style complexes known as *vecindades*. Within these, almost half lived in single rooms and studio suites (*cuartos*), while nearly a quarter lived in more spacious *accesorias*, which typically provided room for an artisan's workshop. Accesorias varied in quality and often had an opening onto the street, facilitating business operations for artisans.

---

[17] The population sample included 731 individuals distributed in 111 households.

[18] The moriscos (especially morisca household heads) in the sample were more likely to live in households of their own than were members of the other extreme castas. The 30 household heads in the sample who were lobos, moriscos, coyotes, moros, or chinos represented some 20 percent of the adult population of these groups. A full 27 of the 30 household heads were moriscos, and there were two moros and one chino. Of the household heads, 19 were moriscas, 1 was a moro woman, and the remaining 10 were males.

TABLE 5.3 *Age Structure of Lobos, Coyotes, Moriscos, Moros,*
and Chinos in Mexico City, 1811

Race	Girls Age 0–12	Boys Age 0–14	Adults	Total
Chino	0	0	2	2
Coyote	5	7	9	21
Lobo	11	8	13	32
Morisco	21	17	122	160
Moro	5	1	5	11
Totals	42	33	151	226

Source: AGN, Padrones, vols. 53, 54, 55, 56, 57, 58, 60, 62, 62, 63, 64, 65, 66, 67, 68, 69, 70, 71, 72, 73, 78.

The extreme castas were truly a small presence in Mexico City. Even in the aggregate, they represented less than one-half of 1 percent of the sampled population of 45,280 individuals. Given that our sample probably represents just less than one-third of the total population at the time, it is highly unlikely that extreme castas would have constituted much more than 1 percent, even if complete census information were available for Mexico City. The rarity of these caste classifications points to their special nature. For a census taker to record someone as a chino or a morisco, it seems that circumstances beyond the ordinary had to exist.

Table 5.3 offers additional clues into what census takers confronted as they conducted their work and how it tempered their tabulations. Here, the sample is subdivided by casta classification and age.[19] Apart from chinos and moriscos, the table reveals that a significant number of the extreme castas in Mexico City were children. There are several implications to this finding. First, it suggests that the categories of coyote, lobo, and moro may have been labels that frequently did not follow people into adulthood, at least in the capital. Second, in a world where caste was lived plurally, we might also be glimpsing individuals whose casta categorizations were on the brink of transition. Being called a coyote, lobo, or moro may not have had much meaning to these individuals as children, but as adults the same people might have chosen to alter their caste status, blended it with another, or found that the circumstances of their lives would automatically prompt a change in caste. Again, the very rarity of

[19] The age criteria used to categorize boys and girls comes from the census itself. AGN, Padrones, vol. 62, fols. 1–94.

these categories in adulthood in Mexico City suggests that any of these possibilities may have been true.

A third observation to draw from this data is that the adults who appeared in the census as coyotes, lobos, and moros must have had a low level of social influence. Standing face to face in front of the census takers, many may have felt themselves to be of origins so humble that they could not bring themselves to contest being assigned a coyote or lobo label.[20] For the record, successful contestations were commonplace, although they sometimes resulted in a stalemate, given that census takers always held the power to edit any claims. Take the case of don Miguel Ferras, an *indio cacique* and carpenter with a white wife. He was a man of importance in the city of Texcoco. Most likely without his knowledge, his enumerator inserted a snide parenthetical note in the census: "He runs about as if he is a *mestizo*."[21] Yet even so, confronted with Ferras's impressive connections and a residential address next to that of the leading government official in the province, the census taker simply could not deny him the honorific "don" before his name, despite the earnest effort to cleanse the record.

In contrast, the coyotes, lobos, and moros of Mexico City in 1811 had no equivalent social capital to call upon. Half of them had come to the city from elsewhere, an indication that they may not have had deep social networks in the capital. Although a small number lived as domestic laborers in elite households, these associations were insufficient to warrant a different caste designation. Consider Nicolás Blas, who lived on Escalerillas Street in the fashionable center of Mexico City. He was employed as a servant in the household of José Joaquín de Arguinsonis, a respected young merchant who was born in Durango but had come to the city from Vizcaya. Arguinsonis's house was filled with other young merchants, all bachelors in their twenties and thirties who were building their fortunes in the capital. All appear to have come to the city with José Joaquín, or slightly afterward. Despite being associated with this somewhat prosperous and upstart group, Nicolás was labeled a coyote, and his wife, also a servant, was classified as a castiza. There was another servant in the household, José Ramón Sandoval, an español.[22] From this brief

---

[20] An insight derived from Stewart R. King, *Blue Coat or Powdered Wig: Free People of Color in Pre-Revolutionary Saint-Domingue* (Athens: University of Georgia Press, 2001), 158–168. This section discusses the use of titles and names among free people of color and how social status was used to acquire access to certain titles.

[21] AGN, Padrones, vol. 43, fol. 24. The phrase used is "que corre por mestizo."

[22] Information on the Arguinsonis household is taken from AGN, Padrones, vol. 53.

TABLE 5.4 *Examples of Caste Labeling, 1811*
Mexico City Census

Racial Mixture	Caste
Español with morisca	Español
Español with morisca	Mestizo
Español with morisca	Morisco
Indio with español	Coyote
Indio with mestiza	Coyote
Indio with pardo	Coyote
Mestizo with india	Coyote
Mestizo with mulata	Lobo
Mestizo with mulata	Lobo
Mestizo with mulatto	Coyote
Morisco with castiza	Mulato
Morisco with española	Morisco
Morisco with india	Morisco
Mulato with española	Morisco
Pardo with castizo	Morisco
Pardo with indio	Lobo

Source: AGN, Padrones, vol. 62, fols. 8v, 17v, 20v, 59v, 78v;
vol. 63, fol. 142v; vol. 68, fols. 10, 55, 115; vol. 66, fols. 25, 95;
vol. 72 fols. 16, 98, 104v, 176v; and vol. 78, fols. 34, 44, 46.

glimpse, one might surmise that patronage networks did not work to the racial advantage of Nicolás Blas. In fact, rather than enhancing his caste status, the household, filled with young social strivers, may have had a heightened sensitivity toward differentiating between caste labels and a greater wish to use them to demarcate social distance. This, in part, explains the level of granularity that distinguished the caste status of the servants. Indeed, in all of the elite households where extreme castas were employed, similar concerns may have prevailed. Having coyotes, lobos, and moros working in and around the house made a public statement about the household head's personal and social cachet, but cultivating this social status was predicated upon carefully regulating social distances.

Further analysis of the 1811 census shows that in deducing the casta status of children, the formulas used by enumerators were not necessarily standardized and could vary appreciably. These categorizations could even deviate from the conventional templates that guided caste labeling more broadly in the colony (see Table 3.1 in Chapter 3). Table 5.4 provides an overview of some of the caste-labeling formulas used in the 1811 census for lobos, coyotes and moriscos. By and large, individual census takers remained consistent with their own labeling, but the evidence also suggests that casta formulas might have varied due to differing norms for identifying castas in various neighborhoods.[23]

It is important to recognize that the caste assignments of children were comments not only on the lineage of their parents but also on a family's entire social trajectory.[24] For example, when the census taker arrived at the home of don Juan Lizama, a white *armero* (gunsmith) living in a relatively spacious accessoria on the street of San Juan, he took special note of Lizama's marriage choice. Lizama had married Felipa Cárdenas, a 45-year-old washerwoman who was classified as a morisca. Perhaps to comment on Lizama's social breach (he was a "don"), and perhaps to discourage any notion of Felipa's social ascent or even to remark on their poverty, the enumerator classified their child as a morisco.[25] In another instance, the family of José Pérez, a white *cantero* (stonecutter) living in cramped quarters in an apartment complex on the street of El Zapo, was not penalized for his marriage to Maria Victoria Varela. She too was a morisca, and officially unemployed. However, their daughter, who had just come of age, was generously classified as an española in the census.[26] Perhaps José, since he was not a "don" and was even poorer than Lizama, simply had less to protect. This made his situation less a threat to the social order. Or maybe, phenotypically, José's daughter was just much fairer in complexion than Lizama's son. In both these cases, we see the census taker making conscious, off-script, perhaps even whimsical and free-style choices to render casta. The practices and habits of the census compilation process that had evolved over time afforded enumerators the license to make such decisions in these special cases. And within

---

[23] It would be important to further examine neighborhood culture in Mexico City during the late eighteenth century. One component might entail an attempt to understand whether and how caste correlated to socioeconomic status within selected neighborhoods. Another way to consider the influence of neighborhood culture in caste classification would be to search for subtle differences in how terminologies appeared and disappeared within Mexico City's cuarteles over time. The use of caste terminology could be compared (cuartel by cuartel) with previous census records, to the extent that these are available. An interesting study using this type of analysis is Dana V. Murillo, Mark Lents, and Margarita R. Ochoa, *City Indians in Spain's American Empire: Urban Indigenous Society in Colonial Mesoamerica and Andean South America, 1530–1810* (Brighton: Sussex Academic Press, 2012). Among other topics, this collection contains essays on ethnogenesis, property, and Afro-indigenous labor.

[24] When located within a larger household, these children may have served to index and categorize the status of the group as a whole.

[25] AGN, Padrones, vol. 78, fol. 16.

[26] AGN, Padrones, vol. 72, fol. 98.

the realm of a census, issuing extreme casta labels could serve purposes beyond trying to accurately identify individuals. This may have been the case with the progeny of certain families in Mexico City on the eve of Independence.

ACT II: VANISHING NUMBERS

One perplexing riddle posed by the censuses in colonial Spanish America is that the population categories into which people were placed did not fully reflect the phenotypic variety of places like colonial Mexico, which was broader than ever by the end of the colonial period. In a world where generations of intermixture should have yielded legions of racially mixed individuals, accompanied by rampant growth in casta categorizations, their variety and numbers as captured in demographic records were in fact small. We can recall from the earlier discussion of the 1777 census that extreme castes represented just less than 3 percent of central Mexico's populace. If castizos (arguably a borderline core caste group) are excluded from this measure, the proportion of extreme castas plummets further, to barely 1 percent (see Table 5.5), roughly akin to the proportions found in the Mexico City sample of 1811. Instead of documenting a rich blossoming of extreme casta population groups, the story emanating from the

TABLE 5.5 *Population by Casta, Archbishopric of Mexico, 1777*

Albino	164
Castizo	23,936
Chino	509
Coyote	1,770
Español	168,411
Indio	802,371
Lobo	5,176
Mestindio	384
Mestizo	110,340
Morisco	1,392
Mulato	67,795
Negro	1,428
Total	**1,191,753**

Source: Ernest Sánchez Santiró, *Padrón del Arzobispado de México, 1777* (Mexico: Archivo General de la Nación and Secretaría de Gobernación, 2003).

late eighteenth-century census record is that at some point the colonial project of labeling and creating new population groups stalled, in spite of the forces of caste pluralism, the creation of compound castes, and other forms of caste morphing that were at play.

Patterns encountered in other census records shed some light as to why these numbers were so low. But before delving into the data, it is important to revisit and understand a few of the features and challenges of working with this invaluable historical resource. Colonial Spanish American census drafting was a delicate act; consequently, the information censuses contained was not always the most accurate or the cleanest. When an upcoming census was publicly announced, colonists (especially men) were known to protest or avoid enumerators by fleeing their homes, finding hideouts, or feigning illnesses. These practices persisted despite efforts to impose jail terms on absentees or restrict populations from escaping into adjoining provinces. Military censuses particularly aroused suspicion, as able-bodied men feared impressment. People also spoke mistruths to census takers in order to alter their status and evade obligations. Being placed on a tribute register, for instance, could place substantial financial burdens on the poorest sectors of society and, as we have seen in other contexts, could permanently mar the reputations of society's better-heeled members.

During the second half of the eighteenth century, there was a general uptick in census activity, thanks to sweeping fiscal and military reforms (known as the Bourbon Reforms). These changes demanded ever greater information about the general population. Further, the new climate of empiricism, stemming from the scientific inquiries inspired by the Enlightenment, spurred efforts to establish a refined knowledge base of the world by means of careful surveillance and voluminous data collection.[27] At their best, census registers were believed to facilitate good order and administration.[28] Moreover, having intricate knowledge of the population

---

[27] Some insightful works on these trends include Neil Safier, *Measuring the New World: Enlightenment Science and South America* (Chicago: University of Chicago Press, 2008); Gabriel B. Paquette, *Enlightened Reform in Southern Europe and Its Atlantic Colonies, c. 1750–1830* (Burlington, UK: Ashgate, 2009); Paquette, *Enlightenment, Governance, and Reform in Spain and Its Empire, 1759–1808* (New York: Palgrave MacMillan, 2008); and Jorge Cañizares-Esguerra, *Nature, Empire, and Nation: Explorations of the History of Science in the Iberian World* (Stanford: Stanford University Press, 2006).

[28] For instance, they worked to exclude "unwanted and dangerous" members from communities, especially closed native communities like pueblos de indios. A great example comes from the town of Santa María Atipac, a native village in the jurisdiction of Coatepec. Here, a morisco (or coyote) by the name of Joseph Antonio had become

could supposedly help devise strategies to stimulate fertility and curb the impact of epidemics. New Spain entered this period of increased recordkeeping with a decree by Viceroy Pedro Cebrián, the fifth Count of Fuenclara, to launch the census of 1743–46. Subsequently, the pace of enumeration efforts picked up, as did the depth of the imperial gaze. Fuenclara sought mainly high-level information on families, but the 1777 census commissioned by Viceroy Antonio Maria de Bucareli y Ursúa, and executed by Mexico's bishops, sought to record details on every individual. Subsequent colonial censuses probed still deeper.[29] The steady flow of nearly overlapping censuses, tribute counts, parish registers, and military musters created a level of caste accountability and anxiety that was palpably higher than before the Bourbon Reforms.

Individual enumerators handled their duties differently. There was a preference for census takers to work in adequately staffed teams, to be of good birth and strong social standing, and to perform their jobs with honesty, trustworthiness, and efficiency, but the truth is more complex. The lines of authority delineating responsibility for the various aspects of the tabulation process were not always clear, precipitating competition, feuds, and even graft. When it came to the work itself, there were certainly those who scrupulously performed their tasks: cross-checking their information with available sources, listening carefully to the population, and approaching their jobs as objectively as possible. If mistakes were made, some census takers sought out additional evidence (death, burial, and

a powerful and abusive figure in the town. He arrived in Atipac when he was quite young, grew up there, and eventually took a native bride. In his subsequent rise to power, he made strategic alliances, one of which was with the *alcalde mayor*. Eventually, through his connections, Joseph Antonio was named *alguacil mayor* (chief bailiff), against the wishes of the community. Once installed, he reportedly embarked upon a string of abuses, including beating elders, seizing land, whipping widows, and jailing people unjustly in order to procure fines. Given his casta status, some argued that he should not have been a resident of the community at all, under definitions articulated in the Real Cédula of June 4, 1683. To curb abuses like these, and to ensure that only authorized residents lived in native communities, a solution was proposed on June 9, 1773: to create and administer regular censuses. These would help establish greater order in society so that colonial legislation could function as intended. In Indian villages, the census was supposed to help identify the people who were officially eligible to vote and stand for election. As the enumerators (drawn from the *justicias*) conducted their work, they operated under special provisions intended to track individuals who were racially mixed. See AGN, Bandos, vol. 8, exp. 39, fols.139–142. On the topic of encouraging fertility rates, see Jordi Nadal, *La población española (siglos XVI a XX)* (Barcelona: Editorial Ariel, 1986).

[29] An excellent summary discussion of New Spain's censuses is in Cecilia Rabel, "Oaxaca en el siglo dieciocho: población, familia, y economía" (PhD diss.: Colegio de México, 2001), 31–52.

marriage registers) to make corrections.[30] But others rushed or glossed over the enumeration process, making assumptions about populations and creating inconsistencies in the documents. Further, censuses were drawn for different purposes and by different colonial institutions and could yield notable discrepancies when describing the same population.[31] For instance, the 1777 ecclesiastical census in Mexico rarely used the term *pardo* to describe individuals of African descent. Yet little more than a decade later, in the Revillagigedo census of 1790–93, both the government and military censuses routinely used the term *pardo*.

With cautions duly raised, I have pulled together a sample of nine jurisdictions from Mexico's 1791 census to explore the reasons for a paucity of extreme castes in the registers of late colonial Mexico. These jurisdictions were selected because they offer an accessible and convenient means of gauging caste interactivity in colonial households (see Figure 11).

In each jurisdiction, enumerators carefully distinguished between español, mestizo, and castizo households and those of pardos, morenos, mulattos, and related castas (see Table 5.6).[32] The grouping of castas into this binary arrangement (white/mestizo vs. black) was far from arbitrary. Part of the rationale involved tribute payments and the effort to separate tribute-paying castes from nontributary ones.[33] The 1791 census

---

[30] See changes made to the record in Chilapa (1791). AGN, Padrones, vol. 16, exp. 2, fol. 202. Church records constituted a critically important repository and archive for verifying data collected by the government.

[31] A good discussion of discrepancies in census records in Mexico can be found in Sánchez Santiró, *Padrón del Arzobispado de México 1777*, 15–31. In an edict published in 1793, the rationale offered for annual parish censuses was that such counts facilitated the parishioners' observance of communion and confession, something everyone was expected to do at least once per year. The Church would use the censuses to keep track of individuals who did not comply with their religious obligations. See AGN, Bandos, vol. 17, fols. 15–25. In 1793, a very specific and detailed ordinance described the process by which tribute censuses were to be taken. The rules were designed to clean up abusive practices and modernize the process. See AGN, Bandos, vol. 17, exp. 55 and 56, fols. 228–249v.

   In 1786, a wonderful synopsis of the military census process in Tezcuoco made a case for updating census counts every six months so as to ensure a reliable and steady reserve army and to safeguard against high degrees of vagrancy. The document also discusses how the census was designed to improve what were deemed to be shoddy militia forces. AGN, Padrones, vol. 43, exp. 1, fols. 197v–235v.

[32] By and large, this is the precise terminology for the groupings found in the census.

[33] The two groups were seen differently not just because of their phenotype (both blacks and Indians paid tribute), but also because of their roles within the fiscal structure of the empire. Tribute brought substantial revenue to the royal coffers, although black tribute remissions paled in comparison to those of Indians. Some scholars have noted that certain

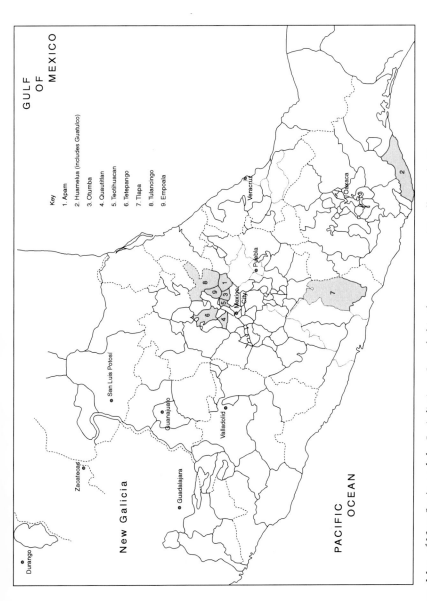

FIGURE 11 Map of New Spain and the Jurisdictions Sampled in the 1791–1793 Revillagigedo Census.
Source: Adapted by the author from Peter Gerhard, *Geografía histórica de la Nueva España, 1519–1821* (Mexico: Universidad Autónoma de México, 1986), 16.

TABLE 5.6 *Casta Populations Sampled, Revillagigedo Census, 1791–93*

Jurisdiction	Españoles, Mestizos, and Castizos	Español, Mestizo, and Castizo Families	Pardos, Morenos, and Mulatos	Pardo, Moreno, and Mulato Families
Apam	1,946	435	1,059	220
Huamelula	174	58	336	91
Otumba	2,053	436	130	20
Quautitlán	3,251	762	219	62
Teotihuacan	1,291	280	266	56
Tetepango	4,220	994	297	85
Tlapa	2,143	569	1,870	504
Tulancingo	15,093	3,259	1,161	253
Zempoala	953	200	736	162
Total	31,574	6,693	6,074	1,453

Source: AGN, Padrones, vols. 1, 5, 6, 12, 20, 22. The 1791–93 census is commonly known as the Revillagigedo census, named after one of New Spain's late-colonial viceroys.

determined whether a family was part of the black household group or the white/mestizo group by evaluating the casta status of household heads. If the household head was an español, mestizo, or castizo, then the entire family was tallied under the white/mestizo group. If the head was a mulato, pardo, or moreno, then the household was recorded in the black group.[34] Given that the primary purpose of this census was for militia recruitment, indigenous household heads were not counted, since they were technically barred from military duty.[35]

segments of the indigenous population had incorporated their timely payment of tribute as part of their socio-political identity. While tribute still remained a stigma for these populations, their regular payment of the levy could be leveraged to acquire privileges from the crown. See Michael T. Ducey, "Viven sin ley ni rey: rebeliones coloniales en Papantla, 1760–1790," in *Procesos rurales e historia regional*, ed. Victoria Chenaut (Mexico City: CIESAS, 1996), 19–20. For more on free-colored tribute in Mexico, see Andrews, "Taxing Blackness"; Andrews, "Calidad, Genealogy, and Disputed Free-Colored Tributary Status"; Vinson, *Bearing Arms for His Majesty*, chap. 4; and Cynthia Milton and Ben Vinson III, "Counting Heads: Race and Non-Native Tribute Policy in Colonial Spanish America," *Journal of Colonialism and Colonial History* 3, no. 3 (2002): 1–18.

[34] I use the terms "black group" and "white/mestizo group" merely as a means of simplifying the categorizations of *mulatto/pardo/moreno* and *español/castizo/mestizo* as they appear in this text.

[35] Indigenous forces comprised an important element of colonial defense, particularly in frontier settings. See Vinson and Restall, "Black Soldiers, Native Soldiers: Meanings of

The majority of household heads, though not all, were male. Families of widows and single women were included.[36] In these instances, a family's casta status became that of the female. The nine jurisdictions chosen for the sample represent a cross-section of racial and casta environments. Huamelula was a region where Afro-Mexicans comprised a majority of the nonindigenous population. Zempoala and Tlapa were both areas where the combined number of mestizos, castizos, and whites was just slightly larger than that of the black population. The remaining six jurisdictions, however, were heavily dominated by the nonblack castes, at a ratio greater than 8:1.

One remarkable find in the 1791 census data is that African-based populations had minimal impact on the family structure of white and mestizo society. Households from the white/mestizo group had an infinitesimal amount of close contact with African-based peoples, regardless of the black population's size in their jurisdictions. I am measuring here not only levels of marital exogamy, but the total numbers of black kin, children, marital partners, and, in some cases, close friends who lived within the family structure of the white/mestizo group. Just 2.7 percent of these families had such contact with blacks. The extremely low level of cross-racial (or intercaste) interaction is even more remarkable when we consider that mestizos, an important presence in the sample, have been construed as one of the most likely nonblack groups to intermarry with peoples of African descent.[37] Yet this household-level contact was negligible in the Revillagigedo data sample. By contrast, the sample shows that pardo, moreno, and mulato households were nine to ten times more likely

---

Military Service in the Spanish American Colonies," in *Beyond Black and Red: African-Native Relations in Colonial Latin America*, ed. Matthew Restall (Albuquerque: University of New Mexico Press, 2005), 15–52.

[36] A number of laws made it possible for women to head households. *Patria potestad* (the legal principle of custody or guardianship, rooted in early Roman legal codes) granted women significant power when it came to broken marriages and widowhood. A brief mention of the phenomenon can be found in Daviken Studnicki-Gizbert, *A Nation upon the Open Sea: Portugal's Atlantic Diaspora and the Crisis of the Spanish Empire, 1492–1640* (Oxford: Oxford University Press, 2007), 82.

[37] Cope, *The Limits of Racial Domination*, 82. Note that in places like Jalapa, Guanajuato, Charcas, and San Luis Potosí, scholars have found that Indian spouses were statistically important marriage partners for all shades of free-coloreds. In most of these centers, the Indians' low social position placed them within easy reach of Afro-Mexicans. See Patrick J. Carroll and Jeffrey Lamb, "Los mexicanos negros: el mestizaje y los fundamentos olvidados de la 'raza cósmica', una perspectiva regional," *Historia Mexicana* 44, no. 3 (1995): 411; and David A. Brading, "Grupos étnicos, clases y estructura ocupacional en Guanajuato," *Historia Mexicana* 21, no. 3 (1972), 258.

to have a member of the white/mestizo group within their families. Indeed, between 25 and 30 percent of all pardo/moreno households included at least one mestizo, español, or castizo. A substantial number of these individuals were whites.

Given the limitations of the census data, an assessment of the presence of indigenous people in the households of both groups could not be fully completed for each jurisdiction.[38] Regardless, some interesting observations can be made from what information is available. The contact of the white/mestizo sector with Indians was substantially greater than that with blacks, but still fairly low. As many as 9.1 percent of all white/mestizo households included at least one Indian member. The ties between blacks and Indians were more numerous, with between 14 and 19 percent of black households including indios. Almost all of this contact represented marital exogamy, since nearly every indigenous person encountered within the black group was the spouse of a household head.

The major divergent case within the sample came from Huamelula, the only area possessing a black majority. Here, the white/mestizo group exhibited a much greater proclivity for incorporating blacks and Indians into their households than anywhere else. A full 27 of the 58 households (46 percent) were interracial (or intercaste), with 9 households (16 percent) including mulattos. By contrast, the black household group exhibited far less contact with whites and mestizos. While indios were present in 37 of their 91 households, just 3 (3 percent) included mestizos, and none included whites. Some of this data is not surprising. Although it contrasts with the other patterns found in the sample, the contours of Huamelula's black interracial behavior appears typical for the Pacific coastal provinces in the late eighteenth century, especially in the regions south of Acapulco and stretching toward Tehuantepec. In Igualapa, for instance, another jurisdiction where blacks comprised the majority, cross-racial (or intercaste) contact with whites and mestizos was virtually nonexistent. However, the main difference from Huamelula was that Igualapa's blacks had barely any contact with the indigenous population either.[39] In short, even taking into account the outlier data from Huamelula, the impact of family-level, cross-racial contact within the black sector was profound in

---

[38] A study of the presence of the indigenous population in the households of españoles, castizos, and mestizos was completed for seven jurisdictions. For the households of pardos, morenos, and mulatos, eight jurisdictions were analyzed.

[39] Ben Vinson III, "The Racial Profile of a Rural Mexican Province in the 'Costa Chica': Igualapa in 1791," *The Americas* 57, no. 2, (October 2000): 269–282.

the regions studied. Almost half of their families included members of a nonblack caste group. Most were spouses.

To sum up, the sample of nine jurisdictions offers only a glimpse at the central regions of New Spain, but it is a provocative late-colonial view. If sustained, it would demonstrate the almost negligible long-term impact of miscegenation with African-descendant persons on mainstream mestizo and white family household structure. It is remarkable that this could have been the case as late as the 1790s. At the same time, there remained various pockets of blackness throughout Mexico where blacks preserved an internal, endogamous household integrity or brought only Indians into their family sphere with any frequency. However, apart from these enclaves (primarily located along the Pacific coast), people of African descent proved far more amenable on a colony-wide basis to opening their households to the other caste groups. These trends were probably foundational to the growth of modern mestizaje.

Because the 1791 census sample suggests that the greatest opportunities in society for generating caste complexity rested in black households (nearly half of their families exhibited cross-racial contact), it is to this group that our attention necessarily turns. Virtually all of the miscegenated Afro-Mexican members of black households could be categorized as pardo or mulato. In essence, therefore, the census exhibits strikingly little caste variety among blacks.[40] A few coyotes and mestindios were counted in the 1791 census, but that was rare. So, returning to the paradox outlined at the beginning of this section, although it seems that the colonial population should have been constantly transforming and evolving, becoming ever richer in caste complexity, this was not the case, even among the group exhibiting the greatest degree of cross-racial contact. Indeed, the 1791 census did not reflect even the complexities captured in the earlier 1777 ecclesiastical census.

The caste uniformity found in the written record had partly to do with the titles assigned to subsections of the census and the labels supplied therein. The practices of drafting the census, especially the preprinted labeling, seem to have influenced the casta description of the adults who were recorded. For example, in the jurisdiction of Tlapa, the black population was logged in a register called *Padrón de las familias de* mulatos *que existen en dicha jurisdicción, 1791* (Census of mulatto families ...; emphasis mine). Subsequently, almost every adult in that jurisdiction

---

[40] Even among the small number of white and mestizo families that openly exhibited miscegenation within their households, the overwhelming majority of castas found in their homes were mulatos and pardos, not members of extreme castes.

who was identified as having African ancestry was categorized as a mulato (see Figure 12).[41] In Apam, therefore, by contrast, the register was named *Padrón de familias* morenas y pardas, *jurisdicción de Apam* (emphasis mine). Almost all persons with any African ancestry in Apam were labeled as pardos (see Figure 13).[42] Figure 14 shows an example from the Revillagigedo census of the Haciendas of San Nicolás.

Such labeling patterns were not unique to the nine jurisdictions in the sample.[43] And, of course, there were some variances in what enumerators recorded. In Guanajuato, Acambaro, and San Juan del Río, the census's title specified pardos, but significant portions of the population, if not the vast majority, were classified instead as mulatos. Interestingly, however, in the final summary sheets, rather than maintaining the subtle differences enumerated between the mulato and pardo caste groups, census takers reclassified the entire population as pardos, regardless of what had actually been written alongside individual names.[44]

Clumping black casta groups into a single category represented a special act. The finer caste distinctions that were likely to be operative in homes, bars, streets, and workplaces did not ultimately trump the overriding similarities of certain castas in the eyes of higher officials in the colonial government, and it was they who were responsible for making use of the region-wide census data. Hence, for the purposes of military recruitment, pardos and mulatos were essentially perceived as the same by the central colonial bureaucracy: they were tributary castes of African ancestry that could be recruited for military duty. Of course, at the local government level, or from the perspective of individual census takers, subtle differences could assume more meaning. A pardo may have enjoyed a slightly higher social station within a regional context than a mulato, for instance. Such apparently conflicting perspectives could comfortably coexist within the pages of the census document.[45] The summary sheets,

[41] AGN, Padrones, vol. 22, fols. 54–93.
[42] AGN, Padrones, vol. 5, fols. 316–398.
[43] For examples, see AGN, Padrones, vols. 5, 16, 17, 22, 23, 25, and 32.
[44] The best example is the jurisdiction of Acambaro. AGN, Padrones, vol. 23. See also vols. 32 and 35.
[45] Two excellent examples come from the provinces of Motines and Tochimilco. In both cases, the censuses advertised that the population of pardos was being tallied. In Motines, out of 540 individuals, a lone mulato, Luciano Gómez was registered. He was a 24-year-old *tirador* living in the town of Coacoman, and he was married to Petra Manulea, an india. In Tochimilco, there were additional mulatos recorded. See AGN, Padrones, vol. 21, exp. 3, fols. 346v–347; and AGN, Padrones, vol. 12, exp. 4, fols. 114–116v.

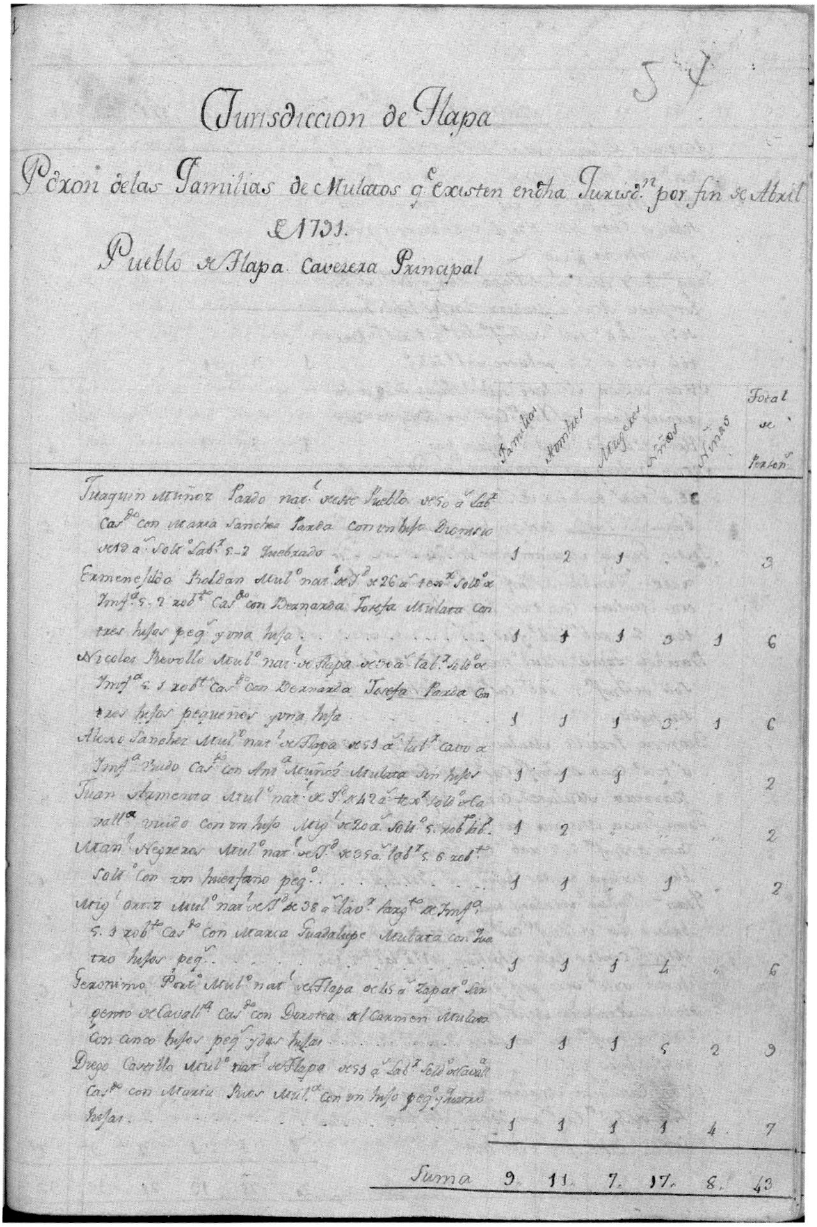

Jurisdiccion de Tlapa

Padron delas Familias de Mulatos q.e existen en dha Jurisd.n por fin de Abril de 1791.

Pueblo de Tlapa Cavezera Principal

	Familias	Hombres	Mugeres	Niños	Niñas	Total de Personas
Joaquin Muñoz Pardo nat. deste Pueblo ...	1	2	1			3
Ermenegildo Roldan Mul.o ... con tres hijos peq.s y una hija	1	1	1	3	1	6
Nicolas Revollo Mul.o nat. de Tlapa ... con tres hijos pequeños y una hija	1	1	1	3	1	6
Alonso Sanchez Mul.o nat. de Tlapa ... Cas.do con Ant.a Muñoz Mulata sin hijos	1	1	1			2
Juan Armenta Mul.o ... viudo con un hijo ...	1	2				2
Juan Negreros Mul.o ... con un huerfano peq.o	1	1		1		2
Mig.l Ortiz Mul.o ... Cas.do con Maria Guadalupe Mulata con quatro hijos peq.s	1	1	1	4		6
Geronimo Peralta Mul.o nat. de Tlapa ... con cinco hijos peq.s y dos hijas	1	1	1	5	2	9
Diego Castillo Mul.o nat. de Tlapa ... con un hijo peq.o y quatro hijas	1	1	1	1	4	7
Suma	9	11	7	17	8	43

FIGURE 12 Title Page for Tlapa, Revillagigedo Census, 1791–1793. Source: AGN, Padrones, vol. 21, no expediente, fol. 84.

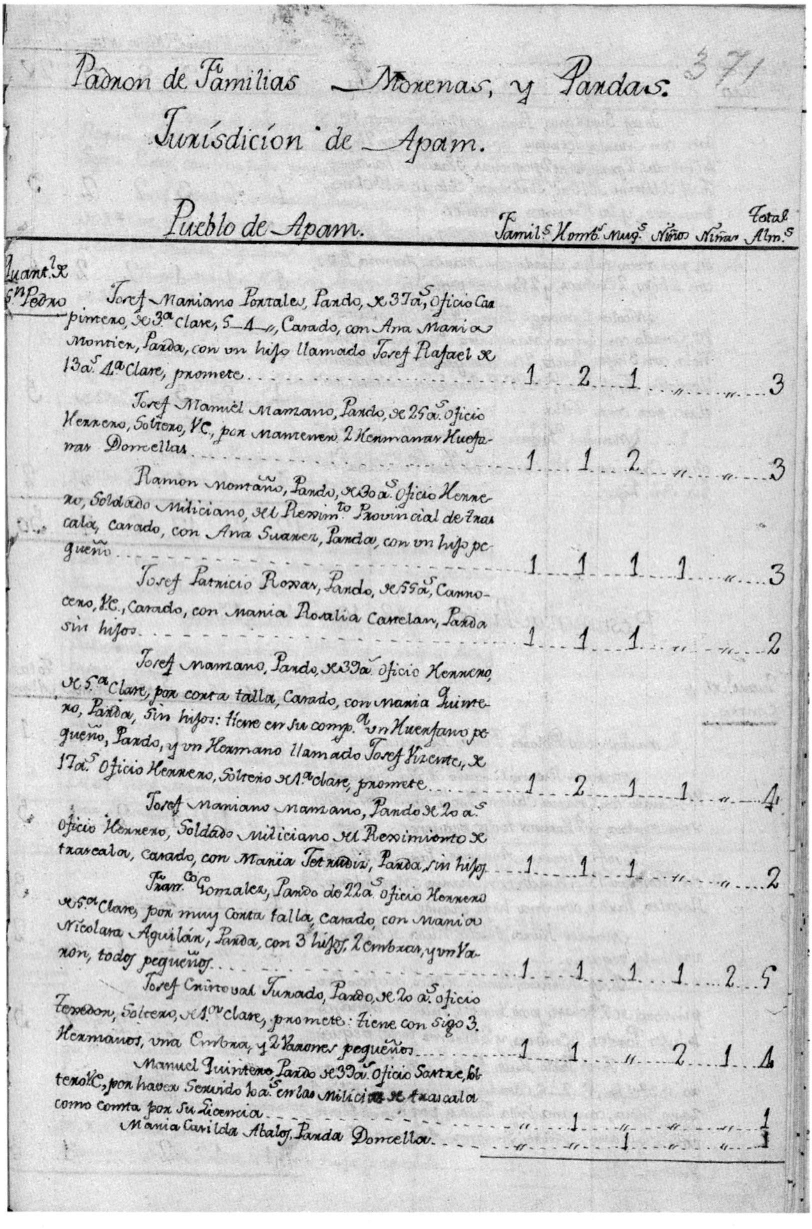

FIGURE 13 Title Page for Apam, Revillagigedo Census, 1791–1793.
Source: AGN, Padrones, vol. 5, exp. 2, fol. 371.

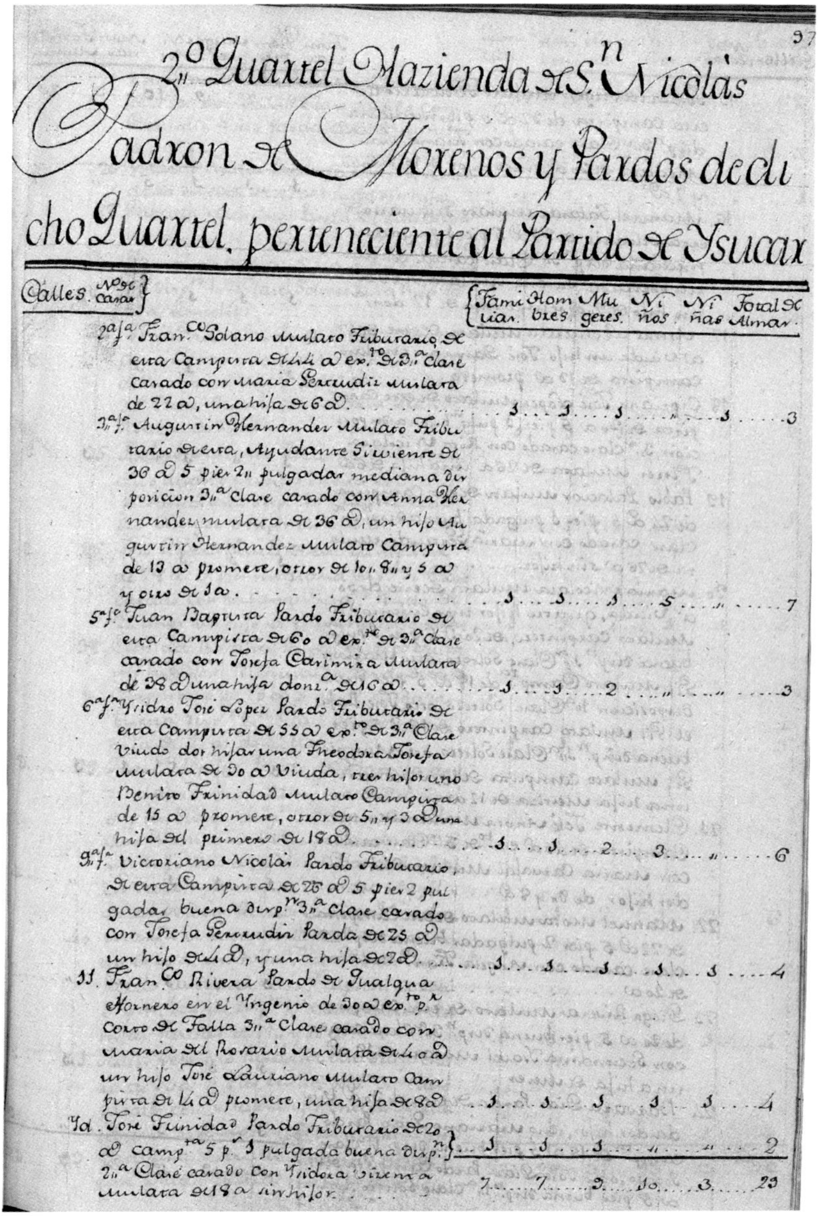

FIGURE 14   Title Page, Haciendas of San Nicolás, Partido of Isucar, Revillagigedo Census, 1791–1793.
Source: AGN, Padrones, vol. 28, no expediente, fol. 97.

with all of their homogenizing and caste smoothing, reflected the labeling patterns that were most important for the central bureaucracy, based on the purposes of the census. On the other hand, the subtleties found within the individual pages of the census could reflect the casta categories that were important locally and in the minds of specific enumerators.

That said, many census summary sheets on which blacks were recorded did make the effort to identify morenos (pure blacks). This tells us that the central colonial state, insomuch as it cared about degrees of blackness, was concerned principally with delineating a difference between "pure blackness" and black mixtures. Remarkably, the central bureaucracy could be unusually persistent in seeking knowledge on morenos, even though their numbers were microscopic. The jurisdiction of Tulancingo, for instance, had over 16,000 residents, just one of whom was a moreno. Nevertheless, the crown cared that this person was properly registered and accounted for.

At the other end of the spectrum, there was equal concern over white purity. In the censuses of white/mestizo households, provisions were made to keep accurate records of castizos. The flexibility of having three categories (mestizo, castizo, and español) provided census takers a broader framework within which to capture differences in phenotype – presumably in hopes of closely regulating entry into the coveted español caste. Even people with markedly fair complexions could be assigned castizo status to keep them from claiming to be españoles; at the same time, their castizo status allowed them to maintain their social elevation in contrast with the broader mestizo mainstream.[46]

One of the few jurisdictional censuses that broke with the patterns described here was taken in Aguascalientes by Felix Calleja in 1792. With part of it labeled the "Padrón de mulatos y demás castas" (Census of mulattos and other castes), the census's title failed to adhere to the traditional formula that separated blacks from whites and mestizos. Rather,

---

[46] Of course, individual census takers could struggle with the centripetal and centrifugal pull of their work. Local perspectives challenged their goals both as agents and instruments of the central imperial bureaucracy. In Tezcuoco, the 1786 military census found enumerators working hard to conform to the rules of the census process while also accommodating local customs. In the town of Tepetlastoc, nestled within the jurisdiction of Tezcuoco, the enumerator mentioned that he had recorded the town as "full of *españoles*, [because] whether true or not, the people there enjoy comforts [and] live honorably." Although this case took place a few years before the 1791 census, the census taker's airy summation was far from unique in late eighteenth-century Mexico. See AGN, Padrones, vol. 43, exp. 1, fols. 234–235.

the title conveyed that all racial mixtures were to be amassed together with the black group. Diving into the details, within the census's pages some individuals were given no caste assignment, leaving their identity open to question, whereas others were described with great care. In contrast to what was recorded for most provinces in the Revillagigedo census, we encounter in Aguascalientes handfuls of coyotes, lobos, and even a morisco.[47] One cannot help but wonder if the census's title, by announcing its goal to capture a broad (albeit unspecified) population spectrum, might have opened the door for including greater casta variety, while also discouraging caste specificity in some cases.[48]

Another important factor affecting how caste diversity was reported involved the ways in which certain enumerators recorded offspring. Rather than providing children with specific caste labels, some enumerators left them raceless (or casteless) in their records. The casta status of children mattered only in census summary sheets, where they were jumbled together indiscriminately as pardos and mulatos (if their parents belonged to the black household group) or mestizos and españoles (if their parents belonged to the white/mestizo group). In our sample, the enumerators' lack of concern over the caste status of children effectively smoothed and flattened the general population into a more homogenous form. In the case of Afro-Mexicans, the effect was to preserve the pardo and mulato categories as mainstream caste designations for subsequent generations of recordkeeping. If children regularly appeared in the summary sheets as pardos and morenos regardless of their degree of racial mixture, those two categories would very likely be carried forward into subsequent censuses, and other, more specific caste classifications would tend to fall away.

In colonial Mexico, the lack of concern over precise caste labeling of children was a feature of both tributary and military census records. The 1791–93 Revillagigedo census showed little interest in labeling children, since its primary purpose was to identify adult males between the ages of 16 and 39 for military duty. Only the names of children were recorded, except for males who had already reached 15 years of age; for them, a note was made that they would soon be eligible for military service. These practices differed from the more careful scrutiny of children that took place in censuses like the 1811 Mexico City municipal register.

---

[47] These castas tended to be clustered in particular geographic pockets within the province, especially certain haciendas or towns.

[48] AGN, Padrones, vol. 5, fols. 288–313v.

As always, there were exceptions. The 1791 censuses taken in Coyoacán, Quautitlán, Zempoala, Otumba, and Tochimilco did attempt to record the casta of children, but in ways that did not follow customary practices.[49] That is, the outcomes of racial mixture were not described in typical ways. Instead, enumerators used the census to channel racial mixtures into outcomes that fit their needs and overemphasized blackness. In Quautitlán, for instance, the marriage of the parda María Gonzáles to 50-year-old don Gabriel Ierresuelos, a white European from the Canary Islands, produced nine children. The taxonomy of the sistema de castas suggested that they all be qualified as moriscos, but they were instead relegated to the caste status of their mother: all emerged as pardos. Less-dramatic inter-casta marriages in the same jurisdiction, such as unions between mestizos and pardos, also routinely produced pardo children. In another example, taken from the jurisdiction of Tochimilco, Ignacio Hernández, a 30-year-old mulato fieldworker who married his sweetheart, an india named Inés, yielded progeny who were all recorded as mulatos, as were the offspring of other couples who had similar casta backgrounds.[50]

Scholars of Latin American history have used the term *hypogamy* (literally, marrying into a lower caste) to capture and describe situations wherein a spouse's phenotype was recorded as defaulting to the status of the darker marital partner (racial drift). Although hypogamy has typically been used to index drifts in racial status that occurred at the time of marriage, it is clear that a family's offspring could be similarly affected by receiving what amounted to a caste demotion.[51] When enumerators systematically catalogued hypogamy and downward racial drifting for both spouses and their children, as they did in several regions in the 1791 census, the result was to blacken a province's population. Consequently, when all censuses in a region or colony were finally rolled up and presented to officials at the highest rungs of the colonial government, the effect was cumulative, giving blackness an unwonted weight. This fact helps explain certain features encountered in the demography of late colonial Mexico. Between 1793 and 1800, the Afro-Mexican population numbered between 370,000 and 635,000 individuals, or roughly

---

[49] Note that the Tochimilco and Coyoacán censuses are not a part of the nine-jurisdiction sample I utilized for this study. The information can be located in AGN, Padrones, vol. 12, exp. 4, fols. 114–116v, and AGN, Padrones, vol. 6, no. 1, exp. 1, fols. 133–146v.

[50] AGN, Padrones, vol. 12, exp. 4, fol. 115.

[51] AGN, Padrones, vol. 6, no. 2, exp. 4, fol. 338v.

10 percent of the colony's total population.[52] Since most of these individuals were freedmen, it can be said that Mexico represented one of the largest concentrations of free-coloreds in the New World. However, this large number may have been a function of the possible overcomputation of blackness and the consequent eclipsing of many extreme casta statuses.

A second broad effect of indexing hypogamy across census documents has been less discussed. In absorbing large numbers of light-skinned individuals as mulatos and pardos, Mexican blackness itself was effectively transformed. As individual provinces were blackening in the documentary record, the physical and phenotypic configuration of blackness was simultaneously whitening, as lighter and lighter hues slipped and became enveloped into black categories.

Let's pause here to tie this discussion into some of the larger themes of this book. The census practices described in this chapter exhibit castizaje at work and set into motion processes that would eventually undergird the emergence of mestizaje in the nineteenth century. The road to modern Mexican mestizaje ultimately inherited the results of caste flattening and smoothing, as well as the capability to deploy precise caste categorizations in local settings. Mexican mestizaje was formed in part by a heritage wherein black households served as key cross-casta and inter-casta incubators, and it featured the incorporation of a blackness that was itself whitening and probably also becoming more indigenous as it evolved. As seen in this chapter, the census data of the late eighteenth century shows that the utilization of caste in such documents was flexible.

It is important to underscore that the government itself exercised its own version of caste flexibility, expanding and contracting caste categories as it saw fit for the needs of the regime. We have seen this at play in the context of military recruitment and, tangentially, in that of the assessment of tribute. There were many more instances. Ultimately, the colonial bureaucracy kept close to its core caste categories, which could be found in nearly every count. Españoles, mestizos, pardos, mulatos, and morenos were everywhere, and the crown found ways to replicate them in its official documents abundantly and from generation to generation, despite the intense pace of miscegenation and its accompanying population changes. On the one hand, caste simplification made bureaucratic

---

[52] Gonzalo Aguirre Beltrán, *La población negra en México: estudio etnohistórico* (Mexico City: Fondo de Cultura Económica, 1972), 222–230; Andrews, *Afro-Latin America*, 41.

paperwork easier, since a few basic categories persisted from one era to the next. It also mitigated the need for census takers to account for scores of different caste types on every census occasion. However, in the event that special circumstances warranted the need, racial and caste details, along with additional casta labels, could always be added to the normative inventory. Certainly at the local level, regional nuance could be, and often was, routinely accounted for in appraisals of caste (see Appendix C).

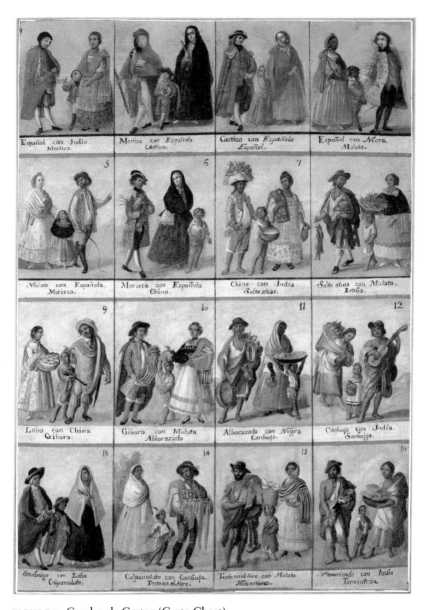

FIGURE 1 Cuadro de Castas (Caste Chart).
Source: Museo Nacional del Virreinato, Tepotzotlán, Mexcio, 18th Century (anonymous painter). Castas Painting, Oil on canvas H 148 × W 105 cm, Courtesy of Art Resource.

FIGURE 2 Mestizo and India Produce Coyote.
Source: Juan Rodríguez Juárez (1675–1728), *De Mestizo, y India Produce Coyote*, ca. 1720, Castas Painting, Oil on canvas H 103.8 × W 146.4 cm, Courtesy of The Hispanic Society of America, New York.

FIGURE 3 Negro and India Produce Lobo.
Source: Juan Rodríguez Juárez (1675–1728), *De Negro, y India Produce Lobo*, ca. 1715; Castas Painting, Oil on canvas, Courtesy of Breamore House, Hampshire, UK/Bridgeman Images.

FIGURE 4 Español and Mulata Produce Morisca.
Source: Juan Rodríguez Juárez (1675–1728), *De Español, y Mulata Produce Morisca*, ca. 1715; Castas Painting, Oil on canvas, Courtesy of Breamore House, Hampshire, UK/Bridgeman Images.

FIGURE 5 Indio y Loba Produce Grifo, Which Is "Tente en el Aire."
Source: Juan Rodríguez Juárez (1675–1728), *De Indio, y Loba Produce Grifo, que es Tente en el Aire*, ca. 1715; Castas Painting, Oil on canvas, Courtesy of Breamore House, Hampshire, UK/Bridgeman Images.

THE CARES OF A GROWING FAMILY
SEEN THROUGH THE BEE'S PROPHESCOPIC SCOOPOGRAPH

FIGURE 6 "The Cares of a Growing Family."
Source: "The cares of a growing family seen through the Bee's prophescopic scoopograph," New York Public Library, General Research Division, Digital Collections, http://digitalcollections.nypl.org/items/9400421e-c06c-4fc1-e040-e0 0a18065ca1, accessed May 5, 2016. The *Bee* was published in Earlington, Kentucky.

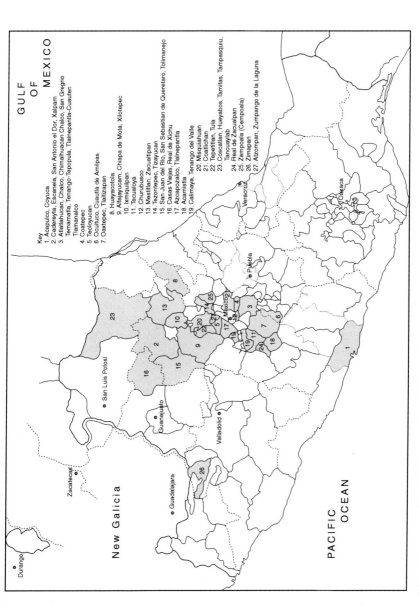

FIGURE 9 Map, Dioceses of the Archbishopric of Mexico that Housed Extreme Castas, Ecclesiastical Census, 1777.

Source: Adapted by the author from Peter Gerhard, *Geografía histórica de la Nueva España, 1519–1821* (Mexico: Universidad Autónoma de México, 1986), 16, and from Ernesto Sánchez Santiró, *Padrón del Arzobispado de México, 1777* (Mexico: Archivo General de la Nación and Secretaría de Gobernación, 2003).

FIGURE 10 Map of Mexico City, Divided Into 32 Cuarteles, 1782.
Source: John Carter Brown Library, Brown University, Providence, RI.

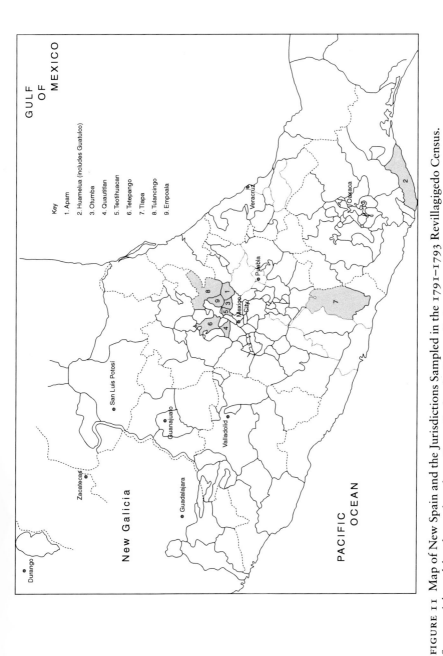

Key

1. Apam
2. Huamelua (includes Guatulco)
3. Otumba
4. Quautitlan
5. Teotlhuacan
6. Tetepango
7. Tlapa
8. Tulancingo
9. Empoala

GULF
OF
MEXICO

PACIFIC
OCEAN

New Galicia

Durango
Zacatecas
Guadalajara
San Luis Potosí
Guanajuato
Valladolid
Mexico City
Puebla
Veracruz
Oaxaca

FIGURE 11 Map of New Spain and the Jurisdictions Sampled in the 1791–1793 Revillagigedo Census.
Source: Adapted by the author from Peter Gerhard, *Geografía histórica de la Nueva España, 1519–1821* (Mexico: Universidad Autónoma de México, 1986), 16.

FIGURE 23 Emiliano Colón Torres in Corralero, 1995.
Source: Photo by author.

6

Betrothed: Marrying into the Extremes

Up to this point in our discussion of racial mixture and its extremes, marriage has occupied an important but not a central role. However, marriage was undoubtedly a principal driver of miscegenation, warranting special attention in any treatise on caste groups. Marriage was critical not only for what it produced, but also for what it stood for. From the perspective of the elite, marriage was elemental to strategies of preserving and enhancing wealth and status, since marital alliances often created the networks and extended family ties that harnessed power in the realms of business and politics. Any slips through imprudent marriage choices could endanger an entire family's honor and wealth.[1]

Marriage was also deemed crucial to creating the ideal unified Christian community that was zealously sought by the Church. In the years immediately after the conquest, the Church actually promoted the sacrament of marriage for both natives and black slaves, not just for the purposes of upholding the tenets of Christian doctrine, but also as an instrument for transmitting Christian values and encouraging domesticity.[2] For many in the colonies, marriage became a means of

---

[1] For extended treatment of this subject, see Verena Stolcke, *Marriage, Class and Colour in Nineteenth-Century Cuba: A Study of Racial Attitudes and Sexual Values in a Slave Society* (Cambridge: Cambridge University Press, 1974).

[2] Classic works on Latin American native experiences include James Lockhart, *The Nahuas after the Conquest: A Social and Cultural History of the Indians of Central Mexico, Sixteenth through Eighteenth Centuries* (Stanford: Stanford University Press, 1992); Matthew Restall, *The Maya World: Yucatec Culture and Society, 1550–1850* (Stanford: Stanford University Press, 1997); Kevin Terraciano, *The Mixtecs of Colonial Oaxaca: Ñudzahui History, Sixteenth through Eighteenth Centuries* (Stanford: Stanford University Press, 2001); Charles Gibson, *The Aztecs under Spanish Rule: A History of the Indians of*

navigating social worlds, expressing love, fostering family, and building community. At times these goals aligned with those of the elite and the Church, and at others they did not. With competing visions of marriage at play (even the Church and the elite could be at odds), it is no surprise that marriage patterns would assume lives of their own, despite efforts at formal regulation and informal oversight.[3] Especially through nuptials that took place between people of different classes and casta groups, marriage also served as a crucible for altering the fabric of society.[4] In these situations, the sacramental nature of marriage unexpectedly gave miscegenation a sacrosanct endorsement – even a measure of acceptability that would help situate racial mixture prominently in the Latin American heritage in ways not readily seen in places like British North America.

The primary focal point of this chapter and the next is to consider the event of marriage as a means of deepening our understanding of the extreme castas. Given that marriage was a time of life when one's casta status was recorded in the colonial record, alongside testimony from the marriage applicants and their circle of friends, marriage documents provide a goldmine of information for scholars seeking to better understand casta relationships, identity, and labeling. Our task here is to consult this

---

the *Valley of Mexico, 1519–1810* (Stanford: Stanford University Press, 2000); and Yanna Yannakakis, *The Art of Being In-Between: Native Intermediaries, Indian Identity, and Local Rule in Colonial Oaxaca* (Durham: Duke University Press, 2008). See also Bennett, *Africans in Colonial Mexico.*

[3] Especially before the eighteenth century, and despite the fact that the Church was the primary institution responsible for managing marriage, Church doctrine itself challenged some of the aspirations of the governing classes. In interpreting love as the expression of individual will rather than the tool of powerful families, in striving to uphold codes of honor that did not always conform to the views of the elite, and in serving as a Catholic protector of female virtue by enforcing the sacrament of marriage when premarital sex occurred, the Church found itself defending marriage choices that were routinely met with scorn from the upper classes. These arguments are presented masterfully in Patricia Seed, *To Love, Honor, and Obey in Colonial Mexico: Conflicts over Marriage Choice, 1574–1821* (Stanford: Stanford University Press, 1988). This tenet of Church doctrine was to be reversed in the eighteenth century – dramatically so with the issuance of the Royal Pragmatic decree of 1778, which enabled parental intervention in marriages of unequal station. However, the argument can be made that a baseline of sanctioned, fluid interracial marital activity had already been established, especially among the lower classes, and that it was not easy to undermine. As marriage patterns assumed a life of their own, they served as indicators of cultural forces that brewed beneath the regularity of established social norms.

[4] It is true that much miscegenation took place in consensual unions, which was sometimes seen as a better option than marriage.

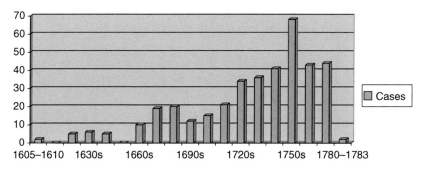

FIGURE 15 Marriages of Lobos and Moriscos in Mexico City by Decade, 1605–1783.
Source: Derived from table of marriage cases in Appendix A.

repository to discover its insights into the behavior and larger impact of Mexico's lobos, moriscos, chinos, and coyotes.

The Mexican national archives have preserved the records of close to 400 marriages celebrated by moriscos, lobos, coyotes, and chinos between the early seventeenth and late eighteenth centuries, primarily in Mexico City and its greater environs. The vast majority occurred in the eighteenth century, especially between 1720 and 1780 (see Figure 15).

In fact, just over half of all recorded marriages involving the extreme castas were celebrated between 1740 and the early 1780s, with the last case in 1783, shortly after the issuance of the Real Pragmática.[5] Only a small number of extreme casta nuptials were recorded prior to 1660, but from 1660 to 1720, there was a fairly steady (albeit small) flow of marriage petitions, averaging about 16 per decade. The unions brought together roughly 770 brides and grooms and called on 1,095 witnesses to testify to the character of the marriage supplicants as well as the legitimacy of their nuptials (see Table 6.1).

Immediately striking in the population sample covered in the marriage applications is the degree to which moriscos predominated among the brides and grooms. Since lobos and coyotes were more of a presence elsewhere in the colony, we might have expected to find at least a few more of them in the Mexico City marriage record. Lobos in particular were found in appreciable numbers in the 1777 census (see Table 5.1). That they did not contract more nuptials in the capital might not have been due solely to

[5] Asunción Lavrin, *Sexuality and Marriage in Colonial Latin America* (Lincoln: University of Nebraska Press, 1989); Patricia Seed, *To Love, Honor, and Obey*; Steinar A. Saether, "Bourbon Absolutism and Marriage Reform in Late Colonial Spanish America," *The Americas* 59, no. 4 (2003): 475–509.

TABLE 6.1 *Brides, Grooms, and Witnesses in Marriages of Extreme Castas, Mexico City, 1605–1783*

	Brides	Grooms	Female Witnesses	Male Witnesses	Subtotal
Castizo	20	21	1	61	103
Chino	16	8	2	10	36
Coyote	1	3	0	0	4
Español	42	75	17	497	631
Indio	13	1	2	41	57
Lobo	21	8	0	1	30
Mestizo	45	38	12	140	235
Moreno	0	0	0	2	2
Morisco	201	149	5	41	396
Mulato	15	56	10	157	238
Negro	7	9	10	22	48
Pardo	1	8	0	21	30
Unknown	3	9	4	39	55
Totals	385	385	63	1,032	1,865

Source: Derived from the table of marriage cases in Appendix A.

demography. One of the great criticisms of marriage evidence is its failure to capture consensual unions, which were probably more prevalent than marriages themselves.[6] Marriage could be costly, with clerical fees amounting to nearly six weeks of an ordinary laborer's salary. Additionally, the betrothed had to display mastery over Church doctrine – perhaps less a problem in Mexico City with its army of clerics than in remote rural areas with limited access to priests.[7] Under these pressures, it may be that the capital's lobos and coyotes, already fewer in number than moriscos, embarked upon consensual unions with frequency, rendering them even more invisible in the archival marriage record.

Table 6.2 displays the marriage patterns of the extreme castas. Noteworthy here is the extent to which lobos and moriscos were exogamous. No lobos intermarried with each other, and just 19 (13 percent) of moriscos did so. Coyotes exhibited the same tendencies, but their numbers are simply too small to permit drawing firm conclusions.

[6] Seed, *To Love, Honor, and Obey*, 25–26.
[7] William Taylor, *Magistrates of the Sacred: Priests and Parishioners in Eighteenth-Century Mexico* (Stanford: Stanford University Press, 1996), 244, 660–661. Of course, in rural areas priests may have adapted their expectations regarding knowledge of Church doctrine to the abilities and level of learning of their congregations.

TABLE 6.2 *Marriage Patterns of Extreme Castas in Mexico City, 1605–1783*

	Mestiza	Loba	Morisca	Española	Castiza	China	India	Negra	Parda	Mulata	Unknown	Coyota	Total
Castizo	1		20										21
Chino		1	1	1				5		1			9
Coyote				2			1						3
Español		3	68			2							73
Indio													0
Lobo	3			2	1		1			1			8
Mestizo		5	31			1							37
Morisco	40	3	19	35	18	1	11	2	1	13	3	1	147
Mulato		6	44		1	4							55
Negro		2				7							9
Pardo			8										8
Unknown		1	7			1							9
Total	44	21	198	40	20	16	13	7	1	15	3	1	379

Source: Derived from the table of marriage cases in Appendix A.

The data is particularly arresting when we consider that endogamy was normative for most of New Spain's major casta groups, especially Indians, whose sheer number facilitated the highest endogamous intermarriage rates in the colony. Although far scarcer than Indians, whites exhibited the second-greatest degree of endogamy, followed by mestizos, and finally by people of African descent. The rate of endogamy varied by region and time period. In seventeenth-century Guanajuato and eighteenth-century Antequera, free-colored endogamy exceeded that of mestizos and castizos. In Mexico City, indigenous endogamy proved difficult to maintain, in part due to a larger and more diverse urban populace. Depending on the moment, endogamy might be more common among mestizos than among indios. Similarly, in Charcas and Zamora, rates of native endogamy could be lower than that of whites.[8] By and large, though, the colony-wide trend was for people of African descent to be the least endogamous group. Among blacks and free-coloreds, endogamy was strongest in the sixteenth and seventeenth centuries, with rates declining steadily after 1650 and plunging further over the course of the eighteenth century.[9] The shrinking

[8] See Vinson, *Bearing Arms for His Majesty*, p. 264 n. 108; and Leon Yacher, "Marriage Migration and Racial Mixing in Colonial Tlazazalca (Michoacán, Mexico), 1750–1800" (PhD diss.: Syracuse University, Department of Geography, 1977), especially 7–9.

[9] The prevalence of early seventeenth-century slavery in Mexico, with annual imports averaging around 1,871 persons per annum, combined with patterns in the transatlantic slave trade that tended to import Africans in ethnic clusters (rather than as disparate groups), meant that first-generation African populations residing in places like Mexico City were not just able to marry with other blacks but also with individuals who shared their ethnic moniker. It is true that that these interethnic unions probably did not closely mimic those of Africans living on the continent. Indeed, they could be deemed interethnic only by applying the labels used by the African slave trade. With this understanding, we can find in the marriage record clusters of "Biafara" slaves wedded to each other and parallel cases for the Bran, Congolese, Angolans, and others. Concomitant with this notion of enforced endogamy was a rise in the number of slaves born in Mexico and a surge in the colony's free people of color. By 1646, there were 116,529 creole free-coloreds and slaves in New Spain in addition to 35,089 Africans, who were mainly slaves. The creole sector would grow throughout the colonial period, spiking to over 370,000 in the 1790s. Many of the creoles married other creoles during the heyday of the Mexican transatlantic slave trade (1595–1639); some offered themselves as marriage partners to African-born slaves. See Herman Bennett, *Africans in Colonial Mexico*, 23, 79–125; Gwendolyn Midlo Hall, *Slavery and African Ethnicities in the Americas: Restoring the Links* (Chapel Hill: University of North Carolina Press, 2005); John K. Thornton, *Africa and Africans in the Making of the Atlantic World, 1400–1800* (Cambridge: Cambridge University Press, 1998); Frank T. Proctor, "Afro-Mexican Slave Labor in the Obrajes de Panos of New Spain, Seventeenth and Eighteenth Centuries," *The Americas* 60, no. 1 (2003): 33–58; and Proctor, *Damned Notions of Liberty*, 37–67. For patterns of demography, see Aguirre Beltrán, *La población negra en México*, 222–230; and Shelburne F. Cook and Woodrow Borah, *Essays in Population*

transatlantic slave trade has been credited for delivering fatal blows to black efforts to sustain higher marital endogamy rates and propelling exogamous unions.[10] Such patterns uphold the notion posited in Chapter 5 that miscegenation within formal family and household structures was probably more prevalent among Mexico's black population than among other groups in New Spain.

Armed with this knowledge, we can take a second look at Mexico City's extreme casta marriage patterns to better understand their inordinately strong leanings toward exogamy. Have we taken a viewpoint that is simply too narrow? Was it even plausible to expect greater degrees of endogamy from esoteric groups whose numbers were so low to start with? If we were to take a slightly different approach in examining the evidence, how would marriage patterns among Mexico City's extreme castas compare against what we know about the broader trends found in other parts of New Spain? Taking all of this into consideration, I would like to suggest that in order to understand extreme casta endogamy in the city, we might need to broaden our frame. Given that moriscos and lobos, the two largest groups encountered in our source documents, were fundamentally understood within the framework of blackness, I would like to posit that endogamy for these two groups might be best conceived as embracing intermarriages within the larger set of Afro-castas. This would mean that we can consider marriages between mulatos and moriscos, or between lobos and moriscos, as endogamous, an approach that has been followed by many historians previously.[11]

History: Mexico and the Caribbean, Vol. 2 (Berkeley: University of California Press, 1971), 180–269. Analyses of patterns of endogamy and exogamy have offered important critiques on the limitations of marriage evidence. Some scholars believe that we have not paid enough attention to consensual unions. What we may find is that there were scores of such unions that connected people of African descent to a wider spectrum of society. If so, this militated against arguments for endogamy amongst Afro-castas. An important work along this line of thought is María Elisa Velázquez and Ethel Correa Duró, *Poblaciones y culturas de origen africano en México* (Mexico City: Instituto Nacional de Antropología e Historia, 2005), 229–309.

[10] For discussion on the decline of slavery, see Dennis N. Valdés, "The Decline of Slavery in Mexico," *The Americas* 44, no. 2 (October 1987): 167–194; Proctor, "Afro-Mexican Slave Labor"; Carroll, *Blacks in Colonial Veracruz*, 28–39; and Naveda Chávez-Hita, *Esclavos negros en las haciendas azucareras de Córdoba*. Note that Frank Proctor has strong criticism for those who have assigned great value to the declining slave trade as a major reason for slips in black endogamy. He suggests that such studies adopt an overly narrow understanding of black endogamy. See Proctor, *Damned Notions of Liberty*.

[11] As mentioned earlier, historians have often aggregated these groups because of the small number of extreme castas, vis-à-vis the numbers in the more normative categories. For ease of demographic analysis, bringing these groups together has often made sense.

I offer this wider framework with caution. One of my reasons for writing this book is to work toward a better understanding of the finer nuances that may have existed between castas. For instance, there could sometimes be appreciable differences between negros and mulatos, and in some communities it might even be true that mulatos and lobos shared a greater cultural connection with indios and mestizos than with negros. Regardless, as I've noted in this book's Preface, I find good reason to believe that a broader black cultural sphere may have emerged in colonial Mexico over time.[12] This is not to suggest that connections among blacks bound the Afro-casta groups into a single community or anything close to one. Rather, the bonds were more scattered, inconsistent, and protean in nature. Some people of African descent felt a sense of affinity to one another, even if highly leveraged through institutions, economic relationships, or different types of connections. Meanwhile, other people of African descent were at best indifferent to each other.[13]

---

[12] For works that I feel seem to suggest the emergence of a black cultural sphere, see Joan Cameron Bristol, *Christians, Blasphemers, and Witches*; Laura A. Lewis, *Chocolate and Corn Flour: History, Race, and Place in the Making of "Black" Mexico* (Durham: Duke University Press, 2012); Bristol and Restall, "Potions and Perils: Love-Magic in Seventeenth-Century Afro-Mexico and Afro-Yucatan," in Vinson and Restall, *Black Mexico*, 155–179; Nicole von Germeten, "Corporate Salvation in a Colonial Society: Confraternities and Social Mobility for Africans and Their Descendants in New Spain" (PhD diss.: University of California, Berkeley, 2003); von Germeten, *Black Blood Brothers: Confraternities and Social Mobility for Afro-Mexicans* (Florida: University Press of Florida, 2006); Bennett, *Colonial Blackness*; Restall, *The Black Middle*; Andrew Fisher, "Negotiating Two Worlds: The Free-Black Experience in Guerrero's Tierra Caliente," in *Black Mexico*, 51–71; von Germeten, "Colonial Middle Men? Mulatto Identity in New Spain's Confraternities," in *Black Mexico*, 136–154; Carroll, "Black Aliens and Black Natives in New Spain's Indigenous Communities," in *Black Mexico*, 72–95; Norma Angélica Castillo Palma, "Cohabitación y conflictividad entre afromestizos y nahuas en el México central," in *Pautas de convivencia étnica en la América Latina colonial: (indios, negros, mulatos, pardos y esclavos)*, ed. Juan Manuel de la Serna (Mexico City: Universidad Nacional Autónoma de México, 2005), 163–185; R. C. Schwaller "Mulata, Hija de Negro y India"; Herman L. Bennett, "The Subject in the Plot: National Boundaries and the 'History' of the Black Atlantic," *African Studies Review* 43, no. 1 (April 2000): 101–124; Bennett, "Sons of Adam: Text, Context, and the Early Modern African Subject," *Representations* 92, no. 1 (Fall 2005): 16–41; Bennett, "Genealogies to a Past: Africa, Ethnicity, and Marriage in Seventeenth-Century Mexico," in *New Studies in American Slavery*, eds. Edward E. Baptist and Stephanie M. H. Camp (Athens: University of Georgia Press, 2005), 127–147; Pablo Sierra, "Urban Slavery in Colonial Puebla de los Ángeles, 1536-1708," (PhD diss.: UCLA, 2013); Danielle Terrazas Williams, "Capitalizing Subjects: Free African-Descended Women of Means in Xalapa, Veracruz during the Long Seventeenth Century," (PhD diss.: Duke University, 2013).

[13] Even through marriage, the union of Afro-castas did not necessarily generate a distinct Afro-Mexican culture.

Bearing the possible existence of a black cultural sphere in mind (fragmented though it may be), some have posited ethnicity as a more useful focus for understanding colonial relationships.[14] I will expand on this notion here to consider the Afro-castas as a broad ethnic group in the context of the archival marriage evidence. In this light, it can be said that roughly one-quarter (26 percent) of morisco marriages were to other members of the Afro-castas, as were just over one-third (36 percent) of morisca marriages. Applying the same principle, lobas emerge as the most endogamous group, with over half marrying moriscos, mulatos, or negros. Moriscas provided a strong marriage option for mulatos, whom they wedded with frequency. Moriscas also married morisco men; among the Afro-castas, they were the most frequent marriage partners of such men. Again drawing from the sample, we can say that women of the extreme castas who were of partial African ancestry demonstrated the greatest propensity to building ties among the broader Afro-castas, with the overwhelming majority of their spouses being free-coloreds rather than slaves.

The remaining nuptials tell a different story. The extreme castas exhibited striking vaults across the major ethnic boundaries. Close to half of all moriscas contracted marriages with either españoles (34.3 percent) or castizos (10 percent); marriages to mestizos were also frequent (15.6 percent). Morisco men, unlike women, chose mestiza spouses with the greatest frequency (27 percent), but their unions with españolas (24 percent) and castizas (12 percent) were also significant, representing over one-third of their total marriages. The near parity between mestiza and española

---

[14] According to this view, there probably existed a set of Indian and African castas that exhibited more interactions with members of their own group than not. It is also likely that Spaniards comprised a third "ethnicity," albeit attached to a smaller complement of castas, since any major expansions of Spanish ethnicity threatened the primary objective of the casta regime: preserving whiteness. While not necessarily constituting an ethnicity per se, mestizos represented another critical force in the larger social order, bearing strong links to the Indian and Spanish worlds. Considering the several core ethnicities, scholars such as Douglas Cope have persuasively argued that one of the most important arenas of interethnic interaction was along the mestizo-mulato boundary, since crossings between these groups represented true movement between ethnic categories, especially the Indian and African sectors. Equally important were interactions that bridged the boundary of the españoles – one we might label the español-casta boundary. Other forms of casta movement potentially had less meaning in the larger casta system, since they were essentially contained within the parameters of the broad ethnic framework These basic ideas are outlined by Douglas Cope in *The Limits of Racial Domination*, 76–85. Note that Patrick Carroll has been developing an important idea that corresponds well with the discussion here, describing colonial Mexico's three anchor ethnicities as "New Spain's social trinity." My observations would certainly dovetail with this idea.

brides is revealing in that both served as virtually equal-opportunity spouses for morisco males.

How does all of this stack up against the trends we find in the larger city, and against the general understanding that New Spain's Afro-castas were highly exogamous? First, it becomes clear that morisco males represented a vanguard of exogamy. Consider the general black marriage patterns in the capital: between 1670 and 1704, 62 percent of Afro-casta women in Mexico City's Sagrario Metropolitano parish were endogamous, as were 47 percent of the men.[15] Between 1720 and 1800, the spouses of 44 percent of the city's married mulatas, moriscas, negras, and lobas were other blacks, and just 31.5 percent were españoles.[16] Afro-casta men exhibited almost the exact same rate of marital endogamy as black women, though their marriages to españolas was considerably lower – just 22 percent. Black men did marry mestizas to a significant extent (34 percent) during this period.[17] Regardless, our sample shows that morisco male exogamy substantially outpaced baseline Afro-casta norms.

Consequently, another story emerging from our analysis of extreme casta marriage patterns is that if a broader black cultural community was being shaped in Mexico City, moriscos were at its edges. And while morisca women were welcome choices for Afro-casta grooms, they were also prime spousal partners for creole and castizo men. Marriages to castizos present an interesting situation: castizos too could represent a form of extreme casta. Whereas the category was widely recognized by the eighteenth century, castizos still did not appear in great numbers even though they were widely distributed throughout New Spain. While the number of castizos marrying morisco brides and grooms was a very small part of the larger marriage picture in Mexico City, the proportion of nuptials they contracted with the moriscos and moriscas in our sample was relatively high. Typically, New Spain's castizos did not marry

---

[15] Part of the explanation for greater rates of female endogamy, particularly prior to 1700, had to do with slavery. Many mulata and negra women who approached the altar were themselves slaves and marrying enslaved men, who tended to be black. By contrast, Mexico City's male slaves had more marriage options, taking brides from both the enslaved and free populations after 1650, thereby opening up for themselves a wider spectrum of casta possibilities. Slavery, however, did not pose a major factor in influencing marriage patterns among the extreme castas. Just nine moriscos and lobos encountered in the marriage applications were slaves, and of those, just three intermarried with other Afro-castas.

[16] Juan Javier Pescador, *De bautizados a fieles difuntos: familia y mentalidades en una parroquia urbana, Santa Catarina de México, 1568–1820* (Mexico City: Colegio de México, Centro de Estudios Demográficos y de Desarrollo Urbano, 1992), 147–148.

[17] Ibid., 151. Note that Pescador combines mestiza and castiza data in his assessment.

members of the Afro-castas. In Guanajuato, Cholula, Jalapa, Orizaba, and even parts of Mexico City during the middle to late eighteenth century, castizos explicitly preferred mestizos, españoles, or fellow castizos as spouses.[18] What our Mexico City data seemingly demonstrate is that moriscos, at least in the capital, may have provided a niche source of partners within the Afro-castas for castizo nuptials.

Similarities between moriscos and castizos may have served to attract each group to the other. Both were the nearest castas to whites in terms of their racial mixture. In 1753, castizos and moriscos exhibited similar employment patterns in the Mexico City, and these were often associated with upward social mobility.[19] In the 1790s, moriscos held some of the highest occupational status among the Afro-castas, with more than 60 percent being artisans.[20] In fact, morisco employment in artisan positions at this time actually significantly outpaced that of castizos, of whom just 12.7 percent were occupied in these trades.[21] Although African admixture stood as an obvious difference separating these two casta groups, this phenotypic fact alone may not have prevented relationships across the divide, especially given the commonalities in their urban lives.

In general, the social status of the whites and castizos who married Mexico City's moriscos was not at the higher end of society. So while there was certainly movement across somatic lines, it is unclear whether it translated into significant social and economic advancement for moriscos.

---

[18] See Pilar Gonzalbo, *Familias iberoamericanas: historia, identidad y conflictos* (Mexico City: Colegio de México, 2001), 246; Brading, "Grupos étnicos," 246; Castillo Palma, *Cholula, sociedad mestiza en ciudad india: un análisis de las consecuencias demográficas, económicas y sociales del mestizaje en una ciudad novohispana (1649–1796)* (Mexico City: Plaza y Valdés, 2001), 394–397. Note that castizo endogamy increased over the course of the eighteenth century. Pescador does not isolate castizos from mestizos but rather treats them as one group. Pescador, *De bautizados,* 145–147, 150–151; Matilde Souto Mantecón and Patricia Torres Mez, "La población del la antigua parroquia del pueblo de Xalapa (1777)," in Pérez Toledo and Klein, *Población y estructura urbana en México,* 96–97. In *The Limits of Racial Domination* (82–83), Cope shows that castizos in the late seventeenth century tended to marry mestizos. The idea of a castizo escape hatch is developed in Bruce Castleman, "Social Climbers in a Colonial Mexican City: Individual Mobility within the Sistema de Castas in Orizaba, 1777–1791," *Colonial Latin American Review* 10, no. 2 (2001): 229–249.

[19] Patricia Seed, "Social Dimensions of Race: Mexico City, 1753," *Hispanic American Historical Review* 62, no. 4 (November 1982): 598.

[20] Vinson, "From Dawn 'til Dusk: Black Labor in Late Colonial Mexico," in Vinson and Restall, *Black Mexico,* 111–112.

[21] The data for both moriscos and castizos is drawn from analyses of Cuarteles 1, 20, and 23. For more on the occupational structure of Mexico City during 1790, see Pérez Toledo and Klein, *Población y estructura social de la Ciudad de México,* 147–191.

TABLE 6.3 *Illegitimacy Rates for Spouses of Morisco Men and Women in Mexico City's Marriage Cases, 1605–1783*

Casta of Spouse	Moriscos	Moriscas
Afro-casta	10 (26)	34 (48)
Mestizo/castizo	18 (31)	8 (16)
Español	13 (37)	14 (21)

Source: Derived from the table of marriage cases in Appendix A.
The number in parentheses is the percentage of the whole represented by the number beside it.

Of the españoles marrying moriscas, 14 (21 percent) could not readily confirm their parentage and were probably illegitimate (see Table 6.3). One was formally listed as an orphan; others may have been abandoned as children (*expósitos*) and incorporated into households of limited financial means and social position.[22]

Many of the men who married moriscas, particularly españoles, also tended to be much older than other men who married in Mexico City. The median age of the whites marrying morisca women was 30; their average age was 42. By contrast, the typical español who approached the altar in the capital, at least in the eighteenth century, was about 25 years old.[23] The advanced age of the moriscas' white grooms might indicate greater stability and economic security, since their position in the labor arena was probably in large part already established. On the other hand, their economic opportunities may have been lower than those of younger men who were setting out to make their mark; little of this can be determined definitively from the evidence. What we do know is that despite being older, the vast majority of these men were not taking moriscas as second brides – just ten were widowers. Morisca spouses were essentially first-choice options, and

[22] For interesting recent perspectives on *expósitos*, see Ondina E. González and Bianca Premo, *Raising an Empire*, and Premo, *Children of the Father King: Youth, Authority, and Legal Minority in Colonial Lima* (Chapel Hill: University of North Carolina Press, 2005). Uncertain lineage could also place casta status in doubt. Illegitimacy rates, high for Mexico City and much of New Spain, reflected escalating rates of cross-racial contact in the empire, as well as the proliferation of consensual unions. See Castillo Palma, *Cholula, Sociedad Mestiza*, 338–358. For some published illegitimacy rates in Mexico City, see Pescador, *De bautizados*, 138–141; Gonzalbo Aizpuru, *Familia y orden colonial*, 164–165; and Twinam, *Public Lives, Private Secrets*, 10–13. Finally, note that the illegitimacy rate for españoles who married moriscas was probably the same or lower than the rate for the city as a whole. Twinam cites this rate as 30 percent, but the rate was subject to great annual fluctuation.

[23] The average age was 25.6; the median age was 24. See Pescador, *De bautizados*, 148.

given the wide age disparity in a number of cases, many moriscas were probably trophy wives. In addition, the late age of marriage suggests that some of these españoles were also perhaps finally formalizing consensual unions that had existed for some time. This was certainly the case in 1764, when 75-year-old Manuel Ortega, the oldest groom in the group, finally married his consort of five years, the 27-year-old María Paula Otañes.[24]

Only a few españoles seem to have been goaded into marriage by extenuating circumstances. Five had landed in jail for having premarital sex with their fiancées and were subsequently coerced by the authorities to contract nuptials. Two men desperately sought marriage on their deathbeds after contracting grave illnesses, a move that supposedly cleansed their souls of sinful cohabitation and illicit sex. In short, white male grooms in the sample wanted and desired their morisca mates, whom they considered attractive brides in a variety of senses. While the majority of the español grooms and suitors of the city's moriscas were not well-to-do, some had pretensions of grandeur, substantiated or not. Pedro Peralta, who married in Mexico City's Sagrario Metropolitano parish in 1764, was thoroughly insulted when he was asked by the notaries to sign his name on his marriage application papers. Being a Spaniard, he perhaps felt entitled to an exemption from dealing with such trifling matters.[25] In 1680, Domingo Cortés, the son of Fernando Cortés y Moctezuma, and the fiancé of Bernabella de Huertas, a morisca, presumably bore the lineage of the great conquistador Hernán Cortés. While there were many self-fashioned progeny of the Cortés line living in Mexico City, Domingo did appear to have some of the right connections – particularly links to the governor of an Indian barrio who may have been his in-law or a close acquaintance.[26] Five more español grooms carried the honorific title of *don*. Although not always a faithful indicator of status and wealth, the don and doña titles were successfully used to demarcate social distance frequently enough to suggest that they were meaningful distinctions.[27] Such was probably the case with don Pedro

---

[24] AGN, Matrimonios, vol. 163, exp. 68.

[25] AGN, Matrimonios, vol. 38, exp. 78, fols. 314–316v.

[26] AGN, Matrimonios, vol. 96, exp. 37, fols. 225–228.

[27] Rodney Anderson, "Race and Social Stratification: A Comparison of Working-Class Spaniards, Indians, and Castas in Guadalajara, Mexico in 1821," *Hispanic American Historical Review* 68, no. 2 (1988): 209–243. Note that in my sample all the marriages of *don* and *doña* brides and grooms to members of the extreme castas took place after 1729, somewhat late in the colonial period. This fact accentuates the rarity of the phenomenon in Mexico City. Note as well that even the men in the sample who carried the title *don* were not always free of a dubious lineage. The español don Joseph de Herrera, who married María Josepha Guerrero in 1729, serves as a prime example. Both his birth origins

López, the 19-year-old who in 1774 married doña María Josepha Vélis, one of Mexico City's few morisca doñas.[28] In this instance, however, it was probably his wife's connections and status that were socially superior. Don Pedro's own ties, as revealed by his witnesses, included two artisans of lower standing, one a carpenter and the other a tailor (relatively common occupations within Mexico's City's working class). Doña Maria's witnesses included two silversmiths, members of one of the most respected and lucrative artisan professions in the colony. We can conjecture that don Pedro was eager to wed doña Maria – not only for love, but also as an opportunity to cement and enhance his own network. The same may have been true of don Joseph de la Luna Montilla, who in 1750 wed María Gertrudis de Zúñiga y Mora, the morisca daughter of a well-connected military captain.[29]

As has been noted earlier, morisco men, unlike moriscas, were more prone to choose spouses who were mestizas. Next in line were españolas and then castizas. As with their morisca counterparts, a morisco's status could be important, for good or for ill, in obtaining matches with españolas. In 1765, the 20-year-old morisco merchant Joseph de Montalbán applied for marriage with doña María Raphaela Andre Olivia, a 15-year-old white *doncella* from Cuernavaca. Despite his youth, Joseph was accomplished and had great connections. He had traveled extensively on business trips throughout the colony with one of his marriage witnesses, don Blás Andreu de Olivar, a prominent trader and patrician.[30] Also in the groom's corner was an attorney of the Real Audiencia, don Jacobo Montejano. The young

---

and parentage were unclear. It is likely that he and his morisca wife were illegitimate, but don Joseph's skin color and occupational success nonetheless earned him the title, as unequivocally confirmed by the three white witnesses to the couple's marriage.

[28] AGN, Matrimonios, vol. 150, exp. 86. I found only one morisca in the marriage record who was listed as a *doña*.

[29] AGN, Matrimonios, vol. 199, exp. 18. Another español, don Cristobal Cuenca y Mollero, from Castile, sought marriage with the 18-year-old María de la Encarnación Narváez, a morisca libre. The social imbalance that one might presume existed between a mainland Spaniard and an Afro-casta was not readily apparent in this instance. María de la Encarnación took great care to stress that she was not a slave, describing herself as "libre de cautiverio." Of course, merely announcing this fact as late as 1731 immediately raised suspicions about her provenance, status, and social standing. Yet she and her husband seemed to share a common social network that included a Church musician, a master coachmaker, and a tailor. None of these were particularly distinguished ties; instead, they suggested a sort of lower-middling position in the urban hierarchy for both the bride and groom. Their union essentially confirmed this status for them in the city. AGN, Matrimonios, vol. 120, exp. 54, fols. 265–279v.

[30] AGN, General de Parte, vol. 39, exp. 15, fol. 9v; AGN, Bienes Nacionales, vol. 91, exp. 43; AGN, General de Parte, vol. 43, exp. 80, fols. 43v–44; AGN, Indiferente Virreinal, caja 1888, exp. 14, fols. 1–14; AGN, General de Parte, vol. 37, exp. 244, fols. 205v–206.

María Raphaela, although a Spaniard, was of less than patrician background, being an orphan. Even if she had been a member of an elite family, her condition might have incited the prejudices of the upper class, but it might also have made her more accessible to Joseph.[31] Regardless, it is clear that he was among the better-heeled moriscos in the city and that he utilized his social capital for an advantageous marriage.[32]

María is the only white or castiza recorded as a doña who married someone of the extreme castas in Mexico City. Others tended to be of lower social station, such as the seven women who declared poverty in their marriage petitions or lived scandalously with their morisco male partners.[33] Thirteen españolas were either illegitimate or did not demonstrate sufficient proof that they knew both of their parents.[34] This number represents a higher proportion of illegitimacy than that among the white males who were married to moriscas. In fact, the illegitimacy index of these white brides was higher than those of the mestiza and Afro-casta spouses of Mexico City's moriscos (shown in Table 6.3).

While the sample is small, it seems to indicate that morisco grooms exhibited more-relaxed standards in accepting the illegitimacy of white women than they did for other potential brides. The high illegitimacy rate among white females also tended to mean that their kinship networks were weaker, which probably reduced the social capital that they could theoretically bring to a marriage. Weaker family ties could also mean that there were fewer layers of protection surrounding these women, making them easier to court and marry. On the flip side, greater legitimacy among Afro-casta women implied that these brides may have enjoyed a higher status (though not necessarily greater wealth), based on deeper and more-reliable family connections. Legitimacy was also a badge of honor – one in which they held an edge over their white female counterparts in their nuptials with morisco grooms. The española brides of morisco men were much younger and more normative than the white males who married moriscas. These women's average age was 23, with a median age of 21.5. In eighteenth-century Mexico City, most white women approached the altar at the age of 20.[35]

---

[31] Ann Twinam, "The Church, the State, and the Abandoned: Expósitos in Late Eighteenth-Century Havana," in González and Premo, *Raising an Empire*, 167.

[32] He may have been the same individual who until the 1780s was also an "escribano del juzgado privativo de tierras y aguas." See AGN, Indiferente Virreinal, caja 657 (Oficios Vendibles), exp. 9, fols. 1–52. If this is the case, then over time he became a *don* himself.

[33] Note that there were orphans among them.

[34] This was the case for 13 españolas, or 37 percent of the sample.

[35] Pescador, *De bautizados*, 144.

TABLE 6.4 *Casta of Witnesses for Morisco Brides and Grooms, Mexico City, 1605–1783*

	Brides	Grooms	Subtotal
Español	220	155	375
Castizo	20	22	42
Mestizo	57	54	111
Mulato	71	65	136
Pardo	8	12	20
Negro	4	4	8
Morisco	18	28	46
Indio	11	14	25
Chino	2	0	2
Unknown	19	16	35
Total	430	370	800

Source: Derived from the table of marriage cases in Appendix A.

The slightly higher ages of the españolas in our sample can be partly credited to the presence of seven widows. Without them, morisco-española marriage patterns appear perfectly normative, with the women's averaging 20.8 years of age at marriage. For both morisco brides and grooms, a presumed affinity to whites and mestizos through kinship ties and social connections (even stronger than those of mulatos) may have partly accounted for their increased pairing with españoles. Perhaps few other Afro-castas, apart from mulatos blancos, enjoyed such closeness.

Marriage witnesses, often cited as a reliable source for understanding the relationships of the betrothed by revealing friendships and important patron-client networks, help substantiate such claims. The largest casta group that testified for morisco marriage celebrants was españoles, who represent almost half of all their witnesses (see Table 6.4).

It is possible that in the colonial world the importance of having españoles serve as witnesses to binding legal documents skewed the evidence, causing them to be overrepresented as witnesses in marriage applications throughout the colony. When an español male, especially a well-connected elder, attested to the veracity of one's claims, credibility was instantly enhanced in the eyes of the government and the clergy, who were themselves largely españoles. But even after factoring in the over-representation of español witnesses, the marriage evidence shows that moriscos had very wide access to this group, signaling that españoles were probably also a solid presence in their social worlds – as friends, confidants, employers, overseers, relatives, and coworkers.[36] Women appear to have had deeper access to these white witnesses than men did. Over half of their testifiers were españoles, as opposed to 44 percent of their male counterparts' attestants. However, morisco men tended to know their white witnesses better. Approximately 55 percent of the español witnesses said that they had known the morisco groom for their entire lives, while only 33 percent claimed to have known the brides for as long.[37]

The data also reveals that morisco men incorporated Afro-casta witnesses into the marriage application process more often than moriscas did. But in a situation almost inverse to with the one cited previously, the morisca brides knew their Afro-casta witnesses better. Over half (51 percent) of all black witnesses for morisca brides had known them for their entire lives, in contrast to just 28 percent of the black testifiers for morisco grooms.[38]

While the overwhelming number of witnesses for all the marriages of moriscos and moriscas were españoles, the preponderance of Afro-castas and the extent to which they knew the marriage supplicants confirms their strong connection to this extreme casta group. Again, it is necessary to note that the nature and uses of the archival record necessarily shaped the witness pool. In all likelihood there was an underrepresentation of Afro-castas for the purpose of presenting to the Church the most compelling assortment of witnesses. Mestizos too were affected by these priorities, slipping to a distant third in the ranking of witnesses.[39] Natives and chinos were rarely called to serve as attestant – perhaps a reflection of their low affinity with moriscos, their weaker demographic presence in certain parts of the city (particularly for chinos), and their diminished suitability as witnesses for these cases.

---

[36] Although slaves sometimes had fairly ready access to the white patricians who were their masters, this was not the case for the moriscos in this sample since there were so few slaves among them.

[37] Among witnesses who had not been early childhood friends of the bride or groom, morisca women tended to have known their español witnesses for slightly longer (10.6 years) than morisco men had known their own español witnesses (9.6 years). But given that women married earlier than men, this may have meant that they had known their español witnesses throughout adulthood, sometimes even stretching back into early adolescence.

[38] Of witnesses who had known morisco brides and grooms for shorter periods of time, moriscos tended to have been acquaintances for longer (10.2 years) than had moriscas (9 years).

[39] If one were to add castizos to their number, the margin narrows. But given the proximity of castizos to whiteness, a convincing argument can be made that they should better be aggregated to the españoles.

7

Betrothed: Identity's Riddle

One surprising feature of the marriage evidence is that the number of morisco marriage applications in Mexico City far overshadowed those of pardos. Pardos comprised an important Afro-Mexican population in other contexts, being found regularly in the ranks of confraternities and militias.[1] But in the marriage record for Mexico City, less than 1 percent of all marriage applications generated in the seventeenth and eighteenth centuries were requested by pardos. This figure was about the same as the number of marriage applications submitted by the more obscure lobos, which also stood near 1 percent. Mulato marriage requests ran highest at 10 percent of all marriage applications, with moriscos second at 5 percent.[2] One might conclude from this data that in New Spain's capital, mulatos and moriscos were the groups of African descent most prone to seek the sacrament of marriage.

What precisely does this mean? If moriscos were so prominent in the marriage market, why was their impact felt so lightly upon society, especially when compared to pardos, for instance? Was it that moriscos became meaningful as a social group primarily at the moment of marriage, only later (and in different contexts) to dissipate as they morphed into other casta groups? This idea would certainly be consistent with the position of those who contend that marriage was one of the moments in life in which casta categories mattered most, when greater care was taken in recording them, and when the degree of genealogical and somatic specificity needed to categorize an extreme casta became most useful in capturing the nuances of

---

[1] Vinson, *Bearing Arms for His Majesty*; von Germeten, *Black Blood Brothers*.
[2] There were 710 recorded mulato marriage petitions and 15 pardo marriage petitions.

one's background.[3] This idea is also consistent with the thinking of those who have observed that at the moment of marriage some mestizos and mulatos received a racial boost. Mulatos of lighter skin could find themselves elevated to moriscos, and mestizos might become castizos or Spaniards. These new somatic facts, preserved in the marriage record, could contradict statuses found in other government and ecclesiastical documents where one's casta remained unchanged.[4] Continuing to pursue the deeper meaning of the prevalence of moriscos in the marriage record, we ask this: Is it possible that their prominence reveals the morisco category as being especially meaningful principally to the Church? Was it mainly through the efforts of the Church and not the bride and groom that morisco identity was grafted onto individuals approaching the altar? Further, if this was the case, after those identified as moriscos wed, did they retain their caste status in everyday interactions, or did they revert back to living as members of another casta group?

Such questions are tricky and admittedly difficult to answer. Yet the archives provide us clues to the significance of what it meant to be a morisco, as well as that of bearing other casta labels. To explore those clues, we need to consider all the layers of evidence available to us, in light of the procedures involved in the marriage process. When a couple first visited their priest to declare their intent to marry, they were called on to answer a series of questions. Priests explained to the supplicants the seriousness of the process and emphasized the need to present accurate information under the eyes of God. After taking an oath, they were asked where they were from, where they resided, their calidad or casta, and their marital status. Each supplicant was also asked questions to determine whether or not they were of legitimate birth, as well as their age and the name of their fiancé. Equally important were questions related to the couple's degree of consanguinity. The Church defined and codified the degrees quite explicitly, allowing for some measure of intermarriage, especially in remote communities where intermarriage was nearly impossible to avoid.[5]

---

[3] Jason Frederick has found for the town of Teziutlan that casta was not always recorded at baptism. He has concluded that people likely entered the sistema de castas at the time of marriage, when their casta was more or less fully formed. This is an interesting suggestion, implying that casta needed its own process of evolution; i.e., as peopled developed, so did their casta. See Jason Frederick, "Without Impediment: Crossing Racial Boundaries in Colonial Mexico," *The Americas* 67, no. 4 (2011): 495–515.

[4] For the idea of a racial boost, or enhancement at marriage, see Seed, *Social Dimensions of Race*, 394.

[5] As a general principle, the closest relatives were barred from marrying.

As the questioning process (*diligencia*) unfolded, grooms were asked if they had been in any prior illicit relationships, if they had issued any pending and competing marriage proposals, and if they knew of any impediment that might otherwise interfere with the marriage. The priest also tried to establish that the bride and groom were choosing to marry of their own free will.[6] The Church's success in protecting the will of the bride and groom oscillated over time, given shifts in the ability of the Church to ward off the coercive influences of family and society, but at least in principle, complying with the wishes of the marriage celebrants remained a goal. Witnesses were further interrogated to affirm the accuracy of the claims they had made, after which, according to the mandates of the Council of Trent, the banns of marriage were announced from the pulpit on three successive Sundays. If no objections were raised within 24 hours following the publishing of the last banns, the couple was free to wed.[7]

The information gleaned by the priest was carefully recorded by a series of notaries and scribes. In the sixteenth century and for most of the seventeenth, diocesan notaries in Mexico City were responsible for taking care of these cases for secular parishes. It was preferred that these ecclesiastical notaries not be Church officials but rather, as articulated in the Laws of the Indies, *escribanos reales* (official recorders), who bore royal appointments that enabled them to practice throughout the Spanish realm. This differentiated them from public notaries, who typically operated solely within the confines of a town or city.[8] By the end of the 1600s and into the eighteenth century, the volume of work had escalated so much that marriage licenses and the application process itself had to be handled by the ecclesiastical notaries of the parishes.[9]

The documents reveal what seem to be three basic types of notaries involved in assembling the testimony of marriage applications in the Mexico City area. In the eighteenth century, the *notario mayor* of the Santo Oficio (Holy Office) would have been the chief notary involved in

---

[6] Seed, *To Love, Honor, and Obey*.

[7] Secret marriages were sometimes authorized by the Church without announcement of the banns. These were conducted in circumstances in which the will of the couple could be compromised if public announcements were made. Such marriages were done mainly in the sixteenth and seventeenth centuries and declined in the eighteenth century as the ability of the Church to act as an enforcer waned.

[8] Kathryn Burns, *Into the Archive: Writing and Power in Colonial Peru* (Durham: Duke University Press, 2010), 160 n. 73; and *Recopilación de leyes de los reynos de las Indias, mandadas imprimir y publicar por la Majestad Católica del Rey don Cárlos II*, 3 vols. (Madrid: Consejo de la Hispanidad, 1943), libro 5, tít. 8, ley 37.

[9] Seed, *To Love, Honor, and Obey*, 247.

gathering information and was typically present to hear the testimony of the bride and groom. A notario mayor frequently worked with one or more assistants who captured the couple's testimony. The notario mayor also stepped in to ratify and confirm all testimony, ensuring that the process and recordkeeping conformed to proper protocol and procedures. He seems to have been responsible for ensuring that the case file was read aloud or otherwise reviewed by the *juez provisor y vicario general del arzobispado*, who was ultimately responsible for dispatching marriage licenses to be granted by individual parish priests.[10] The notario mayor worked closely with the juez provisor. Ranked just below the notario mayor was the *notario receptor*, whose chief responsibilities included taking the testimony of marriage witnesses. There were instances where a single notario mayor handled the entire testimony of a case, but the notario receptor offered much-needed support and relief to his superiors in the task of completing marriage applications. Not infrequently, more than one notario receptor might be found working a marriage case.

In the seventeenth century and the first decade of the eighteenth century, *notarios públicos* could also sometimes be found working on case files. A notario público might be responsible for overseeing all testimony collection, ratifying the information, and (less frequently) dispatching licenses. Duties sometimes shifted. A notario público could be less involved in taking the testimony of the bride and groom than in gathering and ratifying witness testimony. Overall, the detailed panoply of job descriptions and responsibilities of the notary team could be stupefying, and between the end of the seventeenth century and the beginning of the eighteenth, there was frequent overlap and flux in their roles. Indeed, by the 1720s, the role of the notario público had largely vanished, in favor of a two-tiered system of collecting and processing information through a notario receptor and a notario mayor.

Notaries as well as scribes moved in and out of cases, and marriage applications were typically written by several different hands. The end product, the marriage file (*expediente*), was almost always a patchwork of information and opinions on the case, arranged into a set of formulaic documents. With several people involved in preparing each case, the information communicated in any marriage application could be subject to change at a variety of stages along the way. The numerous administrative details that had to be addressed presented opportunities for inconsistencies to arise in the text.

---

[10] The *juez provisor* or *vicario general* was the primary ecclesiastical judge of a diocese.

What made the process work was the overriding commitment to ascertaining accuracy. The complex layers and phases of a marriage application production all served that goal: to standardize information and convey the truth to match the purposes of the inquiry. In a perfect world, the mechanisms by which the information was collected and conveyed should have been largely invisible to the outside world. Whenever a notary's opinion, voice, or hand is detected in the documents, it was supposed to derive from their role as authenticators, inspiring confidence that what one read in the record was indeed true.[11]

All of this background information serves to help formulate a methodology to approach the marriage documentation for information on caste identity. By carefully examining witness and spousal testimonies, and by taking into account the role of notaries and scribes in shaping a marriage application, we can arrive at a sense of how brides, grooms, and witnesses understood their casta. If we chip away at some of the formulaic structure of the documents, we find that there were instances wherein people provided affirmation of their own casta and others in which their casta classifications were determined more by others. Scrutinizing marriage petitions for responses in which individuals (especially brides and grooms) used the first-person singular or plural form to describe their casta helps bring these distinctions to light. Descriptions in the first person make it likely that individuals were conveying their own sense of status in the caste hierarchy.

Examining the documents themselves is not enough to gain a handle on casta identity. It is also useful to analyze the notaries' data collection practices. Were certain types of testimony not admitted by specific notaries? Did some notaries seem more open than others to letting brides and grooms speak for themselves? What trends do we find in the notary evidence that testify for or against the veracity of the petitioners' allegations? It is true that these questions may not reveal ironclad truths, but used consistently they can help us get at a better sense of casta identity. Where it is possible, we have attempted to assess and evaluate the statements of lobo and morisco brides and grooms, as shown in Table 7.1.

The record tells us that the majority of brides and grooms (some 76 percent) probably declared their own casta; and in most instances, they seem to have done so as a couple. In contrast (and not shown in Table 7.1), just 20 percent of the witnesses declared their casta. This low number seems to

---

[11] Kathryn Burns's *Into the Archive* demonstrates many shortcomings in our ability to confide in the neutrality and objectiveness of notaries. They were not always distanced authenticators of testimony.

TABLE 7.1 *Declaration of Casta Status by Lobos and Moriscos, Brides and Grooms, Mexico City, 1605–1783*

	Moriscas	Moriscos	Lobos	Lobas	Subtotal
Self-declaration	145	119	7	15	286
	(72.5)	(80.4)	(87.5)	(75)	(76)
Declared by spouse	48	1	1	4	54
	(24)		(12.5)	(20)	(14.3)
Declared by other	3	26	0	1	30
	(1.5)	(17.5)		(5)	(7.9)
Unknown	4	2	0	0	3
	(2)				
Total	200	148	8	20	376
	(100)	(100)	(100)	(100)	(100)

Source: Derived from the table of marriage cases in Appendix A. The number in parentheses is the percentage of the whole represented by the number just above it.

have much to do with the manner in which their testimony was presented. It is very difficult to determine exactly who was articulating the witnesses' casta status.[12] It is likely that more witnesses expressed their own casta, but the structure of the documents does not allow us to prove this. Ultimately, therefore, the matrimonial record enables us to penetrate deeper into the claims of casta identity for brides and grooms than for witnesses.

Most brides and grooms articulated their casta during the opening phases of a marriage request, sometimes known as the *petición* (premarital investigation). Typically, the groom presented the request for marriage and thus often exercised a considerable amount of control over the testimony of the bride when the couple presented their case to clerics. Nonetheless, the language of many applications suggests that men and women appeared together before the authorities and that when they conveyed information such as their age, name, place of residence, birth, and calidad (casta), the information had been agreed upon jointly and accurately reflected the woman's opinion. Take for instance the petición of Sebastián Cortés y Moctezuma, a mestindio (a mixture of mestizo and indio) who sought the hand of María Plácida Therrasas in 1774. The opening of their application reads as follows:

[12] To determine if witnesses had declared their own casta or calidad, I located all instances in the documentation where a notary recorded phrases like "que dijo ser pardo," or "que dijo ser mestizo." In instances where these phrases were not recorded, I have assumed that we cannot know with certainty whether or not the witnesses were declaring their own casta or calidad.

Sebastian Manuel Cortés y Moctezuma, mestindio, soltero, natural y vecino de esta ciudad sin faltar, hijo legítimo de Pascual de Espiritu Santo Cortés y Moctezuma y Manuela de la Trinidad, *mi* edad veinte y cuatro años; y María Plácida Therrasas mestiza doncella, natural y vecino de esta ciudad sin haber ausencia, hija legítima de Manuel Therrasas y de María de Guadalupe Pérez, *mi* edad veinte y tres años, *parecemos* ante V.S. y *decimos* que para mejor servir a Dios nuestro Señor *tenemos* tratado matrimonio según orden de nuestra Santa Madre Iglesia para su efecto [emphases mine].[13]

The document excerpted here presents the marriage request as a joint endeavor of the couple and differs from that of Antonio de Roa, a morisco libre from Tecpan who sought the hand of Ana Dorantes in 1727. Recently widowed, Antonio presented all of the initial case proceedings himself, taking the liberty to describe Ana's casta. Later, however, Ana was interviewed separately by a notary to confirm that the information Antonio presented about her was correct, including her mestiza caste status.[14] This mode of cross-checking the groom's testimony was quite common and also served to help confirm, in a low-pressure, private setting, that the bride truly wanted to marry the groom.

To what extent did notaries influence the testimony of brides and grooms? Given the nature of the information that we have at our disposal, the question must be handled obliquely. Of the 85 identifiable notaries who compiled and produced the paperwork for the marriages of the extreme castas, there were 26 before whom brides and grooms sometimes failed to report their casta (see Table 7.2). Among these were 13 notaries before whom brides virtually never recorded their own casta. It is likely but not certain that the notaries themselves were responsible for the omissions and aberrations, either in the way they opted to present the information they gathered or in the manner in which they chose to collect it. If that is true, these notaries may have affected the testimonies of up to

---

[13] AGN, Matrimonios, vol. 6, exp. 8, fol. 22.

[14] AGN, Matrimonios, vol. 4, exp. 5, fols. 24–28v. For comparative purposes, the beginning of this case reads as follows: "Antonio de Roa, *morisco* libre, vecino del pueblo de Tecpan y viudo de Magdalena María que a quien fallecío nueve meses, y le enterro en est Sta. Iglesia Cathedral (como consta de la certificasion qu con la de vida solemnidad present), *mi* edad mayor de viente y cinco, paresco ante V.S. en la mayor forma que haya lugar y digo que como tal viudo pretendo contraher matrimonio con Ana Dorantes, *mestiza*, natural y vecina de el Pueblo de San Francisco Tizapan, hija legítima de Juan Dorantes y de María de la Encarnación, *su* edad veinte anos, y para que tenga efecto se ha de server V.S. demander se me reciva informacion de mi viudez y de la libertad y solteria ... se me despache comision para que el padre cura ministro de doctrina del pueblo de Tlalnepantla le reciba su declaración a la suso dicha y queriendo contraher dicho matrimonio de su libre voluntad, nos amoneste, case y vele y por tanto."

TABLE 7.2 *Notaries before Whom Marginal Castes Did Not Self-Declare Their Casta, Mexico City, 1605–1783*

Name	Known Years of Operation
Juan de P.	1605
Cornejo	1610
Alonso De Cavala R.	1628–1633
Alonso De Canea Jal.	1628–1633
Francisco de Gálves	1628–1633
Ruiz de Salvatto	1628–1647
Francisco de Bermedez	1629–1647
Joseph Beltrán	1646
Antonio de Esguar.	1667
Luis de Perea	1667–1678
Lorenzo de Guido	1669
Francisco de Villena	1669–1682
Gerónimo de Heredias	1672
Francisco González Macona	1675
Bernardo de Amelaga	1682–1694
Bernabé Uscarrez	1699–1718
Juan Antonio de Espejo	1702–1708
Juan Limenzo Guerrero	1717–1729
Antonio Sánchez	1722
Joseph Ambrocio de Lima	1725
Julio Clemente Guerrero	1726
Antonio Cisneros	1726–1729
Martin Domínguez	1733–1766
Salvador Monzón	1749–1764
Julías Ortiz	1752–1764
Miguel Pérez Cabello	1778

Source: Derived from the table of marriage cases in Appendix A. "Juan de P." may also be spelled "Joan de P"; "Luis de Perea" may also be spelled "Luis de Peroa." The spelling of "Bermedez" may be "Bermúdez." The last name of Lorenzo de Guido may be misspelled; he is also identified as a notary in Taxco.

207 people in our sample, representing around 27 percent of the total number of brides and grooms.

A second look at the evidence offers a variation in the story – one that is perhaps of greater consequence in understanding the outcomes of the testimonial process. Over half the notaries before whom brides and grooms failed to provide their own casta worked in the seventeenth century. Stunningly, nearly eight out of every ten brides who approached the altar prior to 1700 appear not to have relayed their own casta; for men the ratios are equally impressive, with approximately seven out of every ten grooms failing to do so.[15] The situation would change a great deal over the course of the eighteenth century, but not abruptly. For brides, the ratio actually increased slightly between 1700 and 1720 before plummeting rapidly to one in ten between 1730 and 1783. As for men in the first two decades of the 1700s, only four of ten grooms did not declare their own casta, a ratio that dropped to less than one in ten for the rest of the century.[16]

The best explanation has to do with the introduction of procedural changes in the marriage application process, or at least changes in what was recorded. It is significant that the groom almost always initiated the petition and was the nonecclesiastical person whose name appeared first in a marriage application. Before 1700, women were rarely visible in the petition at all: either the men spoke for them or the notary simply took down their information in the third person, as an observer of events. This is to say that there was seldom space on paper for women's voices to be recorded prior to 1700, even if they were present and spoke up. Men too were susceptible to being muzzled by the method of recordkeeping. After 1700, men still initiated the petitions, but information collection practices now allowed women's voices to be heard. Another major change that apparently began in the 1690s and picked up pace after the 1720s was the practice of allowing the bride and groom to present their petition together as a couple, or at least recording them as having done so. In this way the female voice finally entered the process – not necessarily on her own, but in concert with that of her fiancé.

In sum, we can say that the casta descriptors conveyed in the documentation for Mexico City were probably decent reflections of the way individuals thought of themselves – at least at the moment of marriage. This was true more for men than women prior to 1720, and then equally for both afterwards. Notaries and, more important, notarial practices stood the greatest chance of influencing casta testimony in the seventeenth century. In the 1700s, spousal testimonies provided a more useful guide to casta status. Given that brides bundled their casta testimony with that of their grooms on many occasions, greater doubt lingers over their casta claims. But thanks to the notaries' own cross-checking practices I believe that we can still rely on jointly presented petitions as reasonable indicators of what women thought to be their casta identity.

---

[15] The sample before 1700 has 162 individuals, representing 81 marriages.

[16] The sample taken from the years 1700 to 1720 has 68 individuals in 34 marriages; between 1720 and 1783 there were 530 individuals in 265 marriages.

TABLE 7.3 *Caste Shifting in the Matrimonial Record, Mexico City,*
1605–1783

	Grooms	Brides	Witnesses	Subtotal
Castizo to lobo		2		2
Castizo to mestizo	1			1
Castizo to morisco		2		2
Coyote to mestizo	1			1
Español to morisco		4		4
Lobo to mestizo		1		1
Mestizo to mestindio	1			1
Mestizo to mulato			1	1
Morisco to mestizo	1	1		2
Morisco to mulato	4	9		13
Mulato to morisco	3	2		5
Mulato to pardo	1		3	4
Pardo to morisco	1			1
Pardo to morisco to mulato	1	1		2
Pardo to mulato	3			3
Unknown to morisco	1			1
Total	21	22	6	49

Source: Derived from the table of marriage cases in Appendix A. All witnesses are male.

In about a tenth of the extreme casta marriages, modifications to casta classifications during the marriage application process, both subtle and overt, leave doubts about caste status, as shown in Table 7.3.[17] Certainty deteriorated further throughout the eighteenth century, especially between 1715 and 1783. Previously, there had been few detectable shifts of casta status among marriage applicants and witnesses in the record, with just three nuptials doing so before 1700. Arguably, the eighteenth-century increase in adjustments to calidad was partly a by-product of larger changes taking place in New Spain. As this book makes clear, generations of racial mixture had added immeasurably to the array of hues that populated the colony by the 1700s. At the same time, well-documented changes in access to employment, the growth of the colonial economy, and broad increases in miscegenation and exogamous unions worked to further break down the socio-racial barriers of the colonial world. As social jockeying grew among nonwhites, and as the privilege

---

[17] There were 41 cases where one person's casta status was changed, involving 49 individuals. In the historical literature, some of what I describe as caste shifting has been discussed as "racial variability." See Cope, *The Limits of Racial Domination*, 76–85.

structure of the elite was increasingly threatened, officials made efforts to curb upward social striving. Colonial documents, serving as the footprint of such processes, capture both the attempts to stabilize the social order and its new fissures. In truth, none of what I describe here was entirely new. However, the pace of change increased in the eighteenth century, as did the visibility of caste movement, enabling us to appreciate the events more clearly than in the years before.

In the matrimonial records evaluated here, the majority of instances of caste shifting took place among brides and grooms (as opposed to their witnesses), and within the categories of morisco, mulato, and pardo. Caste shifting between these categories represented just over half of all such cases. Movement within these groups seems to make sense, since they were proximate to each other in the casta hierarchy and could correlate easily in phenotype and lineage.[18] There were also a few documented cases of caste shifting between castizos and mestizos, between coyotes and mestizos, and between mestizos and mestindios; these entailed the same type of near-horizontal movement among casta categories. Underscoring eighteenth-century efforts to manage the pace of social mobility and reduce the upward racial drifting that sometimes took place in hypergamous marriages, there were four allegedly white brides, all married to Spanish men, who had their status reclassified to morisca.[19] All but one of these women had initially testified (or their husbands had testified for them) to being españolas, a likely indicator that their marriages presented an opportunity to elevate their casta status to better match that of their spouses.

In another third of the marriage applications, caste flattening took place – that is, a process of reverting extreme castas back to more normative ones. The best evidence comes from 13 moriscos who were reclassified as mulatos. Typically, flattening involved reining in extreme casta groups in ways that realigned them more closely to their parent categories, especially the repositioning of blacks back into the core terminologies that described Afro-castas. However, the record reveals that for nearly every case of caste flattening there was a concomitant instance in which a core caste classification was transformed into an extreme casta. Apparently, as seen in the 1791 census discussed in Chapter 5, as much as casta categories were in need of

---

[18] *Diccionario de autoridades*, p. 126; Manuel Alvar, *Léxico del mestizaje en Hispanoamérica* (Madrid: Ediciones Cultura Hispánica; Instituto de Cooperación Iberoamericana, 1987), 182–183; Gonzalo Aguirre Beltrán, *La población negra de México: estudio etnohistórico* (Mexico City: Fondo de Cultura Económica, 1972), 173.

[19] Hypergamy describes the action of a spouse who seeks to marry upward in social station.

being contained and restrained, at the same time, the full template of extreme casta labels was available for notaries and others to use when greater precision about casta was required.

The main evidence for caste shifting (sometimes known as racial variability) comes not from the main text of marriage applications but from the cover pages and summary sheets that accompanied them (see Figure 16). These were usually prepared independently by the local church's notarial staff.[20] It was in moments like these, after a marriage application had effectively concluded, that the impact of a notary's hand (or that of his scribe) on casta was most strongly felt. Notaries and their teams modified testimonies silently – after the fact and after individuals might have directly confronted and contested what was said about them. It might be years before the affected persons knew about the change, if they found out about it at all.

It was unlikely that such a switch would have a tangible effect on a person's daily life, since the couples were probably oblivious to it.[21] Casta switches might be exposed in the context of litigation, or at times when individuals needed to supply proof of casta. Announced at these junctures, the results could be jarring, traumatic, even catastrophic. However, because the modifications to casta that were made on cover pages and summary sheets were typically considered supplemental to the *expediente* itself, the additions did not necessarily override the testimony presented by marriage applicants or their friends; rather, it constituted an expert "second opinion" that took its place alongside the words of the marriage party. It is unclear the extent to which those who created the cover pages and summaries had direct contact with any of the marriage petitioners, their witnesses, or the clergymen who were closest to the case. So while notaries and their staffs commanded broad respect as the voice of authority in authenticating marital proceedings, their reliability as first-person witnesses was not always consistent.

Some of the cover-page and summary-sheet emendations that contradicted casta testimonies resulted from clerical error. This was probably the cause of the predicament of Juana Manuela Villasana from Taxco, a self-described morisca, who in 1768 was upgraded to castiza in her marriage application summary sheet (see Figure 17).[22] At a later date

---

[20] Of the 41 cases where a caste status was changed, 27 involved notaries modifying an individual's caste on a file's cover page or summary sheet.

[21] The emendations may have detracted from the accuracy of parish demographic records and related documents.

[22] AGN, Matrimonios, vol. 103, exp. 49, fols. 214–222v.

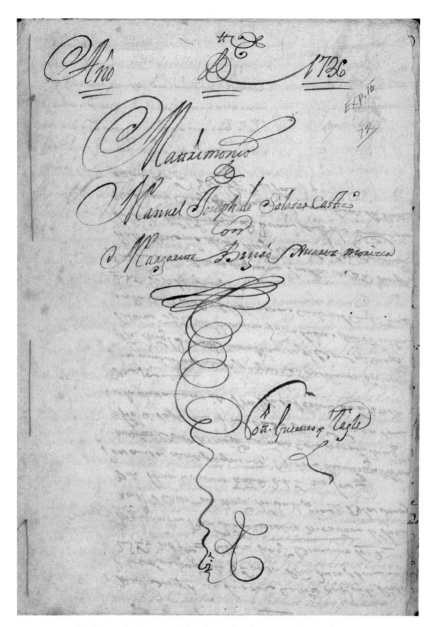

FIGURE 16 Eighteenth-Century Marriage Application Cover Sheet.
Source: AGN, Matrimonios, vol. 72, exp. 15.

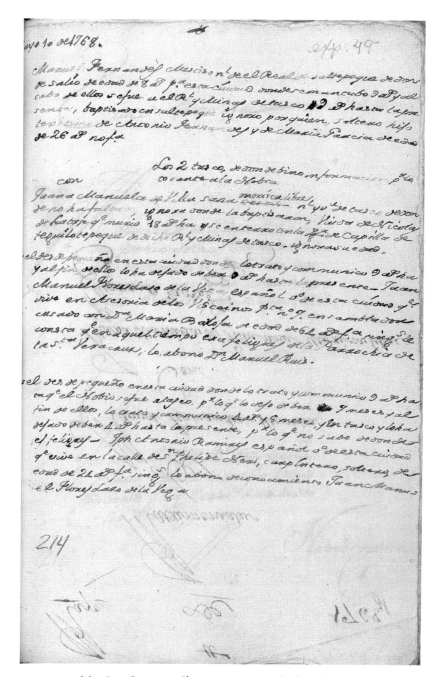

FIGURE 17 Marriage Summary Sheet, Juana Manuela de Villasana, 1768.
Source: AGN, Matrimonios, vol. 103, exp. 49, fol. 214.

the mistake was caught, and Juana was returned to her declared status of morisca.

Witnesses could also generate confusion over casta, as their testimonies sometimes contradicted the statuses articulated by the marital couple. In the summer of 1733, in Mexico City's parish of Santa Veracruz, 18-year-old Joseph Prieto, an orphaned mulato, filed to marry 15-year old Juana de Dios Chávez after he had taken her virginity. As was common in the colony, the couple felt entitled to having premarital sex after he had issued a *palabra de casamiento* (marriage proposal). Such a proposal offered a measure of security for the woman. Dutifully, although perhaps under pressure, Joseph complied with his proposal to his fiancée, whom he described to the Church as a loba libre. In a private interview, Juana confirmed that she was legitimate, knew both of her parents, and that she was indeed a loba libre. However, doubt over her casta status emerged from witness testimonies. The three witnesses, all of whom had known the couple for their entire lives, held different opinions about Juana's casta. Two men affirmed that she was a mestiza, while only one described her as a loba libre. Clearly, they all recognized strands of indigenous ancestry in her heritage, yet they were unsure about whether she also bore African ancestry. In the end, the authorities corroborated her declaration, but for a time her status was unclear.[23]

In other circumstances, the motives precipitating changes in casta could be more questionable. In January of 1773, the 19-year-old Joseph Andrés Ortiz, a self-described mestizo, submitted an application to marry María Gertrudis Hernández, a morisca, in Mexico City's Sagrario parish.[24] Circumstances did not allow María Gertrudis to join him in presenting the application, but in a private interview somewhat later she described herself as a mulata libre, not a morisca libre.[25] Was the groom intentionally seeking to upgrade her casta as well as his own? The summary sheets suggest so. The notarial staff swiftly modified Joseph's testimony, first demoting him to an indio and then switching him, a second time, into a mestindio – effectively accentuating the indigenous element of his mestizo heritage. The notaries then remolded María Gertrudis into a parda. In making the adjustment, indigenous bloodlines were likely being

---

[23] AGN, Matrimonios, vol. 32, exp. 3, fols. 10–13v.

[24] AGN, Matrimonios, vol. 177, exp. 67, fols. 301–305v.

[25] The inverse of this situation can be seen in the marriage documents of Pedro Vicente Sánchez (morisco libre) to María de la Encarnación in Mexico City in 1732. Here, the groom declared that his wife was a morisca libre. In a private interview she declared herself a castiza. See AGN, Matrimonios, vol. 227, exp. 18, fols. 88–93.

introduced into her mixture. In sum, the complicated set of correctives in this case proved confusing at best, with no clear picture emerging as to the identity of the marriage applicants.

The type of caste shifting just described could become decidedly more contentious and invasive when alterations permeated the pages of a document more thoroughly and were not relegated solely to emendations on summary sheets and cover pages. In November of 1780, Antonio Pioquinto de Herrera, a 32-year-old literate slave in Osumba (province of Chalco), applied to marry María Gertrudis Balcazar, also a slave. Antonio appears to have presented himself to the authorities as a morisco libre (freedman), while his wife was known to be a mulata. Antonio's casta claims did not take long to unravel. An unusually high number of witnesses (12 in all) testified in the case, hailing from regions as far flung as Guadalajara, Aguascalientes, Atlixco, and Guanajuato. The sweeping range of this geography reflected the itinerant upbringing of the bride and groom. Both abandoned early in their lives, they had roamed the colony extensively. As the marriage process unfolded, it did not take long for the fact of Antonio's slave status to surface. Just before the banns of marriage were announced, his *liberto* (free) status was rescinded and he was rapidly reclassified back into a mulato. He had initially approached the clergy as a free morisco; just days later he would embark on married life as a mulato slave. The reasoning behind the clergy's decision to re-label Antonio a mulato is not fully clear. But we can guess that his status as an orphan occluded any deep knowledge about his lineage. Neither he nor his wife knew their parents, much less any ancestors who could have affirmed the degree of mixture needed to claim the status of morisco.

Other attempts at casta flattening or compression can be found elsewhere in the matrimonial record. In 1742, 42-year-old Joseph Orduña Aviles, who described himself as a morisco libre, sought the hand of the 25-year-old mestiza María Gerónima Desa.[26] Among the witnesses were two tailors, lifelong friends of Orduña, who described themselves as moriscos libres. The final two witnesses, longtime acquaintances of the bride, described themselves as mulatos. As the case file was being compiled, the notaries reclassified Joseph Orduña to pardo on the cover sheet. In the adjoining marriage application summary, which provided a thumbnail sketch of the case, the notaries further proceeded to reclassify one of Orduña's witnesses to a mestizo libre and both of the bride's attestants to pardos. Only one member of the original group remained

[26] AGN, Matrimonios, vol. 123, exp. 19, fols. 75–79.

a morisco. In this complex reshuffling of casta, it is hard to discern clear patterns. If every morisco had been transformed into a pardo, it would be easier to say that a flattening process had taken place. Instead, the work of the notaries made everything more perplexing by blurring the lines between mulatos, mestizos, pardos, and moriscos.

Maybe there was no need for an underlying logic in the notary activity. A point to consider here is that when notaries recategorized the casta status of a witness, the stakes and consequences were low. There was considerable room for slippage and movement, because shifts and inconsistencies in a witness's casta did not directly affect many major forms of colonial records. Censuses and tribute rosters, for instance, did not draw information on casta statuses that were conveyed in witness testimonies. Similarly, a witness's casta claims were seldom parlayed into affirming or leveraging status in other situations. When casta credentials were needed to validate background, lineage, and overall suitability for particular positions and privileges, the person's record as witness was almost never scrutinized. In marriage situations, then, the casta of witnesses served more to complete the portrait of the bride and groom than to validate any social fact about the witnesses themselves. In repositioning their own casta, witnesses told new stories about the marital couple, but what they communicated with respect to their own status and caste was not as binding in other spheres of activity. Thus, except for situations where people of very high esteem were found testifying, witnesses' casta could be adjusted with little consequence to themselves, but with great possible consequences to the couple.

The impetus for caste flattening could just as likely originate from among the castas as from the colonial authorities. In some cases, either the bride or the groom desired to be flattened, particularly when their sense of self was wrapped into institutional identities that encouraged affiliations with the more amorphous core casta designations. The following examples come from two militiamen for whom casta identity was associated with and fortified by corporate ties.[27] In 1768, Joseph Anselmo Millán, a self-declared mulato and a soldier in the pardo militia of Mexico City, found that his wife's status and his own straddled the divide between two castas. In her marriage application she had declared herself a morisca, but in his militia marriage license (one soldiers sometimes had to procure) she was identified as a parda libre. This second classification was fully in line with her husband's social status as a militiaman in the pardo regiment.

[27] Vinson, *Bearing Arms for His Majesty*, various.

Apparently, the statuses were not at odds. Rather, they seemed to complement each other.[28]

During the waning days of the summer of 1779, Joseph Zambrano, another pardo in Mexico City, began the process of applying for marriage from the confines of a jail cell. As a long-serving member of the free-colored militia, his identity as a pardo militiaman was literally stamped on him. It was part of his esprit de corps, and he presented himself as a pardo to the authorities. However, near the end of October, as the case wound through the channels of the Church and as witness testimonies were being gathered, the clergymen altered Zambrano's casta from pardo to morisco. According to the authorities, the confusion emanated from Zambrano himself, who presented himself before the court of the Archbishop declaring that he was a "*morisco, pardo* soldier."[29]

Previous records of Zambrano's testimony show no record of such claims. A few weeks later, in submitting his final marriage petition, Zambrano reclassified himself again, now stating that he was a mulato libre. The witnesses from Mexico City and Puebla (where he had lived for seven years) who gathered to testify on his behalf remained uncharacteristically vague about Zambrano's true casta identity. There seemed to be a general consensus that his status should be whatever the authorities in Mexico City dictated. When the case ended in February of 1780, Church officials in Puebla finally inscribed Zambrano's caste as mulato.

Needless to say, the fixity of casta was gravely problematic here. Zambrano's service in the militia probably conditioned his identity, favoring his initial embrace of being pardo, which was somewhat interchangeable with mulato, a description he reverted to later. However, as the case unfolded, neither terminology proved necessarily exclusive to the notion of being a morisco. It is telling that Zambrano could be thought of as a "morisco, pardo" person to some. As with other instances of compound castas that we have seen (as in Chapter 4), this very conception suggested that there was latitude given in conjoining lineage-based and phenotypic indicators of casta. Zambrano's genealogy might make him a pardo, but he might nonetheless have a morisco appearance, or vice versa. While the archives do not let us know if Zambrano actually embraced such ideas, it is interesting that the Church authorities apparently saw no contradiction

---

[28] AGN, Matrimonios, vol. 147, exp. 50.

[29] "[P]arecio ante nos, (audiencia Arzopisbal) y declare ser *morisco* soltero soldado *pardo* natural y vecino de esta ciudad, de la que solo ha faltado año que estuvo en esa ciudad." See AGN, Matrimonios, vol. 102, exp. 16, fols. 100–118v.

in the juxtaposition of the castes. Again, it was they who took the early initiative of registering his casta identity in the marriage documents.

It is also telling that that there was little scuffle raised by the authorities as to possible contradictions between mulato-ness and pardo-ness. Zambrano's case may have been just another in which the lived realities of casta seemed unduly complex but did not warrant deeper correction, especially given that the stakes were low. If we step back for a broader view, it is clear that legions of situations like Zambrano's must have been encountered daily. Projecting these ambiguities up to the scale of the entire colony, and fully recognizing that such equivocations were allowed to thrive, we are therefore compelled to conclude that Spanish America's colonial authorities were at times administering a realm of regulated unregulation – a veritable contradiction in terms. They must have often found themselves caught up in contradictions as they tried to regulate something so amorphous as caste. In the world of colonial Spanish casta, there were moments when the prescribed rules and outcomes of mixture simply ceased to apply. At these junctures, society, officials, and individuals riffed on the theme: they continued forth in defining mixture and identity guided by general principles, ad hoc logic, their own needs, and the experiences they had acquired in their lived interactions. This mixed set of actions then melded with the colonial order as best it could – sometimes eventually guiding policies and behavior, and sometimes standing at a distant remove.

8

Betrayed

The caste fluidity sometimes observed at the altar could spin into overdrive when husbands and wives left each other for reasons of lust, spousal abuse, or adventure. Many times, departures led to a second marriage, authorized or not. Bigamy offered another avenue for casta change, and following bigamy cases can tell us a good deal about how caste pluralism and mobility operated on the ground. Because the officials who judged on these matters often tracked bigamists as they circulated throughout the colony over time, these cases yield more-dynamic views than do marriage petitions.[1] Entering this motile world allows us to better appreciate how individuals such as moriscos, lobos, and coyotes might be received as they came into different communities, under an array of life situations and circumstances.

For this chapter, I have analyzed 47 of the seventeenth- and eighteenth-century bigamy cases found in Mexico's national archives and listed in Appendix A. They represent virtually all instances of bigamy found in the Archivo General de la Nación (AGN) in which the alleged perpetrators were lobos, moriscos, or coyotes.[2] The overwhelming majority of the cases were filed in the eighteenth century and prior to 1789, when the Inquisition lost jurisdiction over bigamy. Cases were distributed fairly

---

[1] Richard E. Boyer, *Lives of the Bigamists: Marriage, Family, and Community in Colonial Mexico* (Albuquerque: University of New Mexico Press, 1995); Herman L. Bennett, *Colonial Blackness: A History of Afro-Mexico* (Bloomington: Indiana University Press, 2009), 114–136.

[2] It is entirely possible that new cases of bigamy for these groups may emerge in the Indiferente General section of the AGN or in the scores of regional and parish archives located outside of Mexico City.

TABLE 8.1 *Instances of Caste Change among Bigamists in Colonial Mexico,*
1690–1790

Original Casta Specifications	Casta in Second Marriage
Coyote	Mestizo
Coyote/mulato	Mestizo/mulato/lobo
Español	Coyote
India	Mulata/morisca
India	Mulata/morisca
Indio	Coyote
Indio/lobo	Mestizo/mulato
Indio/lobo	Indio
Loba	India
Loba	Coyota
Loba (actually india)	India
Loba/mestiza/mulata	Coyota
Lobo	Mulato/mestizo
Lobo/Indio	Chino/indio
Lobo/mulato	Mestizo
Lobo/mulato prieto/pardo	Mulato cocho/mestizo
Mestizo	Blanco de nación coyote/mulato
Mestizo	Coyote/lobo
Mestizo/morisco/lobo	Mestizo/morisco/lobo
Mulata loba	Mestiza
Mulato	Coyote
Mulato blanco/mulato	Morisco
Mulato libre	Coyote

Source: Derived from table in Appendix A.

evenly in the decades between the 1710s and the 1780s (except for
a noticeable rise in depositions during the 1750s), followed immediately
by a steep drop in the 1760s. The bigamists under scrutiny probably
represent an atypical subset of the cases that came before the ecclesiastical
courts: nearly half experienced some sort of shift in their casta during the
periods covered by their trials (see Table 8.1).[3] It is unlikely that most of
these changes represented conscious efforts at passing; they seem to have
instead been adaptations people made when they entered communities
that held to somatic rules different from those to which they were

---

[3] By contrast, the bigamists landing in court who were españoles, mestizos, and in some
cases mulatos enjoyed more stability of caste. In Richard Boyer's pioneering study of
bigamists, caste remained fairly consistent from marriage to marriage. See Boyer, *Lives of
the Bigamists*, 7–8.

accustomed. For members of the extreme castas, even neighboring townships might offer very different interpretations of caste. Hence, when lobos, moriscos, and coyotes journeyed, they probably lived through a more diverse set of casta experiences than others in the colony who were somatically nearer to the mainstream.

Almost to a fault, the purported bigamists in this sample were of the working classes. By and large, their first and second marriages took place in rural or semiurban settings, including small villages, remote parishes, haciendas, and lesser townships. The few that took place in major metropolises such as Mexico City, Guadalajara, and Valladolid were exceptions, as is demonstrated in Table 8.2. While bigamy in the colony was largely a man's affair, given that women were monitored more carefully and their movements more often constrained, over a quarter of the bigamists in our sample were women, significantly exceeding colonial norms.[4]

Bigamy cases have been expertly mined for their invaluable information on the social history of various segments of colonial society. These documents have also richly illuminated the institutional history of the Church. But here our focus is caste: How do the records proffer glimpses into appreciating caste transformations and maneuvers? To answer this, we first need to examine the testimonies and expressions of caste within the flow and structure of bigamy case files. As with most Inquisition proceedings, bigamy cases typically followed a pattern. They began with a denunciation, followed by the gathering of evidence and the presentation of an accusation (the *sumario*). Next came a trial (*prueba*) and, if the accusation was upheld, the sentencing (*sentencia*).[5] As the inquisitors gathered evidence, it was important to ensure that the witnesses were properly interrogated, that the physical traits of both spouses were carefully described, that each marriage was fully verified (preferably with marriage licenses), and that a timeline be established to demonstrate a period of overlap between the marriages. Without these proofs, bigamy could not be ascertained.[6]

Most important for understanding casta fluctuations was the part of the case preceding the trial and sentencing. This phase offered moments

---

[4] Silvia Marina Arrom, *The Women of Mexico City, 1790–1857* (Stanford: Stanford University Press, 1985); Boyer, *Lives of the Bigamists*, 7.

[5] Boyer, *Lives of the Bigamists*, 17–18. See also John F. Chuchiak, *The Inquisition in New Spain, 1536–1820: A Documentary History* (Baltimore: Johns Hopkins University Press, 2012). Officials occasionally expressed concern that alleged bigamists were being thrown in jail prematurely, before the necessary proofs of guilt were completed.

[6] AGN, Inquisición, vol. 817, exp. 18, fol. 411.

TABLE 8.2 *Towns and Cities of Residence of Extreme Casta Bigamists, 1690–1790*

Town or City Name
Cardereyta
Cariabapa (in the Sierra de Topia)
Chiguagua
Cuernavaca
Fresnillo
Guadalajara
Guanajuato
Guejozingo
Gutiérrez (in Villanueva)
Hacienda Ciénega de Mata
Hacienda de Sn. Mateo (in Villanueva)
Harascla
Havana
Hoyo del Agua
Huizuco (in Tlaxmalacac)
Isthlauacan
Linares (Guadalajara)
Magdalena (in Guadalajara)
Malinalco
Matehuala
Mexico City
Mireles (N. León)
Misión de San Ignacio
Monterrey
Nuestra Señora de las Nieves
Ojocaliente
Olatitan
Pahuatlan
Paraje de Piedra Gorda (Villa de León)
Pátzcuaro
Penjamillo
Piedra Gorda (León)
Presidio de San Joseph (New Mexico)
Presidio del Paraje
Querétaro
Real Minas de Fresnillo
Salto del Agua
San Antonio de los Llanos (in N. León)
San Felipe
San Joseph Cardereyta
San Juan de los Llanos (in Villa de los Lagos)
San Juan Huetamo (Zahuayo, Valladolid)

(continued)

TABLE 8.2 *(continued)*

San Juanico (Guchiapan)
San Luis Potosí
San Miguel Mesquitic
San Nicolás Tolentino (Celaya)
San Pedro
Santa Clara (Charcas)
Santa Eulalia de Mérida de Chiguagua
Santa María de Río Verde (Valladolid)
Santiago Chimaltitan (Totatiche)
Santiago Papasquiano (Durango)
Santiago Xalpam
Silão
Temascalcingo
Tenestepango
Tiripito
Tlacolula (Mestitlan)
Tlasasalca
Tlaxcala
Trapiche de Huertas
Tupataro (Pátzcuaro)
Turicato (in Cinagua)
Vacubirito (Sinaloa)
Valladolid
Veracruz
Villa de Lagos
Villa de San Phelipe (Charcas)
Xalmolonga (a sugar mill and estate)

Source: Derived from table in Appendix A.

for witnesses, plaintiffs, defendants, and bureaucrats to speak, react, and air opinions on matters of caste. During the denunciation, inquisitors routinely asked witnesses about the casta and the appearance of the alleged bigamists. If it was not possible to conduct questioning immediately at the site of the denunciation, officials in one of the Inquisition's regional seats, such as Mexico City or Guadalajara, received the depositions and initiated a full investigation. Notifications, dispatches, and requests for verification were then sent to commissioners in the towns and parishes where the first and second marriages reportedly took place.

Verifying nuptials was not always easy, given that those who made denunciations did not always have accurate facts. Once the commissioners received the charge to initiate a local investigation, they appointed notaries and commenced with questioning and interviews. Simultaneously, they launched searches for marriage documents in their parish registers. If possible, they lined up the parties' *padrinos* for questioning. They also tracked down spouses and key witnesses who could describe the couple's married life. Ideally, the authorities tried to corral three or four "people of trust" who could testify to the "public" aspects of a couple's marriage and caste and also confirm their place of residence and occupation. When possible, the witnesses, who sometimes included the priest who had officiated at the marriage, were asked to confirm wedding dates.

The Inquisition placed a premium on expediency. Ideally, testimony had to be ratified within three days, and the resulting information was promptly dispatched back to an Inquisition office in a city like Mexico City or Guadalajara.[7] The distances covered by documents circulating throughout New Spain could be great, which constantly threatened to slow a case. In 1735, a denunciation was made against Agustín Miguel in the town of Nuestra Señora de Guadalupe, located in the *partido* of Río del Norte. The trajectory of the paperwork in the case, from Guadalajara to the valley of Buenaventura (between Chiguagua and Xanos) and on to Mexico City and Paso del Río, among other towns in northern Mexico, was nearly 400 leagues in length. One league was approximately the distance a person could walk in an hour. Unsurprisingly, the case dragged on into 1741, without resolution.[8]

The initial casta status recorded during a denunciation was key to how Inquisition officials would view suspected bigamists during the early phases of a case. Additional casta information, drawn from the first local parish investigation, could help solidify or put in question a caste status in the minds of inquisitors. Altering these initial impressions could be difficult. At the same time, the early accounts of casta provided by denouncers and witnesses were sometimes nebulous and could cause inquisitors to suspend judgment on a person's casta. This could delay the investigatory process. For example, when Agustín Miguel was denounced in 1735, his accuser told the local commissioner that the accused was "moreno in color, like a chino, and he appears to be lobo [which] in these parts we call chino."[9] In rendering this caste description, the denouncer's personal impressions of Agustín's casta reflected the traditions of caste classification found in his home community (Río del

---

[7] For an outline of the steps to be taken by commissioners, see AGN, Inquisición, vol. 980, exp. 12, fols. 173–174.

[8] AGN, Inquisición, vol. 872, vol. 1, exp. 2, fols. 36–73v.

[9] Ibid., 37.

Norte). He tried to interpret these localisms for the benefit of the court, but the result was not clear. Not all descriptions were quite this complex.

Cases like Agustín's had to be handled delicately, and the ecclesiastical courts, and most likely bureaucratic culture as well, were prepared for these occasions. By the late eighteenth century, there had been devised a provisional casta category known as *caldidad de por ahora* that assigned temporary casta or calidad statuses to individuals under the premise that future evidence might effect a change.[10] Calidad de por ahora was employed in several contexts having little to do with caste, but it gradually found utility in the realm of casta – especially with respect to tribute collection policies.[11] Although not referenced specifically, the basic concept of calidad de por ahora seemed to apply in some bigamy cases. The casta initially recorded for an individual could implicitly be understood as a placeholder; change might take place as a case progressed over the long term. A morisco, for example, might be discovered to have been both a mestizo and a lobo over the course of the proceedings. Faced with vague or conflicting evidence, the inquisitors could temporarily assign

---

[10] In ordinances issued in the 1790s and early 1800s, people who were exempt from paying tribute on the basis of their calidad officially included Indian caciques, the firstborn sons of caciques, mestizos (specifically, the sons of españoles and indias), castizos, and españoles. However, the authorities made provisions for the Junta Superior of the Real Hacienda to examine and evaluate a wider scope of exemption claims. A commissioner was free to openly challenge any individual's claim to a specific casta or calidad, even if they had never paid tribute or appeared on any tribute rosters before. As was made clear in the legislation of the 1790s, commissioners were effectively granted the authority to recalibrate calidad when necessary and if proof could be given, and thus they became arbiters and enforcers of casta. People disputing a commissioner's assessment of their casta and tributary status had the right to demonstrate proof of their presumed calidad using all of the records they could obtain (including marriage and baptismal registers), supplemented with interviews and testimony. Clergymen from a person's place of origin, *alcaldes*, and *gobernadores de indios* were prime candidates to be called in as casta authenticators. All materials were passed on to the *promotor fiscal*. The *asesor* then wrote his opinion. In cases of doubt, a "calidad de por ahora" could be assigned. The full deposition was then sent to the Junta Superior de la Real Hacienda and the *fiscal* of the Real Hacienda for a final decision. This assessment was then passed down to the local commissioners, who could make corrective annotations on the *matrícula*, or tribute register. During the final deliberations over a person's casta status, their calidad remained in limbo, defaulting to whatever designation was articulated as the calidad de por ahora. AGN, Bandos, vol. 17, exp. 55 and 56, especially fols. 235v–236.

[11] For some other examples showing uses of the term, see Charles W. Polzer and Thomas E. Sheridan, *The Presidio and Militia on the Northern Frontier of New Spain,* Vol. 2, Pt. 1, *The Californias and Sinaloa-Sonora, 1700–1765* (Tucson: University of Arizona Press, 1997), 436; Fray Eudaldo Jaumeandreu, *Rudimentos de economía política dispuestos por el M. Fr. Eudaldo Jaumeandreu* (Barcelona: A Brusi, 1816), 332; AGN, Indios, vol. 66, exp. 3, fols. 4v–5v; and AGN, Reales Cédulas Originales, vol. 182, exp. 6.

such a person one of these statuses while awaiting further verification. Meanwhile, as testimonies were presented, the individual could morph (on paper) in and out of a variety of caste conditions, according to the claims of those involved in the case. If the proceedings reached trial and sentencing, then the morphing processes culminated into a final evaluation by the court. Yet even this status could still be contested. Nonetheless, the assignment of a calidad de por ahora allowed the Inquisition to freeze caste to a certain degree in their records while final assessments were hammered out collectively and collaboratively by the authorities, witnesses, plaintiffs, and defendants.

The courts also had the option to adjust or simplify the caste information they received at the outset of a case. Agustín, for instance, could have been designated a lobo on the spot, for convenience's sake, with the expectation that his casta status would be better identified later. What actually happened when Agustín's file was forwarded to Mexico City was that Church officials left room for doubt in their caste appraisal, describing Agustín as either a lobo or chino. And when the inquisitors in Mexico City reviewed the deposition and began preparing his file for further distribution, the ambiguities prompted them to add new questions of their own to the investigation. They asked that as additional details of the case were collected elsewhere in the colony, witnesses provide a clearer answer as to whether Agustín was a lobo, mestizo, or indio puro.[12]

Introducing the possibility that Agustín was an indio radically changed matters. Real confusions existed in the colony around individuals like him, as some lobos were truly mislabeled indios, while others were people who may have lived as indios for stints in their lives.[13] Some members of the clergy facilitated these confusions when they proceeded to marry as indios people who were otherwise classified or publicly known to be lobos and coyotes, or even mulatos and moriscos.[14] The concern over whether

---

[12] AGN, Inquisición, vol. 872 (1), vol. 1, exp. 2, fols. 39–40.
[13] A discussion of lobos living as indios, or having that reputation in the community, is in AGN, Inquisición, vol. 1292, exp. 17, fols. 1–101, and AGN, Inquisición, vol. 780, exp. 10, fols. 414–485v, especially the revelation found on folio 460v. In one instance, a coyote named Juan Antonio Lombardo who claimed to be an orphan had the nickname "el indio," which raised questions among inquisitors as to whether he might be indigenous. Inquiries were made into his lineage. See AGN, Inquisición, vol. 811, exp. 3, fols. 229, and especially 263 and 267. Finally, an example of someone who was "reputed to be a *lobo*" but was actually an indio can be found in AGN, Inquisición, vol. 921, exp. 15, fols. 221–236.
[14] For examples, see AGN, Inquisición, vol. 941, exp. 25, fols. 262–276v; and AGN, Inquisición vol. 1133, exp. 5, fols. 42–47v.

a suspected bigamist might be an indio stemmed from the fact that natives were not subject to the Inquisition's jurisdiction (recall the case of Bernardo Carrillo from Chapter 3). If it seemed plausible that an alleged perpetrator was an indio, the search for corroboration intensified. Inquisitors sought additional information about birthplace, baptismal records, and upbringing. They wanted a firmer understanding of one's parents and caste background as well as precise information about where the family lived. Residence in an Indian parish or township (*pueblo de indios*) could support claims to native identity.[15]

Ordinarily, the bar for establishing proof of casta was not so high. Keep in mind that the purpose of verifying casta in bigamy cases was to ensure that the correct individuals were being identified for trial and brought to justice. Beyond that, referencing casta could help accurately identify the spouses of an accused bigamist so that they could be located and questioned. Outside of this, precision about casta did not have much additional value – a point the inquisitors understood. On many occasions, Church officials handled caste with a certain laxity, which could sometimes spell trouble.

When María de la Cruz denounced her husband Salvador Rangel for bigamy in the Villa de San Phelipe (in the Minas de Charcas) in September of 1730, the indictment was quickly followed by routine investigation into the nature of the marriage. When Briceño don Balthasar de Fonseca, San Phelipe's local commissioner, completed his work and sent the case file to Mexico City, he corroborated María de la Cruz's initial testimony that her husband was a lobo. Shortly thereafter, Mexico City's inquisitors crafted their own description of Salvador: "He appeared to be a *mulato*, of medium build, curly hair, dark color (*prieto*), approximately 30 years old."[16] It is unclear how they arrived at this description. Perhaps it was conjured to provide additional details to help locate Salvador, as he had not yet been found and apprehended. Perhaps calling him a mulato uncovered the biases of Mexico City's Inquisition staff, revealing their perceptions of what the term *lobo* really described. Maybe the new label represented an effort to conflate the lobo category into more-standard casta language. Whatever the motivation, as the officials in Mexico City prepared orders to send to the commissioners in Charcas and San Phelipe, they immediately started to struggle over Salvador's caste. Someone inserted a note in the text saying that Salvador appeared to be a mulato

[15] AGN, Inquisición, vol. 830, exp. 4, fols. 53–54.
[16] Ibid., 59.

but might also be a lobo. Another annotation, made later, asked regional officials to pay special attention to the following question as they gathered evidence: "What caste is he, *mulato, indio* or *lobo?*"[17]

Witnesses in Charcas responded consistently that Salvador was not a mulato but a lobo, even though the commissioner dutifully followed his instruction from Mexico City exactly, inquiring if anyone knew a "mulato" named Salvador who fit specific physical criteria. No one in town knew a mulato with those traits, but they did know a lobo. By the third interview, Charcas's commissioner started changing his line of questioning: he now asked witnesses if they knew a lobo named Salvador. Through the force of testimony in this case, witnesses' impressions slowly sculpted the casta outlook of the Inquisition.[18]

Salvador's case was not unique. Here, and in other instances, when dispatches were sent to regional and local commissioners to gather testimonies, early court impressions of a bigamist's casta were typically put to their greatest test. As competing descriptions of casta emerged – sometimes from marriage registers but mainly from witnesses – the courts found themselves having to rethink and manage changing caste information over the duration of the proceedings. While witness testimony could nudge or even sway inquisitors' views of a suspected bigamist's casta, rarely was a witness's outlook on casta similarly challenged – simply because the court didn't press the issue. In the bigamy trials evaluated here, the Inquisition tended to absorb local and individual perspectives on casta rather than dispute them.[19] This meant that there was not necessarily a conflict if a defendant was considered a morisco in one town and a lobo in another; those viewpoints were respected locally and were not brought forward and into conflict with each other. This characteristic embodies the essence of a process that might best be described as caste management: the courts sifted through, weighed, arbitrated, and navigated a sea of opinions from different locations on the caste of accused bigamists to arrive at their own

---

[17] Ibid., 6ov. For the full case, see fols. 52–82.

[18] I present this as a representative case. I think it is also important to note that in his second marriage, Salvador and his wife were both considered indios (Salvador claimed that both of his parents were indios). The impact of local testimony on the perspective of the inquisitors can be seen in the majority of cases surveyed for this chapter. Another excellent example of the process can be traced in the transformations of casta in Agustín Miguel's case. AGN, Inquisición, vol. 872 (1), exp. 2, 36–73.

[19] This said, the ways in which inquisitors phrased questions sometimes conditioned responses by providing both a vocabulary and a format for an individual's answers. This outcome may have been unintended by the inquisitors and their staff.

views. They did not seek caste resolution for its own sake, but rather as progress toward resolution of the bigamy case.

In so doing, caste management and its effort to reach resolution in bigamy cases allowed ample latitude for contradictory casta opinions to exist on the ground, unchecked. It is clear that simply reaching a minimum threshold of casta accuracy sufficed to keep a case moving toward its end, which was the primary goal. This relaxed attitude even enabled witnesses to approach the courts to declare that a suspected bigamist was simultaneously of several castes.[20] Under the influence of witnesses, members of the ecclesiastical courts themselves seemed to accept that individuals could plausibly have two or more casta identities. The archival documentation is riddled with examples in which scribes and clergy described individuals as being composites of several castas or of compound castas, or otherwise carrying multiple recognized caste statuses.[21]

There were exceptions to that rather open approach when the court directly confronted bigamists during their trials and sentencing. Interrogations might be peppered with questions like "Have you ever been known by another name?" or "Have you ever been known as a *coyote* or *morisco*?" Questions like these sought to compel the accused to reconcile casta variances and other discrepancies in their identity. In addition, witnesses were occasionally pressed before their sentencing to verify their own casta.[22] Yet, while the excavation of casta profiles in case proceedings tends to reveal very detailed descriptive information, it was the more superficial content – the broadest glosses of a person's casta identity – that seemingly mattered most to the Inquisition.

---

[20] Occasionally, such descriptions melded into depicting certain bigamists as being of compound casta, like a *mulato lobo*. Some examples can be found in AGN, Inquisición, vol. 586, fols. 502–572; and AGN, Inquisición, vol. 780, exp. 10, fols. 414–485v.

[21] In several case records – even on the title pages – the purported bigamist could be referred to as both lobo and mulato, or as mulato lobo, or as both morisco and mulato. For examples, see AGN, Inquisición, vol. 862, exp. 1, fol. 196; AGN, Inquisición, vol. 586, exp. 8, fol. 502; AGN, Inquisición, vol. 781, exp. 8, fol. 373; and AGN, Inquisición, vol. 980, exp. 12, fol. 170. As these cases unfolded, one can trace the shifts and maneuverings of casta at each stage.

[22] AGN, Inquisición, vol. 875, exp. 5, fol. 122. In this case, Balthasar de los Reyes Pacheco, a witness and a hacienda worker in Sierra de Pinos (Guadalajara) was asked if he had ever been referred to as a lobo or negro. He said that this had never happened and that only when he got married was he referred to as an indio. He also stated that he was the son of mestizos. Here, a jarring phenotype prompted a line of questioning that did not have much to do directly with the case. However, this was the only example of such witness interrogation that I was able to find, although there is likely more evidence in the archives.

BALANCING ACTS: ON SEEKING CASTA ACCURACY
AND ITS EFFECTS

There were times when problems arose with the information that the courts acquired about casta, especially for members of the extreme castes. When the quality of the data was compromised, a range of factors might account for the problem. One issue was the veracity and thoroughness of the information recorded at the time of marriage – not all nuptials were performed judiciously. When Pedro Nolasco de Vega married for the second time in 1751, quite aware that he was already married, the priest rushed the process because he was in a hurry. There was no notary to record the event properly, the couple's declaration was not taken in proper form, and Pedro was asked only for his name, his birthplace, and his parents' identity.[23] It is not clear if he was ever asked his casta, and the inquisitors could never seem to decide whether he was an indio or a coyote.

Couples too could raise barriers, especially when priests insisted on following formal marriage protocols. Some openly argued with the clergy, while others tricked, manipulated, and pressured priests into conducting marriages without verifying their casta identity.[24] To complicate matters, not all clerics knew their flocks well, while others bore prejudices that they exercised when assigning casta labels. When Juan Francisco and Lucía Casimira (both known to be coyotes) exchanged wedding vows in September of 1745, the officiating priest simply labeled them as mestizos. In his testimony, he confessed to not having much interpersonal contact with people "of low color" (*de color bajo*). He recognized them primarily by sight (*de vista*) rather than through knowledge of their sustained relationships.[25] We can easily appreciate how this priest's view of casta obscured his understanding of its nuances and function among parishioners, especially those who were as deeply miscegenated as the extreme castes.

It is not a stretch to assert that the people who surrounded the accused bigamists – their friends, neighbors, coworkers, family, and communities – probably had a more textured impression of their casta than did some Church officers. But the documents exhibit a core tension in how these acquaintances fundamentally understood casta. On the one hand was the knowledge of casta derived from familiarity with an individual's lineage.

---

[23] AGN, Inquisición, vol. 1122, exp. 3, fols. 75v–80. In Pedro's testimony, he recounted that he was married the second time "en un instantito" (instantly).

[24] AGN, Inquisición, fol. 539, exp. 9, fols. 80–86v; AGN, Inquisición, vol. 941, exp. 25, fols. 262–276v.

[25] AGN, Inquisición, vol. 927, exp. 7, fols. 341v–342.

Witnesses sometimes referred to cues of "casta y generación" in their evaluations, relying essentially on a summative assessment of casta achieved through genealogy.[26] On the other hand, witnesses also evaluated casta by interpreting phenotypic features. Those interpretations might be further correlated with the individual's social station and socioeconomic standing (*calidad*).[27] In this mode, witnesses might remark that "according to appearances" (*según aspecto*) or "according to reputation" (*reputado por*) someone was of a particular casta.[28] Such subjective caste assessments echoed the larger tensions between phenotype and lineage that figured into other discussions about the conception of caste (see Chapter 3).

Bigamy proceedings demonstrate that the interrogation process itself could further facilitate friction between different forms of casta assessment. At times inquisitors clearly asked for one's *casta y generación*, encouraging responses of a genealogical type.[29] But since the Inquisition also requested descriptive data on individuals, there was a parallel tendency to meld physical appearances with caste conceptions. Predictably, respondents in their testimonies began merging information in their answers – for example, saying that someone was "*mulato* in *calidad* but leans toward black [in the phenotypic sense]."[30] Alternatively, one might find an individual who was "white but of *nación coyote*" or even "[the person] is white, [and] looks more [so] than a *coyote*."[31]

Inquisitors were also inconsistent in specifying to witnesses whether they were seeking information on casta, calidad, or nación, and they were equally unclear as to whether they sought differentiation between these

---

[26] AGN, Inquisición, vol. 539, exp. 9, fols. 80–86v.

[27] This conflation of somatic and socioeconomic measures to evaluate a person's casta has been discussed at length in the scholarly literature as revelatory of a person's calidad. See the classic article by Robert McCaa, "Calidad, Clase, and Marriage in Colonial Mexico: The Case of Parral, 1788–90," *Hispanic American Historical Review* 64, no. 3 (1984): 477–501. See also an excellent discussion on shifts that occurred between casta and calidad in María Elena Martínez, *Genealogical Fictions*, 247–248.

[28] AGN, Inquisición, vol. 952, exp. 34, fols. 367–368. María Francisca Arrieta denounced her son-in-law for bigamy, describing him as "según aspecto, de casta lobo." AGN, Inquisición, vol. 817, exp. 18, fol. 413. Don Juan de Herrera, testified that the accused bigamist Juan Joseph was "reputado por *indio*." These were both fairly common terms of referencing individuals.

[29] For examples, see AGN, Inquisición, vol. 830, exp. 4, fols. 53–54; AGN, Inquisición, vol. 811, exp. 3, fols. 263–267; and AGN, Inquisición, vol. 927, exp. 7, fols. 364–374.

[30] For use of the descriptive phrase "mulato de calidad que tira a negro," see AGN, Inquisición, vol. 980, exp. 12, 178v–179.

[31] AGN, Inquisición, vol. 907, exp. 23, fols. 384; AGN, Inquisición, vol. 1068, exp. 9, fol. 68. The phrases were "blanco de nación coyote," and "es blanco, parece más que coyote."

categories. Often, inquisitors asked for all at the same time, as when they prompted witnesses to describe the casta and calidad of Agustín Miguel in 1737.[32] In the 1720s, during the proceedings of Josepha Rodríguez, one commissioner asked witnesses to convey her *nación*, while others sought her *casta*; essentially, they were using two terms to extract the same information.[33] With such lack of clarity and direction, it is unsurprising that when witnesses described someone's casta in error, little effort was made to make corrections. Obviously, there were arenas where caste nomenclature was used more deliberately and consistently than in others.[34] But in the context of the bigamy trials examined here, the porous distinctions among these terms served to encourage a rampant blending of phenotype, genealogy, and even social status in individual casta profiles.

This was not always the case, however. Witnesses less informed about an accused bigamist's lineage sometimes made an effort to differentiate between the genealogical information that they did have and visible phenotype. Witnesses and inquisitors alike sometimes used the phrase *al parecer* ("appears to be") to qualify casta classifications that were primarily based on visual cues. The archival record is packed with people who "appear to be" lobo, coyote, or morisco. However, when lineage was supported by firm proof, genealogy took precedence. Reexamining Juan Francisco's marriage to Lucía Casimira in the 1740s, when Juan Manuel Christomo (a mestizo witness) testified for the couple, he carefully underscored that Juan Francisco was a mestizo al parecer but that his wife was an outright mestiza, presumably based on stronger genealogical certainties that he had at his disposal. In the same case, the witness Martín Arellano, an indio ladino, stated that Juan Francisco was a lobo al parecer, while Lucía Casimira was an unqualified mestiza. It is hard to know exactly what prompted each witness's evaluation of Juan Francisco and his wife. Everyone worked and lived on the same hacienda. However, Juan Francisco was a relatively new immigrant to the estate and region of Silão, and Lucía Casimira was a long-time resident of the hacienda, raised there by her mother and stepfather. Juan Francisco, therefore, was an outsider whose lineage could not be definitively known in the same way as Lucía Casimira's.

---

[32] AGN, Inquisición, vol. 872 (1), exp. 2, fols. 69–70.

[33] AGN, Inquisición, vol. 780, exp. 10, fols. 446–455.

[34] In the context of tribute collection, for example, *calidad* acquired greater significance and even definitional precision, particularly during the latter half of the eighteenth century. See N. Andrews, "Taxing Blackness."

Juan Francisco never knew his real father and generally considered himself a coyote, although in other parts of the colony he easily passed for indio (his mother's caste). Knowing nothing of Juan Francisco's mother, it is significant that Martín, the indio witness in the case, darkened Juan Francisco's casta to be more closely aligned with his own. Meanwhile, Manuel, the mestizo witness, believed that Juan Francisco looked more like him. Although we cannot know exactly why this occurred, we can postulate for cases in which lineage was unclear that the subject position of the witnesses, their experiences, their own casta status, and their worldview may have influenced them to produce slightly different interpretations of the same person, even in the same setting. Back in the town of San Phelipe (Michoacán) where Juan Francisco had married his first wife and where his mother was well known, some deciphered him as a coyote al parecer. Others, such as Joseph Antonio Hernández, a mulato blanco (white mulatto), provided considerably more-refined appraisals, labeling Juan Francisco an "indio blanco acoiotado" (coyotized white Indian).[35] Here again we must wonder if Joseph's status as a mulato blanco preconditioned him to detect supposed blanco traits in other individuals like Juan Francisco.

The situations just described show that in evaluating one's casta, as witnesses alternated between basing their assessments on lineage, lifestyle, or phenotype (or all three), knowledge of lineage was not something to be taken for granted. Even when known, lineage connections and their attendant social value did not transfer easily as people moved from one place to the next. Particularly for members of the nonelite, a change of place could effectively negate lineage and some of its benefits, or perhaps necessitate the creation of new lineage networks.

[35] AGN, Inquisición, vol. 927, exp. 7, fols. 316–383, especially fols. 334–335 and 341–354. One cannot help but wonder if Joseph Antonio's status as a mulato blanco primed him to see the blanco quality in other individuals. It is also fascinating that both of Juan's spouses considered him to be a "mulato al parecer." It is unclear if they were using the term *mulato* to denote African ancestry or simply to express that he was a person of racially mixed descent. Another good example in which witnesses made fine distinctions between knowing a person's casta through lineage and using phenotype to assess casta is in AGN, Inquisición, vol. 872 (1), exp. 2, fol. 54v–55. This is the case of Agustín Miguel, mentioned earlier in the chapter, accused of bigamy in the partido of Río del Norte in 1735. Agustín was the legitimate son of Miguel de la Cruz Solóranzo from Guadalajara, an "indio ladino, alobado, and muy ladino," and Sebastiana de los Reyes, a "mulata alobada." According to informants who knew Agustín Miguel and his family, he was a "lobo legítimo" (officially recognized lobo) with a public reputation for being such. "This is public knowledge although they [the family] would like to be taken for *indios*, since this is [of] more noble blood." Again, for the witness, proof based on lineage constituted certainty regarding Agustín's lobo background.

New Spain's colonists did not usually travel great distances alone. In the bigamy cases surveyed here, men frequently journeyed in groups that kept them connected to a prior life, at least through the group's collective memory. Itinerant workers, often muleteers, frequently traveled together and might consider themselves a sort of alternative family, aware of each other's relationships and contacts as they circulated about the colony. Women rarely traveled alone but were typically escorted (sometimes forcibly) to new places by men, who introduced them to new communities. In short, there were many potential brokers who might accompany individuals from one life into a new one. These people became substitutes for long-standing lineage connections.

At times, colonists who entered new communities were able to appropriate lineage networks in those places, thereby acquiring surrogate lineages that affected their casta identity. In the Real Minas de Fresnillo in 1740, María Gertrudis Ranjel married for the second time, presenting herself as an india. Although at the time of the marriage she claimed to be the legitimate daughter of Nicolás Ranjel and María Arsinega, whom she alleged were both indios and deceased, the truth was that she did not know her parents. Abandoned by her father, María Gertrudis was placed in the care of a priest, who in turn sent her to live with a woman in San Luis Potosí, ostensibly "for the benefit of her education." While still young, María Gertrudis was snatched by another woman who lived in Lagunillas, near Mezquitic. María Gertrudis eventually married in Mezquitic (likely against her will), enduring a stormy relationship with a man whom she did not love. Lacking knowledge of her parents, she was described by those who knew her as, variously, a coyota, mestiza, mestirita, morisquita, and mulatita blanca. After finally fleeing her first husband and relocating to Fresnillo (where she believed she was from), María Gertrudis met Miguel Briceño, with whom she began an amorous relationship. Miguel helped her "recover" her identity. After speaking with his father and a host of town elders, the community of Fresnillo collectively concluded that María Gertrudis was the long-lost daughter of the deceased Nicolás Ranjel. Never able to fully confirm this, María Gertrudis nonetheless embraced the story, as did the surviving members of the Ranjel family. Since the story was subscribed to by the wider Fresnillo community, she was accepted as an india by all. With a place in the community literally carved out for her, any doubts about María Gertrudis's casta and phenotype soon faded.[36]

[36] AGN, Inquisición, vol. 875, exp. 5, fols. 101–149.

Another telling case is that of Rita Vitoriana Andrade, who in 1757 married Joseph Manuel Hernández in the town of Tupataro (Valladolid). As with María Gertrudis, Rita Vitoriana needed a broker to help her gain entrée into her new world. Shortly after arriving in the town, she befriended an indio, Juan Lucas Moreno. Assuming the role of her protector, he announced suddenly to the community that she was his sister. This newly acquired status of surrogate sibling radically altered the community's view of her phenotype, since many now believed that she too was an india. Not everyone was so easily convinced, of course, since her somatic features suggested that she was a mulata. Rita Vitoriana herself knew this to be closer to the truth; after all, her father was a well-known mulato. Those who knew her from her previous residence also perceived her to be a mulata, and she even officially presented herself to the Inquisition as a morisca. However, in both of her marriages, she was registered by the clergy as an india.[37]

These cases underscore that when witnesses deliberated how they were going to describe someone using the genealogical and phenotypic information that they had at their disposal, the unexpected malleability of lineage could distort the data. Moreover, as increasing value was placed on physical features in colonial society over the course of the eighteenth century, knowledge of a person's true lineage did not necessarily retain its worth for navigating casta in everyday society.[38]

---

[37] AGN, Inquisición, vol. 941, exp. 25, fols. 262–276v, especially 270v.

[38] To explore these concepts as they were depicted in art, see Magali Carrera, *Imagining Identity*; and Ilona Katzew, *Casta Painting*. María Elena Martínez discusses this as a phenomenon in *Genealogical Fictions*. Among the lower-class social sectors, there were situations in which siblings born of the same parents openly presented themselves as belonging to different castas. Some consciously downgraded their casta status, even in the face of provable lineage. Consider the case of two sisters originally from Guatitlan who were living in Mexico City in the 1730s. María Theresa and Gerónima Micaela Campos were the children of Nicolasa de la Encarnación (española) and Miguel Campos (mestizo). According to their lineage, both were castizas, but life circumstances prompted each to depict themselves differently. See AGN, Inquisición, vol. 845, exp. 16, fols. 212–214v, and fols. 219–219v. The types of relationships that individuals maintained within their families also conditioned their casta outlook; there could be rivalries on issues of skin color that prodded one brother or sister to favor a particular casta identity. In witness testimony from the case of Juan Joseph (lobo), it emerged that his father's differential treatment of his children, based on skin color, left lasting impressions. The mulato father apparently favored his darker children. Consequently, Juan Joseph felt that he lacked his father's love growing up. See AGN, Inquisición, vol. 817, exp. 18, fols. 413v–414v.

TOWARD A THEORY OF HYPERHYBRIDITY

A case that came before the Inquisition in 1693 in many ways encapsulates and extends the themes explored in this chapter. That year, Thomasa Gerónima, from the town of Huexotzingo, between Puebla and Mexico City, was denounced and eventually prosecuted for bigamy. Her first husband, Joseph de la Cruz, was an indio from the same town. After they wed in 1679, the young couple lived together blissfully, albeit briefly. Joseph's job as a muleteer kept him on the road, and soon he ignited an old flame. Confronted with the news of his adultery and disappointed with her husband's missteps, Thomasa fled her home and engaged in a liaison of her own, befriending Antonio López in the town of San Phelipe. The two lived together for two years before deciding to move to Mexico City. Never married, their consensual union produced three children. Thomasa's relationship with Antonio soured, and they eventually parted. In the meantime, Thomasa claimed to have learned that her husband had been violently killed by a bull in the annual bullfight celebrated on the feast day of San Diego. Liberated from her marriage, or so she thought, Thomasa began a romantic courtship with Sebastián Fabián, the mulato slave of a hacienda owner. The relationship was consummated by marriage on July 27, 1693.

Sebastián's master was extremely suspicious of Thomasa. They had known each other for roughly six years, and he had independently made multiple inquiries into her marital status during this time, probably knowing that she had several children. As the master's questioning intensified, the couple resorted to near desperate measures. After a trip to Thomasa's hometown of Huexotzingo (where Sebastián's master had asked him to investigate Thomasa's history thoroughly), the couple produced a fake letter detailing and confirming the death of Thomasa's husband. Sebastián presented it to his master, who was not reassured and became all the more suspicious. The case became even more dramatic with Thomasa's daring jailbreak at the outset of the official inquisitorial process, but for the purposes of this chapter, what is most intriguing are the details of the sinuous shifts to Thomasa's casta.

She proved to be a chameleon. While awaiting trial, she unequivocally claimed indio status, declaring that her parents were the indios Juan de la Cruz Escudero and María Vázquez and that her grandparents were also all indios. This was never confirmed. At the time of her first marriage, Thomasa's casta was, curiously, never mentioned. Her second marriage license was never found. Meanwhile, at the moment of her denunciation,

Thomasa's accuser, from her hometown of Huexotzingo, stated that she was a loba – a status change that made a lasting impression on certain Church officials in Mexico City. As they prepared requests to obtain further information for the case, they too used the term loba to describe her. However, before interrogating any witnesses, Huexotzingo's local commissioner recast Thomasa's identity as that of mestiza, following the caste of her mother. As testimony in the town unfolded, the commissioner's classification was confirmed by several witnesses, who likewise described Thomasa as a mestiza. The primary cleric who was managing the case in Mexico City was not persuaded. He continued to refer to Thomasa as a loba, a status he would later confuse by calling her a mulata. Other inquisitors in Mexico City oscillated between describing Thomasa as a loba, mestiza, coyote, or mulata. In the meantime, witnesses of the second marriage described her as a mestiza. By the time the case concluded and she was banished from Mexico City, Thomasa had rotated through a full cycle of casta identities.[39]

This final case exemplifies in wonderful detail the net effect of the scrutiny that individuals endured in the midst of the legal process. As a person's casta was repeatedly interpreted, reinterpreted, and reclassified, he or she effectively endured a process of hyperhybridity wherein their somatic features, in conjunction with cues taken from their lineage, could precipitate an exponential proliferation of casta statuses. Hybridity has meant many things in the scholarly literature. At its most basic level, the term entered academic and intellectual discourse as a means to discuss racial mixture and its effects – a usage that has still not disappeared.[40] However, as a discursive tool, the meaning of hybridity has undergone several transformations. In its broadest form, hybridity essentially refers to processes of cultural, social, and biological interactivity that resist the formation of coherent ethnic and racial identities.[41]

---

[39] AGN, Inquisición, vol. 451, exp. 1, fols. 1–122.

[40] See R. C. Young, *Colonial Desire: Hybridity in Theory, Culture, and Race* (London: Routledge, 1995).

[41] Multiculturalism has been described as the antithesis of hybridity. The *multi-* prefix implies discreet identities interacting with one another, presumably in a nation-state. In the early 1990s, a flurry of theoretical refinements combined with widespread adoption of "hybridity" across academic discourses produced different "schools" of hybridity, as well as a backlash to its presumed premises. Some major figures include Homi Bhabha, *The Location of Culture* (London: Routledge, 1994); Néstor García Canclini, *Hybrid Cultures: Strategies for Entering and Leaving Modernity*, trans. C. Chiappari and S. López (Minneapolis and London: University of Minneapolis Press, 1995 [Spanish original, *Culturas híbridas, estratégias para entrar y salir de la modernidad*, 1989]);

Thomasa's hyperhybridity (and that of others like her) was enabled by
miscegenation but also transcended the forces of racial mixture. In other
words, while the range of casta categories through which a person like

Anne Stoler, *Carnal Knowledge and Imperial Power: Race and the Intimate in Colonial
Rule* (Berkeley: University of California Press, 2002); Paul Gilroy, *The Black Atlantic:
Modernity and Double Consciousness* (Cambridge, MA: Harvard University Press,
1993); and Aijaz Ahmad, *In Our Time: Empire, Politics, Culture* (London: Verso,
2007). Bhaba's *The Location of Culture* is a seminal text in hybridity studies. Using
postcolonial literature, he discusses how colonial subjects' appropriation of imperial
language and culture should be understood as inherently destabilizing. This "mimicry,"
he argues, is not capitulation; through replication of imperialist enunciations, slippages
inevitably occur, and thus a hybrid subject necessarily results from such interactions.
In this way, colonial discourse is not represented but dynamically replicated by those who
use the gap between the "original" and the "copy" to bring into being a "third space" –
one that embodies and enables subversive colonial resistance. Bhabha's theories of
mimicry, based in textual, post-Lacanian analysis, are similar to Judith Butler's concept
of "performativity" – the replication of normative gender (with the attendant power
dynamics involved in hetero-normativity and patriarchy) and the potential for resistance
in the slippages inherent in the continual reenactment of the gendered body. See
Judith Butler, *Gender Trouble: Feminism and the Subversion of Identity* (New York:
Routledge, 1999). An important difference is that for Bhabha, mimicry necessarily
produces the strategies of resistance (at least rhetorical strategies), whereas for Butler
performativity demonstrates the potential for resistance but does not necessarily lead to
active subversion. Bhabha is sometimes said to represent the "psychoanalytic and literary
side" of hybridity studies and García Canclini to be the exemplar of the "anthropological
and sociological" use of the concept. García Canclini's most influential works concerning
hybridity studies (influential at least for the English-speaking world; they are his only
translated books) are *Consumers and Citizens: Globalization and Multicultural Conflicts*
(1991) and *Hybrid Cultures: Strategies for Entering and Leaving Modernity* (1995). For
García Canclini, an anthropologist, hybridity underscores how modernity in Latin
America is composed of heterogeneous, hybrid temporalities – that is, ways in which
contemporary cultures and socioeconomic structures in postcolonial Latin America are
marked by blends and mixtures of "tradition" and innovation. Anne Stoler and Paul
Gilroy are heavy hitters in hybridity studies, and their work has more directly influenced
historians. Stoler incorporates subaltern theorists such as Gayatri Spivak, along with
Foucault and others, to interrogate sexuality and regulation in colonial spaces, particularly in Southeast Asia. Her 2002 book *Carnal Knowledge and Imperial Power: Race and
the Intimate in Colonial Rule* most directly engages with the "hybrid turn." Gilroy's
The Black Atlantic engages with the history of transatlantic African migrations and
movements to present a "counterculture of modernity" that rejects nationalism and
ethnic purity and instead embraces hybrid spaces, races, and self-identifications. He
focuses on African American and black British intellectuals, and his work with music
has been particularly influential. For Gilroy, the ship at sea (now carrying people on
voluntary migrations) serves as a key metaphor for hybrid selves and liminal encounters.
See in addition Jeremy H. Bentley, *Old World Encounters: Cross-Cultural Contacts and
Exchanges in Pre-Modern Times* (New York and Oxford: Oxford University Press,
1993); Paul Gilroy, *The Black Atlantic*; Marwan Kraidy, *Hybridity, or the Cultural
Logic of Globalization* (Philadelphia: Temple University Press, 2005); Ann Stoler,
Carnal Knowledge; and Young, *Colonial Desire*.

Thomasa passed could not exist without miscegenation, her multiple permutations of casta had much to do with other factors. It was through institutionally underwritten activities, orchestrated primarily by bureaucrats who were seeking caste information about colonists, that hyperhybridity was enacted, eventually compelling people like Thomasa to be seen kaleidoscopically.

The prismatic outcomes of hyperhybridity were not visible to all. It is doubtful that Thomasa (and people like her) ever grasped the full range of castes she projected or that were projected onto her. She probably had little idea that she was being classified as a coyote, mulata, or loba, but this did not make the process or its effects any less real. Hyperhybridity probably entailed a great price on colonial ideologies of difference. It did not radically change elite culture or affect colonial outlooks writ large. Rather, hyperhybridity was subtler, probably delivering its most significant impact within the circuitry of the colonial system, especially in the operation of its courts and offices at the midmanagerial level and below. In an inversion of what Homi Bhabha has termed "mimicry" – wherein colonial subjects appropriated imperial language, systems, and culture and used them toward destabilizing ends – the process of hyperhybridity effectively turned the cycle around.[42] It reappropriated what colonists had already absorbed and "mimicked." Then it deployed these remastered conceptions to stabilizing effect in the arena of the courts. In bringing forth a cacophony of possible identities that bureaucrats embraced and even expanded on, hyperhybridity generated an unusual openness to individual casta shifts for certain members of society, especially those from the popular masses. Below the ranks of the elite, hyperhybridity was daily testimony to the elasticity of colonial perspectives on casta and racial mixture, while at the same time serving to further extend that malleability. This feature, detectable in the context of the bigamy cases of the extreme castas, may have had wider ramifications for other colonial situations and contexts. It was also emblematic of a unique type of caste mobility harbored under castizaje – one that loosened casta enough to help it serve as a credible precursor to mestizaje.

---

[42] Bhabha, *The Location of Culture.*

9

Colonial Bequests

A DEATH'S KNELL

Caste, at least as it was articulated, lived, and practiced in Mexico, should have died by 1822. From September 16, 1810, when the insurgency movement that led to Mexican independence began, until the early 1820s, the country underwent a bloody struggle that claimed the lives of countless individuals who fought not only for political liberty but also for the end of a social order that had tried to control vast population groups by maintaining a caste-based hierarchy. Caste's demise was articulated triumphantly at both ends of the revolutionary effort. Not long after the priest and rebel leader Miguel Hidalgo first summoned his parishioners to take arms against the Spaniards in 1810, his movement, which swelled to include nearly 60,000 Indians and those of mixed-race castes, quickly reinterpreted his *grito* as a cry for ending all-white rule and its accompanying caste disparities. As his followers became radicalized around tribute collection and other powerful symbols of inequity, the white creole population had much to fear.

In the aftermath of a bloody massacre in the streets of Guanajuato in which whites were isolated and targeted for extermination by Hidalgo's followers, the creole elite counterattacked viciously, with the help of the Spaniards. Hidalgo's motley movement buckled under the pressure, and shortly thereafter the leader was executed. But the message that caste hierarchy was an abomination had been duly received and would be picked up by future rebel leaders, including José María Morelos and Vicente Guerrero, themselves of mixed-race origins. On September 14, 1813, in a memorable document titled *Sentimientos de la Nación*

(Sentiments of the Nation) delivered to the Revolutionary Congress at Chilpancingo, Morelos stated, "Slavery is forbidden forever, as well as the distinction of *casta*, leaving everyone equal; Americans will be distinguished from one another only by virtue and vice."[1] Although Morelos's bold declaration was followed by years of alternating vacillation and struggle, there was a dramatic resolution when in July 1822 the newly crowned Mexican emperor, Agustín Iturbide, issued a statement declaring that everyone, regardless of race – except for Indians – was to be considered a full citizen. In October of that year, Church officials were ordered to stop using caste labels for identifying and recording their parishioners. The only exception allowed was for categories recorded during the ceremony of matrimony.[2] In 1824, the newly drafted Mexican constitution upheld and formalized this position by decreeing civil equality regardless of race and origin.

The final legislative blows to caste came with the efforts to abolish slavery. As long as slavery persisted, society retained a structural need to preserve aspects of caste hierarchy and nomenclature so as to demarcate the place of slaves. Gradually, slavery crumbled. In July 1824, the slave trade was outlawed, although Mexican slave owners were permitted to keep slaves already in their possession. In 1825, to accelerate the emancipation process, the government began purchasing slaves from landholders. Slaves were issued their freedom amid much fanfare, in a public ceremony commemorating the anniversary of independence. Finally, on September 15, 1829, President Vicente Guerrero banned slavery completely in Mexico. Through these acts, the foundations for a new and potentially harmonious society, largely bereft of caste, were laid.

Despite the legal end of casta in Mexico, time and truth would reveal an alternate fate. The new nation's large indigenous population and the persistence of some colonial-era recordkeeping practices for native groups, especially in remote areas, meant that some places would preserve caste distinctions in documents well into the 1830s. Certain church parishes also consciously violated their mandate to use casta labels only

---

[1] Quoted in Felipe Tena Ramírez, *Leyes fundamentales de México, 1808–1971* (Mexico City: Porrúa, 1971), 30.

[2] Álvaro Ochoa Serrano, "Los africanos en México antes de Aguirre Beltrán (1821–1924)," *Afro-Latin American Research Association (PALARA)* 2 (1998): 80; and Ochoa Serrano "Los africanos en México antes de Aguirre Beltrán (1821–1924)," in *El rostro colectivo de la nación mexicana*, ed. by María Guadalupe Chávez Carvajal, 169–189 (Morelia, Michoacán: Instituto de Investigaciones Históricas de la Universidad Michoacana de San Nicolás de Hidalgo), 1997.

in matrimonial records. At least until 1840, various other records bearing caste classifications could be found. There was also an unquantifiable persistence of casta terminologies in the Mexican public's everyday conversations, even well after independence. In places like Mexico City, a number of colonial-era institutions that had been organized along casta principles survived independence in somewhat altered form; of these, some, in a striking and ironic turn, were partially appropriated by local populations to shape interpersonal relations, interactions with powerbrokers, and even relationships with the state.[3] So caste continued to function in the early national period, albeit repurposed for other ends. Finally, casta designations persisted sporadically in census records into the latter half of the nineteenth century.[4] While caste unquestionably sustained nearly fatal blows in the 1820s, it did not vanish entirely, or even quietly.

GLIMPSES OF CASTA'S AFTERLIFE

The century between the end of the colonial regime in 1821 and the last years of the Mexican Revolution bore dramatic political and ideological contrasts as a range of governance philosophies and approaches to national development were explored. Mexico would ride a veritable carousel of ruling forms and rulers – strongman dictatorship, constitutional monarchy, foreign monarchy, liberal reform, government by conservative principles, federal rule, and centralism. The century saw some of the darkest, most unstable, and economically challenging moments of Mexican history, with no fewer than ten presidents governing the country between 1835 and 1846. Upon the conclusion of a catastrophic war with the United States in 1848, Mexico lost over half of its national territory.

The country was both devastated and demoralized, leaving intellectuals and politicians largely pessimistic about the nation's future and unsure what to try next. The government of Benito Juárez (1861–1872) offered a few glimmers of hope as Mexico entered a much-needed reform period after defeating the French, who had briefly occupied the nation. Under Juárez, some of the liberal principles championed by members of Mexico's

---

[3] This insight is found in the intriguing work of Matthew D. O'Hara, *A Flock Divided: Race, Religion, and Politics in Mexico, 1749–1857* (Durham: Duke University Press, 2010).

[4] Moisés González Navarro, "El mestizaje mexicano en el periodo nacional," *Revista Mexicana de Sociología* 30, no. 1 (January–March 1968): 35–52; O'Hara, *A Flock Divided*.

progressive political cliques were adopted. Yet it was clear that there were serious shortcomings: Juárez's actions were not palatable to all, and his attempts to centralize power in Mexico City came at the expense of state autonomy. With powerful factions estranged from the central government, the stage was set for the rise of General Porfirio Díaz, a mestizo war hero who seized power in 1876, four years after Juárez died of a heart attack.

For the next 35 years, a desperately needed peace fell over Mexico. Some of the nation-building projects that had commenced earlier began to take full shape. In the intellectual realm, the publication of Vicente Riva Palacio's multivolume masterwork of Mexican history, *México a través de los siglos*, represented a signature feat (Figure 18). It assembled for the first time a coherent national narrative that synthesized and rationalized what had been construed up to this point as a series of fractured and disjunctured events. Widely known and broadly popularized, the landmark work also successfully folded a largely forgotten native past into what had been deemed a maligned and reviled era of colonial rule. Presenting primary documents and copious illustrations, and employing a largely balanced historical writing style that intentionally veered away from the polemically written histories of Mexico's past, *México a través de los siglos* traced a progressive and positive arc in the Mexican saga, moving steadily through the struggle of independence and turbulent early nationalism to the years of Díaz's reign. Mexicans could now see that what may have seemed to be missteps in their history were actually encouraging strides along an evolutionary track. *México a través de los siglos* also openly conveyed Mexico's ethnic fusion and accretion of cultures as favorable, thereby positioning the nation for what was to come and defining it as good. Though it did not provide a blueprint, this influential and widely read masterwork offered a structure for the development of mestizaje by situating the mestizo near the center of Mexican history.[5]

It is important to remember that this unforeseen climax (the emergence of mestizaje) was long in the making. Although mestizos rose considerably in prominence and stature during the nineteenth century, the full meaning of their ascendance was not immediately grasped in wider society. The period leading up to the 1910 Mexican Revolution was very much

---

[5] A superb synthesis showing how Mexico envisioned itself and its future in the period between independence and the Mexican Revolution can be found in a brilliant book by Enrique Florescano, *National Narratives in Mexico: A History* (University of Oklahoma Press, 2002), 261–309. The book examines the full sweep of Mexican history.

FIGURE 18 Vicente Riva Palacio.
Source: Courtesy of the Library of Congress.

a time when streams of ideas about national image, race, and nationhood were being defined and then tested against each other in both the public sphere and private forums. Before the rise of mestizaje, these debates would have an inevitable effect on the perception and application of caste. Stripped of its anchor in colonial-era ideology, caste was now afloat in a milieu in which the firm ideological compass of mestizaje was not yet clearly formulated.

Indeed, much like the colonial notion of casta itself, *mestizaje* was one of several terms used interchangeably and loosely – for example, *mestización*, hybridization, and *cruzamiento* (crossing). The confusions these terms produced probably afforded a more fertile situation than one might surmise, in that as all of these terms competed, any one of them stood a chance to usurp the primacy of mestizaje. Nineteenth-century science started to help clarify the differences between them. Because in the realms of zoology and botany the act of uniting two different species was said to produce "hybrids," it was eventually determined that mestizos could not be considered the by-product of "hybridization." Mestizos were instead deemed the outcome of racial mixing *within* a species (humans). Meanwhile, *cruzamiento* was seen to describe the process where members of a "pure race" (typically male) mated with a hybrid or a mestizo.[6] The term *cruzamiento*, therefore, emerged as more constraining than the type of mixture that mestizaje would later connote. In short, as time progressed, *mestizaje* and *mestización* gradually surfaced as the best candidates for conveying the processes of everyday interracial mixing.[7] However, a great assortment of other options still remained. And survivor as it was, the idea of casta did not disappear, but instead found a place in the nineteenth century.

Casta's new life in the postindependence era became closely tied to the political struggles and issues of the times. Invoking the term *casta* and any adherence to it became a way for liberal politicians and reformers to efface the Church and the military, and for conservatives to reference and historicize certain principles that they held dear, such as the preservation of corporate privilege. While invocations of casta in the colonial period could certainly possess political dimensions, arguably "casta politics" during these times tended to be more rooted in the daily lives and local maneuverings of officials and colonists.[8] Simply put, the colonial politics

---

[6] *El Cultivador*, November 1, 1873, Mexico City, 129. I did not find a consensus on this view, and certainly there are counterexamples to take into consideration.

[7] Nineteenth-century discussion surrounding the terms *mestizaje* and *mestización* often involved trying to determine at what point cross-breeding either improved or perfected races, or yielded pure races. Originating in the spheres of plant and animal husbandry, this discussion came to involve humans as well. For examples, see *Boletín de Agricultura Minera e Industrias*, October 1, 1891, Mexico City, 56–58; and *Semana Mercantil*, Mexico City, December 13, 1886.

[8] *Casta's* entry into Mexico's political arena was by no means new. Although imperial rule conditioned the ways in which casta operated politically in the colonial period, its presence was felt. For instance, viceregal officials worried openly about the menace that disgruntled casta masses might pose, particularly if their plight somehow aligned with that of Indians. The 1692 grain riots in Mexico City provide a good example. A series of meager harvests, the pinch of inflation, and food scarcity sparked alliances between natives and castas (among other groups) who cried death to all *gachupines* (white Spaniards) and bad

of casta was tied up in real people in new and changing situations, and in pressing problems that demanded resolution in real time.

In the postindependence era, casta was spoken about more conceptually, as an idea or value decoupled from actual people. Invoking caste in politics targeted abstract characteristics of society. Certainly, these issues were not altogether absent in the colonial period. Statesmen, intellectuals, and clerics alike often wondered about the long-term effect of the racial mixing on their world, but they were also mired in the practicalities of managing caste and thus did not have the luxury of distancing themselves to ponder what a world without castas would be like. The vantage of the postindependence era offered exactly this type of historical distance and hindsight.

Almost to a person, the writers and thinkers of the nineteenth century conceived of casta as belonging to a different time, connoting different experiences. In fact, some authors mentioned casta almost exclusively when referencing history, as if to support the notion that Mexico had moved well beyond this age.[9] One of the great conservative thinkers of his times, Lucas Alamán (1792–1853; Figure 19), did precisely that in *Historia de México*. The book offers trenchant insight into how caste structured the colonial world but provides virtually no understanding of what casta meant to the author's contemporaries.[10] Others who adopted

government. For an excellent treatment of the 1692 grain riots, see Cope, *The Limits of Racial Domination*, 125–160. This study demonstrates how the riot brought together a complex set of alliances that cannot be neatly described as an alignment of Indians and castas against Spaniards. In the rural sphere, as we have seen in other chapters of this book, crown officials were equally leery of casta-Indian political ties, especially in situations where castas held political offices in predominantly native communities. As independence drew near, a number of Church figures and crown bureaucrats expressed fears over policies that they thought overly circumscribed the castas, potentially converting them into a hostile force. Don Manuel Abad y Queipo, a cleric from Michoacán, wrote extensively on these matters between 1790 and 1810. On his mind, and a concern to others who shared his opinion, were most likely such recent violent upheavals as the Lambayeque tax revolt in Peru and the Comunero rebellion in New Granada. For Abad y Queipo's republished writings, see José María Luis Mora, *Obras sueltas de José María Luis Mora, ciudadano mexicano*, Vol. 1 (Paris: Librería de Rosa, 1837), 54–69, 148–150. Another exemplary instance of colonial casta politics is the use by elites of the caste heritage of their rivals to discredit their candidacy for specific offices or to reveal them as unfit for special business opportunities, marriage alliances, and privileges.

[9] Two works that exemplify this trend are Juan Antonio Mateos, *Sacerdote y caudillo: memorias de la insurrección, novela histórica mexicana*, 9th edition, illustrated (Mexico and Buenos Aires: Maucci Hermanos, 1902); and Gabino Barreda, *Opúsculos, discusiones y discursos* (Mexico City: Impr. del Comercio, 1877), esp. 96, 104.

[10] Lucas Alamán, *Historia de México*, Vol. 1 (Mexico City: Imprenta de Victoriano Agüeros y Comp., 1883), 29, 32, 39.

FIGURE 19 Lucas Alamán.
Source: Courtesy of the Library of Congress.

a historical approach to caste tended to highlight its pitfalls and faults, juxtaposing them against what they believed was their own more progressive era. In his *México y sus revoluciones*, the influential liberal thinker and cleric José María Luis Mora (1794–1850) reflected on how small numbers of Spaniards were able to exert wide control over vast territories and populations during the colonial period, reasoning that it was largely by opportunistically melding Old World and New World whites that a strong bloc of caste-bound elites was formed, with each group fortifying the other so as to survive.[11] Not only were caste distinctions abolished after independence, Mora noted, but along with them the colonial state's tendency to assign noble privileges to oligarchies, which is what had made caste distinctions so meaningful in the preindependence years. This important accomplishment of the colonial period was to be celebrated but never repeated, he wrote.[12] Fellow liberal thinkers Melchor Ocampo (1814–1861) and Guillermo Prieto (1818–1897) essentially agreed with Mora, adding that casta had also been crucial for determining how the colonial government apportioned land and labor. However, Prieto argued that caste had been overly influential in structuring the colonial economy – another fate to be avoided at all costs.[13]

Vicente Riva Palacio (1832–1896) – statesman, attorney, novelist, orator, and the author of *México a través de los siglos* – also used a historical approach to caste in his writings. Riva Palacio often incorporated casta to contextualize and provide detail for scenes in his historical novels; his use of caste seems consistent with his objective: to narrate the colonial experience on its own terms. However, Riva Palacio occasionally described the complexity of the various casta nomenclatures for other ends, such as to ridicule the caste scheme itself. Through the language of casta, people of the colonial period, he wrote, were accustomed to describing themselves "like dogs and horses."[14]

[11] José María Luis Mora, *México y sus revoluciones*, Vol. 2 (Mexico: Porrúa, 1977), 228–229, 258. Some of these viewpoints were shared by Ignacio L. Vallarta – especially the idea that caste derivations resulted from the effort to tailor privileges to certain groups. See Vallarta, *Obras completas* (Mexico City: José Joaquín Terrazas e Hijas, 1897), 79.

[12] Mora, *México y sus revoluciones*, Vol. 1, clxxxviii.

[13] Melchor Ocampo, *Obras completas*, Vol. 1 (Mexico City: J. de Elizade, 1900), 20–21; Guillermo Prieto, *Memorias de mis tiempos, 1828–1840* (Mexico City and Paris: Librería de la Vda. de C. Bouret, 1906), 45.

[14] Vicente Riva Palacio, *Memorias de un impostor. Don Guillén de Lampart, rey de México: novela histórica* (Mexico City: Porrúa, 1872), 18. Note that Riva Palacio believed that casta terms were used in this manner because there was little conception of equality amongst people in the colonial period. See Vicente Riva Palacio, *Las dos emparedadas: memorias de los tiempos de la Inquisición* (Mexico City: T. F. Neve, 1869), 322. See also Riva Palacio, Manuel Payno, Juan E. Mateos, and Rafael Martínez de la Torre, *El libro rojo, 1520–1867*, Vol. 1 (Mexico City: A. Pola, 1905), 414, which shows again how caste was relegated to a different time. Another subtlety evident in Riva Palacio's writings, and manifested in others' work as well, was the tendency to conflate race and casta in discussing how the various caste groups originated. Riva Palacio noted that there were

Francisco Bulnes (1847–1924; Figure 20), a member of Porfirio Díaz's elite team of *científicos* (technocrats), worried about the effect of Mexico's legacy of colonial hierarchy on the nation's future and looked outside of Mexico in an attempt to understand caste more broadly. China, India, Persia, Peru, and Egypt provided Bulnes with examples of what he termed an "imperio de castas," or a form of caste regime. Each of these nations had been governed by a caste order that had cycled in and out of favor through time. Bulnes advocated the notion that caste-based societies were not necessarily bad, noting that the imperios de castas had been able to produce prolonged periods of stability and prosperity during which empires had enjoyed relatively peaceful existences, sometimes lasting centuries.[15] Problems came, Bulnes observed, when the descendants of these older societies clung to past glory in more modern times. These nostalgics, whom he labeled traditionalists, became the prime inhibitors of progress. They threatened modern patriotism, which he argued demanded progressive thinking and an obligation on the part of citizens to sacrifice their individual needs for those of the nation. Traditionalists were trained to obey – they lacked leadership, entrepreneurial drive, and initiative. They possessed what he believed was a natural human instinct to preserve the past and edify old customs.[16] Those who heeded their teachings risked becoming zombies, incapable of generating the type of rational reflection demanded by an advanced nation-state. Bulnes believed that this fate had been avoided in Brazil, Argentina, and Chile – due in no small measure to their successful immigration policies – but that the rest of Latin America had much to fear from the dreaded traditionalists. In *El porvenir de las naciones hispanoamericanas*, Bulnes wrote disparagingly of the people of other nations in the region:

groups of core "races" from which the castas sprang: españoles, indios, and negros. The mixture of these races, then, was primarily responsible for engineering castas. It is highly doubtful that Riva Palacio or others would have paid close attention to how they were merging the two concepts, and this is precisely the point. We have already noted a robust tradition in the colonial period for combining concepts and terminologies. Early on, race and caste were interchangeable, and probably more so in the eighteenth century than in the 1600s. In the nineteenth century, with the rise of sharper understandings about what race meant, both race and casta grew more mutually descriptive, if not symbiotic, in the minds of many Mexican thinkers. Certainly, this entwining was displayed in the writings of Riva Palacio.

[15] Francisco Bulnes, *El verdadero Juárez y la verdad sobre la intervención y el imperio* (Paris: C. Bouret, 1904), 480.
[16] Ibid., 459

FIGURE 20 Francisco Bulnes.
Source: Courtesy of the Library of Congress.

A mass of anonymous individuals, formed out of the empires of *castas*; not ancient empires, [but] modern ones, from almost yesterday. The Conquest encountered Incan and Aztec empires organized along *casta* lines; the Spanish system [both] sought and achieved [the prolongation] of this *casta* arrangement. What [does it mean] to have [the] popular masses modeled into *castas*? ... The "*hombre de casta*" [man of caste] does not know, nor does he have the capacity to know, what a government is; nor does he think, nor is he able to think about making law and legislation; this is because he is already formed. All barbarians believe the past to be superior to the present and the future, and the public and private rights of the *sociedad de castas* stems from this [past], like eternal cordilleras in the midst of near prehistoric times. In such [casta] societies there is only one great police force that patrols the world; and that is the memory of what our fathers did. ... *Casta* is a fence, and within it [there is] a cage, the *sub-casta*. Within the cage is a department, the rural farm; within the department is a starving trunk, the family. ... A society of *castas* is governed like battalions, with flags [and] drumbeats, [and with] customs, like government, to tie it up, prostrate it, vilify and debase it without making it suffer. Nothing refines [the society], but nothing destroys it. ... It is true that these societies remain intact for fifty centuries, but when they end, their people are useless prostitutes for the nation. ... There is not a single case in which a society of *castas* has developed into a great civilization, bearing the heart of liberty. The remains of *casta* that have endured in the world have only enslaved others; it is not possible to transform it without transfusing another form of blood."[17]

In some ways, these musings on casta were wholly predictable. Mexico's leaders needed to sow the ground for the future. Caste was a symbol of structural inequality embedded in an ancient regime, and as such it had to be removed to allow society to move forward. But those who studied and reflected on casta from a safe historical distance tended not to see its malleability and fluidity. They especially failed to see the degree of elasticity described in this book. In some ways, they couldn't. The condition of the archives and the types of questions being asked by scholars at the time were not conducive to opening up that vision. These intellectuals were also prone to being influenced by their readings of international caste systems in places like India. Many found it hard to isolate Mexico's particular casta experience from what they knew about caste worldwide. Therefore, it was hard to particularize, situate, and distinguish the character and outcome of Mexico's casta fluidity in the larger course of history, making it appear more rigid than it was. Moreover, Mexico's intellectuals were facing immediate and sweeping challenges that did not call for unpacking the intricacy and nuance of colonial-era casta. Often, the nature of their work demanded conveying quick, rough, and broad strokes of history, leaving finer points aside. Hence, these thinkers wrote about what casta symbolically represented and what the sistema de castas

---

[17] Francisco Bulnes, *El porvenir de las naciones latino-americanas ante las recientes conquistas de Europa y Norteamérica: estructura y evólucion de un continente* (Mexico City: Imprenta de Mariano Nava, 1899; Pensamiento Vivo de América, 1940), 234–236.

had achieved (or at least was supposed to have achieved) in terms of maintaining the position of the colonial elite. They also described the price Mexico was paying for its legacy of caste policy. Many, including Bulnes, took to heart the words of the Prussian naturalist and geographer Alexander von Humboldt, whose journey through Latin America in the late eighteenth century produced a number of incisive observations about its political system on the eve of independence. In his *Political Essay on the Kingdom of New Spain*, Humboldt wrote that one of the major fissures holding Latin America back was its division into castas. The cancerous hatred it produced had to be addressed, he said, if Mexico, or any other part of the Spanish New World, was to enjoy long-term success.[18]

The end of the struggle for independence produced another twist. Postindependence discussions of casta prioritized an understanding of power relationships, especially of how caste oppressed populations. Interestingly, the growing prominence of mestizos gave them an important voice in this conversation, following on its suppression during colonial times. Among the new, strong critical voices was the liberal activist Ignacio Manuel Altamirano (1834–1893; Figure 21). An Amerindian born into poverty, Altamirano went on to receive an education, eventually becoming an important man of letters during the regime of Benito Juárez. Altamirano's background is important in establishing his outlook and passion for exalting all things Mexican. He was committed to the task of creating a Mexican national literature by harvesting the country's unique regional cultures and languages. As with other intellectuals we have discussed, Altamirano was skilled at depicting caste as a fossil of history and using it as a means to lodge subtle criticisms at society, past and present. With this in mind, in his novel *Clemencia*, Altamirano uses the term "naturaleza casta" (found abundantly in colonial records) to

---

[18] Alexander von Humbolt, *Political Essay on the Kingdom of New Spain*, book 2 (Paris, 1811; London, 1811; publisher not identified), chap. 7, pp. 196–197. The full quote is as follows: "The want of sociability so universal in the Spanish colonies, and the hatreds which divide the castes of greatest affinity, the effects of which shed a bitterness over the life of the colonists, are solely due to the political principles by which these regions have been governed since the sixteenth century. A government aware of the true interests of humanity will be able to diffuse information and instruction, and by extinguishing gradually the monstrous inequality of rights and fortunes, will succeed in increasing the physical well-being of the settlers [and] gradually eliminate that monstrous inequality of right and wealth, but it will have to overcome immense difficulties when it wishes to make the inhabitants sociable and teach them to treat each other mutually as citizens." This passage was definitely on the mind of Bulnes, who quoted it in its entirety in *El porvenir de las naciones hispanoamericanas*, 70.

D. Ignacio Manuel Altamirano

FIGURE 21 Ignacio Manuel Altamirano.
Source: Courtesy of the Library of Congress.

discuss one of the characters in the book. Set against the backdrop of the French occupation of Mexico in the mid-nineteenth century, this classic story of Mexican literature was heralded as one of the great novels of its time. It concerns the tragic love quadrangle between Enrique Flores, a handsome, blond soldier whose character fails to measure up to his good looks; Fernando Valle, a dark, ugly, and sickly man of glowing inner qualities; Clemencia, a classic dark-haired bombshell who is hopelessly in love with Enrique; and Isabel, a pallid woman of exceptional good looks who is also enthralled by Enrique. As the story unfolds to its tragic end (Fernando dies for Enrique's missteps, leaving Isabel forlorn and lonely, and Clemencia goes to a convent), Enrique advises Fernando about where he should direct his love. Predictably, Fernando is smitten by the fair Isabel, but Enrique tries to persuade him that he should be channeling his energies and feelings toward Clemencia. The conversation thickly discusses physical characteristics and racial stereotypes. Altamirano uses Enrique's voice to make a sage comment on Fernando's caste identity and how it should fit into solving the puzzle of this tragic love story:

> You should forget about Isabel, and this won't be a significant sacrifice since the beautiful, divine *morena* [Clemencia], who is the type of woman who would make a Dn. Juan content, will fling open her arms to you, smiling with all the promises of an ardent and intoxicating love. How happy you will be, Fernando! You, being of *casta* birth [*naturaleza casta*], a sad dreamer, finding yourself suddenly at the gate of an oriental paradise, guided by a houri devoted solely to you, with her black eyes, who will inebriate you with her breath of roses, who will slay you with her caresses of fire. C'mon man! Do you find this an unfortunate situation?[19]

In this passage, casta offered a commentary on aspirations. From the perspective of the white Enrique, someone of Fernando's features and background could certainly aspire to love, but within certain parameters. Ultimately, therefore, caste sealed Fernando into a fate that was not of his own desire. However, what Altamirano may have also been reaching for was of slightly greater register. It was Fernando, regardless of his looks and caste, who was, of the two men, the true gem. From the way the book was written, it did not take much for Altamirano's readers to recognize Mexico herself in such an assessment. Despite the fate that Europe, the United States, and others were assigning to Mexico due to its indigenous and mixed racial ancestry, as in the case of Fernando, there was a marvelous treasure embedded within that could someday be released, if properly guided.

In his writings, Altamirano construed casta primarily as divisive and oppositional.[20] Yet poetically he was capable of describing the full irony of caste – not just as figments of the past but also as an enduring, if muted, feature of modern Mexican democracy. In a telling passage in his *Paisajes y leyendas: tradiciones y costumbres*, he wrote that anyone who wanted an authentic picture of Mexican life, with its varied customs and peoples, could get it simply by boarding an outbound train from Mexico City's Plaza de Armas. Departing every ten minutes for some remote village or town, a passenger invariably encountered a "cataract of people spill[ing]

---

[19] Ignacio M. Altamirano, *Clemencia* (Mexico City and Paris: Imprenta de la Vda. de C. Bouret, 1907), 113.
[20] Ignacio M. Altamirano, *Paisajes y leyendas: tradiciones y costumbres de México* (Mexico City: Imprenta y Litografía Española, 1884), 87.

from the twenty wagons that constitute each train [as they arrived at the Villa de Guadalupe]," the whole forming a "picturesque," "riotous," "multi-colored," but "difficult to describe" mass. "On this train one will find all of the races of the old colony, all of the classes of the New Republic, all of the *castas* that live in our Democracy, all of the various forms of dress of our civilization, all of the opinions of our political scene, all the verities of vice, and all of the masks of our virtue."[21]

Although his vision was a fleeting comment in a much longer treatise, the irony of juxtaposing casta with democracy was likely not lost on Altamirano, who so carefully deployed the term in other settings. It seems that he deliberately used the three chief elements of social description – race, class, and casta – to suggest that, while the modern democratic republic seemed to be characterized by class distinctions rather than casta, it was nonetheless just as much the home of the sociedad de castas as colonial New Spain had been. In summoning race rather than casta to describe the inhabitants of the colonial era, he continued to blur lines, and did so intentionally. Although it would have been more accurate for him to have used *casta* to discuss the "old colony," he instead brought it to bear on the modern democracy, where it had supposedly gone dormant. This clever use of phrase heightened the impact of his point. Finally, by depicting the "races of the old colony" riding in a nineteenth-century, modern mass transit system, Altamirano juxtaposed modernity with tradition, alluding to the possibility that Mexico was figuratively carrying its past on its journey (and vessel) of modernity. This implied that the modern Mexican people were a by-product of the old. The conclusion of his passage is packed with cynicism. Altamirano insinuated that whatever virtues Mexico managed to display to the world constituted a farce; in truth, the nation had found ways to inappropriately infuse vice into qualities that might otherwise have had a redeeming effect on the nation, its posture, and its body politic.

In a different treatise, Altamirano's gaze sometimes took another turn. Seeking to understand why so many literary men and intellectuals came to disdain patriotism shortly after independence, he concluded that blame should be assigned to the civil conflicts and turmoil that had gripped the nation after Mexico's final victory over the Spaniards. What his peers had failed to fathom, he thought, was the true "tempestuous nature of democracy."[22] They expected, unrealistically, too rapid a rise to prosperity.

---

[21] Ibid., 85.

[22] Ignacio M. Altamirano and C. Sierra Casasús, *Obras completas* (Mexico City: Secretaría de Educación Pública, 1986), 332.

In the face of lackluster results, some began currying favor with the old regime, which was "easy to explain since the royalists were still alive, and they had not truly accepted independence themselves, except in the most hypocritical way."[23] So Altamirano painted a postindependence version of history wherein the old privileged classes – the clergy, the army, and members of the aristocracy – continued to dominate.

But in a shrewd flip of script, Altamirano proceeded to describe the members of the dominant classes themselves as castas: "[These were the] *castas* that hated the people [*el pueblo*], this is to say, the masses that had followed Hidalgo in his heroic uprising. ... The hate erupted in more threatening forms each day between these *castas* and the popular majority of the nation."[24] To appreciate the deftness of Altamirano's literary move, we must consider all the various meanings of *casta* and how they suited his purposes. Casta, of course, could mean all the masses of mixed-raced individuals who populated the colony; in fact, by many accounts they constituted the very masses who Altamirano and others described as staffing Hidalgo's army. Altamirano explicitly recast this group as "el pueblo" (the people), a true upgrade in their status: now the former castas comprised not the dominated masses, but the heart of the young nation. Meanwhile, in describing members of the aristocracy as the new castas of the postindependence era, Altamirano saddled them with all the negative baggage associated with sustaining caste hierarchy. Altamirano's aristocratic club, a corrosive vestige of the colonial regime, now constituted its own casta in his mind – one that intended to rule as their colonial counterparts did, through the subjugation of others to their corporate will and authority.[25]

As Altamirano would assert in still other works, education for the masses was essential. Without it, "There will always be an aristocracy that will dominate with all of the *fueros* (exemptions, rights) of a privileged *casta*; there will be patricians as in oligarchic republics."[26] Perpetual vigilance was needed to ensure that these privileged groups would not reemerge. The pulse of the nation lay elsewhere, Altamirano asserted, and with other, more-representative population groups. In Altamirano's writings, casta seemingly reached an inversion point from how it was conceived in

---

[23] Ibid.

[24] Ibid. The description reads, "castas que odiaban cordialmente al pueblo, es decir a las masas que habían seguido a Hidalgo en su levantamiento [heroico]."

[25] Note the similarities between these "castas" and Bulnes's traditionalists.

[26] Ignacio M. Altamirano, *Discursos: pronunciados en la tribuna* (Paris: Biblioteca de la Europa y América, 1892), 255.

FIGURE 22 Justo Sierra Méndez.
Source: Courtesy of the Library of Congress.

colonial times; now the former elite became the reviled castas, and the racially mixed masses constituted the young nation's best hope.

Justo Sierra Méndez (1848–1912; Figure 22) built on themes encountered in Altamirano's writings. A renowned technocrat and occasional critic of Porfirio Díaz's regime, as well as one of Mexico's seminal educators and historians, Sierra published a set of reflections in the *Revista Nacional de Letras y Ciencias* (1889). Here, he outlined how the privileges of the castas were under full assault, as they were being dismantled by what he classified as the *"mestizo* family."[27] Like

[27] Justo Sierra Méndez et al., *Revista Nacional de Letras y Ciencias*, Vol. 1 (Mexico City: Imprenta de la Secretaría de Fomento, 1889), 170–181.

Altamirano, Sierra frequently used multiple meanings of *casta* to describe different populations and circumstances. In this instance, he used it to characterize a segment of the aristocracy that had survived independence. Sierra brilliantly connected certain colonial conceptualizations of casta (specifically, references to a broad and amorphous mixed-race population) with emerging modern views about the character of the Mexican people. In fact, Sierra identified his "*mestizo* family" (which he also dubbed the "mestizo world" or the "neo-Mexicans") as direct descendants of the "antiguas castas" of viceregal times. These people, he noted, constituted a minority of Mexico's rural population, but they formed the bulk of urban residents and comprised the industrial backbone of the country. Hence, like Altamirano but even more explicitly, Sierra traced a direct lineage from the colonial castas to the center of national identity. Yet, in a feat of irony, he observed that "the neo-Mexicans, the *antiguas castas* ... in the colonial period suffered like Indians, but even more so because they were conscious of their sufferings. Now, this population governs the country; this population has done little for their [Indian] brothers for a century."[28] These newly empowered castas, therefore, were just as capable of oppression as the aristocratic club had been. The next phase of their development, he reasoned, would entail their embracing and elevating the Indian, for the greater sake of the nation.[29]

Sierra's writings on the topic of casta are of profound importance. He was part of a cadre of individuals attempting to build national unity around the figure of the mestizo. As a person who had held prominent posts within the government and was recognized as one of Mexico's primary intellectuals, Sierra was a prime candidate for translating the heritage of the colonial enterprise into emergent ideologies of national consensus. The connections Sierra made between the castas and the mestizo figure stand admittedly quiet within the broader annals of history, especially when placed alongside the other vast contributions he made as an intellectual figure. Regardless, his pontifications form an element of the story of casta's integration, rounding

---

[28] Ibid., 178.
[29] Another thinker who proffers an insight into how casta figured in the development of Mexico's classes is Ignacio Ramírez, *Obras de Ignacio Ramírez*, Vol. 2 (Mexico City: Oficina Tip. de la Secretaría de Fomento, 1889), 58. His connection to the theme is admittedly oblique, but we can see here how Ramírez's thinking about casta and the structure class disparities formed a backdrop to the fuller elaboration of caste in Mexico in the postindependence years.

out the picture of how casta skipped across time into the final product of mestizaje.[30]

CONCLUSION: THE COLONIAL BEQUEST

Before mestizaje, there was caste, changing ever so much through the vessel of castizaje. The world of the Spanish colonies was one that struggled for order amidst massive transformations and population change. Racial mixture constituted one of those disruptive forces. Amidst hazy beginnings and competing terminologies, the concept of caste emerged as the best tool to both describe and control New World peoples. But almost from inception, caste competed with itself to fulfill divergent goals. On the one hand were the local needs and objectives of colonists and minor bureaucrats, trying to make sense of their lives and experiences. For this, caste needed precision, which led to increased categorization, refinement, and even the proliferation of caste terminologies and expressions. Then there were the goals of the grander Church, the central government, and the broader apparatus of empire. In this register,

---

[30] The pages of the Mexican press in the nineteenth and early twentieth centuries, when it (rarely) entertained the notion of casta, tended to uphold the various depictions described throughout this chapter. A good example is the article "Nueva Obra Redentora" by Francisco Manríquez, published in *El Abogado Cristiano Ilustrado*, September 12, 1907, Mexico City. Much like Bulnes's work, this article discusses how Mexico's "imperio de castas" produced a miserable mass of agricultural laborers who were largely removed from the mainstream of civilization. It is possible that some writings of prominent intellectuals were simply republished (or originally published) in newspaper form. In other cases, it is clear that columnists were influenced by the work of leading thinkers and borrowed both their language and ideas as they commented on newsworthy matters. Since so many articles appearing in the press were satirical in nature, casta inevitably came into the line of fire. In an 1877 broadside taunting the congress in the wake of a tax hike on mescal and sugarcane rum producers, the author of an article titled "El congreso" lamented that this miserable lot of rowdy politicians, who consistently found themselves deadlocked like a "rat caught in a trap," demonstrated an extreme insensitivity to the people and their castas. Clearly, this article used *casta* much like race, implying that there was a gulf of distance between politicians and their constituency. "El Congreso," *Novena Broma*, Mexico City, April 8, 1877. In another article, in 1899, titled "Subasta pública" (public auction), the anonymous author metaphorically depicted Mexico as a man longing to marry and enjoy the pleasures of a woman. To make matters worse, everyone he knew was getting married. Ultimately, the man became so desperate that he announced that he would kill himself at the end of the month unless he found a woman. Trawling the depths of desperation, he confessed that any woman would do: "Inés, Juana, they are all the same." Finally, readers were hit with the punch line: "Girls, I am on auction: who wants me? who wants me?" Of course, the point was that no one would take him (Mexico) because of his casta. See "Subasta pública," *Cómico*, Mexico City, July 30, 1899.

the need for caste complexity collapsed somewhat, easing the task of how the upper echelons of colonial administration could manage the colonies on the whole. Ultimately, standing atop unsettled foundations, caste became slippery, enabling identities to become fluid in the process.

At its extremes, caste's fluidity became most apparent. People hopped into and out of categories. They lived caste plurally. Some even became hyperhybridized as the courts and multiple constituencies struggled over identity interpretations. Castes were flattened, smoothed, compounded, expanded. Meanings varied regionally, locally, individually. Caste, never hard and fast to begin with, loosened even more. Mobility became its modality. And a curious end was reached. As it segmented colonial society, caste also came to index and encompass the phenomenon of hybridity in its grandest form, occasionally making casta almost synonomous with racial mixture. Castizaje had helped casta reach this point.

Such was the state of affairs by the era of independence. Caste, as reviled a symbol as it was for many, stood on the brink of anticipating mestizaje. As the idea wove through the trials of the nineteenth century, this lost history, seen well at the margins of colonial caste, faintly prefigured what was to come.

Historian's Coda: Casta States of Mind

Almost 20 years ago, I had the unique experience of conducting and filming ethnographic interviews on the west coast of Mexico, in an area called the Costa Chica, a region with a history tightly linked to an Afro-Mexican past. Living in the small community of El Ciruelo with Fr. Glyn Jemmot Nelson, a Trinidadian priest who since 1984 had been a major protagonist in promoting a black-identity movement in the region, I vividly remember the answers my respondents gave when the line of questioning turned to matters of racial identity. "Somos mexicanos, somos cristianos" (we are Mexican, we are Christian). Nearly absent from the interviews were any specific mentions of blackness. Allusions to Christianity were predictable, even obligatory given the company that I was keeping.

In these responses, nationalism too spoke volumes. Mexico's goal of eradicating race after 1821 and building a national citizenry took hold firmly and deeply in these remote rural communities. But these very people, outside of the formal context of an interview, could be quick and unsparing in their descriptions of phenotype. In casual late-evening conversations around a hammock or on leisurely walks in the *milpas* (agricultural plots), residents conveyed nuances and understandings of racial difference that reminded me of what I had seen in the archives of colonial times. I was told that "in these parts some people are described as *negro fino* [fine black], *negro claro* [light/clear black], and *negro papayaste* [analogous to a coarse or rough blackness]." There was an equally deep understanding of who among them were indios and who were not. In general, people recognized subtle ethnic differences. And many mestizos were identified to me as important business owners, living on paved roads in the downtown sections of the area's villages.

These are impressions from the two decades past. Times have certainly changed. Black identity in Mexico now exists differently than before. Even at the time of my interviews, it was visibly shifting. Mexico has a black movement, and since 2015 blacks have been able to self-identify on the national census. But for me, my interviewees' impressions remind me that even in modern times, beneath all of the accomplishments of mestizaje in forging a national citizenry, a great deal of differentiation – not uncasta-like in its quality – persists. The Mexican scholar Gonzalo Aguirre Beltrán noticed it too, when he visited the Costa Chica for fieldwork around the mid-twentieth century. He wrote then that degrees of whiteness could serve as social markers in Afro-Mexican communities in the Costa Chica. *Cuculustes* were the darkest, most phenotypically proximate to "pure blacks" (*negros puros*). Racial mixture introduced other configurations, like *negradita, blanquito*, and *aindiado*. As with the colonial period, the forces of phenotype, social context, class status, distinguishing physical features, and culture could allow people to move within and between statuses. Aguirre Beltrán treats this subject in his study of the town of Cuijla (*Cuijla: esbozo etnográfico de un pueblo negro*, Mexico: Fondo de Cultura Económica, 1995), on pages 65–76.

Have these vestigial vocabularies evolved into terms of endearment? Maybe. Are they terms of survival? Perhaps. In my interview with Emiliano Colón Torres (age 95) in the town of Corralero, I was repeatedly told that "todos somos iguales" (we are all the same/equal) and that "aquí no hay raza" (we don't have race here). See Figure 23.

Some of Emiliano's family members who assisted with the interview even struggled with what the concept of race meant. However, after the filming in Emiliano's house concluded, a young boy sprinted across floor, making his way out of the door and off the veranda. His mother quickly yelled, "Oye, negro ¡Ven acá!" (Hey, blackie, come back here!). Stunned by the sudden juxtaposition of what I had been told with what I had just witnessed, I asked why, if racial language was not routinely used in Corralero, she was calling the boy "negro." Her response was that as the darkest child of the family, he was likely going to be called a negro in school, "So we are trying to get him ready for this early, while he is young."

These memories have lived with me for quite some time. Obviously, the days of living in the presence of full-blown casta are long gone in Mexico. Mestizaje itself has also changed over the course of time; but shadows of the deep past linger into the present for those able to see them. Caste-like terminologies, different today than before, do not enjoy the same sanction

FIGURE 23 Emiliano Colón Torres in Corralero, 1995.
Source: Photo by author.

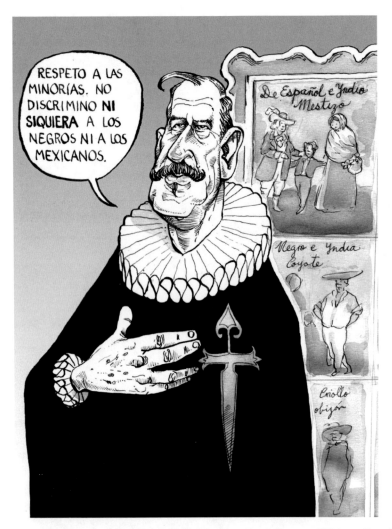

FIGURE 24 *A Modern Rendition of the Mexican Caste System: "Viceroy Fox de Quezada."*
Source: Drawn by Rafael Barajas Duran, aka "El Fisgón," *La Jornada (México)*, Cartones, Mexico City, May 17, 2005. Then-president Vicente Fox is shown in the role of a colonial Mexican viceroy, standing before a series of casta paintings. His pious expression and words evoke deep irony: "I respect minorities. I don't discriminate against blacks or Mexicans." El Fisgón drew this cartoon shortly after Fox issued a comment that Mexican immigrants in the United States were taking jobs that "not even blacks would do." Reproduced courtesy of *La Jornada*.

they once enjoyed in the colonial regime, but neither have caste language and thought disappeared from Mexican life altogether, as Figure 24 shows. Casta swims in an undercurrent alongside more modern ideologies, statist politics, and the doings of everyday life – all the while adapting, changing, and adjusting into the future.

APPENDIX A

Core Records Consulted from the Archivo General de la Nación

TABLE A.1

Archival Branch	Casta	Volume	Expediente	Folios	Theme
Alcaldes mayores	Chino(s)	5	s/e	180–181 v	Aprehensión chino
Archivo histórico de Hda.	Chino(s)	723	s/e	s/f	Varios
Archivo histórico de Hda.	Chino(s)	947	s/e	s/f	Reclamo bienes
Archivo histórico de Hda.	Chino(s)	971	s/e	s/f	Venta esclavo chino
Bienes nals.	China(s)	14	644	18	Testamento
Bienes nals.	Lobo(s)	93	111	s/f	Dispensa parentesco
Bienes nals.	Morisco(s)	93	180	s/f	Dispensa parentesco
Bienes nals.	Lobo(s)	93	296	s/f	Dispensa parentesco
Bienes nals.	Lobo(s)	353	3	s/f	Querella acreedores
Bienes nals.	Morisco(s)	441	28	s/f	Dispensa parentesco
Bienes nals.	Chino(s)	509	12	s/f	Solicitud libertad chino
Bienes nals.	Lobo(s)	538	20	s/f	Fiadores
Bienes nals.	Lobo(s)	549	6	s/f	Venta casa
Bienes nals.	Lobo(s)	564	3	s/f	Querella acreedores
Bienes nals.	Lobo(s)	630	14	s/f	Juramento matrimonial
Bienes nals.	Morisca(s)	810	101	s/f	Amancebados
Bienes nals.	Morisco(s)	911	48	s/f	Dispensa parentesco
Bienes nals.	Lobo(s)	1523	10	s/f	Censo p/convento
Clero Reg y Sec.	Morisco(s)	48	4	96–101	Partida bautismo
Correspondencia Virreyes	Chino(s)	17bis	s/e	139–140 v	Remisión indios chinos

(continued)

Criminal	Chino(s)	139	2	37–106	Acusación de homicidio
Criminal	Chino(s)	187	19	289–303	Acusación de homicidio
Criminal	Coyote(s)	206	40	364bis–374	Delito coyotes
Criminal	Chino(s)	692	3	26–57	Encubrimiento esclavo
Filipinas	Chino(s)	7	7	216–335 v	Ajuste sueldos chinos
Gral de partes	China(s)	6	566	210 v	Entrega esclavo
Gral de partes	Chino(s)	7	221	147	Permiso para venta
Gral de partes	Chino(s)	8	66	46 v	Solicitud protección
Gral de partes	Chino(s)	9	61	38 v	Entrega esclavo
Gral de partes	Chino(s)	9	116	78	Autorización protección
Gral de partes	Chino(s)	14	40	38 v	Autorización barberos chinos
Gral de partes	Chino(s)	15	36	28 v	Acusación extracción perlas
Gral de partes	Chino(s)	28	88	79 v–88	Acusación vs. teniente
Gral de partes	Chino(s)	35	180	141–142	Alcabala milicianos chinos
Gral de partes	Coyote(s)	36	76	64–64 v	Averiguación población
Gral de partes	Chino(s)	47	19	20	Capitán de chinos
Gral de partes	Chino(s)	47	143	77–78 v	Capitán de chinos
Gral de partes	Chino(s)	47	144	78–78 v	Alférez de chinos
Gral de partes	Chino(s)	70	193	156–156 v	Licencia buceo
Hospitales	Chino(s)	30	15	163–168	Fondo bautizo chinos
Indios	Chino(s)	5	1022	331 v	Licencia para montar caballo indio chino
Indios	Chino(s)	6	1200	330	Solicitud tenencia mulas indio chino
Indios	Chino(s)	6	1202	331	Licencia p/montar caballo indio chino

(continued)

TABLE A.1 *(continued)*

Archival Branch	Casta	Volume	Expediente	Folios	Theme
Indios	Chino(s)	10	249	142	Permiso venta aguardiente
Indios	Chino(s)	10	273	155–155 v	Expulsión chinos
Indios	Chino(s)	11	166	136 v	Pago alcabala indios chinos
Indios	Chino(s)	13	112	92	Pago alcabala indios chinos
Indios	Chino(s)	13	126	111	Pago tributos
Indios	Chino(s)	13	248	219	Pago alcabala
Indios	Chino(s)	15	28	20 v	Permiso barbería indios chinos
Indios	Chino(s)	15	29	20 v–21	Permiso barbería indios chinos
Indios	Chino(s)	15	62	44 v	Permiso barbería chinos
Indios	Chino(s)	15	86	154–155 v	Permiso barbería indios chinos
Indios	Chino(s)	16	28	27–28 v	Permiso venta indios chinos
Indios	Chino(s)	17	40	62 v–63	Protección vs. ganado indio chino
Indios	Chino(s)	17	19bis	31 v–32 v	Permiso p/espada
Indios	Chino(s)	19	172	90 v–91	Portación armas
Indios	Chino(s)	19	336	190–190 v	Autorización ventas indio chino
Indios	Chino(s)	20	63	38–38 v	Autorización ventas indio chino
Indios	Chino(s)	21	220	192	Autorización ventas indio chino

(continued)

Indios	Chino(s)	23	375	351 r–351 v	Solicitud libertad
Indios	Chino(s)	24	85	48 v–49 r	Permiso venta
Indios	Morisca(s)	30	106	98 r–98 v	Posesión tierras
Indios	Chino(s)	32	337	297 v–298 r	Reelección gobernador
Indios	Chino(s)	32	350	386 v–387 r	R\reelección gobernador
Indios	Morisco(s)	36	176	160–161 v	Salida habs.
Indios	Coyote(s)	56	226	323 v–324	Negativa participación elecciones
Infidencias	Chino(s)	172	80	492	Solicitud liberación
Inquisición	Morisca(s)	16	7	10	Blasfemia
Inquisición	Morisca(s)	38	9	207–211 v	Hechicería
Inquisición	Lobo(s)	271	8	24	?
Inquisición	Morisca(s)	276	7	167–176	Blasfemia
Inquisición	Chino(s)	285	61	258	Bigamia
Inquisición	Lobo(s)	292	2	2–4, 12–18	Denuncia maltrato esclavos
Inquisición	Lobo(s)	292	38	174–175	Querella criminal
Inquisición	Chino(s)	293	49	335–336	?
Inquisición	Morisca(s)	308	61	380	Supersticiones
Inquisición	Chino(s)	312	45	228	Blasfemia
Inquisición	Morisco(s)	328	25	106–111	?
Inquisición	Chino(s)	328	55	378–379	Blasfemia
Inquisición	Chino(s)	355	18	382–383	Renegado
Inquisición	Chino(s)	356	20	27	Renegado
Inquisición	Morisco(s)	356	109	326–185	?
Inquisición	Morisco(s)	356	110	186	?
Inquisición	China(s)	365	3	4	Blasfemia
Inquisición	Morisca(s)	368	133	510–511 v	Blasfemia

(continued)

TABLE A.1 *(continued)*

Archival Branch	Casta	Volume	Expediente	Folios	Theme
Inquisición	Chino(s)	372	20	20	Blasfemia
Inquisición	Chino(s)	435	36	94–94 v	Bigamia
Inquisición	Chino(s)	435	253	s/f	Supersticiones
Inquisición	Loba(s)	451	1	1–122	Bigamia
Inquisición	Chino(s)	456	2	55–98	Hechicería
Inquisición	Chino(s)	486	39	201	Hechicería
Inquisición	Coyote(s)	498	19	196–198 v	Blasfemia
Inquisición	Lobo(s)	539	9	80–86 v	Bigamia
Inquisición	Chino(s)	583	5	520–568	Renegado
Inquisición	Chino(s)	598	15	169–171 v	Renegado
Inquisición	Chino(s)	600	23	521–528	Renegado
Inquisición	Chino(s)	612	4	495–499	Bigamia
Inquisición	Chino(s)	626	4	120–128	Supersticiones
Inquisición	Chino(s)	673	37	315–320	Solicitud matrimonio
Inquisición	Loba(s)	713	12	310–323	Adulterio
Inquisición	Loba(s)	713	14	341–349	Adulterio
Inquisición	Loba(s)	715	18	485–570	Idolatría
Inquisición	Loba(s)	715	s/e	447–450	Idolatría
Inquisición	Chino(s)	718	s/e	340–342 v	?
Inquisición	China(s)	746	s/e	600–608	?
Inquisición	Morisca(s)	753	s/e	440	Bigamia
Inquisición	Loba(s)	758	15	458–467	Bigamia
Inquisición	Loba(s)	758	17	475–492	Bigamia
Inquisición	Chino(s)	769	15	325–333	Brujería

(continued)

214

Inquisición	Coyote(s)	777	11	68–92	Bigamia
Inquisición	China(s)	781	44	517–523	Bigamia
Inquisición	Chino(s)	789	23	361–366	Blasfemia
Inquisición	Coyote(s)	799	28	519–530	Faltas respeto
Inquisición	Coyote(s)	811	3	216–309	Bigamia
Inquisición	Loba(s)	820	14	280–295	Bigamia
Inquisición	Loba(s)	829	9	589–611	Fuga
Inquisición	Lobo(s)	862	s/e	196–212	Bigamia
Inquisición	Loba(s)	885	18	206–211	Hechicería
Inquisición	Coyote(s)	893	s/e	215–301	Bigamia
Inquisición	Coyote(s)	901	36	327–337	Hechicería
Inquisición	Coyote(s)	907	23	384–391	Bigamia
Inquisición	Coyote(s)	919	10	258–270	Bigamia
Inquisición	Lobo(s)	921	15	221–236	Bigamia
Inquisición	Loba(s)	935	2	265–377 v	Bigamia
Inquisición	Coyote(s)	939	9	338–446	Hechicería
Inquisición	Morisco(s)	948	30	454–457 v	Bigamia
Inquisición	Chino(s)	968	11	30	Venta esclavo chino
Inquisición	Coyote(s)	979	13	239–273	Hechicería
Inquisición	Chino(s)	999	6	335–336	Supersticiones
Inquisición	Loba(s)	1000	25	319–321 v	Bigamia
Inquisición	Coyote(s)	1018	5	165–173 v	Testigo falso
Inquisición	Coyote(s)	1043	s/e	s/f	Bigamia
Inquisición	Morisco(s)	1046	14	207	Supersticiones
Inquisición	Loba(s)	1051	s/e	125–126	?
Inquisición	Coyote(s)	1061	3A	194–201	Bigamia
Inquisición	Loba(s)	1065	13	272–404	Bigamia

(continued)

TABLE A.1 *(continued)*

Archival Branch	Casta	Volume	Expediente	Folios	Theme
Inquisición	Coyote(s)	1068	9	68–90 v	Bigamia
Inquisición	Coyote(s)	1069	4	108bis–168 v	Bigamia
Inquisición	Loba(s)	1089	1	1–108	Bigamia
Inquisición	Loba(s)	1097	8	218bis–233	Maléficas
Inquisición	Lobo(s)	1097	16	270–273 v	Bigamia
Inquisición	Loba(s)	1100	s/e	88	?
Inquisición	Coyote(s)	1120	12	179–276 v	Bigamia
Inquisición	Coyote(s)	1121	12	271–277 v	Bigamia
Inquisición	Loba(s)	1122	3	71–98	Bigamia
Inquisición	Coyote(s)	1133	5	42–47 v	Bigamia
Inquisición	Morisco(s)	1141	1	1–8	Blasfemia
Inquisición	Morisca(s)	1168	8	187–203	Curandero
Inquisición	China(s)	1169	s/e	261	Brujería
Inquisición	Chino(s)	1169	s/e	263–263 v	Brujería
Inquisición	Lobo(s)	1176	4	69–79 v	Hechicería
Inquisición	Loba(s)	1180	17	380–382 v	Curandero
Inquisición	Coyote(s)	1184	22	192–288 v	Bigamia
Inquisición	Lobo(s)	1237	5	156–259	Bigamia
Inquisición	Coyote(s)	1257	2	1–131	Bigamia
Inquisición	Chino(s)	1259	14	309–314 v	Bigamia
Inquisición	Loba(s)	1264	3	146–155	Hechicería
Inquisición	Morisca(s)	1271	2	53–119	Bigamia
Inquisición	Morisca(s)	1273	6	72–77	Herejía
Inquisición	Loba(s)	1292	17	1–101	Bigamia

(continued)

216

Inquisición	China(s)	1297	10	42–47	?
Inquisición	Chino(s)	1297	13	82–100 v	Maléfico
Inquisición	Morisco(s)	1299	13	179–187 v	?
Inquisición	Lobo(s)	1299	s/e	64–64 v	Bestialidad
Inquisición	Chino(s)	1319	s/e	s/f	?
Inquisición	Morisca(s)	1328	s/e	260	?
Inquisición	Coyote(s)	1364	15	371–418	Bigamia
Inquisición	Loba(s)	1378	2	5–17 v	Permiso casamiento
Inquisición	Loba(s)	1447	7	134–135	Curandero
Inquisición	Loba(s)	1504	5	214–237	Idolatría
Inquisición	China(s)	1551	37	546–550 v	Blasfemia
Inquisición	China(s)	1552	s/e	193	?
Judicial	Morisco(s)	32	35	116–117	Demanda por maltrato
Marina	Chino(s)	2	4	4–4 v	Nombramiento grumete indio chino
Marina	Chino(s)	2	5	5–5 v	Nombramiento grumete indio chino
Marina	Chino(s)	2	15	6	Nombramiento grumete indio chino
Marina	Chino(s)	2	21	7	Nombramiento grumete indio chino
Marina	Chino(s)	2	22	8	Nombramiento grumete indio chino
Marina	Chino(s)	23	56	94	Cía. lanceros chinos
Marina	Chino(s)	78	13	189–202 v	Marineros chinos
Matrimonios	Morisca(s)	1	62	285–288	Licencia matrimonio
Matrimonios	Morisca(s)	1	66	306–309 v	Licencia matrimonio

(continued)

TABLE A.1 *(continued)*

Archival Branch	Casta	Volume	Expediente	Folios	Theme
Matrimonios	Morisco(s)	4	30	136–140	Licencia matrimonio
Matrimonios	Morisca(s)	4	37	168–170 v	Licencia matrimonio
Matrimonios	Morisca(s)	4	55	241–243 v	Licencia matrimonio
Matrimonios	Morisca(s)	4	76	327–330 v	Licencia matrimonio
Matrimonios	Morisca(s)	4	87	374–377 v	Licencia matrimonio
Matrimonios	China(s)	5	94	264–265	Licencia matrimonio
Matrimonios	China(s)	5	116	317–318	Licencia matrimonio
Matrimonios	Morisco(s)	5	127	340–341 v	Licencia matrimonio
Matrimonios	Morisco(s)	6	20	58–62	Licencia matrimonio
Matrimonios	Loba(s)	6	53	170–172	Licencia matrimonio
Matrimonios	Morisco(s)	6	63	207–209 v	Licencia matrimonio
Matrimonios	Morisco(s)	6	96	316–317 v	Licencia matrimonio
Matrimonios	Morisca(s)	6	97	318–320	Licencia matrimonio
Matrimonios	Morisco(s)	7	8	38–40	Licencia matrimonio
Matrimonios	China(s)	7	56	203–204	Licencia matrimonio india china
Matrimonios	Chino(s)	7	73	247–248	Licencia matrimonio
Matrimonios	Morisca(s)	7	103	346–349	Licencia matrimonio
Matrimonios	Morisca(s)	9	26	351–354 v	Licencia matrimonio
Matrimonios	Chino(s)	10	106	245–246	Licencia matrimonio
Matrimonios	Morisco(s)	11	2	4–6 v	Licencia matrimonio
Matrimonios	Morisco(s)	11	28	135–139	Licencia matrimonio
Matrimonios	Morisca(s)	11	40	201–204 v	Licencia matrimonio
Matrimonios	Morisco(s)	11	43	214–219	Acusación de incontinencia

(continued)

Matrimonios	Morisca(s)	11	48	238–243	Licencia matrimonio
Matrimonios	Morisco(s)	11	76	418–421	Licencia matrimonio
Matrimonios	Morisco(s)	12	8	27–30 v	Licencia matrimonio
Matrimonios	Morisca(s)	12	11	37–40 v	Licencia matrimonio
Matrimonios	Morisca(s)	13	9	49–51 v	Licencia matrimonio
Matrimonios	Morisco(s)	13	45	228–231 v	Licencia matrimonio
Matrimonios	Morisco(s)	14	19	52–53	Licencia matrimonio
Matrimonios	Morisca(s)	14	47	132–133 v	Licencia matrimonio
Matrimonios	Morisca(s)	14	112	344–346 v	Licencia matrimonio
Matrimonios	Morisca(s)	14	124	381–382 v	Licencia matrimonio
Matrimonios	China(s)	19	16	83–84	Licencia matrimonio
Matrimonios	China(s)	19	62	193–194	Licencia matrimonio
Matrimonios	Morisco(s)	19	100	316–317 v	Licencia matrimonio
Matrimonios	Morisca(s)	20	23	142–145 v	Licencia matrimonio
Matrimonios	Morisca(s)	20	29	176–181	Licencia matrimonio
Matrimonios	Morisca(s)	20	30	182–187	Licencia matrimonio
Matrimonios	Morisca(s)	21	38	171–174 v	Licencia matrimonio
Matrimonios	Morisca(s)	21	70	335–339	Licencia matrimonio
Matrimonios	Morisco(s)	23	32	161–163 v	Licencia matrimonio
Matrimonios	Morisca(s)	24	79	359–365	Licencia matrimonio
Matrimonios	Morisca(s)	25	63	325–329 v	Licencia matrimonio
Matrimonios	Morisco(s)	25	78	392–394 v	Licencia matrimonio
Matrimonios	Morisca(s)	25	79	395–397	Licencia matrimonio
Matrimonios	Morisco(s)	25	82	406–408 v	Licencia matrimonio
Matrimonios	Morisco(s)	26	19	330–333 v	Licencia matrimonio
Matrimonios	Morisca(s)	27	85	306–307	Licencia matrimonio
Matrimonios	China(s)	29	106	247–248	Licencia matrimonio

(continued)

Archival Branch	Casta	Volume	Expediente	Folios	Theme
Matrimonios	Morisco(s)	29	122	388–390 v	Licencia matrimonio
Matrimonios	Morisca(s)	30	9	30–33	Licencia matrimonio
Matrimonios	Morisca(s)	30	12	41–43 v	Licencia matrimonio
Matrimonios	Morisco(s)	30	23	84–86 v	Licencia matrimonio
Matrimonios	Loba(s)	30	24	87–90 v	Licencia matrimonio
Matrimonios	Morisco(s)	30	44	163–166 v	Licencia matrimonio
Matrimonios	Coyote(s)	30	66	338–341 v	Licencia matrimonio
Matrimonios	Morisca(s)	31	23	113–117 v	Licencia matrimonio
Matrimonios	Chino(s)	31	43	200	Licencia matrimonio
Matrimonios	Morisca(s)	31	51	225–226 v	Licencia matrimonio
Matrimonios	Loba(s)	32	3	9–13 v	Licencia matrimonio
Matrimonios	Loba(s)	32	43	242–244 v	Licencia matrimonio
Matrimonios	Morisca(s)	32	48	268–274 v	Licencia matrimonio
Matrimonios	Morisca(s)	32	64	345–348 v	Licencia matrimonio
Matrimonios	Morisca(s)	32	69	376–379 v	Licencia matrimonio
Matrimonios	Morisca(s)	32	71	384–387	Licencia matrimonio
Matrimonios	Morisca(s)	32	78	409–412 v	Licencia matrimonio
Matrimonios	Morisco(s)	33	15	61–63 v	Licencia matrimonio
Matrimonios	Morisca(s)	33	47	204–207 v	Licencia matrimonio
Matrimonios	Coyote(s)	33	56	239–241	Licencia matrimonio
Matrimonios	Morisca(s)	34	27	101–104	Licencia matrimonio
Matrimonios	Morisca(s)	34	83	396–399	Licencia matrimonio
Matrimonios	Coyote(s)	36	1	2–4	Licencia matrimonio
Matrimonios	Morisca(s)	36	30	128–131	Licencia matrimonio

(continued)

Matrimonios	Morisca(s)	36	37	155–159	Licencia matrimonio
Matrimonios	Morisco(s)	38	19	63–66	Licencia matrimonio
Matrimonios	Morisco(s)	38	65	262–267	Licencia matrimonio
Matrimonios	Morisca(s)	38	78	313–316 v	Licencia matrimonio
Matrimonios	Morisca(s)	38	85	340–343 v	Licencia matrimonio
Matrimonios	Morisco(s)	40	11	41–43 v	Licencia matrimonio
Matrimonios	Morisca(s)	41	10	230–232 v	Licencia matrimonio
Matrimonios	Morisco(s)	42	56	353–356	Licencia matrimonio
Matrimonios	Morisca(s)	42	59	365–368 v	Licencia matrimonio
Matrimonios	Morisca(s)	45	55	239	Licencia matrimonio
Matrimonios	Morisca(s)	46	51	271–274	Licencia matrimonio
Matrimonios	Morisco(s)	46	55	283–284 v	Licencia matrimonio
Matrimonios	Morisca(s)	46	63	307–310	Licencia matrimonio
Matrimonios	Morisco(s)	47	4	8–9 v	Licencia matrimonio
Matrimonios	Chino(s)	47	57	162–165 v	Licencia matrimonio
Matrimonios	Chino(s)	48	88	239–240	Licencia matrimonio
Matrimonios	Loba(s)	49	88	256–257 v	Licencia matrimonio
Matrimonios	Morisco(s)	49	121	332–336 v	Dispensa afinidad
Matrimonios	Morisca(s)	50	2	4–7	Licencia matrimonio
Matrimonios	Morisca(s)	51	2	5–9	Licencia matrimonio
Matrimonios	Morisco(s)	52	15	376–381	Licencia matrimonio
Matrimonios	Morisca(s)	54	10	56–59	Licencia matrimonio
Matrimonios	Morisco(s)	54	28	133–136	Licencia matrimonio
Matrimonios	Morisca(s)	54	39	173–177	Licencia matrimonio
Matrimonios	Morisca(s)	55	10	54–57 v	Licencia matrimonio
Matrimonios	Morisca(s)	55	11	58–60	Licencia matrimonio
Matrimonios	Morisca(s)	55	54	247–248 v	Licencia matrimonio

(continued)

TABLE A.1 (continued)

Archival Branch	Casta	Volume	Expediente	Folios	Theme
Matrimonios	Morisco(s)	55	57	256–257 v	Licencia matrimonio
Matrimonios	Morisca(s)	56	11	35–37 v	Licencia matrimonio
Matrimonios	Morisca(s)	56	26	85–87 v	Licencia matrimonio
Matrimonios	Morisca(s)	56	49	187–189 v	Licencia matrimonio
Matrimonios	Morisca(s)	56	62	238–240 v	Licencia matrimonio
Matrimonios	Loba(s)	58	37	178–181	Licencia matrimonio
Matrimonios	Coyote(s)	59	6	69–88	Licencia matrimonio
Matrimonios	Morisco(s)	59	13	105 v–106 v	Licencia matrimonio
Matrimonios	Morisco(s)	60	32	67–70	Licencia matrimonio
Matrimonios	Morisco(s)	60	41	105 v–107 v	Licencia matrimonio
Matrimonios	Morisca(s)	60	55	164–167	Licencia matrimonio
Matrimonios	Loba(s)	60	68	206–210	Licencia matrimonio
Matrimonios	Morisco(s)	60	81	243–244	Licencia matrimonio
Matrimonios	Chino(s)	61	27	142–144 v	Licencia matrimonio
Matrimonios	Morisca(s)	61	61	245–248	Licencia matrimonio
Matrimonios	Chino(s)	61	73	288–290	Licencia matrimonio
Matrimonios	Coyote(s)	62	48	439–444 v	Violencia vs. sacerdote
Matrimonios	Morisca(s)	63	37	196–198 v	Licencia matrimonio
Matrimonios	Morisco(s)	64	109	337–338 v	Licencia matrimonio
Matrimonios	Morisco(s)	65	86	339–342 v	Licencia matrimonio
Matrimonios	Morisca(s)	65	98	392–395	Licencia matrimonio
Matrimonios	Morisca(s)	67	19	83 v–88 v	Licencia matrimonio
Matrimonios	Morisco(s)	67	103	397–398 v	Licencia matrimonio
Matrimonios	Morisca(s)	69	22	137–140	Licencia matrimonio

(continued)

Matrimonios	Morisco(s)	69	54	327–331	Licencia matrimonio
Matrimonios	Morisca(s)	69	67	392–397 v	Licencia matrimonio
Matrimonios	Morisca(s)	70	15	223–224 v	Licencia matrimonio
Matrimonios	Morisco(s)	71	27	122–126 v	Licencia matrimonio
Matrimonios	Morisco(s)	71	54	242–245 v	Licencia matrimonio
Matrimonios	Morisca(s)	71	69	302–304	Licencia matrimonio
Matrimonios	Morisco(s)	71	70	305–308 v	Licencia matrimonio
Matrimonios	Morisco(s)	71	75	327–331 v	Licencia matrimonio
Matrimonios	Morisca(s)	71	78	339–342	Licencia matrimonio
Matrimonios	Morisco(s)	72	45	233–236 v	Licencia matrimonio
Matrimonios	Morisca(s)	72	58	296–299 v	Licencia matrimonio
Matrimonios	Morisca(s)	72	62	325–327 v	Licencia matrimonio
Matrimonios	Morisca(s)	73	15	88–93 v	Arresto por amancebados
Matrimonios	Morisca(s)	73	25	145–148 v	Licencia matrimonio
Matrimonios	Morisca(s)	73	39	246–248 v	Licencia matrimonio
Matrimonios	Morisco(s)	73	44	290–294 v	Licencia matrimonio
Matrimonios	Morisca(s)	73	71	426–428 v	Licencia matrimonio
Matrimonios	Morisco(s)	75	23	88–90 v	Licencia matrimonio
Matrimonios	Morisca(s)	75	52	219–235	Licencia matrimonio
Matrimonios	China(s)	75	93	323	Licencia matrimonio
Matrimonios	Chino(s)	75	93	323	Licencia matrimonio
Matrimonios	Morisco(s)	76	25	129–130 v	Licencia matrimonio
Matrimonios	Morisco(s)	76	27	133–134 v	Licencia matrimonio
Matrimonios	Morisco(s)	76	58	219–221	Licencia matrimonio
Matrimonios	Morisco(s)	76	81	278–281 v	Licencia matrimonio
Matrimonios	Morisca(s)	76	119	423–424	Licencia matrimonio
Matrimonios	China(s)	76	130	458–459 v	Licencia matrimonio

(continued)

TABLE A.1 (continued)

Archival Branch	Casta	Volume	Expediente	Folios	Theme
Matrimonios	Morisco(s)	78	59	321–324 v	Licencia matrimonio
Matrimonios	Morisca(s)	79	23	222–224 v	Licencia matrimonio
Matrimonios	Morisco(s)	79	31	262–265 v	Licencia matrimonio
Matrimonios	Loba(s)	79	46	325–327 v	Licencia matrimonio
Matrimonios	Morisco(s)	79	52	354–359	Licencia matrimonio
Matrimonios	Morisca(s)	80	54	272–276 v	Licencia matrimonio
Matrimonios	Morisco(s)	80	55	277–280 v	Licencia matrimonio
Matrimonios	Morisca(s)	80	57	286–288 v	Licencia matrimonio
Matrimonios	Morisco(s)	81	68	183–184 v	Licencia matrimonio
Matrimonios	Morisca(s)	81	100	252–254	Licencia matrimonio
Matrimonios	Loba(s)	81	107	269–270	Licencia matrimonio
Matrimonios	Morisca(s)	82	7	23–26 v	Licencia matrimonio
Matrimonios	Morisca(s)	82	43	195–197 v	Licencia matrimonio
Matrimonios	Morisca(s)	82	45	201–204	Licencia matrimonio
Matrimonios	Morisco(s)	82	47	209–213 v	Licencia matrimonio
Matrimonios	Morisca(s)	82	67	295–299	Licencia matrimonio
Matrimonios	Morisco(s)	82	69	304–319	Licencia matrimonio
Matrimonios	Morisco(s)	82	70	320–324	Licencia matrimonio
Matrimonios	Morisco(s)	83	5	268–275 v	Licencia matrimonio
Matrimonios	Morisca(s)	84	9	43–50 v	Licencia matrimonio
Matrimonios	Morisca(s)	84	44	256–259 v	Licencia matrimonio
Matrimonios	Morisca(s)	85	69	396–398	Licencia matrimonio
Matrimonios	Morisca(s)	85	70	399–405	Licencia matrimonio
Matrimonios	Morisca(s)	86	11	66–71	Licencia matrimonio

(continued)

224

Matrimonios	Morisco(s)	86	37	291–295	Licencia matrimonio
Matrimonios	Morisco(s)	87	29	155–157 v	Licencia matrimonio
Matrimonios	Morisco(s)	87	53	353–354	Licencia matrimonio
Matrimonios	Morisco(s)	89	4	14–16 v	Licencia matrimonio
Matrimonios	Morisco(s)	89	31	113–115 v	Licencia matrimonio
Matrimonios	Morisco(s)	89	65	198–201 v	Licencia matrimonio
Matrimonios	Morisco(s)	89	87	316–320	Licencia matrimonio
Matrimonios	Loba(s)	89	91	331–337 v	Licencia matrimonio
Matrimonios	Morisca(s)	90	2	3–4 v	Licencia matrimonio
Matrimonios	Morisca(s)	90	45	113–114 v	Licencia matrimonio
Matrimonios	Morisca(s)	90	137	324–325 v	Licencia matrimonio
Matrimonios	Morisca(s)	90	165	427–430	Licencia matrimonio
Matrimonios	Loba(s)	93	11	72–76	Licencia matrimonio
Matrimonios	Morisca(s)	93	71	348–350 v	Licencia matrimonio
Matrimonios	Morisco(s)	93	88	408–412	Licencia matrimonio
Matrimonios	Morisco(s)	94	13	110–112 v	Licencia matrimonio
Matrimonios	Morisca(s)	95	29	387–388 v	Licencia matrimonio
Matrimonios	Morisca(s)	96	37	225–228	Licencia matrimonio
Matrimonios	Morisca(s)	96	43	243–244 v	Licencia matrimonio
Matrimonios	Morisco(s)	96	80	348–350 v	Licencia matrimonio
Matrimonios	Morisco(s)	96	82	353–354 v	Licencia matrimonio
Matrimonios	Morisco(s)	96	94	378–380 v	Licencia matrimonio
Matrimonios	Morisca(s)	96	95	381–382 v	Licencia matrimonio
Matrimonios	Morisca(s)	98	34	89–90 v	Licencia matrimonio
Matrimonios	Morisco(s)	98	41	103–104 v	Licencia matrimonio
Matrimonios	Morisca(s)	98	46	113–114 v	Licencia matrimonio
Matrimonios	Morisco(s)	100	8	60–63 v	Licencia matrimonio

(continued)

TABLE A.1 *(continued)*

Archival Branch	Casta	Volume	Expediente	Folios	Theme
Matrimonios	Morisco(s)	100	33	171–174	Licencia matrimonio
Matrimonios	Morisco(s)	102	16	100–118 v	Licencia matrimonio
Matrimonios	Morisca(s)	102	42	361–366 v	Licencia matrimonio
Matrimonios	Morisco(s)	103	12	41–44	Licencia matrimonio
Matrimonios	Morisca(s)	103	27	102–104 v	Licencia matrimonio
Matrimonios	Morisca(s)	103	49	214–222 v	Licencia matrimonio
Matrimonios	Morisco(s)	103	85	376	Demanda cumplimiento matrimonio
Matrimonios	Morisca(s)	104	2	6–13	Licencia matrimonio
Matrimonios	Morisca(s)	104	7	47–50	Licencia matrimonio
Matrimonios	Morisca(s)	105	28	341–344 v	Licencia matrimonio
Matrimonios	Morisca(s)	106	30	141–143	Licencia matrimonio
Matrimonios	Morisca(s)	108	10	48–50 v	Licencia matrimonio
Matrimonios	Morisco(s)	108	20	107–109 v	Licencia matrimonio
Matrimonios	Loba(s)	108	24	125–127 v	Licencia matrimonio
Matrimonios	Morisco(s)	108	25	128–131 v	Licencia matrimonio
Matrimonios	Morisca(s)	108	64	318–321 v	Licencia matrimonio
Matrimonios	Morisco(s)	108	78	382–385 v	Licencia matrimonio
Matrimonios	Morisco(s)	109	27	103–106 v	Licencia matrimonio
Matrimonios	Morisco(s)	109	81	355–357 v	Licencia matrimonio
Matrimonios	Morisco(s)	112	5	28–43 v	Licencia matrimonio
Matrimonios	Morisca(s)	112	32	266–273	Licencia matrimonio
Matrimonios	Morisca(s)	112	40	327–330 v	Licencia matrimonio
Matrimonios	Chino(s)	113	135	345–346	Licencia matrimonio

(continued)

Matrimonios	Morisca(s)	114	45	194–197	Licencia matrimonio
Matrimonios	Morisco(s)	114	58	244–247	Licencia matrimonio
Matrimonios	Morisco(s)	114	63	262–265	Licencia matrimonio
Matrimonios	Morisca(s)	114	68	282–284 v	Licencia matrimonio
Matrimonios	Loba(s)	114	99	402–408	Licencia matrimonio
Matrimonios	Morisco(s)	115	25	184–187	Licencia matrimonio
Matrimonios	Morisco(s)	117	16	56–58 v	Licencia matrimonio
Matrimonios	Morisca(s)	117	20	69–71 v	Licencia matrimonio
Matrimonios	Morisco(s)	117	50	203–209	Licencia matrimonio
Matrimonios	Morisca(s)	117	56	234–242 v	Licencia matrimonio
Matrimonios	Morisca(s)	117	67	301–305 v	Licencia matrimonio
Matrimonios	Morisco(s)	118	47	105–106 v	Licencia matrimonio
Matrimonios	Loba(s)	118	51	114–115 v	Licencia matrimonio
Matrimonios	Loba(s)	118	54	120–121 v	Licencia matrimonio
Matrimonios	Morisca(s)	118	79	175–176 v	Licencia matrimonio
Matrimonios	Morisca(s)	118	86	195–196 v	Licencia matrimonio
Matrimonios	Morisca(s)	118	115	302–303 v	Licencia matrimonio
Matrimonios	Morisco(s)	118	150	392–394	Licencia matrimonio
Matrimonios	Morisca(s)	120	54	265–279	Licencia matrimonio
Matrimonios	Morisca(s)	120	77	373–375	Licencia matrimonio
Matrimonios	Morisca(s)	121	80	404–407 v	Licencia matrimonio
Matrimonios	Morisco(s)	122	21	75–76 v	Licencia matrimonio
Matrimonios	China(s)	122	59	177–178 v	Licencia matrimonio
Matrimonios	Morisca(s)	122	118	328–329 v	Licencia matrimonio
Matrimonios	Morisca(s)	122	119	330–331 v	Licencia matrimonio
Matrimonios	Morisco(s)	123	19	75–79	Licencia matrimonio
Matrimonios	Morisco(s)	123	28	112–114 v	Licencia matrimonio

(continued)

Archival Branch	Casta	Volume	Expediente	Folios	Theme
Matrimonios	Morisco(s)	125	55	349–354	Licencia matrimonio
Matrimonios	Morisca(s)	126	44	129–130 v	Licencia matrimonio
Matrimonios	Morisco(s)	132	116	1–2	Licencia matrimonio
Matrimonios	Morisca(s)	134	26		Licencia matrimonio
Matrimonios	Morisco(s)	135	52	3–4	Licencia matrimonio
Matrimonios	Morisco(s)	135	80	3–4	Licencia matrimonio
Matrimonios	Morisco(s)	140	16	4	Licencia matrimonio
Matrimonios	Morisca(s)	141	41	6	Licencia matrimonio
Matrimonios	Morisca(s)	141	55	55	Licencia matrimonio
Matrimonios	Coyote(s)	141	60	24	Suspensión matrimonio
Matrimonios	Morisco(s)	141	64	6	Licencia matrimonio
Matrimonios	Morisco(s)	141	72	8	Licencia matrimonio
Matrimonios	Morisca(s)	141	74	74	Licencia matrimonio
Matrimonios	Morisca(s)	142	28	4	Licencia matrimonio
Matrimonios	Morisco(s)	143	7	39–45	Licencia matrimonio
Matrimonios	Morisco(s)	144	7	4 v	Licencia matrimonio
Matrimonios	Morisca(s)	144	31	5 v	Licencia matrimonio
Matrimonios	Morisca(s)	144	49	4 v	Licencia matrimonio
Matrimonios	Morisca(s)	144	57	3 v	Licencia matrimonio
Matrimonios	Morisca(s)	144	58	3 v	Licencia matrimonio
Matrimonios	Morisco(s)	145	15	7–9	Licencia matrimonio
Matrimonios	Morisca(s)	145	54	1–3	Licencia matrimonio
Matrimonios	Morisco(s)	145	75	1–5 v	Licencia matrimonio
Matrimonios	Morisca(s)	145	78	13–17 v	Licencia matrimonio

(continued)

Matrimonios	Morisca(s)	146	25	3	Licencia matrimonio
Matrimonios	Morisco(s)	146	41	4	Licencia matrimonio
Matrimonios	Morisca(s)	147	5	4	Licencia matrimonio
Matrimonios	Morisco(s)	147	36	3	Licencia matrimonio
Matrimonios	Morisca(s)	147	41	3	Licencia matrimonio
Matrimonios	Morisca(s)	147	50	8	Licencia matrimonio
Matrimonios	Morisco(s)	148	7	14–18	Licencia matrimonio
Matrimonios	Morisco(s)	149	24	s/f	Licencia matrimonio
Matrimonios	Morisca(s)	150	4	3	Licencia matrimonio
Matrimonios	Morisco(s)	150	73	5 v	Licencia matrimonio
Matrimonios	Morisca(s)	150	86	5	Licencia matrimonio
Matrimonios	Loba(s)	151	19	4	Licencia matrimonio
Matrimonios	Morisco(s)	151	30	5	Licencia matrimonio
Matrimonios	Morisco(s)	153	10	4	Licencia matrimonio
Matrimonios	Morisco(s)	153	28	3	Licencia matrimonio
Matrimonios	Morisca(s)	153	42	4	Licencia matrimonio
Matrimonios	Morisco(s)	153	44	3	Licencia matrimonio
Matrimonios	Morisca(s)	153	45	4	Licencia matrimonio
Matrimonios	Morisca(s)	153	67	52–119	Licencia matrimonio
Matrimonios	Morisco(s)	153	67	1	Licencia matrimonio
Matrimonios	Morisco(s)	153	85	7	Licencia matrimonio
Matrimonios	Morisca(s)	153	116	5	Licencia matrimonio
Matrimonios	Morisca(s)	153	125	3	Licencia matrimonio
Matrimonios	Morisco(s)	154	27	3	Licencia matrimonio
Matrimonios	Morisca(s)	154	35	3	Licencia matrimonio
Matrimonios	Morisca(s)	157	17	70–72 v	Licencia matrimonio
Matrimonios	Morisco(s)	157	18	4 v	Licencia matrimonio

(continued)

Archival Branch	Casta	Volume	Expediente	Folios	Theme
Matrimonios	Morisca(s)	157	39	5 v	Licencia matrimonio
Matrimonios	Morisco(s)	159	21	4	Licencia matrimonio
Matrimonios	Morisco(s)	159	23	3 v	Licencia matrimonio
Matrimonios	Morisco(s)	159	49	4 v	Licencia matrimonio
Matrimonios	China(s)	160	86	2	Licencia matrimonio
Matrimonios	Loba(s)	160	177	2	Licencia matrimonio
Matrimonios	Morisca(s)	160	179	2	Licencia matrimonio
Matrimonios	Morisco(s)	162	26	3 v	Licencia matrimonio
Matrimonios	Morisca(s)	162	44	5	Licencia matrimonio
Matrimonios	Morisca(s)	162	92	3 v	Licencia matrimonio
Matrimonios	Morisca(s)	163	33	3	Licencia matrimonio
Matrimonios	Morisca(s)	163	68	4	Licencia matrimonio
Matrimonios	Morisca(s)	165	59	1	Licencia matrimonio
Matrimonios	Loba(s)	165	110	1	Licencia matrimonio
Matrimonios	Morisca(s)	165	122	1	Licencia matrimonio
Matrimonios	China(s)	166	29	2	Licencia matrimonio
Matrimonios	Morisco(s)	167	53	3 v	Licencia matrimonio
Matrimonios	Chino(s)	172	112	2	Licencia matrimonio
Matrimonios	Morisca(s)	173	75	2	Licencia matrimonio
Matrimonios	Morisca(s)	173	159	2	Licencia matrimonio
Matrimonios	China(s)	173	161	2	Licencia matrimonio
Matrimonios	Morisco(s)	174	60	4	Licencia matrimonio
Matrimonios	Morisca(s)	174	65	4 v	Licencia matrimonio
Matrimonios	Morisca(s)	174	66	3 v	Licencia matrimonio

(continued)

Matrimonios	Morisco(s)	174	88	3	Licencia matrimonio
Matrimonios	Morisca(s)	175	21	4 v	Licencia matrimonio
Matrimonios	Morisco(s)	175	23	5 v	Licencia matrimonio
Matrimonios	Morisca(s)	175	27	6	Licencia matrimonio
Matrimonios	Morisca(s)	175	37	6 v	Licencia matrimonio
Matrimonios	Morisco(s)	176	7	3	Licencia matrimonio
Matrimonios	Morisco(s)	178	21	3	Licencia matrimonio
Matrimonios	Morisca(s)	178	22	2	Licencia matrimonio
Matrimonios	Morisca(s)	178	46	3	Licencia matrimonio
Matrimonios	Loba(s)	178	60	9	Oposición matrimonio
Matrimonios	Morisca(s)	179	9	2 v	Licencia matrimonio
Matrimonios	China(s)	179	113	5	Licencia matrimonio
Matrimonios	Morisco(s)	180	45	3	Licencia matrimonio
Matrimonios	Morisca(s)	181	14	9	Licencia matrimonio
Matrimonios	Morisco(s)	181	32	7 v	Licencia matrimonio
Matrimonios	Loba(s)	183	116	2 v	Licencia matrimonio
Matrimonios	China(s)	183	131	2	Licencia matrimonio
Matrimonios	Morisco(s)	191	28	4	Licencia matrimonio
Matrimonios	Morisca(s)	191	38	4	Licencia matrimonio
Matrimonios	Morisco(s)	194	60	2	Licencia matrimonio
Matrimonios	Morisco(s)	198	26	4	Licencia matrimonio
Matrimonios	China(s)	198	52	2	Licencia matrimonio
Matrimonios	Morisca(s)	199	18	3	Licencia matrimonio
Matrimonios	Morisco(s)	200	6	1	Licencia matrimonio
Matrimonios	Loba(s)	200	9	61–64	Licencia matrimonio
Matrimonios	Morisco(s)	200	29	4	Licencia matrimonio
Matrimonios	Morisca(s)	200	42	4	Licencia matrimonio

(continued)

Archival Branch	Casta	Volume	Expediente	Folios	Theme
Matrimonios	Morisco(s)	200	45	s/f	Licencia matrimonio
Matrimonios	Morisco(s)	200	59	3	Licencia matrimonio
Matrimonios	Morisca(s)	201	27	5	Licencia matrimonio
Matrimonios	Morisco(s)	201	63	2	Licencia matrimonio
Matrimonios	Morisca(s)	203	18	3	Licencia matrimonio
Matrimonios	Morisca(s)	203	87	6	Licencia matrimonio
Matrimonios	Morisco(s)	205	4	2	Licencia matrimonio
Matrimonios	Loba(s)	205	33	2	Licencia matrimonio
Matrimonios	Morisca(s)	205	50	5	Licencia matrimonio
Matrimonios	Morisca(s)	208	37	5	Licencia matrimonio
Matrimonios	Morisco(s)	209	32	3	Licencia matrimonio
Matrimonios	Loba(s)	211	1	6	Licencia matrimonio
Matrimonios	Morisca(s)	211	30	3	Licencia matrimonio
Matrimonios	Morisca(s)	212	18	5	Licencia matrimonio
Matrimonios	Chino(s)	213	32	1	Licencia matrimonio
Matrimonios	China(s)	213	54	2	Licencia matrimonio
Matrimonios	China(s)	213	76	1	Licencia matrimonio
Matrimonios	Morisca(s)	213	95	2	Licencia matrimonio
Matrimonios	China(s)	215	18	3	Licencia matrimonio
Matrimonios	Coyote(s)	215	49	14	Comparecencia
Matrimonios	Morisca(s)	217	8	9	Negación procedencia divorcio
Matrimonios	Morisca(s)	217	9	38	Divorcio
Matrimonios	Morisca(s)	217	10	6	Divorcio

(continued)

Matrimonios	Morisca(s)	218	16	7	Licencia matrimonio
Matrimonios	Morisca(s)	220	18	102–105	Licencia matrimonio
Matrimonios	Morisco(s)	220	71	283–287	Licencia matrimonio
Matrimonios	Morisco(s)	221	12	52–55 v	Licencia matrimonio
Matrimonios	Morisca(s)	221	47	162–165	Licencia matrimonio
Matrimonios	Morisco(s)	222	3	8–11	Licencia matrimonio
Matrimonios	Morisco(s)	222	9	29–31 v	Licencia matrimonio
Matrimonios	Morisca(s)	222	12	39–41 v	Licencia matrimonio
Matrimonios	Morisco(s)	222	15	49–52	Licencia matrimonio
Matrimonios	Morisca(s)	222	40	138–141	Licencia matrimonio
Matrimonios	Morisca(s)	223	3	12–13 v	Licencia matrimonio
Matrimonios	Morisca(s)	224	2	5–11	Licencia matrimonio
Matrimonios	Morisca(s)	224	6	29–32 v	Licencia matrimonio
Matrimonios	Morisca(s)	224	15	72–75 v	Licencia matrimonio
Matrimonios	Morisco(s)	224	41	178–181	Licencia matrimonio
Matrimonios	Morisca(s)	224	53	231–235 v	Licencia matrimonio
Matrimonios	Morisco(s)	226	37	143–147 v	Licencia matrimonio
Matrimonios	Morisco(s)	226	74	311–314	Licencia matrimonio
Matrimonios	Morisco(s)	226	77	326	Licencia matrimonio
Matrimonios	Morisco(s)	227	6	26–29	Licencia matrimonio
Matrimonios	Morisco(s)	227	18	88–93	Licencia matrimonio
Matrimonios	Morisco(s)	227	40	207–210	Licencia matrimonio
Matrimonios	Morisco(s)	227	42	215–217 v	Licencia matrimonio
Matrimonios	Morisca(s)	227	51	254–256 v	Licencia matrimonio
Matrimonios	Morisco(s)	227	66	317–319 v	Licencia matrimonio
Matrimonios	Morisca(s)	227	69	327–329 v	Licencia matrimonio
Matrimonios	Morisco(s)	229	5	276–282	Licencia matrimonio

(continued)

Archival Branch	Casta	Volume	Expediente	Folios	Theme
Matrimonios	Morisco(s)	229	11	317–323	Licencia matrimonio
Matrimonios	Morisca(s)	229	24	410–416	Licencia matrimonio
Ordenanzas	Chino(s)	5	18	13–14 v	Portación armas
Ordenanzas	Chino(s)	5	19	14	Portación armas
Ordenanzas	Chino(s)	6	39	44 v–52 v	Prohibición gremio pañeros
Ordenanzas	Morisco(s)	14	311	219 v–220 v	Permiso para herrar ganado
Reales Cédulas	Chino(s)	7	90	167–167 v	Pirata chino
Reales Cédulas	Chino(s)	15	178	140	Prohibición armas y grupos
Reales Cédulas	Chino(s)	18	26	35 v	Permiso ventas
Reales Cédulas	Chino(s)	18	27	40	Limitación barberías chinos
Reales Cédulas	Chino(s)	18	507	249 v	Pago tributos
Reales Cédulas	Chino(s)	18	758	287 v	Pago tributos
Reales Cédulas	Chino(s)	20	30	24 v	Prohibición armas
Reales Cédulas	Chino(s)	20	88	55	Prohibición armas
Reales Cédulas	Chino(s)	22	342	356	Plazas chinos oficiales reales
Reales Cédulas	Chino(s)	23	77	199	Prohibición armas
Reales Cédulas	Chino(s)	23	83	206	Prohibición armas
Reales Cédulas	Chino(s)	29	236	383 v	Permiso viaje esclavos
Reales Cédulas	Chino(s)	30	94	133	Liberación esclavos chinos
Reales Cédulas	Chino(s)	30	95	134	Liberación esclavos chinos
Reales Cédulas	Chino(s)	35	238	230	Permiso venta
Reales Cédulas	Chino(s)	35	254	233 v	Permiso venta
Reales Cédulas	Chino(s)	45	179	306 v	Permiso p/herrar ganado
Reales Cédulas	Chino(s)	48	136	56 v–57 r	Permiso barbería

(continued)

Reales Cédulas	Chino(s)	48	323	219	Permiso ventas
Reales Cédulas	Chino(s)	145	275	396	Prisioneros chinos
Tierras	Morisco(s)	2389	39	2	Aprehensión morisco
Tierras	Coyote(s)	2494	7	7	Querella por venta
Tierras	Coyote(s)	2861	3	15	Solicitud expulsión
Tierras	Coyote(s)	2861	5	14	Solicitud expulsión
Tierras	Chino(s)	2862	4	4-4 v	Demanda por camino real
Tierras	Coyote(s)	2873	10	43-45	Disputa por tierras
Tierras	Chino(s)	2956	52	2	Exención impuestos
Tierras	Chino(s)	2963	69	2	Libertad esclavo chino
Tierras	Chino(s)	2984	111	2	Prohibición armas
Tierras	Morisco(s)	2984	116	s/f	Asesinato
Tierras	Chino(s)	3624	6		?
Tributos	Morisco(s)	14	6	90-92 v	Tributos moriscos
Tributos	Chino(s)	51	6	84-100 v	Censo
Vínculos y May.	Lobo(s)	287	1	s/f	Testimonio limpieza sangre

APPENDIX B

Place of Origin of the Extreme Castas
in Mexico City's Marriage Cases, 1605–1783

The following tables show the places of origin for lobos, moriscos, and coyotes who were parties in Mexico City marriage cases for the period studied. The tables are derived from the core sources identified in Appendix A.

TABLE B.1 *Place of Origin of Lobos in Marriage Cases, Mexico City, 1605–1783*

Place of Origin	Number
Cuernavaca	2
Mexico City	13
Minas de San Luis	1
Puebla	1
Pueblo de San Gerónimo	1
San Miguel de Chapultepec	1
Tarasquillo	1
Temascaltepeque	
Tenestepango	1
Tlanepantla	1
Total	22

TABLE B.2 *Place of Origin of Moriscos in Marriage Cases,*
Mexico City, 1605–1783

Place of Origin	Number
Amilpas	1
Atlixco	2
Atrisco	1
Atzcapotzalco	2
Calimaya	1
Celaya	1
Chalco	3
Chalma	1
Chicaruasco	1
Chilquautla (Ismiquilpan)	1
Coyoacán	1
Cuautitlan	1
Cuernavaca	1
Doctrina de Istapaluca	1
Escapusaleo	1
Extremadura (Spain)	1
Guadalajara	1
Guanajuato	1
Guejutla	1
Havana	1
Huichapa (Hacienda Saiz)	1
Istapaluca	1
Lerma	1
Mexico City	218
Minas de Zaqualpa	1
Nstra. Señora de Guadalupe	1
Nueva Veracruz	2
Pachuca	2
Partido de Istlahuaca	1
Popotla (Tacuba)	1
Puebla	8
Pueblo de San Jacinto	1
Querétaro	1
R. de Minas de Sombrerete	1
Real del Monte	4
Remedios	1
Rivera de San Cosme	1
San Agustín de las Cueva	2
San Angel	5
San Bartholomé (Tacuba)	1
San Bartholomé Naocalpam	1

(continued)

TABLE B.2 *(continued)*

Place of Origin	Number
San Jacinto	3
San Luis de Paz	1
San Miguel Cambay	1
San Miguel el Grande	1
Santa Fe	1
Sinacantepeque	1
San Pedro Zacantenco	1
Tacuba	3
Tampico	1
Tantoyuca	1
Taxco	2
Teotihuacan	1
Tepeapulco	1
Tepetitlan	3
Teposotlan	1
Tezcoco	2
Tilapa (Puebla)	1
Tlalmanalco	2
Tlanepantla	1
Toluca	2
Tula	1
Tuliagualco (Iantepec)	1
Valladolid	2
Yautepeque	1
Zacatlan de las Manzanas	1
Total	316

TABLE B.3 *Place of Origin of Coyotes in Marriage Cases, Mexico City, 1605–1783*

Place of Origin	Number
Azcapotzalco	1
Querétaro	1
Tolcayucan	1
Total	3

APPENDIX C

Extreme Casta Slave Sales, from Mexico City Notarial Archive, Seventeenth Century

The data in the following table is taken from records of slave sales in the Archivo de Notarías del Distrito Federal, Mexico City. I would like to thank Tatiana Seijas for allowing me to use and publish this data.

TABLE C.1 *Selected Extreme Caste Slave Sales, Mexico City, Seventeenth Century*

Notary: Volume	Foli page	Date	Name of Slave	Description	Age	Price
F Veedor: 4615	133 v	1671	Francisco	Berberisco	21	300
J Pérez de Rivera: 4368	333 r	1652	Maria de Jesus	Chichimeca	18	100
D de los Ríos: 3843	13 v	1651	Francisco	Chichimeco	10	80
C Muñoz: 2525	1 v	1674	Nicolasa	Loba	35	400
N Bernal: 457	95 v	1673	Maria Clabixo	Morisca blanca	28	400
F de Olalde: 3237	348 v	1647	Juan	Morisco	4	100
D de los Ríos: 3845	67 r	1657	Francisco	Moro de nación	30	310
N Bernal: 461	6 v	1680	Isabel	Mulata amestizada	36	430
N Bernal: 462	12 v	1683	Petronila	Mulata blanca	24	200
N Bernal: 463	108 r	1689	Josepha	Mulata blanca	28	200
C Muñoz: 2526	67 v	1685	Juana de Salacar	Mulata blanca	44	200
M Pacheco de Figueroa: 3367	61 r	1672	Maria de San Antonio	Mulata blanca	19	200
H de Robledo: 3856	—	1688	Agustina de San Joseph	Mulata blanca	25	200
N Bernal: 463	31 v	1686	Maria	Mulata blanca	14	215
F Ramírez de Mendoza: 3863	58 r	1668	Ana	Mulata blanca	11	225
G López Ahedo: 2231	1 r	1656	Luisa	Mulata blanca	9	230
N de Vega: 4637	32 r	1678	Teresa de la Encarnación	Mulata blanca	35	230
N de Vega: 4636	47 r	1666	Cathalina	Mulata blanca	35	250
B Sarmiento de Vera: 4372	6 r	1673	Juana de San Agustín	Mulata blanca	16	290
J de Cartagena Valdivia: 734	85 v	1657	Angela Sol	Mulata blanca	20	300
J de Cartagena Valdivia: 738	46 r	1687	Josepha	Mulata blanca	30	300

(continued)

T Cobián: 730	361 v	1659	Maria Antonia	Mulata blanca	29	300
M Molina: 2485	27 r	1649	Isabel de la Cruz	Mulata blanca	20	300
C Muñoz: 2526	53 v	1690	Josepha Margarita	Mulata blanca	20	300
C Muñoz: 2526	—	1693	Josepha de Olalde	Mulata blanca	34	300
H de Robledo: 3855	—	1681	Theresa de Barrientos	Mulata blanca	13	300
G López Ahedo: 2236	63 r	1670	Ana de la Cruz	Mulata blanca	18	320
M Pacheco de Figueroa: 3368	3 v	1674	Teresa	Mulata blanca	20	320
J Anaya: 16	131 v	1672	Theresa de la Encarnación	Mulata blanca	27	325
N Bernal: 455	65 r	1670	Maria	Mulata blanca	20	325
L de Mendoza: 2493	208 r	1673	Margarita	Mulata blanca	25	325
N de Vega: 4636	—	1668	Francisca de la Cruz	Mulata blanca	18	325
N Bernal: 461	79 r	1680	Manuela	Mulata blanca	22	330
F Ramírez de Mendoza: 3862	193 r	1666	Josepha	Mulata blanca	20	330
F Ramírez de Mendoza: 3866	10 v	1679	Nicolasa	Mulata blanca	20	330
B Sarmiento de Vera: 4373	55 r	1676	Isabel	Mulata blanca	20	330
N Bernal: 458	161 v	1674	Andrea de la Cruz	Mulata blanca	22	340
N Arauz: 12	116 r	1661	Maria	Mulata blanca	22	350
N Bernal: 463	6 r	1689	Clara de la Cruz	Mulata blanca	17	350
M Molina: 2486	15 r	1653	Pasquala	Mulata blanca	26	350
F Veedor: 4616	190 r	1672	Loranza	Mulata blanca	27	350
F Veedor: 4622	2 v	1678	Micaela	Mulata blanca	13	350
N Bernal: 453	5 r	1667	María de la Encarnación	Mulata blanca	18	360
C Muñoz: 2524	51 r	1668	Josepha de Espinosa	Mulata blanca	24	360
F Ramírez de Mendoza: 3863	161 r	1667	Maria de la Cruz	Mulata blanca	17	370

(continued)

TABLE C.1 (continued)

Notary: Volume	Foli page	Date	Name of Slave	Description	Age	Price
M Pacheco de Figueroa: 3370	—	1696	Maria de Mendoca	Mulata blanca	30	390
T Cobián: 731	505 v	1661	Maria de la Cruz	Mulata blanca	35	400
C Muñoz: 2526	60 v	1684	Theresa	Mulata blanca	25	400
F Ramírez de Mendoza: 3866	11 r	1685	Antonia de la Encarnación	Mulata blanca	22	400
D de los Ríos: 3845	30 r	1656	Juana de los Reyes	Mulata blanca	22	400
H de Robledo: 3850	—	1667	Petronila	Mulata blanca	23	400
J Leonardo de Sevilla: 4382	74 v	1669	Juliana	Mulata blanca	27	420
J de la Puebla: 3377	11 v	1694	Juana	Mulata blanca	24	450
T Cobián: 731	260 v	1661	Jusepa	Mulata blanca	19	500
J Anaya: 21	192 r	1677	Pasquala de la Cruz	Mulata blanca	30	550
C Muñoz: 2526	65 r	1689	Juana	Mulata color cocho	24	100
M Molina: 2489	2 r	1666	Lucia	Mulata de color prieto	14	300
L de Mendoza: 2492	316 v	1659	Maria	Mulata prieta	4	156
C Muñoz: 2526	4 v	1683	Mariana	Mulata prieta	12	250
J Leonardo de Sevilla: 4382	77 v	1668	Magdalena	Mulata prieta	13	270
B Sarmiento de Vera: 4373	71 v	1677	Úrsula	Mulata prieta	16	284
J de Cartagena Valdivia: 734	23 v	1667	Juana de la Cruz	Mulata prieta	19	300
T Cobián: 728	106 r	1656	Sebastiana	Mulata prieta	32	300
F Veedor: 4617	398 v	1673	Juana de los Reyes	Mulata prieta	46	300
F Veedor: 4621	12 v	1677	Andrea	Mulata prieta	20	300
G Rueda: 3840	274 r	1638	Juana	Mulata prieta	18	325
B Sarmiento de Vera: 4376	179 r	1683	Ana de Santiago	Mulata prieta	14	325
T Cobián: 731	454 r	1661	Augustina	Mulata prieta	30	330

(continued)

Source	Folio	Name	Description	Year	Age	Price
H de Robledo: 3851	—	Joana	Mulata prieta	1662	25	340
N Bernal: 461	19 r	Dominga Gutiérrez	Mulata prieta	1682	18	350
F Ramírez de Mendoza: 3862	68 v	Francisca de la Cruz	Mulata prieta	1666	16	350
F de Rivera: 3858	40 v	Maria	Mulata prieta	1666	21	350
J Piedras Cortés: 3372	151 r	Maria	Mulata prieta	1673	18	365
N Bernal: 454	237 v	Jerónima de San Miguel	Mulata prieta	1669	20	370
N Arauz: 12	190 r	Juana	Mulata prieta	1662	22	380
L de Mendoza: 2493	113 r	Maria	Mulata prieta	1673	32	385
C Muñoz: 2526	66 r	Juana de la Cruz	Mulata prieta	1680	21	400
M Pacheco de Figueroa: 3369	59 r	Angela de Fuentes	Mulata prieta	1686	49	400
J de la Puebla: 3375	147 r	Nicolasa	Mulata prieta	1685	28	400
T Cobián: 729	436 r	Juana	Mulata prieta	1658	38	425
M Pacheco de Figueroa: 3369	40 v	Juana	Mulata, color cocho	1686	22	330
L de Mendoza: 2492	189 r	Teresa	Mulata, color	1659		
prieta membrillo	20			320		
F Veedor: 4620	864 r	Sebastiana	Mulatilla blanca	1676	5	100
H de Robledo: 3856	—	Eugenia	Mulatilla blanca	1670	7	175
N Bernal: 461	73 v	Francisca	Mulatilla blanca	1681	8	200
M Molina: 2489	2 v	Nicolassa	Mulatilla blanca	1666	8	200
N Bernal: 458	150 v	Isabel de Santa Rosa	Mulatilla blanca	1674	17	250
B Sarmiento de Vera: 4375	160 r	Inés de Biberos	Mulatilla prieta	1682	8	200
T Cobián: 732	303 v	Nicolás de la Cruz	Mulato albino	1662	22	300
F Ramírez de Mendoza: 3863	203 r	Nicolás	Mulato blanco	1667	3	50
J Piedras Cortes: 3373	276 r	Cristóbal	Mulato blanco	1689	8	125
N Bernal: 463	134 r	Joseph	Mulato blanco	1688	36	150
H de Robledo: 3854	86 r	Francisco	Mulato blanco	1679	22	150

(continued)

TABLE C.I (*continued*)

Notary: Volume	Foli page	Date	Name of Slave	Description	Age	Price
F Veedor: 4618	389 r	1674	Antonio	Mulato blanco	12	150
H de Robledo: 3853	53 v	1672	Pascual de la Cruz	Mulato blanco	24	200
B Sarmiento de Vera: 4376	94 v	1684	Francisco	Mulato blanco	12	200
F Ramírez de Mendoza: 3864	170 r	1669	Juan de la Cruz	Mulato blanco	11	210
J Piedras Cortes: 3371	141 r	1672	Francisco	Mulato blanco	18	230
B Sarmiento de Vera: 4371	100 r	1670	Juan de Dios	Mulato blanco	14	240
J de Cartagena Valdivia: 739	12 r	1689	Antonio Sánchez	Mulato blanco	16	250
J Cruz: 720	26 v	1623	Lorenzo	Mulato blanco	16	250
G López Ahedo: 2228	10 r	1649	Sebastián	Mulato blanco	15	250
M Pacheco de Figueroa: 3369	3 v	1690	Pablo	Mulato blanco	14	250
F Ramírez de Mendoza: 3863	142 v	1667	Joseph	Mulato blanco	13	250
F Ramírez de Mendoza: 3864	105 v	1669	Antonio	Mulato blanco	15	250
N Bernal: 463	99 v	1687	Juan	Mulato blanco	25	260
N Bernal: 463	93 v	1687	Juan Grande	Mulato blanco	31	275
J Anaya: 22	227 v	1678	Juan	Mulato blanco	36	280
G López Ahedo: 2228	5 r	1647	Antonio de la Cruz	Mulato blanco	15	280
T Cobián: 726	118 r	1653	Felipe	Mulato blanco	18	285
L de Mendoza: 2493	138 r	1673	Juan de la Cruz	Mulato blanco	16	290
N Bernal: 455	146 v	1670	Francisco	Mulato blanco	25	300
N Bernal: 459	189 v	1676	Pedro de la Cruz	Mulato blanco	18	300
N Bernal: 460	42 v	1678	Pedro de los Reyes	Mulato blanco	31	300
L de Mendoza: 2492	16 v	1659	Domingo	Mulato blanco	13	300
J Leonardo de Sevilla: 4382	36 v	1668	Antonio de la Cruz	Mulato blanco	17	300
M Pacheco de Figueroa: 3370	1 r	1693	Nicolás de la Rosa	Mulato blanco	22	320
F Veedor: 4606	216 v	1662	Thomas de la Cruz	Mulato blanco	19	320

(*continued*)

N Bernal: 462	98 v	1683	Miguel de Torres	Mulato blanco	22	325
F Veedor: 4615	400 v	1671	Juan de Gálvez	Mulato blanco	19	325
L de Mendoza: 2492	83 v	1659	Joseph	Mulato blanco	27	330
F Ramírez de Mendoza: 3863	6 r	1667	Nicolás Ambrosio	Mulato blanco	17	330
J de la Puebla: 3377	77 v	1694	Nicolás	Mulato blanco	18	350
F Ramírez de Mendoza: 3864	36 v	1670	Juan de Belasco	Mulato blanco	22	350
H de Robledo: 3849	128 v	1660	Juan Gallegos	Mulato blanco	24	350
F Veedor: 4617	808 r	1673	Juan	Mulato blanco	22	350
J Piedras Cortes: 3371	5 v	1671	Joseph	Mulato blanco	28	360
J de la Puebla: 3376	33 v	1686	Juan Antonio	Mulato blanco	22	360
J de la Puebla: 3377	9 v	1694	Esteban de la Cruz	Mulato blanco	20	360
J de Cartagena Valdivia: 735	19 v	1680	Juan de los Sanctos	Mulato blanco	27	380
H de Robledo: 3851	—	1663	Salvador	Mulato blanco	29	380
H Arauz: 9	256 r	1636	Diego	Mulato blanco	35	400
D de los Ríos: 3846	37 r	1660	Salbador	Mulato color membrillo	30	380
N Bernal: 460	4 v	1678	Joseph Martínez	Mulato membrillo cocho	40	150
N Bernal: 461	1 r	1681	Pedro	Mulato membrillo cocho	27	230
J Piedras Cortes: 3372	102 r	1673	Matheo de Paderes	Mulato moreno	23	330
N Bernal: 457	160 r	1672	Joseph de los Reyes	Mulato morisco blanco	28	280
T Cobián: 732	165 r	1662	Nicolás	Mulato prieto	28	150
N Bernal: 461	125 r	1682	Thomas de los Ríos	Mulato prieto	15	190
F Ramírez de Mendoza: 3863	96 v	1667	Domingo	Mulato prieto	10	230
F Veedor: 4617	98 r	1673	Antonio de la Cruz	Mulato prieto	34	230

(continued)

TABLE C.1 *(continued)*

Notary: Volume	Foli page	Date	Name of Slave	Description	Age	Price
N de Vega: 4638	—	1682	Luis de la Cruz	Mulato prieto	11	250
J Pérez de Rivera: 3362bis	315 r	1626	Pedro	Mulato prieto	16	260
J de la Puebla: 3375	4 r	1682	Lorenzo de la Cruz	Mulato prieto	24	280
N Bernal: 463	127 r	1687	Nicolás	Mulato prieto	20	290
T Cobián: 731	395 r	1661	Pedro	Mulato prieto	16	300
M Molina: 2486	35 r	1653	Ignacio	Mulato prieto	22	300
B Sarmiento de Vera: 4376	188 r	1683	Manuel Pacheco	Mulato prieto	14	300
F Veedor: 4615	134 r	1671	Francisco	Mulato prieto	18	300
L de Mendoza: 2492	352 r	1659	Ramón	Mulato prieto	18	315
C Muñoz: 2526	4 v	1691	Francisco	Mulato prieto	14	320
L de Mendoza: 2493	37 r	1673	Juan de Dios	Mulato prieto	?	330
F Veedor: 4618	75 v	1674	Juan de Velasco	Mulato prieto	29	340
L de Mendoza: 2493	285 r	1673	Nicolás	Mulato prieto	14	350
T Cobián: 730	378 r	1659	Gerónimo	Mulato prieto	23	356
J de la Puebla: 3377	43 r	1694	Manuel	Mulato prieto	20	400
F Ramírez de Mendoza: 3865	68 r	1671	Andrés de Santiago	Mulato prieto	30	525
M Molina: 2485	43 r	1650	Francisco	Mulato, "color membrillo"	19	330
G López Ahedo: 2236	75 r	1670	Bernardo de la Cruz	Mulato, "más blanco que prieto"	11	190
M Pacheco de Figueroa: 3369	77 r	1687	Salvador	Mulato, color cocho	28	350
J de la Puebla: 3375	8 r	1685	Joseph	Muleque	12	310
T Cobián: 732	172 v	1662	Juan Bautista	Nación berberisca	40	150
J Leonardo de Sevilla: 4382	1 r	1671	Bernardo	Negro amulatado	21	270

(continued)

T Cobián: 732	346	1662	Bernabé de la Cruz	Negro amulatado	13	340
F Veedor: 4621	397 r	1677	Francisco Muñoz	Negro bicho	60	140
F Veedor: 4615	348 r	1671	Domingo	Negro cafre de pasa	16	330
F Veedor: 4621	658 r	1677	Antonio	Negro cafre de pasa	28	335
C Muñoz: 2525	36 v	1673	Pedro Benito	Negro, color loro	19	380

APPENDIX D

Identity Reconsidered: Factoring Lineage into Declarations of Casta

In pondering the notion of identity among the extreme casta groups, the marriage cases outlined in Appendix A enable us to study another important element of the puzzle: Just how conscious were certain castas, especially Afro-castas, of their parentage and heritage? To what extent were their births legitimate or not? How did this knowledge, or lack of it, translate into declarations of lineage at the altar?

There are three conventional modes of thinking in this regard. The first convention follows on the long-standing cultural assumption in colonial society that members of the Afro-castas and other extreme castes were illegitimate and barely knew their lineage. It was often supposed that they were the bastard progeny of slaves and masters, the fruit of unions, often nonconsensual, between individuals of unequal social station or the product of casual and otherwise unsanctioned sexual liaisons. The second convention is associated with a more modern and scholarly perspective: many marginal castas lived in a plebeian world in which most lives did not revolve around formal knowledge of lineage. This seems to have been the case in late seventeenth-century Mexico City, where even the use of surnames among those castes was seemingly uncommon, as Douglas Cope has noted (*The Limits of Racial Domination*, 56–67). The third convention embodies a very different and logically opposing notion: that bearing a caste label such as morisco or lobo implied very intimate and precise intergenerational knowledge – an intricate recipe of lineage, relationships, and caste status – that was often passed down by informal means such as reputational race and gossip. Often, neighbors and acquaintances became the gatekeepers of such knowledge, carrying it on into the collective memory of local communities.

The marriage application data reveals that the majority of moriscos and lobos knew both of their parents. Chinos, on the other hand, overwhelmingly did not report knowing their parents. Unfortunately, the limited number of coyotes prevents us from arriving at any clear picture of their parental knowledge. Nonetheless, it is evident that knowledge about parentage generally increased in the eighteenth century. Prior to 1700, approximately half of morisco men and women did not report their parents' identity in their marriage petitions, but by the eighteenth century, just 16 percent of women and 7 percent of men failed to record their parents. Lobas, who were far fewer in number, followed similar trends. Tracing the representation of chinos in the marriages of marginal castes is not possible, as they slipped almost entirely from view in the eighteenth century.

The dramatic increase in parental knowledge after 1700 is probably not wholly due to a sudden change in intergenerational understandings of lineage. It appears that completeness and accuracy increased as Church notaries adopted different questioning procedures during the eighteenth century. With these improvements in recordkeeping came better tracking of parental knowledge at the time of marriage. The difference is shown in Tables D.1 and D.2.

Another method of determining the extent to which castas knew their lineage is to study orphans, especially among the Afro-castas, where the data is richest, as shown in Tables D.1 and D.2. The number of orphans among lobos and moriscos increased from the seventeenth to the eighteenth centuries, but at least for moriscos the proportion of brides and grooms who married as orphans remained roughly the same. In other words, anywhere between 18 and 19 percent of morisca brides were orphans during the seventeenth and eighteenth centuries, as were between 9 and 11 percent of morisco grooms. In contrast, no lobos were recorded as orphans in the seventeenth century, but in the eighteenth, 20 percent of lobas fell into this category, as did 14 percent of lobo men.

What can we learn from this data? When compared to published data on illegitimacy for the entire population of Mexico City, we find that lobo and morisco orphans in the marriage applications were fewer than what we might expect. Research on the central Mexico City's Sagrario parish reveals that illegitimacy rates for mulatos and castas ranged between 30 and 50 percent between 1724 and 1811. However, in the parish of Santa Catarina, illegitimacy rates for all casta groups hovered around 20 percent. More work is needed to explore this issue, but one might

TABLE D.1 *Marginal Castes' Knowledge of Lineage, 1605–1700*

	Moriscas	Moriscos	Lobos	Lobas	Chinos	Chinas	Coyotes	Coyotas	Total
Knew both parents	12	9	1	2	0	1	0	0	25
	(35)	(41)	(100)	(40)		(6)			(30)
Orphans	6	2	0	0	0	1	0	0	9
	(18)	(9)				(6)			(11)
Did not report knowing parents	16	11	0	3	7	13	0	0	50
	(47)	(50)		(60)	(100)	(87)			(59)
Total	34	22	1	5	7	15	0	0	84
	(100)	(100)	(100)	(100)	(100)	(100)			(100)

Source: Derived from the marriage cases in Appendix A. The number in parentheses is the percentage of the whole represented by the number just above it.

TABLE D.2 *Marginal Castes' Knowledge of Lineage, 1700–1783*

	Moriscas	Moriscos	Lobos	Lobas	Chinos	Chinas	Coyotes	Coyotas	Total
Knew both Parents	108	95	4	13	0	0	1	0	221
	(65)	(76)	(57)	(65)					(68)
Orphans	32	14	1	3	0	0	1	0	51
	(19)	(11)	(14)	(15)					(16)
Did not report knowing parents	27	16	2	4	1	0	1	1	52
	(16)	(13)	(29)	(20)	(100)				(16)
Total	167	125	7	20	1	0	3	1	324
	(100)	(100)	(100)	(100)	(100)				(100)

Source: Derived from the marriage cases in Appendix A. The number in parentheses is the percentage of the whole represented by the number just above it.

TABLE D.3 *Casta Declarations of the Marginal Castes Who Did Not Report Parentage*

	Moriscas	Moriscos	Lobos	Lobas	Chinos	Chinas	Coyotes	Coyotas	Total
Self-Declared Casta	41 (51) 14 widows	31 (72) 12 widowers	1 (33)	3 (30) 1 widower	1 (13) 1 widower	0	2 (100) 1 widower	0	79 (49)
Did Not Self-Declare Casta	40 (49) 2 widows	12 (28) 3 widowers 1 widower	2 (67) 1 widower	7 (70) 1 widow	7 (87)	14 (100)	0	1 (100) 1 widow	83 (51)
Total	81 (100)	43 (100)	3 (100)	10 (100)	8 (100)	14 (100)	2 (100)	1 (100)	162 (100)

Source: Derived from the marriage cases in Appendix A. The number in parentheses is the percentage of the whole represented by the number just above it.

argue that lobos and moriscos who contracted nuptials in the eighteenth century, excluding those who were in consensual unions, probably had a better understanding of their lineage than colonial opinion might lead us to expect.

Firmer understandings of lineage should mean that members of marginal castes who self-reported could do so with the backing of genealogical evidence and could be less reliant on phenotypic criteria or social position. The evidence suggests that a strong nucleus of moriscos and lobos seeking marriage who self-declared their casta had (more so in the eighteenth century than in the 1600s) an understanding of their background that covered at least one generation, if not more. Such knowledge did not, of course, prevent individuals who had a lesser understanding of their lineage from identifying their casta (see Table D.3). Nearly half of all individuals who self-declared their casta to notaries did not profess their lineage or were orphans. Hence, it was almost an even draw as to whether lineage or phenotype prevailed as the main factor for determining casta among the extreme castas in the sample. Individuals with weak genealogical knowledge who nonetheless articulated their casta might have used a combination of somatic criteria and status considerations to gauge their status.

A closer look at the evidence reveals a slightly more nuanced picture. Nearly three-quarters of all male moriscos whose lineage was uncertain spoke up to self-declare their casta. Moriscas dominated the overall sample but were reticent in following suit. Data for other members of the extreme castas is too small to be conclusive. But by and large, it was morisco men who took the lead and felt most comfortable articulating their casta, regardless of the completeness of their intergenerational knowledge.

The cases involving widowed persons reveal another aspect of casta marriage. From analyzing the record, it appears that it may not have been customary for remarrying widows and widowers to provide knowledge of their lineage to the notaries. Undoubtedly, some number of them were legitimate and knew their parents. Since the number of widows and widowers was greatest among those individuals who declared their casta (especially moriscos and moriscas, who represented about one-third of those widowed), it is quite possible that we may have an inaccurate perception of how many individuals lacking full knowledge of their parental background proceeded to convey their casta status. Nearly all of the widows and widowers in our sample come from the 1700s. Therefore, the influence of the "widow effect" on the data was largely a phenomenon of the eighteenth century.

References

ARCHIVAL SOURCES

The National Archives of Mexico (hereafter AGN) and the Notarial Archive of Mexico City (hereafter ANM) constitute the two primary repositories used for this study. In the AGN, an effort was made to locate as many references to lobos, moriscos, and coyotes in the colonial record as possible. It is likely that there are other references to be found, especially in the Indiferente Virreinal section of the archives. Additionally, there are more references to be identified in the parish and regional archives throughout Mexico.

AGN, Bandos, vol. 8, exp. 39, fols. 139–142.
AGN, Bandos, vol. 17, fols. 15–25.
AGN, Bandos, vol. 17, exp. 55 and 56, fols. 228–249v.
AGN, Bienes Nacionales, leg. 88, exp. 13, fols. 1–6.
AGN, Bienes Nacionales, vol. 91, exp. 43.
AGN, Bienes Nacionales, vol. 113, exp. 10, fols. 39–43v.
AGN, Bienes Nacionales, vol. 293, exp. 299.
AGN, Bienes Nacionales, vol. 787, exp. 1.
AGN, Bienes Nacionales, vol. 800, leg. 808, exp. 3, fols. 1–37.
AGN, Bienes Nacionales, leg. 1229, exp. 4, fols. 13–15.
AGN, Californias, vol. 58, fols. 82–117v.
AGN, Clero Regular y Secular, vol. 48, exp. 4, fols. 96–101.
AGN, Criminal, vol. 206, fols. 364bis–374.
AGN, General de Parte, vol. 21, exp. 211, fols. 248v–249v.
AGN, General de Parte, vol. 37, exp. 244, fols. 205v–206.
AGN, General de Parte, vol. 38, exp. 10, fols. 19–19v.
AGN, General de Parte, vol. 39, exp. 15, fol. 9v.
AGN, General de Parte, vol. 41, exp. 329, fols. 253v–254.
AGN, General de Parte, vol. 43, exp. 80, fols. 43v–44.
AGN, General de Parte, vol. 73, exp. 216, fols. 235–237v.
AGN, General de Parte, vol. 79, exps. 275–277, fols. 239v–241v.
AGN, Indiferentes de Guerra, vol. 53-A.

AGN, Indiferente Virreinal, caja 599, exp. 16, fols. 1–7v (1781).
AGN, Indiferente Virreinal, caja 657 (Oficios Vendibles), exp. 9, fols. 1–52.
AGN, Indiferente Virreinal, vol. 726, exp. 26, fols. 1–3v.
AGN, Indiferente Virreinal, caja 1355, exp. 34, fols. 1–4v.
AGN, Indiferente Virreinal, caja 1888, exp. 14, fols. 1–14.
AGN, Indiferente Virreinal, caja 1975, exp. 1.
AGN, Indiferente Virreinal, caja 2486, exp. 18, fols. 1–16.
AGN, Indiferente Virreinal, vol. 3431, exp. 40, fols. 1–1v.
AGN, Indiferente Virreinal, caja 4045, exp. 26, fols. 1–2v.
AGN, Indiferente Virreinal, caja 4077, exp. 9, fols. 1–6.
AGN, Indiferente Virreinal, caja 5257, exp. 36, fols. 1–3v.
AGN, Indiferente Virreinal, caja 5679, exp. 18.
AGN, Indiferente Virreinal, caja 5868, exp. 4, fols. 1–2v.
AGN, Indiferente Virreinal, caja 6295, exp. 15, fols. 1–8.
AGN, Indiferente Virreinal, caja 6512, exp. 50.
AGN, Indiferente Virreinal, vol. 6596, exp. 138, fol. 1.
AGN, Indios, vol. 6, exp. 989.
AGN, Indios, vol. 11, exp. 166, fols. 136v–137v.
AGN, Indios, vol. 25, exp. 499, fols. 346v–347v.
AGN, Indios, vol. 66, exp. 3, fols. 4v–5v.
AGN, Inquisición, vol. 281, exp. 10, fols. 532–537, 717–719.
AGN, Inquisición, vol. 312, exp. 45, fol. 228.
AGN, Inquisición, vol. 362 second series, exp. 133, fols. 510–511v.
AGN, Inquisición, vol. 451, exp. 1, fols. 1–122.
AGN, Inquisición, vol. 539, exp. 9, fols. 80–86v.
AGN, Inquisición, vol. 586, exp. 8, fols. 502–572.
AGN, Inquisición, vol. 705, exp. 7, fol. 52.
AGN, Inquisición, vol. 715, exp. 18, fol. 489v.
AGN, Inquisición, vol. 758, exp. 15, fol. 463.
AGN, Inquisición, vol. 775, exp. 45, fols. 553–556.
AGN, Inquisición, vol. 777, exp. 28, fols. 81–82.
AGN, Inquisición, vol. 780, exp. 10, fols. 414–485v.
AGN, Inquisición, vol. 781, exp. 5, fol. 388v.
AGN, Inquisición, vol. 781, exp. 8, fol. 373.
AGN, Inquisición, vol. 781, exp. 26, fols. 267–270.
AGN, Inquisición, vol. 781, exp. 44, fols. 517–523.
AGN, Inquisición, vol. 808, exps. 11 and 12, fols. 458–491v.
AGN, Inquisición, vol. 811, exp. 3, fols. 229, 263–267.
AGN, Inquisición, vol. 817, exp. 18, fols. 411, 413–414v.
AGN, Inquisición, vol. 826, exp. 42, fols. 413–431v.
AGN, Inquisición, vol. 829, exp. 9, fols. 589–611.
AGN, Inquisición, vol. 830, exp. 4, fols. 52–82, 59, 60v.
AGN, Inquisición, vol. 845, exp. 16, fols. 212–214v, 219.
AGN, Inquisición, vol. 862, exp. 1, fol. 196.
AGN, Inquisición, vol. 872 (1), exp. 2, 36–73.
AGN, Inquisición, vol. 875, exp. 5, fols. 101–149.
AGN, Inquisición, vol. 890, fols. 52–66v.
AGN, Inquisición, vol. 907, exp. 23, fols. 384.

AGN, Inquisición, vol. 921, exp. 15, fols. 221–236.
AGN, Inquisición, vol. 927, exp. 7, fols. 364–374.
AGN, Inquisición, vol. 941, exp. 3, fols. 10–30.
AGN, Inquisición, vol. 941, exp. 25, fols. 262–276v.
AGN, Inquisición, vol. 951, exp. 7, fols. 81–104v.
AGN, Inquisición, vol. 952, exp. 34, fols. 367–368.
AGN, Inquisición, vol. 980, exp. 12.
AGN, Inquisición, vol. 1065, exp. 13, fols. 296–298.
AGN, Inquisición, vol. 1068, exp. 9, fol. 68.
AGN, Inquisición, vol. 1097, exp. 8, fols. 218v–233.
AGN, Inquisición, vol. 1122, exp. 3, fols. 75v–80.
AGN, Inquisición, vol. 1133, exp. 5, fols. 42–47v.
AGN, Inquisición, vol. 1169, exp. 7, fols. 94–97.
AGN, Inquisición, vol. 1176, exp. 4, fol. 68–79v.
AGN, Inquisición, vol. 1224, exp. 10, fols. 208–229.
AGN, Inquisición, vol. 1237, exp. 5, fols. 156–259.
AGN, Inquisición, vol. 1256, exp. 1, fols. 1–91.
AGN, Inquisición, vol. 1274, exp. 7, fols. 427–436.
AGN, Inquisición, vol. 1287, exp. 1, fols. 1–16.
AGN, Inquisición, vol. 1292, exp. 17, fols. 1–101.
AGN, Inquisición, vol. 1378, exp. 2, fols 5–17v.
AGN, Inquisición, vol. 1495, exp. 3, fols. 9–21.
AGN, Matrimonios, vol. 4, exp. 5, fols. 24–28v.
AGN, Matrimonios, vol. 6, exp. 8, fol. 22.
AGN, Matrimonios, vol. 32, exp. 77, fols. 405–408.
AGN, Matrimonios, vol. 85, exp. 18, fol. 34.
AGN, Matrimonios, vol. 87, exp. 4 bis., fols. 14–26.
AGN, Matrimonios, vol. 88, exp. 3, fols. 5–6v.
AGN, Matrimonios, vol. 109, exp. 94, fols. 397–400.
AGN, Matrimonios, vol. 113, exp. 62, fols. 162–163v.
AGN, Matrimonios, vol. 159, exp. 52, fol. 7v.
AGN, Matrimonios, vol. 170, exp. 1, fols 1–4.
AGN, Matrimonios, vol. 203, exp. 12, fol. 4.
AGN, Matrimonios, vol. 224, exp. 2, fols. 5–11.
AGN, Matrimonios, vol. 550, exp. 1, fol. 457.
AGN, Padrones, vols. 5, 16, 17, 22, 23, 25, 32, 43, 53, 62, 72, and 78.
AGN, Padrones, vol. 6, no. 1, exp. 1.
AGN, Padrones, vol. 6, no. 2, exp. 4.
AGN, Padrones, vol. 12, exp. 4.
AGN, Padrones, vol. 16, exp. 2.
AGN, Padrones, vol. 21, exp. 3.
AGN, Provincias Internas, vol. 240, exp. 11, exps. 156–166v.
AGN, Reales Cédulas Originales, vol. 182, exp. 6, 2 fojas.
ANM, C. Muñoz 2525, fol. 1v.
ANM, Fernando Veedor 4601, fol. 212v.
ANM, Fernando Veedor 4618, fol. 32v.
ANM, Martin Sariñana 4362, fol. 196.
ANM, Nicolás Bernal 461, fol. 12.

258 References

BOOKS AND ARTICLES

Aguilar, Mario I. "Local and Global, Political and Scholarly Knowledge: Diversifying Oromo Studies." *African Affairs* 96, no. 383 (April 1997): 277–280.

Aguilar y Correa, Antonio, Marqués de la Vega de Armijo. *Observaciones del Excmo. Sr. Marqués de la Vega de Armijo sobre la mejora de las castas de caballos en España.* Madrid: Imp. de Don Eusebio Aguado, 1831.

Aguirre Beltrán, Gonzalo. *Cuijla: esbozo etnográfico de un pueblo negro.* Mexico: Fondo de Cultura Económica, 1995.

Medicina y magia: el proceso de aculturación en la estructura colonial. Mexico City: Instituto Nacional Indigenista, 1963.

El negro esclavo en Nueva España. Mexico City: Fondo de Cultura Económica, 1994.

La población negra de méxico: estudio etnohistórico. Mexico City: Fondo de Cultura Económica, 1972.

Ahmad, Aijaz. *In Our Time: Empire, Politics, Culture.* London: Verso, 2007.

"The Politics of Literary Postcoloniality." *Race and Class* 36, no. 3 (1995): 1–20.

Alamán, Lucas. *Historia de México.* Vol. 1. Mexico City: Imprenta de Victoriano Agüeros y Comp., 1883.

Historia de México desde los primeros movimientos que prepararon su independencia en el año de 1808, hasta la época presente. Vol. 1. Mexico City: Instituto Cultural Helénico, 2000.

Alberro, Solange. *Inquisición y sociedad en México, 1571–1700.* Mexico City: Fondo de Cultura Económica, 1988.

La sociedad novohispana: estereotipos y realidades. Mexico City: Colegio de México, Centro de Estudios Históricos, 2013.

Altamirano, Ignacio M. *Clemencia.* Edited by Elliott B. Scherr and Nell Walker. Boston: D. C. Heath, 1948.

Discursos: pronunciados en la tribuna cívica, en la Cámara de diputados, en varias sociedades científicas y literarias y en otros lugares, desde el año de 1859 hasta el de 1881; coleccionados por la primera vez. Paris: Biblioteca de la Europa y America, 1892.

Paisajes y leyendas: tradiciones y costumbres de México. Mexico City: Imprenta y Litografía Española, 1884; Antigua Librería Robredo, 1949.

Altamirano, Ignacio M., and C. Sierra Casasús. *Obras completas.* Mexico City: Secretaría de Educación Pública, 1986.

Althouse, Aaron P. "Contested Mestizos, Alleged Mulattos: Racial Identity and Caste Hierarchy in Eighteenth-Century Pátzcuaro, Mexico." *The Americas* 62, no. 2 (October 2005): 151–175.

Alvar, Manuel. *Léxico del mestizaje en Hispanoamérica.* Madrid: Ediciones Cultura Hispánica; Instituto de Cooperación Iberoamericana, 1987.

Anderson, Rodney. "Race and Social Stratification: A Comparison of Working-Class Spaniards, Indians, and Castas in Guadalajara, Mexico in 1821." *Hispanic American Historical Review* 68 (1988): 209–243.

Andrews, George R. *Afro-Latin America, 1800–2000*. Oxford: Oxford University Press, 2004.

Andrews, Norah. "Calidad, Genealogy, and Disputed Free-Colored Tributary Status in New Spain." *The Americas: A Quarterly Review of Latin American History* 73, no. 02 (2016): 139–170.

"Taxing Blackness: Free-Colored Tribute in Colonial Mexico." PhD diss.: Johns Hopkins University, 2014.

Ares Queija, Berta and Alessandro Stella, eds. *Negros, mulatos, zambaigos: derroteros africanos en los mundos ibéricos*. Seville: Escuela de Estudios Hispano-Americanos, Consejo Superior de Investigaciones Científicas, 2000.

Armstrong, James C., and Nigel A. Worden. "The Slaves, 1652–1834." In *The Shaping of South African Society, 1652–1840*. Edited by Richard Elphick and Hermann Giliomee. Middletown, CT: Maskew Miller Longman, 1989.

Arrom, Silvia Marina. *The Women of Mexico City, 1790–1857*. Stanford: Stanford University Press, 1985.

Baker, Lee. *From Savage to Negro: Anthropology and the Construction of Race, 1896–1954*. Berkeley: University of California Press, 2007.

Banton, Michael. *Racial Theories*. Cambridge: Cambridge University Press, 1998.

Barkey, Karen. "Aspects of Legal Pluralism in the Ottoman Empire." In *Legal Pluralism and Empires, 1500–1850*, ed. Lauren A. Benton and Richard J. Ross. New York: New York University Press, 2013, 83–108, 95.

Barreda, Gabino. *Opúsculos, discusiones y discursos*. Mexico City: Impr. del Comercio, 1877. Google Books version.

Basarás, Joaquín Antonio. *Origen, costumbres y estado presente de mexicanos y philipinos: descripción acompañada de 106 estampas en colores* (1763). Edited by Ilona Katzew. Mexico City: Landucci, 2006.

Beltrán, Carlos. "Hippocratic Bodies. Temperament and Castas in Spanish America (1570–1820)." *Journal of Spanish Cultural Studies* 8, no. 2: 253–289.

Bennett, Herman L. *Africans in Colonial Mexico: Absolutism, Christianity, and Afro-Creole Consciousness, 1570–1640*. Bloomington and Indianapolis: Indiana University Press, 2003.

Colonial Blackness: A History of Afro-Mexico. Bloomington: Indiana University Press, 2009.

"Genealogies to a Past: Africa, Ethnicity, and Marriage in Seventeenth-Century Mexico." In *New Studies in American Slavery*, edited by Edward E. Baptist and Stephanie M. H. Camp. Athens: University of Georgia Press, 2005.

"Lovers, Family, and Friends: The Formation of Afro-Mexico, 1580–1810." PhD diss.: Duke University, 1993.

"Sons of Adam: Text, Context and the Early Modern African Subject." *Representations* 92, no. 1 (Fall 2005): 1–45.

"The Subject in the Plot: National Boundaries and the History of the Black Atlantic." *African Studies Review* 43 (April 2000): 101–124.

Bentley, Jeremy H. *Old World Encounters: Cross-Cultural Contacts and Exchanges in Pre-Modern Times*. New York and Oxford: Oxford University Press, 1993.

Benton, Lauren A., and Richard J. Ross, eds. *Legal Pluralism and Empires, 1500–1850*. New York: New York University Press.

Bhabha, Homi K. *The Location of Culture*. London and New York: Routledge, 1994.

Boas, Franz. "Mi andina y dulce Rita: Women, Indigenism, and the Avant-garde in César Vallejo." In *Primitivism and Identity in Latin America: Essays on Art, Literature, and Culture*, edited by Erik Camayd-Freixas and José Eduardo González. Tucson: University of Arizona Press, 2000.

The Mind of Primitive Man. Lexington, KY: Forgotten Books, 2011.

Boletín de Agricultura, Minera e Industrias, October 1, 1891, Mexico City: 56–58.

Boyer, Richard E. *Caste and Identity in Colonial Mexico: A Proposal and an Example*. Storrs, CT, Providence, RI, and Amherst, MA: Latin American Consortium of New England, 1997.

Lives of the Bigamists: Marriage, Family, and Community in Colonial Mexico. Albuquerque: University of New Mexico Press, 1995.

Brading, David A. "Grupos étnicos, clases y estructura ocupacional en Guanajuato (1792)." *Historia Mexicana* 21 (January–March 1972): 258, 460–480.

Mexican Phoenix: Our Lady of Guadalupe: Image and Tradition Across Five Centuries. Cambridge: Cambridge University Press, 2001.

The Origins of Mexican Nationalism. Cambridge: Cambridge University Press, 1985.

Brah, A., and Annie E. Coombes. *Hybridity and Its Discontents: Politics, Science, Culture*. London: Routledge, 2000.

Bristol, Joan C. *Christians, Blasphemers, and Witches: Afro-Mexican Ritual Practice in the Seventeenth Century*. Albuquerque: University of New Mexico Press, 2007.

Bristol, Joan C., and Matthew Restall. "Potions and Perils: Love-Magic in Seventeenth-Century Afro-Mexico and Afro-Yucatan." In *Black Mexico: Race and Society from Colonial to Modern Times*, edited by Ben Vinson III and Matthew Restall. Albuquerque: University of New Mexico Press, 2009.

Brockington, Lolita G. *Blacks, Indians, and Spaniards in the Eastern Andes: Reclaiming the Forgotten in Colonial Mizque, 1550–1782*. Lincoln: University of Nebraska Press, 2006.

Buffon, Georges L. *Natural History, General and Particular*. Translated by William Smellie and William M. Wood. London: T. Cadell and W. Davies, 1812.

Bulnes, Francisco. *El porvenir de las naciones latino-americanas ante las recientes conquistas de Europa y Norteamérica: estructura y evólucion de un continente*. Mexico City: Imprenta de Mariano Nava, 1899; Pensamiento Vivo de América, 1940.

El verdadero Juárez y la verdad sobre la intervención y el imperio. Paris: C. Bouret, 1904.

Burns, Kathryn. *Into the Archive: Writing and Power in Colonial Peru*. Durham: Duke University Press, 2010.

"Unfixing Race." In *Rereading the Black Legend: The Discourses of Religious and Racial Difference in the Renaissance Empires*, edited by Margaret R. Greer, Walter D. Mignolo, and Maureen Quilligan. Chicago, University of Chicago, 2007.

Bushnell, Dave, and Neill Macaulay. *The Emergence of Latin America in the Nineteenth Century*. New York: Oxford University Press, 1988.

Butler, Judith. *Gender Trouble: Feminism and the Subversion of Identity*. New York: Routledge, 1999.

Butler, Kim D. *Freedoms Given, Freedoms Won: Afro-Brazilians in Post-Abolition São Paulo and Salvador*. New Brunswick, NJ: Rutgers University Press, 1998.

Cáceres, Rina. *Negros, mulatos, esclavos y libertos en la Costa Rica del siglo XVII*. Mexico City: Instituto Panamericano de Geografía e Historia, 2000.

Cañizares-Esguerra, Jorge. *How to Write a History of the New World: Histories, Epistemologies, and Identities in the Eighteenth-Century Atlantic World*. Stanford: Stanford University Press, 2001.

Nature, Empire, and Nation: Explorations of the History of Science in the Iberian World. Stanford: Stanford University Press, 2006.

"New World, New Stars: Patriotic Astrology and the Invention of Indian and Creole Bodies in Colonial Spanish America, 1600–1650." *American Historical Review* 104, no. 1 (1999): 33–68.

Caro, José E., Arbeláez E. Vargas, and Guillén G. Vargas. *Mecánica social, o, teoría del wmovimiento humano, considerado en su naturaleza, en sus efectos y en sus causas*. Bogotá: Instituto Caro y Cuervo, 2002.

Carrera, Magali M. *Imagining Identity in New Spain: Race, Lineage and the Colonial Body in Portraiture and Casta Paintings*. Austin: University of Texas Press, 2003.

Carrión, Antonio. *Historia de la Ciudad de Puebla de los Angeles*, 2nd edition. Vol. 2. Puebla: Editorial José M. Cajica Jr, 1970.

Carroll, Patrick J. "Black Aliens and Black Natives in New Spain's Indigenous Communities." In *Black Mexico: Race and Society from Colonial to Modern Times*, edited by Ben Vinson III and Matthew Restall. Albuquerque: University of New Mexico Press, 2009.

Blacks in Colonial Veracruz: Race, Ethnicity, and Regional Development. Austin: University of Texas Press, 2001.

"New Spain's Holy Trinity" (Forthcoming).

Carroll, Patrick J., and Jeffrey Lamb. "Los mexicanos negros: el mestizaje y los fundamentos olvidados de la 'raza cósmica', una perspectiva regional." *Historia Mexicana* 44, no. 3 (1995): 411.

Caso, Antonio. *Discursos a la nación mexicana*. Mexico City: Porrúa, 1922.

El problema de México y la ideología nacional. Mexico City: Libro-Mex Editores, 1955.

Caso, Antonio, Felix F. Palavicini, and José Almaraz. *México: historia de su evolución constructiva*. Mexico City: Libro, 1945.

Castillo Palma, Norma Angélica. *Cholula, sociedad mestiza en ciudad india: un análisis de las consecuencias demográficas, económicas y sociales del mestizaje en una ciudad novohispana (1649–1796)*. Mexico City: Plaza y Valdés, 2001.

"Cohabitación y conflictividad entre afromestizos y nahuas en el México central." In *Pautas de convivencia étnica en la América Latina colonial: (indios, negros, mulatos, pardos y esclavos)*, edited by Juan Manuel de la Serna. Mexico City: Universidad Nacional Autónoma de México, 2005.

Castleman, Bruce. "Social Climbers in a Colonial Mexican City: Individual Mobility within the Sistema de Castas in Orizaba, 1777–1791." *Colonial Latin American Review* 10, no. 2 (2001): 229–249.

Castro, Américo. *The Spaniards: An Introduction to Their History*. Berkeley: University of California Press, 1971.

Castro, Juan E. *Mestizo Nations: Culture, Race, and Conformity in Latin American Literature*. Tucson: University of Arizona Press, 2002.

Catlos, Brian A. *Muslims of Medieval Latin Christendom, c. 1050–1614*. Cambridge and New York: Cambridge University Press, 2014, 280.

Chasteen, John Charles. *Born in Blood and Fire: A Concise History of Latin America*. New York: Norton, 2001.

National Rhythms, African Roots: The Deep History of Latin American Popular Dance. Albuquerque: University of New Mexico Press, 2004.

Chávez-Hita, Adriana Naveda. *Esclavos negros en las haciendas azucareras de Córdoba, Veracruz, 1690–1830*. Xalapa: Universidad Veracruzana, Centro de Investigaciones Históricas, 1987.

Chuchiak, John F. *The Inquisition in New Spain, 1536–1820: A Documentary History*. Baltimore: Johns Hopkins University Press, 2012.

Clark, Joseph M. "Veracruz and the Caribbean in the Seventeenth Century." PhD diss.: Johns Hopkins University, 2016.

Clayton, Lawrence A., and Michael L. Conniff. *History of Modern Latin America*. Fort Worth, TX: Harcourt Brace College Humanities, 1999.

Cleary, David. "Race, Nationalism and Social Theory in Brazil: Rethinking Gilberto Freyre." Working Paper TC -99–09. Cambridge: Harvard University, David Rockefeller Center for Latin American Studies, 1999. www.transcomm.ox.ac.uk/working%20papers/cleary.pdf, accessed July 1, 2016.

Coleman, David. *In the Light of Medieval Spain: Islam, the West, and the Relevance of the Past*. New York: Palgrave Macmillan, 2008, 177.

Colonial Latin American Historical Review 8, no. 3 (Summer 1999): 393–394. Review of Robert H. Jackson, *Race, Caste, and Status: Indians in Colonial Spanish America*.

"El Congreso." *Novena Broma*, April 8, 1877.

Cook, Sherburne F., and Woodrow W. Borah. *Essays in Population History: Mexico and the Caribbean*. Berkeley: University of California Press, 1971. Translated as *Ensayos sobre historia de la población: México y El Caribe*. Mexico City: Siglo XXI, 1977.

Cope, R. Douglas. *The Limits of Racial Domination: Plebeian Society in Colonial Mexico City, 1660–1720*. Madison: University of Wisconsin Press, 1994.

Corro, Ramos O. *Los cimarrones en Veracruz y la fundación de Amapa*. Veracruz: Comercial, 1951.

El Cultivador, November 1, 1873.

Curcio-Nagy, Linda A. *The Great Festivals of Mexico City: Performing Power and Identity.* Albuquerque: University of New Mexico Press, 2004.

Curran, Andrew. *The Anatomy of Blackness: Science & Slavery in an Age of Enlightenment.* Baltimore: Johns Hopkins University Press, 2011.

"Rethinking Race History: The Role of the Albino in the French Enlightenment Life Sciences." *History and Theory* 48, no. 3 (October 2009): 151–179.

Davies, Keith. "Tendencias demográficas urbanas durante el siglo XIX en México." *Historia y Población* 21, no. 3 (January-March 1972): 481–524.

Dávila, Arlene. *Latino Spin: Public Image and the Whitewashing of Race.* New York: New York University Press, 2008.

de Berey, C. *Carte de la partie occidentale de l'Afrique: comprise entre Arguin & Serrelionne où l'on a représenté avec plus de circonstances & d'exactitude que dans aucune carte précédente, non seulement le détail de la côte & les entrées des rivières, mais encore un assez grand détail de l'intérieur des terres, jusqu'à une très grande distance de la mer: en sorte qu'on y indique les divers royaumes & les nations des négres, le cours des grandes rivières, notamment de Sénégal & Gambie, et les établissements que les nations Européennes, François, Portugais, & Anglais, ont sur la côte & dans le pays / dressée sur plusieurs cartes & divers mémoires, par le Sr. d'Anville, géographe ordinaire du roi.* Map. Paris: Chez l'Auteur, Rue St. Honoré vis-à-vis la Rue de l'Arbre Sec, à la Coupe d'Or. January 1727.

Díaz, María Elena. *The Virgin, the King, and the Royal Slaves of El Cobre: Negotiating Freedom in Colonial Cuba, 1670–1780.* Stanford: Stanford University Press, 2000.

Ducey, Michael T. "Viven sin ley ni rey: rebeliones coloniales en Papantla, 1760–1790." In *Procesos rurales e historia regional: sierra and costa totonacas*, edited by Victoria Chenaut. Mexico City: CIESAS, 1996.

Earle, Rebecca. *The Body of the Conquistador: Food, Race, and the Colonial Experience in Spanish America, 1492–1700.* Cambridge: Cambridge University Press, 2012.

East, Edward, and Donald Jones. *Inbreeding and Outbreeding: Their Genetic and Sociological Significance.* Philadelphia: Lippincott, 1919.

Elliott, John. *Empires of the Atlantic World: Britain and Spain in America, 1492–1830.* New Haven, CT: Yale University Press, 2006.

Eltis, David. *The Rise of African Slavery in the Americas.* Cambridge: Cambridge University Press, 2000.

Enciso Rojas, Dolores. "La legislación sobre el delito de bigamia y su aplicación en Nueva España." In *El placer de pecar & el afán de normar*, edited by Seminario de Historia de las Mentalidades y Religión en México Colonial. Mexico City: Instituto Nacional de Antropología e Historia, 1988.

Erauso, Catalina, Michele Stepto, and Gabriel Stepto. *Lieutenant Nun: Memoir of a Basque Transvestite in the New World.* Boston: Beacon Press, 1996.

Farber, Paul Lawrence. *Mixing Races: From Scientific Racism to Modern Evolutionary Ideas.* Baltimore: Johns Hopkins University Press, 2010.

Fernández, Justino. *Planos de la Ciudad de México, siglos XVI y XVII. Estudio histórico, urbanístico y bibliográfico.* Mexico City: Universidad Nacional Autónoma de México, 1990.

Ferrer, Ada. *Insurgent Cuba: Race, Nation, and Revolution, 1868–1898.* Chapel Hill: University of North Carolina Press, 1999.

Fisher, Andrew. "Negotiating Two Worlds: The Free-Black experience in Guerrero's Tierra Caliente." In *Black Mexico: Race and Society from Colonial to Modern Times,* edited by Ben Vinson III and Matthew Restall. Albuquerque: University of New Mexico Press, 2009.

Fisher, Andrew B., and Matthew D. O'Hara, eds. *Imperial Subjects: Race and Identity in Colonial Latin America.* Durham, NC; London: Duke University Press, 2009.

Florescano, Enrique. *National Narratives in Mexico: A History.* Norman: University of Oklahoma Press, 2002.

Fontaine, Pierre-Michel. *Race, Class, and Power in Brazil.* Los Angeles: University of California, Center for African American Studies, 1985.

Forbes, Jack D. "Unknown Athapaskans: The Identification of the Jano, Jocome, Jumano, Manso, Suma, and Other Indian Tribes of the Southwest." *Ethnohistory* 6, no. 2 (Spring 1959): 97–159.

Frederick, Jason. "Without Impediment: Crossing Racial Boundaries in Colonial Mexico." *The Americas* 67, no. 4 (2011): 495–515. www.jstor.org/stable/41239107, accessed July 1, 2016.

Fuchs, Barbara. *Exotic Nation: Maurophilia and the Construction of Early Modern Spain.* Philadelphia: University of Pennsylvania Press, 2009.

"The Spanish Race." In *Rereading the Black Legend: The Discourses of Religious and Racial Difference in the Renaissance Empires,* edited by Margaret R. Greer, Walter D. Mignolo, and Maureen Quilligan. Chicago: University of Chicago Press, 2007.

Galton, Francis. *Hereditary Genius.* Bristol, UK: Thoemmes Press, 1998.

Gamio, Manuel. *Forjando patria.* Mexico City: Porrúa, 1960.

García, Jesús C. *Afrovenezolanidad: esclavitud, cimarronaje y lucha contemporánea.* Caracas: Ministerio de Educación, Cultura y Deportes, CONAC, 2001.

Caribeñidad: afroespiritualidad y afroepistemología. Caracas: Ministerio de Cultura, Fundación Editorial el Perro y la Rana, 2006.

Mokongo ma chévere: danzar la historia … danzar la memoria. Caracas: Consejo Nacional de la Cultura, Dirección de la Danza del Fundación Afroamérica, 2004.

García Canclini, Néstor. *Consumers and Citizens: Globalization and Multicultural Conflicts.* Minneapolis: University of Minnesota Press, 2001.

Hybrid Cultures: Strategies for Entering and Leaving Modernity. Translated by C. Chiappari and S. Lopez. Minneapolis and London: University of Minneapolis Press, 1995. Spanish edition: *Culturas híbridas. estrategias para entrar y salir de la modernidad,* Mexico City, Grijalbo, 1990.

Garofalo, Leo, and Rachel O'Toole, eds. Constructing Difference in Colonial Latin America. Special issue, *Journal of Colonialism and Colonial History* 7, no. 1 (Spring 2006).

Gauderman, Kimberly. *Women's Lives in Colonial Quito: Gender, Law, and Economy in Spanish America.* Austin: University of Texas Press, 2003.

Gerhard, Peter. *Geografía histórica de la Nueva España, 1519–1821.* Mexico: Universidad Autónoma de México, 1986.

Gibson, Charles. *The Aztecs under Spanish Rule: A History of the Indians of the Valley of Mexico, 1519–1810.* Stanford: Stanford University Press, 2000.

Gilroy, Paul. *The Black Atlantic: Modernity and Double Consciousness.* Cambridge: Harvard University Press, 1993.

Girard, Pascale. "Les africains aux Philippines aux XVIe et XVIIe siècles." In *Negros, mulatos, zambaigos: derroteros africanos en los mundos ibéricos,* edited by Berta Ares Queija and Alessandro Stella. Seville: Escuela de Estudios Hispano-Americanos, Consejo Superior de Investigaciones Científicas, 2000.

Gómez, Michael Angelo. *Exchanging Our Country Marks: The Transformation of African Identities in the Colonial and Antebellum South.* Chapel Hill: University of North Carolina Press, 1998.

Gonzalbo Aizpuru, Pilar. *Familia y orden colonial.* Mexico City: Colegio de México, 1998.

Familias iberoamericanas: historia, identidad y conflictos. Mexico City: Colegio de México, 2001.

González, Anita. *Jarocho's Soul: Cultural Identity and Afro-Mexican Dance.* Lanham, MD: University Press of America, 2004.

González, Ondina E., and Bianca Premo. *Raising an Empire: Children in Early Modern Iberia and Colonial Latin America,* Albuquerque: University of New Mexico Press, 2007.

González Navarro, Moisés. "El mestizaje mexicano en el periodo nacional." *Revista Mexicana de Sociología* 30, no. 1 (January–March 1968): 32–52.

Gordon, Edmund T. *Disparate Diasporas: Identity and Politics in an African Nicaraguan Community.* Austin: University of Texas Press, 1998.

Graham, Richard, Thomas E. Skidmore, Aline Helg, and Alan Knight. *The Idea of Race in Latin America, 1870–1940.* Austin: University of Texas Press, 1990.

Grijalva, Manuel Miño. "La población de la Ciudad de México en 1790. Variables económicas y demográficas de una controversia." In *La población de la Ciudad de México en 1790: estructura social, alimentación y vivienda,* edited by Manuel Miño Grijalva and Sonia Pérez Toledo. Mexico City: Universidad Autónoma de México Iztapalapa, 2004.

Guardino, Peter. *The Time of Liberty: Popular Political Culture in Oaxaca, 1750–1850.* Durham, NC: Duke University Press, 2005.

Guerra, Lillian. *The Myth of José Martí: Conflicting Nationalisms in Early Twentieth-Century Cuba.* Chapel Hill: University of North Carolina Press, 2005.

Guss, David M. *The Festive State: Race, Ethnicity, and Nationalism as Cultural Performance.* Berkeley and Los Angeles: University of California Press, 2000.

"The Selling of San Juan: The Performance of History in an Afro-Venezuelan Community." *American Ethnologist* 20, no. 3 (1993): 451–473.

Hale, Charles A. *Transmission of Liberalism in Late Nineteenth-Century Mexico.* Princeton: Princeton University Press, 1989.

Hanchard, Michael George. *Orpheus and Power: The Movimento Negro of Rio de Janeiro and São Paulo, Brazil, 1945–1988.* Princeton: Princeton University Press, 1998.

Hargrave, Francis. *An Argument in the Case of James Somersett a Negro.* London: 1772. At John Rylands Library, University of Manchester.

Hassig, Ross. *Trade, Tribute, and Transportation: The Sixteenth-Century Political Economy of the Valley of Mexico.* Norman: University of Oklahoma Press, 1985.

Helg, Aline. *Our Rightful Share: The Afro-Cuban Struggle for Equality, 1886–1912.* Chapel Hill: University of North Carolina Press, 1995.

Herrera, Robinson. *Natives, Europeans, and Africans in Sixteenth-Century Santiago de Guatemala.* Austin: University of Texas Press, 2003.

Herrera Casassús, María Luisa. *Presencia y esclavitud del negro en la Huasteca.* Mexico City: Universidad Autónoma de Tamaulipas; Porrúa, 1988.

Heywood, Linda M., and John K. Thornton. *Central Africans, Atlantic Creoles, and the Foundation of the Americas, 1585–1660.* New York: Cambridge University Press, 2007.

Hickerson, Nancy P. "The Linguistic Position of Jumano." *Journal of Anthropological Research* 44, no. 3 (Autumn 1988), 311–326.

Hill, Jonathan D. *History, Power, and Identity: Ethnogenesis in the Americas, 1492–1992.* Iowa City: University of Iowa Press, 1996.

Hill, Ruth. "Casta as Culture and the Sociedad de Castas as Literature." In *Interpreting Colonialism,* edited by Byron Wells and Philip Stewart. Oxford: Voltaire Foundation, 2004.

Hierarchy, Commerce, and Fraud in Bourbon Spanish America: A Postal Inspector's Exposé. Nashville: Vanderbilt University Press, 2005.

"Towards an Eighteenth-Century Transatlantic Critical Race Theory." *Literature Compass* 3 (2006): 53–64.

Hoig, Stan. *Tribal Wars of the Southern Plains.* Norman: University of Oklahoma Press, 1993.

Hooker, Juliet. *Race and the Politics of Solidarity.* New York: Oxford University Press, 2009.

The Travels and Researches of Alexander von Humboldt: Being a Condensed Narrative of His Journeys in the Equinoctal Regions of America, and in Asiatic Russia: Together with an Analysis of His More Important Investigations. New York: J & J Harper, 1833.

Israel, Jonathan I. *Race, Class and Politics in Colonial Mexico, 1610–1670.* Oxford: Oxford University Press, 1975.

Jackson, Robert. *Race, Caste and Status: Indians in Colonial Spanish America.* Albuquerque: University of New Mexico Press, 1999.

Jaumeandreu, Eudaldo. *Rudimentos de economía política dispuestos por el M. Fr. Eudaldo Jaumeandreu.* Barcelona: A Brusi, 1816.

Jefferson, Thomas. *Notes on the State of Virginia.* Raleigh, NC: Alex Catalogue, 1990.

Jiménez Ramos, Marisela. "Black Mexico: Nineteenth Century Discourses of Race and Nation." PhD diss.: Brown University, 2009.

Kagan, Richard, and Abigail Dyer, eds. *Inquisitorial Inquiries: Brief Lives of Secret Jews and Other Heretics.* Baltimore: Johns Hopkins Press, 2004.

Kamen, Henry. *Empire: How Spain Became a World Power, 1492–1763.* New York: Harper Collins, 2003.

Katzew, Ilona. *Casta Painting: Images of Race in Eighteenth-Century Mexico.* New Haven: Yale University Press, 2004.

——— . "'That This Should Be Published Again in the Age of the Enlightenment?' Eighteenth-Century Debates about the Indian Body in Colonial Mexico." In *Race and Classification: The Case of Mexican America,* edited by Ilona Katzew and Susan Deans-Smith, Stanford: Stanford University Press, 2009.

Keane, A. H. "Ethnology of Egyptian Sudan." *Journal of the Anthropological Institute of Great Britain and Ireland* 14 (1885): 91–113.

King, Stewart R. *Blue Coat or Powdered Wig: Free People of Color in Pre-Revolutionary Saint-Domingue.* Athens: University of Georgia Press, 2001.

Klein, Herbert S., and Ben Vinson III. *African Slavery in Latin America and the Caribbean.* New York and Oxford: Oxford University Press, 2007.

Klooster, Willem. "'Subordinate but Proud': Curaçao's Free Blacks and Mulattoes in the Eighteenth Century." *New West Indian Guide* 67, nos. 3–4 (1994): 283–300.

Kraidy, Marwan. *Hybridity, or the Cultural Logic of Globalization.* Philadelphia: Temple University Press, 2005.

Kurath, Gertrude Prokosch. "Mexican Moriscas: A Problem in Dance Acculturation." *Journal of American Folklore* 62, no. 244 (April–June 1949): 87–106.

Lafaye, Jacques. "La sociedad de castas en la Nueva España." *Artes de México* 8 (1990).

Landers, Jane G. "Cimarrón and Citizen: African Ethnicity, Corporate Identity, and the Evolution of Free Black Towns in the Spanish Circum-Caribbean." In *Slaves, Subjects, and Subversives: Blacks in Colonial Latin America,* edited by Jane G. Landers and Barry M. Robinson. Albuquerque: University of New Mexico Press, 2006.

Lasso, Marixa. *Myths of Harmony: Race and Republicanism during the Age of Revolution, Colombia, 1795–1821.* Pittsburgh: University of Pittsburgh Press, 2007.

Laurencio, Juan. *Campaña contra Yanga en 1608.* Mexico City: Editorial Citlaltepetl, 1974.

Lavrin, Asunción. *Sexuality and Marriage in Colonial Latin America.* Lincoln: University of Nebraska Press, 1989.

Lewis, I. M., and P. A. Jewell. "The Peoples and Cultures of Ethiopia." *Proceedings of the Royal Society of London, Series B, Biological Sciences* 194, no. 1114 (August 27, 1976): 11.

Lewis, Laura A. *Chocolate and Corn Flour: History, Race, and Place in the Making of "Black" Mexico.* Durham: Duke University Press, 2012.

——— . *Hall of Mirrors: Power, Witchcraft, and Caste in Colonial Mexico.* Durham, NC: Duke University Press, 2003.

La Libertad, "Cosas del Dia," Mexico City, November 12, 1879.

"Lista de Castas." *Artes de México* 8 (1990): 79.

Livesay, Daniel. "Children of Uncertain Fortune: Mixed-Race Migration from the West Indies to Britain, 1750–1820." PhD diss.: University of Michigan, 2010.

Lockhart, James. *The Nahuas after the Conquest: A Social and Cultural History of the Indians of Central Mexico, Sixteenth through Eighteenth Centuries.* Stanford: Stanford University Press, 1992: 30–40.

Lohse, Russell. *Africans into Creoles: Slavery, Ethnicity, and Identity in Colonial Costa Rica.* Diálogos Series. Albuquerque: University of New Mexico Press, 2014.

Lokken, Paul. "Marriage as Slave Emancipation in Seventeenth-Century Rural Guatemala." *The Americas* 58, no. 2 (2001): 175–200.

Lomnitz-Adler, Claudio. *Exits from the Labyrinth: Culture and Ideology in the Mexican National Space.* Berkeley: University of California Press, 1992.

López Beltrán, C. "Hippocratic Bodies: Temperament and Castas in Spanish America (1570–1820)." *Journal of Spanish Cultural Studies* 8, no. 2 (2007): 253–289.

Lund, Joshua. *The Impure Imagination: Toward a Critical Hybridity in Latin American Writing.* Minneapolis: University of Minnesota Press, 2006.

Lutz, Christopher H. *Santiago de Guatemala, 1541–1773: City, Caste, and the Colonial Experience.* Norman: University of Oklahoma Press, 1994.

Lynch, John. *Spain under the Habsburgs.* New York: Oxford University Press, 1964.

Manríquez, Francisco. "Nueva Obra Redentora," *El Abogado Cristiano Ilustrado*, September 12, 1907, Mexico City.

Maravall, José A. *Culture of the Baroque: Analysis of a Historical Structure.* Minneapolis: University of Minnesota Press, 1986.

Martínez, María Elena. *Genealogical Fictions: Limpieza de Sangre, Religion, and Gender in Colonial Mexico.* Stanford: Stanford University Press, 2008.

"The Language, Genealogy, and Classification of 'Race' in Colonial Mexico." In *Race and Classification: The Case of Mexican Americans*, edited by Ilona Katzew and Susan Deans-Smith. Stanford: Stanford University Press, 2009.

Martínez-Alier, Verena. *Marriage, Class, and Colour in Nineteenth-Century Cuba: A Study of Racial Attitudes and Sexual Values in a Slave Society.* Ann Arbor: University of Michigan Press, 1989.

Martínez-Echazabal, Lourdes. "Mestizaje and the Discourse of National/Cultural Identity in Latin America, 1845–1959." *Latin American Perspectives* 25, no. 3 (1998): 21–42.

Mateos, Juan Antonio. *Sacerdote y caudillo: memorias de la insurrección, novela histórica mexicana.* 9th edition, illustrated. Mexico City; Buenos Aires: Maucci Hermanos, 1902.

McCaa, Robert. "Calidad, Clase, and Marriage in Colonial Mexico: The Case of Parral, 1788–90." *Hispanic American Historical Review* 64, no. 3 (1984): 477–501.

McCann, James. "The Political Economy of Rural Rebellion in Ethiopia: Northern Resistance to Imperial Expansion, 1928–1935. *International Journal of African Historical Studies* 18, no. 4 (1985): 601–623.

Medina, Charles Beatty. "Caught between Rivals: The Spanish-African Maroon Competition for Captive Indian Labor in the Region of Esmeraldas during the Late Sixteenth and Early Seventeenth Centuries." *The Americas* 63, no. 1 (2006): 113–136.

Midlo Hall, Gwendolyn. *Slavery and African Ethnicities in the Americas: Restoring the Links.* Chapel Hill: University of North Carolina Press, 2005.

Milton, Cynthia, and Ben Vinson III. "Counting Heads: Race and Non-Native Tribute Policy in Colonial Spanish America." *Journal of Colonialism and Colonial History* 3, no. 3 (2002): 1–18.

Miranda, Gloria E. "Gente de Razón Marriage Patterns in Spanish and Mexican California: A Base Study of Santa Barbara and Los Angeles." *Southern California Quarterly* 63, no. 1 (1981): 1–21.

"Racial and Cultural Dimensions of Gente de Razón Status in Spanish and Mexican California." *Southern California Quarterly* 70, no. 3 (1988): 265–278.

Moore, Robin D. *Nationalizing Blackness: Afrocubanismo and Artistic Revolution in Havana, 1920–1940.* Pittsburgh, PA: University of Pittsburgh Press, 1997.

Mora, José María Luis. *México y sus revoluciones.* Mexico: Porrúa, 1977.

Obras sueltas de José María Luis Mora, ciudadano mexicano. Vol. 1. Paris: Librería de Rosa, 1837.

Morales Cruz, Joel. *The Mexican Reformation: Catholic Pluralism, Enlightenment Religion, and the Iglesia de Jesús in Benito Juárez's Mexico (1859–72).* Eugene, OR: Pickwick, 2011.

Moreno Fraginals, Manuel, and Cedric Belfrage. *The Sugar Mill: The Socioeconomic Complex of Sugar in Cuba, 1760–1860.* New York: Monthly Review Press, 2008.

Mörner, Magnus. *Race Mixture in the History of Latin America.* Boston: Little, Brown and Company, 1967.

Murillo, Dana V., Mark Lents, and Margarita R. Ochoa. *City Indians in Spain's American Empire: Urban Indigenous Society in Colonial Mesoamerica and Andean South America, 1530–1810.* Brighton: Sussex Academic Press, 2012.

Muteba Rahier, Jean, ed. *Black Social Movements in Latin America: From Monocultural Mestizaje to Multiculturalism.* New York: Palgrave MacMillan Press, 2012.

Nadal, Jordi. *La población española (siglos XVI a XX).* Barcelona: Editorial Ariel, 1986.

Needell, Jeffrey D. "Identity, Race, Gender, and Modernity in the Origins of Gilberto Freyre's Oeuvre." *American Historical Review* 100, no. 1 (February 1995): 51–77.

Nobles, Melissa. *Shades of Citizenship: Race and the Census in Modern Politics.* Stanford: Stanford University Press, 2000.

Nodín Valdés, Dennis. "The Decline of the Sociedad de Castas in Mexico City." PhD diss.: University of Michigan, 1978.

Norris, Robert. *Memoirs of the Reign of Bossa Ahádee, King of Dahomy, an inland country of Guiney. To which are added, the author's journey to Abomey, the capital; and a short account of the African slave trade.* London: W. Lowndes, 1789.

Ocampo, Melchor. *Obras completas.* Vol. 1. Mexico City: J. de Elizade, 1900.

Ochoa Serrano, Álvaro. "Los africanos en México antes de Aguirre Beltrán (1821–1924). *Afro-Latin American Research Association (PALARA)* 2 (1998): 80.

"Los africanos en México antes de Aguirre Beltrán (1821–1924)." In *El rostro colectivo de la nación mexicana,* edited by María Guadalupe Chávez Carvajal. Morelia, Michoacán: Instituto de Investigaciones Históricas de la Universidad Michoacana de San Nicolás de Hidalgo, 1997.

O'Hara, Matthew D. *A Flock Divided: Race, Religion, and Politics in Mexico, 1749–1857.* Durham: Duke University Press, 2010.

Olliz-Boyd, Antonio. *The Latin American Identity and the African Diaspora: Ethnogenesis in Context.* Amherst, NY: Cambria Press, 2010.

Osorio y Carbajal, Ramón. *La conjura de Martín Cortés y otros sucesos de la época colonial.* Mexico City: Departamento del Distrito Federal, Secretaría de Obras y Servicios, 1973.

Owens, Sarah E., and Jane E. Mangan, *Women of the Iberian Atlantic.* Baton Rouge: Louisiana State University Press, 2012.

Pagden, Anthony. *The Fall of Natural Man: The American Indian and the Origins of Comparative Ethnology.* Cambridge: Cambridge University Press, 1982.

Palavicini, Felix F. *Panorama político de México.* Mexico City: Ediciones del Partido Revolucionario Institucional, 1948.

Palmer, Colin. *Slaves of the White God: Blacks in Mexico 1570–1650.* Cambridge: Harvard University Press, 1976.

Pappademos, Melina. *Black Political Activism and the Cuban Republic.* Chapel Hill: University of North Carolina Press, 2011.

Paquette, Gabriel B. *Enlightened Reform in Southern Europe and Its Atlantic Colonies, c. 1750–1830.* Burlington: Ashgate, 2009.

Enlightenment, Governance, and Reform in Spain and Its Empire, 1759–1808. New York: Palgrave MacMillan, 2008.

Pérez Toledo, Sonia. *Los hijos del trabajo: los artesanos de la Ciudad de México, 1780–1853.* Mexico City: Colegio de Mexico and Universidad Autónoma Metropolitana Iztapalapa, 1996.

Pérez Toledo, Sonia, and Herbert S. Klein. *Población y estructura social de la Ciudad de México, 1790–1842.* Mexico City: Universidad Autónoma Metropolitana Iztapalapa, 2004.

Pescador, Juan Javier. *De bautizados a fieles difuntos: familia y mentalidades en una parroquia urbana, Santa Catarina de México, 1568–1820.* Mexico City: Colegio de México, Centro de Estudios Demográficos y de Desarrollo Urbano, 1992.

Piccato, Pablo. *City of Suspects: Crime in Mexico City, 1900–1931.* Durham, NC: Duke University Press, 2001.

"La pintura de castas." *Artes de México* 8, Summer 1990, dedicated issue, out of print.

Pike, Ruth. *Linajudos and Conversos in Seville: Greed and Prejudice in Sixteenth- and Seventeenth-Century Spain.* New York: Peter Lang, 2000.

Pitt-Rivers, Julian. *Race in Latin America: The Concept of "Raza."* (Paris: Plon, 1973).

"Race in Latin America: The Concept of 'Raza.'" *European Journal of Sociology* 14 (1973): 3–31.

Pollak-Eltz, Angelina. *María Lionza, mito y culto venezolano ayer y hoy, 40 años de trabajo en el campo*, 3rd edition. Caracas: Universidad Católica Andrés Bello, 2004.

Polzer, Charles W., and Thomas E. Sheridan, eds. *The Presidio and Militia on the Northern Frontier of New Spain*. Vol. 2, Part 1: *The Californias and Sinaloa-Sonora, 1700–1765*. Tucson: University of Arizona Press, 1997.

Premo, Bianca. *Children of the Father King: Youth, Authority, and Legal Minority in Colonial Lima*. Chapel Hill: University of North Carolina Press, 2005.

Prieto, Guillermo. *Memorias de mis tiempos, 1828–1840*. Mexico City and Paris: Librería de la Vda. de C. Bouret, 1906.

Proctor, Frank T. III. "Afro-Mexican Slave Labor in the Obrajes de Panos of New Spain, Seventeenth and Eighteenth Centuries." *The Americas* 60, no. 1 (2003): 33–58.

Damned Notions of Liberty: Slavery, Culture, and Power in Colonial Mexico, 1640–1769. Albuquerque: University of New Mexico Press, 2010.

"Slave Rebellion and Liberty in Colonial Mexico." In *Black Mexico: Race and Society from Colonial to Modern Times*, edited by Ben Vinson III and Matthew Restall. Albuquerque: University of New Mexico Press, 2009.

Pupo-Walker, Enrique, ed. *Castaways: The Narrative of Álvar Núñez Cabeza de Vaca*. Berkeley: University of California Press, 1993.

Rabel, Cecilia. "Oaxaca en el siglo dieciocho: población, familia y economía." PhD diss.: Colegio de México, 2001.

Rama, Ángel, and David L. Frye. *Writing across Cultures: Narrative Transculturation in Latin America*. Durham, NC: Duke University Press, 2012.

Ramírez, Ignacio, and Ignacio M. Altamirano. *Obras de Ignacio Ramírez*. Mexico City: Oficina Tip. de la Secretaría de Fomento, 1889.

Ramos, Gabriela, and Yanna Yannakakis, eds. *Indigenous Intellectuals: Knowledge, Power, and Colonial Culture in Mexico and the Andes*. Durham, NC: Duke University Press, 2014.

Rappaport, Joanne. *The Disappearing Mestizo: Configuring Difference in the Colonial Kingdom of New Granada*. Durham, NC: Duke University Press, 2014.

Real Academia Española. *Diccionario de autoridades* (edición facsímil). Vol. 1. Madrid: Editorial Gredos, S.A., 1990.

Recopilacion de leyes 2:153, Book 5, title 8, law 37.

Recopilación de leyes de los reynos de las Indias, 4 vols. Madrid: Julián de Paredes, 1681.

Recopilación de leyes de los reynos de las Indias, mandadas imprimir y publicar por la Majestad Católica del Rey don Cárlos II, 3 vols. Madrid: Consejo de la Hispanidad, 1943.

Restall, Matthew. "Black Conquistadors: Armed Africans in Early Spanish America." *The Americas* 57, no. 2 (2000): 171–205.

The Black Middle: Africans, Mayas, and Spaniards in Colonial Yucatan. Stanford: Stanford University Press, 2009.

The Maya World: Yucatec Culture and Society, 1550–1850. Stanford: Stanford University Press, 1997.

Seven Myths of the Conquest. New York: Oxford University Press, 2003.

Riva Palacio, Vicente. *Las dos emparedadas: memorias de los tiempos de la Inquisición.* Edited by Manuel C. De Villegas. Mexico: T. F. Neve, 1869. Google Books version.

Memorias de un impostor. Don Guillén de Lampart, rey de México: novela histórica. Mexico City: Porrúa, 1872. Google Books version.

Riva Palacio, Vicente, et al. *El libro rojo, 1520–1867.* 2 vols. Mexico City: A. Pola, 1905

Rodó, José Enrique. *Ariel.* Austin: University of Texas Press, 1988.

Rowe, Erin. *Saint and Nation: Santiago, Teresa of Avila, and Plural Identities in Early Modern Spain.* University Park: Pennsylvania State University Press, 2011.

Royer, Clémence. "La question du métissage." *Actes de la Société d'Ethnographie* 10 (1886): 49–57.

Saether, Steinar A. "Bourbon Absolutism and Marriage Reform in Late Colonial Spanish America." *The Americas* 59, no. 4 (2003): 475–509.

Safier, Neil. *Measuring the New World: Enlightenment Science and South America.* Chicago: University of Chicago Press, 2008.

Sánchez, Joseph P. "Between Mestizaje and Castizaje: An Imperial View of the Spanish Vision of Race and Ethnicity in Colonial New Spain." Paper presented at Mestizaje (forum), National Hispanic Cultural Center, Albuquerque, New Mexico, September 26, 2006.

Sánchez Santiró, Ernesto. *Padrón del Arzobispado de México, 1777.* Mexico City: Archivo General de la Nación and Secretaría de Gobernación, 2003.

Schwaller, John. *The Church in Colonial Latin America.* Wilmington, DE: Scholarly Resources Books, 2000.

Schwaller, Robert C. "Defining Difference in Early Colonial New Spain." PhD diss.: Penn State University, 2009.

"'For Honor and Defence': Race and the Right to Bear Arms in Early Colonial Mexico." *Colonial Latin American Review* 21, no. 2 (August 2012): 239–266.

Géneros de Gente in Early Colonial Mexico: Defining Racial Difference. Norman: University of Oklahoma Press, 2016.

"'Mulata, Hija de Negro y India': Afro-Indigenous Mulatos in Early Colonial Mexico." *Journal of Social History* 44, no. 3 (Spring 2011): 889–914.

Seed, Patricia. *Amar, honrar y obedecer en el México colonial: conflictos en torno a la elección matrimonial, 1574–1821.* Mexico City: Conaculta; Alianza Editorial, 1991. Also, English version: *To Love, Honor, and Obey in Colonial Mexico: Conflicts over Marriage Choice,1574–1821.* Stanford: Stanford University Press, 1988.

"Social Dimensions of Race: Mexico City, 1753." *Hispanic American Historical Review* 62, no. 4 (1982): 569–606. Duke University Press: doi:10.2307/2514568.

Seijas, Tatiana. *Asian Slaves in Colonial Mexico: From Chinos to Indians.* New York: Cambridge University Press, 2014.

"Transpacific Servitude: The Asian Slaves of Mexico, 1580–1700." PhD diss.: Yale University, 2008.

Semana Mercantil, December 13, 1886, Mexico City: 579.

Sieder, Rachel, and John-Andrew McNeish, *Gender Justice and Legal Pluralities: Latin American and African Perspectives*. Milton Park, Abingdon, Oxon: Routledge, 2013.

Sierra Méndez, Justo, Francisco Sosa, Nájera M. Gutiérrez, and Jesús E. Valenzuela, eds. *Revista Nacional de Letras y Ciencias* 1. Mexico City: Imprenta de la Secretaría de Fomento, 1889.

Sierra, Pablo M. "Urban Slavery in Colonial Puebla de los Ángeles, 1536–1708." PhD diss.: UCLA, 2013.

Silverblatt, Irene. *Modern Inquisitions: Peru and the Colonial Origins of the Civilized World*. Durham, NC: Duke University Press, 2004, 32–34.

Skidmore, Thomas E., and Peter H. Smith. *Modern Latin America*. New York: Oxford University Press, 1984.

Slack, Edward R. "The Chinos in New Spain: A Corrective Lens for a Distorted Image." *Journal of World History* 20, no. 1 (2009): 35–67.

"Sinifying New Spain: Cathay's Influence on Colonial Mexico via the *Nao de China*." *Journal of Chinese Overseas* 5, no. 1 (2009): 5–27.

Smallwood, Stephanie E. *Saltwater Slavery: A Middle Passage from Africa to American Diaspora*. Cambridge: Harvard University Press, 2008.

Socolow, Susan M. *The Women of Colonial Latin America*. New York and Cambridge: Cambridge University Press, 2015.

Socolow, Susan M., and Louisa S. Hoberman, *The Countryside in Colonial Latin America*. Albuquerque: University of New Mexico Press, 1996.

Solano D., Sergio Paolo. "Usos y abusos del censo de 1777–1780. Sociedad, 'razas' y representaciones sociales en el Nuevo Reino de Granada en el siglo XVIII." PhD diss.: Universidad de Cartagena, 2013.

Souto Mantecón, Matilde, and Patricia Torres Mez. "La población de la antigua parroquia del pueblo de Xalapa (1777)." In *Población y estructura urbana en México, siglos XVIII y XIX*, edited by Carmen Blázquez Domínguez et al. Xalapa: Universidad Veracruzana, 2002.

Spencer, Herbert. *The Classification of the Sciences: To Which Are Added Reasons for Dissenting from the Philosophy of M. Comte*. New York: Don Appleton and Company, 1864.

Stepan, Nancy. *The Hour of Eugenics: Race, Gender, and Nation in Latin America*. Ithaca, NY: Cornell University Press, 1991.

Stewart, C. C. *Creolization: History, Ethnography, Theory*. Walnut Creek, CA: Left Coast Press, 2010.

Stolcke, Verena. *Marriage, Class and Colour in Nineteenth-Century Cuba: A Study of Racial Attitudes and Sexual Values in a Slave Society*. Cambridge: Cambridge University Press, 1974.

Stoler, Ann. *Carnal Knowledge and Imperial Power: Race and the Intimate in Colonial Rule*. Berkeley and Los Angeles: University of California Press, 2002.

Studnicki-Gizbert, Daviken. *A Nation upon the Open Sea: Portugal's Atlantic Diaspora and the Crisis of the Spanish Empire, 1492–1640*. Oxford: Oxford University Press, 2007, 82.

"Subasta pública," *Cómico*, Mexico City, July 30, 1899.

Taylor, William B. *Magistrates of the Sacred: Priests and Parishioners in Eighteenth-Century Mexico*. Stanford: Stanford University Press, 1996.

Tena Ramírez, Felipe, ed., *Leyes fundamentales de México, 1808–1971*. Mexico City: Porrúa, 1971.

Terraciano, Kevin. *The Mixtecs of Colonial Oaxaca: Ñudzahui History, Sixteenth through Eighteenth Centuries*. Stanford: Stanford University Press, 2001.

Terrazas Williams, Danielle. "Capitalizing Subjects: Free African-Descended Women of Means in Xalapa, Veracruz during the Long Seventeenth Century." PhD diss.: Duke University, 2013.

Thornton, John K. *Africa and Africans in the Making of the Atlantic World, 1400–1800*. 2nd edition. Cambridge: Cambridge University Press, 1998. Also, first edition, Cambridge University Press, 1992.

A Cultural History of the Atlantic World, 1250–1820. New York: Cambridge University Press, 2012.

Todorov, Tzvetan. *The Conquest of America: The Question of the Other*. New York: Harper & Row, 1984.

Toussaint, Manuel, Federico Gómez de Orozco, and Justino Fernández. *Planos de la Ciudad de Mexico, siglos XVI y XVII: estudio histórico, urbanístico y bibliográfico*. Mexico City: Universidad Nacional Autónoma de México, 1990.

Tutino, John. *Making a New World: Founding Capitalism in the Bajío and Spanish North America*. Durham, NC, and London: Duke University Press, 2011.

Twinam, Ann. "The Church, the State, and the Abandoned: Expósitos in Late Eighteenth-Century Havana. In *Raising an Empire: Children in Early Modern Iberia and Colonial Latin America*, edited by Ondina E. González and Bianca Premo. Albuquerque: University of New Mexico Press, 2007.

Public Lives, Private Secrets: Gender, Honor, Sexuality, and Illegitimacy in Colonial Spanish America. Stanford: Stanford University Press, 1999.

Purchasing Whiteness: Pardos, Mulatos, and the Quest for Social Mobility in the Spanish Indies. Stanford: Stanford University Press, 2015.

Valdés, Dennis N. "The Decline of Slavery in Mexico." *The Americas* 44, no. 2 (1987): 167–194.

Vallarta, Ignacio L. *Obras completas*. Mexico City: José Joaquín Terrazas e Hijas, 1897.

Vasconcelos, José. *El desastre: terceraparte de Ulises Criollo, continuación de la tormenta*. Mexico City: Ediciones Botas, 1938.

Vasconcelos, José, and Didier T. Jaén, *The Cosmic Race: A Bilingual Edition*. Baltimore: Johns Hopkins University Press, 1997.

Velázquez, María Elisa, and Duró E. Correa, *Poblaciones y culturas de origen africano en México*. Mexico City: Instituto Nacional de Antropología e Historia, 2005.

Velásquez, Melida. "El comercio de esclavos en la Alcaldía Mayor de Tegucigalpa." *Mesoamerica* 22, no. 42 (2001):199–222.

Viera-Powers, Karen. *Women in the Crucible of the Conquest: The Gendered Genesis of Spanish American Society, 1500–1600*. Albuquerque: University of New Mexico Press, 2005.

Villa-Flores, Javier. "To Lose One's Soul: Blasphemy and Slavery in New Spain, 1596–1669." *Hispanic American Historical Review* 82, no. 3 (August 2002): 435–469.

Vinson, Ben III. *Bearing Arms for His Majesty: The Free-Colored Militia in Colonial Mexico.* Stanford: Stanford University Press, 2001.

"From Dawn 'til Dusk." In *Black Mexico: Race and Society from Colonial to Modern Times,* edited by Ben Vinson III and Matthew Restall. Albuquerque: University of New Mexico Press, 2009.

"The Racial Profile of a Rural Mexican Province in the 'Costa Chica': Igualapa in 1791." *The Americas* 57, no. 2 (October 2000): 269–282.

Vinson, Ben, and Matthew Restall, "Black Soldiers, Native Soldiers: Meanings of Military Service in the Spanish American Colonies." In *Beyond Black and Red: African-Native Relations in Colonial Latin America,* edited by Matthew Restall. Albuquerque: University of New Mexico Press, 2005.

"The Medium of Military Service and Encounter." In *Beyond Black and Red: African-Native Relations in Colonial Latin America,* edited by Matthew Restall. Albuquerque: University of New Mexico Press, 2005.

von Germeten, Nicole. *Black Blood Brothers: Confraternities and Social Mobility for Afro Mexicans.* Gainesville: University Press of Florida, 2006.

"Colonial Middle Men? Mulatto Identity in New Spain's Confraternities." In *Black Mexico: Race and Society from Colonial to Modern Times,* edited by Ben Vinson III and Matthew Restall. Albuquerque: University of New Mexico Press, 2009.

"Corporate Salvation in a Colonial Society: Confraternities and Social Mobility for Africans and Their Descendants in New Spain." PhD diss.: University of California, Berkeley, 2003.

von Humbolt, Alexander. *Political Essay on the Kingdom of New Spain.* London: I. Riley, 1811.

von Mentz, Brígida. *Pueblos de indios, mulatos y mestizos, 1770–1870: los campesinos y las transformaciones protoindustriales en el poniente de Morelos.* Centro de Investigaciones y Estudios Superiores en Antropología Social (CIESAS), 2010 (ebook).

Wade, Peter. *Blackness and Race Mixture: The Dynamics of Racial Identity in Colombia.* Baltimore: Johns Hopkins University Press, 1993.

Race and Ethnicity in Latin America. Chicago: Pluto Press, 1997.

"Rethinking 'Mestizaje': Ideology and Lived Experience." *Journal of Latin American Studies* 37, no. 2 (May 2005).

Wagley, Charles. *Race and Class in Rural Brazil.* Paris: UNESCO, 1952.

Wilkerson, S. J. K. "Ethnogenesis of the Huastecs and Totonacs: Early Cultures of North-Central Veracruz at Santa Luisa, Mexico." PhD diss.: Tulane University, 1972.

Wolf, Eric. *Sons of the Shaking Earth.* Chicago: University of Chicago Press, 1959.

Wright, Winthrop R. *Café con Leche: Race, Class, and National Image in Venezuela.* Ann Arbor: UMI Books on Demand, 2003.

Yacher, Leon. "Marriage, Migration, and Racial Mixing in Colonial Tlazazalca (Michoacán, Mexico), 1750–1800." PhD diss.: Syracuse University, 1977.

Yannakakis, Yanna. *The Art of Being In-Between: Native Intermediaries, Indian Identity, and Local Rule in Colonial Oaxaca*. Durham, NC: Duke University Press, 2008.

Young, R. C. *Colonial Desire: Hybridity in Theory, Culture and Race*. London: Routledge, 1995.

Zayas, R. de. "Fisiología del crimen." El Siglo XIX, Mexico City, October 30, 1891.

Zea, Leopoldo. *The Latin-American Mind*. Norman: University of Oklahoma Press, 1963.

Zemon Davis, Natalie. *Trickster Travels: A Sixteenth-Century Muslim between Worlds*. New York: Hill and Wang, 2006.

Zorita, Alonso de. "Breve y sumaria relación de los señores ... de la Nueva España." In *Nueva colección de documentos para la historia de México*, edited by Joaquín García Icazbalceta [1886–1892]. Mexico City: Editorial Chávez Hayhoe, 1941.

OTHER SOURCES

de L'Isle, Guillaume, and l'Academie Royale des Science. *Carte de la Barbarie, de la Nigritie et de la Guinée*. C. Inselin, engraver. Map. Paris: Chez l'Auteur sur le Quai de l'Horloge a l'Aigle d'Or, avec privilege du roi, August 1707 [1718?]. Available at www.loc.gov/resource/g8220.ct001447/, accessed July 4, 2016.

du Trafage, Jean Nicolas, cartographer. *Afrique: selon les Relations les plus Nouvelles dressée Sur les Mémoires du Sr. de Tillemont: Divisée en tousses Royaumes et grands États avec un discours Sur la nouvelle découverte de la Situation des Sources du Nil*. Map. Paris: Jean Baptiste Nolin, reproduced in 1742.

Index